Conformal Prediction for Reliable Machine Learning

Conformal Prediction for Reliable Machine Learning
Theory, Adaptations and Applications

Vineeth N. Balasubramanian
Department of Computer Science and Engineering
Indian Institute of Technology, Hyderabad, India
(formerly at Center for Cognitive Ubiquitous Computing
Arizona State University, USA)

Shen-Shyang Ho
School of Computer Engineering
Nanyang Technological University, Singapore

Vladimir Vovk
Department of Computer Science, Royal Holloway
University of London, UK

AMSTERDAM • BOSTON • HEIDELBERG • LONDON
NEW YORK • OXFORD • PARIS • SAN DIEGO
SAN FRANCISCO • SINGAPORE • SYDNEY • TOKYO

Morgan Kaufmann is an imprint of Elsevier

Acquiring Editor: Todd Green
Editorial Project Manager: Lindsay Lawrence
Project Manager: Malathi Samayan
Designer: Russell Purdy

Morgan Kaufmann is an imprint of Elsevier
225 Wyman Street, Waltham, MA 02451, USA

Notices
Knowledge and best practice in this field are constantly changing. As new research and experience broaden our understanding, changes in research methods or professional practices, may become necessary. Practitioners and researchers must always rely on their own experience and knowledge in evaluating and using any information or methods described here in. In using such information or methods they should be mindful of their own safety and the safety of others, including parties for whom they have a professional responsibility.

To the fullest extent of the law, neither the Publisher nor the authors, contributors, or editors, assume any liability for any injury and/or damage to persons or property as a matter of products liability, negligence or otherwise, or from any use or operation of any methods, products, instructions, or ideas contained in the material herein.

Library of Congress Cataloging-in-Publication Data
Application Submitted

British Library Cataloguing-in-Publication Data
A catalogue record for this book is available from the British Library

ISBN: 978-0-12-398537-8

For information on all MK publications, visit our
website at www.mkp.com or www.elsevierdirect.com

14 15 16   13 12 11 10 9 8 7 6 5 4 3 2 1

Working together
to grow libraries in
developing countries

www.elsevier.com • www.bookaid.org

Copyright Permissions

Chapter 3

Figures 3.4, 3.5, 3.6, 3.9 and Tables 3.1, 3.2: Reprinted with permission from Balasubramanian, Chakraborty and Panchanathan, Generalized Query by Transduction for Online Active Learning, *12th International Conference on Computer Vision Workshops (ICCV Workshops),* © 2009 IEEE.

Figures 3.7, 3.8: Reprinted with permission from Makili et al., Active Learning Using Conformal Predictors: Application to Image Classification, Fusion Science and Technology, *Vol 62 No 2* © 2012 American Nuclear Society, La Grange Park, Illinois.

Chapter 6

Figure 6.4: Reprinted from Artificial Intelligence Applications and Innovations, Meng Yang, Ilia Nouretdinov, Zhiyuan Luo, Alexander Gammerman, Feature Selection by Conformal Predictor, 439–448, Copyright (2011), with kind permission from Springer Science and Business Media.

Chapter 9

Figures 9.1, 9.2, 9.3, 9.4 and Tables 9.1, 9.2: Reprinted from Intelligent Data Analysis, 13.6, Smirnov, Evgueni N., Georgi I. Nalbantov, and A. M. Kaptein, Meta-conformity approach to reliable classification, 901–915, Copyright (2009), with permission from IOS Press.

Figures 9.5, 9.6, 9.7, 9.8 and Table 9.3: Reprinted from Artificial Intelligence: Methodology, Systems, and Applications, Smirnov, Evgueni, Nikolay Nikolaev, and Georgi Nalbantov, Single-stacking conformity approach to reliable classification, 161–170, Copyright (2010), with kind permission from Springer Science and Business Media.

Chapter 10

Figures 10.1 & 10.3: Reprinted with permission from Li and Wechsler, Open Set Face Recognition Using Transduction, IEEE Transactions on Pattern Analysis and Machine Intelligence, © 2005 IEEE.

Figures 10.5, 10.6 & 10.7: Reprinted with permission from Face Authentication Using Recognition-by-parts, Boosting and Transduction, Li and Wechsler, International Journal of Pattern Recognition and Artificial Intelligence, Vol. 23, Issue 3, © 2009 World Scientific.

Figure 10.8: Reprinted with permission from Robust Re-identification Using Randomness and Statistical Learning: Quo Vadis, Nappi and Wechsler, Pattern Recognition Letters, Vol. 33, Issue 14, © 2012 Elsevier.

Chapter 11

Figure 11.1: Reprinted with permission from Qualified Predictions from Microarray and Proteomics Pattern Diagnostics with Confidence Machines, Bellotti, Luo, Gammerman, Van Delft, Saha, International Journal of Neural Systems, Vol. 15, No 4, pp 247–258, © 2005 World Scientific.

Contents

PART 3 APPLICATIONS

Contributing Authors

Vineeth N. Balasubramanian
Department of Computer Science and Engineering, Indian Institute of Technology, Hyderabad, India

Tony Bellotti
Mathematics Department, Imperial College, London, United Kingdom

Shayok Chakraborty
Center for Cognitive Ubiquitous Computing, Arizona State University, AZ, USA

Mikhail Dashevskiy
Computer Learning Research Centre, Department of Computer Science, Royal Holloway, University of London, United Kingdom

Alexander Gammerman
Computer Learning Research Centre, Department of Computer Science, Royal Holloway, University of London, United Kingdom

David R. Hardoon
Ernst & Young, Singapore

Shen-Shyang Ho
School of Computer Engineering, Nanyang Technological University, Singapore

Zakria Hussain
Department of Computer Science, University College London, United Kingdom

Matjaž Kukar
Faculty of Computer and Information Science, University of Ljubljana, Ljubljana, Slovenia

Prasanth Lade
Center for Cognitive Ubiquitous Computing, Arizona State University, AZ, USA

Rikard Laxhammar
Saab AB, Järfälla, Sweden

Fayin Li
CleverSys Inc., VA, USA

Zhiyuan Luo
Computer Learning Research Centre, Department of Computer Science, Royal Holloway, University of London, United Kingdom

Ilia Nouretdinov
Computer Learning Research Centre, Department of Computer Science, Royal Holloway, University of London, United Kingdom

Sethuraman Panchanathan
Center for Cognitive Ubiquitous Computing, Arizona State University, AZ, USA

John Shawe-Taylor
Department of Computer Science, University College London, United Kingdom

Evgueni Smirnov
Department of Knowledge Engineering, Maastricht University, Maastricht, The Netherlands

Hemanth Venkateswara
Center for Cognitive Ubiquitous Computing, Arizona State University, AZ, USA

Vladimir Vovk
Computer Learning Research Centre, Department of Computer Science, Royal Holloway, University of London, United Kingdom

Harry Wechsler
Department of Computer Science, George Mason University, VA, USA

Meng Yang
Computer Learning Research Centre, Department of Computer Science, Royal Holloway, University of London, United Kingdom

Foreword

Traditional, low-dimensional, small scale data have been successfully dealt with using conventional software engineering and classical statistical methods, such as discriminant analysis, neural networks, genetic algorithms, and others. But the change of scale in data collection and the dimensionality of modern datasets has profound implications on the type of analysis that can be done. Recently several kernel-based machine learning algorithms have been developed for dealing with high-dimensional problems, where a large number of features could cause a combinatorial explosion. These methods are quickly gaining popularity, and it is widely believed that they will help to meet the challenge of analyzing very large datasets.

Learning machines often perform well in a wide range of applications and have nice theoretical properties without requiring any parametric statistical assumption about the source of data (unlike traditional statistical techniques). However, a typical drawback of many machine learning algorithms is that they usually do not provide any useful measure of confidence in the predicted labels of new, unclassified examples. Confidence estimation is a well-studied area of both parametric and nonparametric statistics; however, usually only low-dimensional problems are considered.

A new method of prediction with confidence under the i.i.d. assumption—called conformal prediction—has been developed. The main ideas were summarized in a book entitled *Algorithmic Learning in a Random World*, published in 2005. Conformal prediction has attracted interest from many researchers in the field of machine learning, and this interest has been steadily developing over the years. It has now reached a point when it requires a review of different directions in theory and applications. This is the aim of this new book, *Conformal Predictions for Reliable Machine Learning: Theory, Adaptations and Applications*, prepared and edited by Vineeth Balasubramanian, Shen-Shyang Ho, and Vladimir Vovk.

The idea of conformal predictors is relatively simple. As usual, in the case of classification, there is a set of examples with corresponding features that belong to different classes. In the online case, we consider each example in turn and our task is to assign a new example to a certain class assuming that the examples are independent and identically distributed. In order to do this we need a measure of strangeness, which would indicate how "strange" the new example is in comparison with the previously accumulated examples. In other words, how this new example fits (or conforms with) the previous examples. The measure of strangeness (or nonconformity measure) can then be converted into p-values and allows us not just to make predictions, but also to estimate confidence of prediction, or reliability of prediction. The conformal prediction method has a number of very useful features; namely, it:

- gives provably valid measures of confidence;
- does not make any additional assumption about the data beyond the i.i.d. assumption;

- allows us to estimate confidence for individual objects;
- can be used as a region predictor with a number of possible predicted values;
- can be used in both online and offline learning as well as in intermediate types of learning (e.g., slow, lazy).

The possibility of calculating confidence of prediction lies at the heart of "reliability engineering" and allows us to make risk assessments for various applications. Machine learning has traditionally emphasized performance measures like accuracy or the number of false positives or false negatives ignoring issues about confidence in decisions. But it is equally important that decision rules would also give us some limits of predictions with an understanding of risk of outcome. In the medical domain, for example, it is important to be able to measure the risk of misdiagnosis or disease misclassification to ensure low risk of error. This is possible if we provide measures of confidence with predictions. This is the main subject of the book—how to use conformal predictors to make reliable predictions.

Overall, the book is highly recommended to anyone who is involved in making reliable predictions using machine learning algorithms.

Alexander Gammerman
Computer Learning Research Centre
Royal Holloway, University of London

Preface

Reliable estimation of prediction confidence remains a significant challenge in machine learning, as learning algorithms proliferate into difficult real-world pattern recognition applications. The Conformal Predictions (CP) framework is a recent development in machine learning to associate reliable measures of confidence with pattern recognition settings including classification, regression, and clustering. This framework is an outgrowth of earlier work on algorithmic randomness, transductive inference, and hypothesis testing, and has several desirable properties for potential use in various real-world applications. One of the desirable features of this framework is the calibration of the obtained confidence values in an online setting. While probability/confidence values generated by existing approaches can often be unreliable and difficult to interpret, the theory behind the CP framework guarantees that the confidence values obtained using this framework manifest themselves as the actual error frequencies in the online setting (i.e., they are well-calibrated). Further, this framework can be applied across all existing classification and regression methods (such as neural networks, Support Vector Machines, k-Nearest Neighbors, ridge regression, etc.), thus making it a very generalizable approach. Over the last few years, there has been a growing interest in applying this framework to real-world problems such as clinical decision support, medical diagnosis, sea surveillance, network traffic classification, and face recognition. The promising results have resulted in further extensions of the framework to problem settings such as active learning, model selection, feature selection, change detection, outlier detection, and anomaly detection. This book captures the basic theory of the framework, demonstrates how the framework can be applied to real-world problems, and also presents several adaptations of the framework including active learning, change detection, and anomaly detection.

The motivations for this book are as follows.

- The Conformal Predictions (CP) framework was proposed more than a decade ago, and numerous researchers have actively worked on this framework over the last few years. However, there is only one existing book on this topic, *Algorithmic Learning in a Random World*, which explains the theoretical foundations of this work and is intended for a researcher with an advanced mathematical and machine learning background. There is a need for a book that caters to a broader audience, presenting the framework from an applied researcher's perspective. This book has been compiled to address this important need.

- While the CP framework has several desirable properties, the efforts of researchers in applying or adapting this framework have been limited to a few groups of researchers scattered around the world. The framework has been slow in being adopted by the machine learning community due to its mathematical formulation being less conventional to the community, even though the framework has several features that make it attractive from a machine learning perspective. This book has been written to bridge this gap, and to expose the framework to a large base of researchers in machine learning, pattern recognition, and artificial intelligence.

- As mentioned earlier, the last decade has seen several efforts from both practitioners and researchers around the world in applying or adapting the framework. Although there are several common trends in these efforts, there is no in-depth publication that captures these developments, nor is there a survey article that brings together these bodies of work for a new researcher to understand the theory through real-world applications so that new applications or adaptations can further be proposed. This book will provide a platform for researchers to understand the framework as well as the efforts so far in using the framework, thus providing a springboard for further research as well as a handbook for application in real-world problems.

Book Organization

The book is organized into three parts: *Theory*, *Adaptations*, and *Applications*. These three parts, each consisting of multiple chapters, reflect the categorization of the efforts that have been undertaken so far with respect to the CP framework. Part I (*Theory*), composed of Chapters 1 and 2, presents a summary of the theoretical foundations of conformal prediction that have been developed over the years. Part II (*Adaptations*), composed of Chapters 3 through 9, covers the different machine learning settings—such as active learning, feature selection, and change detection—in which the CP framework has been incorporated successfully, along with related theoretical and experimental results. Part III (*Applications*), composed of Chapters 10 through 13, describes the application domains in which the framework has been validated successfully—ranging from biometrics to medical diagnostics/prognostics to network intrusion detection, along with the corresponding experimental results and analysis. We hope that we will continue to expand each of these parts in the near future, to include additional efforts undertaken by researchers in the field, and to make this book a valuable resource for practitioners of conformal prediction.

Part I: Theory

This part briefly covers the theoretical foundations of conformal prediction. Its main goal is to serve the needs of the other chapters, but it also includes several other topics (such as a detailed discussion of conditional validity). The main definitions are given in the simplest possible context, always making the assumption of exchangeability (which is used in the vast majority of papers about conformal prediction). Nontrivial proofs are either avoided altogether or replaced by proof sketches; references to full proofs are always given. Occasionally, gaps in the existing theory are pointed out and stated as open problems; these places are listed in the index under the entry "open problems."

Chapter 1 is an introduction to the basic theory of conformal prediction. It concentrates on the two main properties of conformal predictors, their validity (ensured automatically) and efficiency (enjoyed by different conformal predictors to different degrees).

Chapter 2 discusses various generalizations of conformal predictors, first of all those designed to achieve conditional validity and efficiency. Among other main topics of this chapter are inductive conformal predictors, a computationally efficient modification of conformal predictors, and Venn predictors, a modification that outputs probabilities instead of p-values.

There are important theoretical topics that are not included in this part, and are instead covered in Part II. One of these topics is anomaly detection, which is only briefly mentioned in Part I (see the end of Section 1.4); it is covered in detail in Chapter 4 by Rikard Laxhammar. That chapter states both standard properties of validity for conformal anomaly detectors (see Propositions 4.1 and 4.2 and Theorems 4.1 and 4.2) and an important new property of validity (Theorem 4.3). The efficiency of the constructed conformal anomaly detectors is demonstrated in Chapter 4 empirically.

Another theoretical topic covered in Part II is testing exchangeability (Chapter 5 by Shen-Shyang Ho and Harry Wechsler). The main property of validity is stated as Theorem 5.1. The idea of the conformal approach to testing exchangeability is to use smoothed p-values $p_1, p_2, \ldots$ output by conformal predictors (as explained in Section 1.8) to define a martingale $S_n := \Pi_{i=1}^{n} f_i(p_i)$, where f_i is a nonnegative measurable function satisfying $\int_0^1 f_i(p)dp = 1$ and found (in a measurable way) from $p_1, \ldots, p_{i-1}$. The main theoretical open question in this area is whether this is the only way to obtain nonnegative processes whose initial value is 1, are measurable with respect to the filtration generated by the observations, and are martingales with respect to any exchangeable distribution.

Part II: Adaptations

This part, in general, describes the capability of conformal prediction, as a concept, to be generalized to various machine learning settings, without affecting their individual existing formulations or objectives—and by adding value to the formulations using the framework's theoretical guarantees.

Chapter 3 describes the adaptation of conformal predictors to active learning in the online setting. Active learning methods can broadly be categorized as *online* and *pool-based*, and the guarantees provided by the CP framework in the online setting naturally extends itself to use in the active learning problem. This chapter discusses the Query by Transduction (QBT) and the Generalized Query by Transduction (GQBT) methods, along with multicriteria extensions to both these methods. The chapter also points the reader to the appropriate bibliographic references, which demonstrate the theoretical connection between the discussed methods (QBT, in particular) and existing active learning strategies (Query-by-Committee).

Chapter 4 presents an extension of conformal prediction for anomaly detection applications. From a machine learning standpoint, anomaly detection can be considered as a classification problem, where each data instance belongs to a *normal* or *abnormal* class. However, the difference lies in the fact that it may be possible to only model data from the *normal* class, thus making this also a one-class classification problem. This chapter introduces and discusses the Conformal Anomaly Detector (CAD) and the computationally more efficient Inductive Conformal Anomaly Detector (ICAD), which are general algorithms for unsupervised or semisupervised and offline or online anomaly detection. One of the key properties of CAD and ICAD is that the rate of detected anomalies is well-calibrated in the online setting under the randomness assumption.

Chapter 5 discusses the use of conformal predictors in change detection settings. The problem of change detection, typically studied in the online setting for sequential data, attempts to identify changes in the stochastic homogeneity of data streams, so as to detect a state transition in the data model (see Section 5.2). This chapter explains how this is achieved by using the smoothed p-values obtained from conformal predictors as a martingale to test the exchangeability assumption in the data stream. It also discusses implementation-related issues related to this method, and pointers for future work in this direction.

Chapter 6 reviews the methods proposed so far to achieve feature selection using conformal predictors. Given the high dimensionality of digital data often generated in real-world applications today, feature selection, which attempts to select the salient features (or dimensions) among all, is an important learning problem. This chapter begins with a summary of existing feature selection methods, and points out computational issues that arise when using existing methods with the conformal prediction framework. It then reviews two recently proposed methods: the Strangeness Minimization Feature Selection (SMFS) method, and the Average Confidence Maximization (ACM) method. SMFS minimizes the overall nonconformity values of a sequence of examples, and ACM maximizes the average confidence output by the conformal predictor using a subset of features. The chapter also provides experimental results based on a real-world medical diagnostic problem to validate the proposed methods (see Sections 6.4.1 and 6.4.2).

Chapter 7 proposes the use of the nonconformity measure, as described in Chapter 1, for purposes of model selection in batch learning settings. Model selection is the task of choosing the best model for a particular data analysis task, and is generally based on a trade-off between fit with the data and the complexity of the model. The most popular techniques used by practitioners today are Cross-Validation (CV) and Leave-One-Out (LOO). This chapter compares the performance of the novel nonconformity-based model selection method with CV and LOO using the Support Vector Machine algorithm, and also proves a generalization error bound to upper-bound the loss of each test example using this method (see Theorem 7.1 in Section 7.4).

Chapter 8 describes a general approach to estimating quality of data mining predictions, based on conformal prediction and another closely related framework called transductive reliability estimation. As machine learning and data mining tools become increasingly used in risk-sensitive application domains, failed predictions may cause substantial financial, economic, health, reputational, or other damage. This chapters seeks to address this need by describing the aforementioned method to estimate prediction quality using conformal predictors. This method provides a general strategy that is independent of the particular underlying data mining algorithm.

Chapter 9 seeks to present the other adaptations of the CP framework that do not fit into traditional machine learning settings described in earlier chapters. In particular, the chapter describes two methods that use the idea of a metaclassifier to associate reliability values with output predictions from a base classifier. Both Metaconformal Predictors (see Section 9.2) and Single-Stacking Conformal Predictors (see Section 9.3) use a combination of a base classifier and a metaclassifier (trained on metadata generated from the data instances and the classification results of the base classifier) to associate reliability values on the classification of data instances; but differ in the manner in which metadata are constructed and the way in which reliability values are estimated. The chapter also briefly introduces how conformal predictors can be extended to time series analysis. This topic, however, is described in more detail in Chapter 12.

Part III: Applications

The main objective of this part is to expose the reader to the wide range of applications that have benefitted from the use of the conformal prediction framework in recent years. Chapters 10, 11, and 12 describe applications that have been investigated in significant detail so far, and Chapter 13 summarizes the various other application domains that have been studied in this context.

Chapter 10 provides a comprehensive discussion on the scope, challenges, and vulnerabilities in the use of conformal predictors for biometrics in general, and robust face recognition in particular. The chapter motivates the need for the CP framework for robust biometrics, and describes a novel method, called the Transduction Confidence Machine for Detection and Recognition (TCM-DR), that is built on the traditional Transduction Confidence Machine (TCM). It also discusses the potential of these methods for biometrics settings including closed versus open set recognition, as well as face verification. The chapter concludes with clear pointers to future research directions including reidentification using sensitivity analysis and revision for the purpose of metaprediction (see Sections 10.11 and 10.12).

Chapter 11 describes existing efforts in applying the CP framework to problems of diagnosis and prognosis in the biomedical domain. This domain is an important context for this framework, considering the risk-sensitive nature of predictions (imagine a physician being falsely notified about a patient with cancer, as not being cancerous).

The chapter presents a review of such biomedical applications, ranging from cancer diagnosis to depression diagnosis and prognosis. The chapter concludes with a useful summary of research efforts so far that have applied the conformal prediction framework to medicine and biology (see Table 11.6). This chapter also reviews and identifies the best performing nonconformity measure from literature for each of these problems, which will greatly help a new researcher (or practitioner) in the field.

Chapter 12 presents an application of conformal predictors to a nontraditional setting, namely time series analysis. This is nontraditional because existing methods in this domain depend on the sequential nature of data and violate the exchangeability assumption on which the framework is founded. The way in which the framework is applied is described using the example of reliable classification of network traffic and accurate network demand prediction based on network traffic flow measurements. In particular, the chapter investigates how to make predictions and build effective prediction intervals in time series data, and demonstrates the benefits of conformal prediction on publicly available network traffic datasets.

Chapter 13, the final chapter of this book, summarizes the other real-world applications that have directly used the CP framework for classification/regression tasks or its adaptations to tasks not discussed in the earlier chapters. These applications include clean and safe fusion power generation (Section 13.1); sensor device-based applications such as tea smell classification, total electron content prediction, and roadside assistance decision support system (Section 13.2); sustainability and environment-related prediction tasks (Section 13.3); security and surveillance tasks (Section 13.4); and other prediction tasks in software engineering, forensic science, machine translation, and pharmaceutical industry (Section 13.5).

Companion Website

A companion website for the book is available at http://www.conformalprediction book.com. The website will contain an overview of the book, additional resources related to the topics, and an errata list that will be updated periodically.

Contacting Us

We have endeavored to eliminate typos and other errors from the text to the extent possible. But we would appreciate if you would notify us of any errors or omissions in the book that are not on the current list of errata. We would also be glad to receive suggestions on improvements to the book, and welcome any contributions to the book website that could be of use to other readers, such as new adaptations, new applications, online labs and tutorials, and implementation-related tips. Email should be addressed to authors@conformalpredictionbook.com.

Acknowledgments

Many people have helped us during the process of editing this book. In particular, we thank:

- Students and researchers at the Center for Cognitive Ubiquitous Computing (CUbiC), Arizona State University, for several useful discussions on the topics in the book; and its Director, Prof. Sethuraman Panchanathan, for allowing use of resources toward the realization of this book
- Members of the Computer Learning Research Centre, Royal Holloway, University of London, for their contributions and discussions

We thank the following funding bodies for financial support: Nanyang Technological University for the Start-Up Grant; Ministry of Education (Singapore) through grants AcRF–RG 41/12; Cyprus Research Promotion Foundation; EPSRC (grant EP/K033344/1); US National Science Foundation (IIS Award 1116360).

We take the opportunity to thank the publishing team at Morgan Kaufmann Publishers (an imprint of Elsevier, Inc.) for their efforts in making this book a reality.

On a personal note, the authors thank their respective families for their love, patience, and continued support during all stages of the book from inception to completion.

Vineeth N. Balasubramanian
Department of Computer Science and Engineering
Indian Institute of Technology, Hyderabad
(formerly at Center for Cognitive Ubiquitous Computing, Arizona State University)

Shen-Shyang Ho
School of Computer Engineering
Nanyang Technological University

Vladimir Vovk
Department of Computer Science
Royal Holloway, University of London

Theory

The Basic Conformal Prediction Framework

1

Vladimir Vovk

Computer Learning Research Centre, Department of Computer Science,
Royal Holloway, University of London, United Kingdom

CHAPTER OUTLINE HEAD

The aim of this chapter is to give a gentle introduction to the method of conformal prediction. It will define conformal predictors and discuss their properties, leaving various extensions of conformal prediction for Chapter 2.

1.1 The Basic Setting and Assumptions

In the bulk of this chapter we consider the basic setting where we are given a training set of examples, and our goal is to predict a new example. We will assume that the examples are elements of an *example space* $\mathbf{Z}$ (formally, this is assumed to be a measurable space, i.e., a set equipped with a σ-algebra). We always assume that $\mathbf{Z}$ contains more than one element, $|\mathbf{Z}| > 1$, and that each singleton is measurable. The examples in the training set will usually be denoted $z_1, \ldots, z_l$ and the example to be predicted, *(test example)* z_{l+1}. Mathematically the training set is a sequence, $(z_1, \ldots, z_l)$, not a set.

The basic setting might look restrictive, but later in this chapter we will see that it covers the standard problems of classification (Section 1.6) and regression (Section 1.7); we will also see that the algorithms developed for our basic setting can be applied in the online (Section 1.8) and batch (Section 2.4) modes of prediction.

We will make two main kinds of assumptions about the way the examples z_i, $i = 1, \ldots, l + 1$, are generated. Let us fix the size $l \geq 1$ of the training set for now. Under the *randomness assumption*, the $l + 1$ examples are generated independently from the same unknown probability distribution Q on $\mathbf{Z}$. Under the *exchangeability assumption*, the sequence $(z_1, \ldots, z_{l+1})$ is generated from a probability distribution P on $\mathbf{Z}^{l+1}$ that is *exchangeable*: for any permutation π of the set $\{1, \ldots, l + 1\}$, the distribution of the permuted sequence $(z_{\pi(1)}, \ldots, z_{\pi(l+1)})$ is the same as the distribution P of the original sequence $(z_1, \ldots, z_{l+1})$. It is clear that the randomness assumption implies the exchangeability assumption, and in Section 1.5 we will see that the exchangeability assumption is much weaker. (On the other hand, in the online mode of prediction the difference between the two assumptions almost disappears, as we will see in Section 1.8.)

The randomness assumption is a standard assumption in machine learning. Methods of conformal prediction, however, usually work for the weaker exchangeability assumption. In some important cases even the exchangeability assumption can be weakened; see, for example, Chapters 8 and 9 of [365] dealing with online compression modeling.

1.2 Set and Confidence Predictors

In this book we are concerned with reliable machine learning, and so consider prediction algorithms that output a set of elements of $\mathbf{Z}$ as their prediction; such a set is called a *prediction set* (or a *set prediction*). The statement implicit in a prediction set is that it contains the test example z_{l+1}, and the prediction set is regarded as erroneous if and only if it fails to contain z_{l+1}. We will be looking for a compromise between reliability and informativeness of the prediction sets output by our algorithms; an example of prediction sets we try to avoid is the whole of $\mathbf{Z}$; it is absolutely reliable but not informative.

A *set predictor* is a function Γ that maps any sequence $(z_1, \ldots, z_l) \in \mathbf{Z}^l$ to a set $\Gamma(z_1, \ldots, z_l) \subseteq \mathbf{Z}$ and satisfies the following measurability condition: the set

$$\{(z_1, \ldots, z_{l+1}) \mid z_{l+1} \in \Gamma(z_1, \ldots, z_l)\} \tag{1.1}$$

is measurable in $\mathbf{Z}^{l+1}$.

We will often consider nested families of set predictors depending on a parameter $\epsilon \in [0, 1]$, which we call the *significance level*, reflecting the required reliability of prediction. Our parameterization of reliability will be such that smaller values of ϵ correspond to greater reliability. (This is just a convention: e.g., if we used the *confidence level* $1 - \epsilon$ as the parameter, larger values of the parameter would correspond to greater reliability.)

Formally, a *confidence predictor* is a family $(\Gamma^\epsilon \mid \epsilon \in [0, 1])$ of set predictors that is nested in the following sense: whenever $0 \le \epsilon_1 \le \epsilon_2 \le 1$,

$$\Gamma^{\epsilon_1}(z_1, \ldots, z_l) \supseteq \Gamma^{\epsilon_2}(z_1, \ldots, z_l). \tag{1.2}$$

1.2.1 **Validity and Efficiency of Set and Confidence Predictors**

The two main indicators of the quality of set and confidence predictors are what we call their validity (how reliable they are) and efficiency (how informative they are).[1] We say that a set predictor Γ is *exactly valid at a significance level* $\epsilon \in [0, 1]$ if, under any power probability distribution $P = Q^{l+1}$ on $\mathbf{Z}^{l+1}$, the probability of the event $z_{l+1} \notin \Gamma(z_1, \ldots, z_l)$ that Γ makes an error is ϵ. However, it is obvious that the property of exact validity is impossible to achieve unless ϵ is either 0 or 1:

Proposition 1.1. *At any level* $\epsilon \in (0, 1)$, *no set predictor is exactly valid.*

Proof. Let Q be a probability distribution on $\mathbf{Z}$ that is concentrated at one point. Then any set predictor makes a mistake with probability either 0 or 1. □

In Section 1.8 we will see that exact validity can be achieved using randomization.

The requirement that can be achieved (even trivially) is that of "conservative validity." A set predictor Γ is said to be *conservatively valid* (or simply *valid*) at *a significance level* $\epsilon \in [0, 1]$ if, under any power probability distribution $P = Q^{l+1}$ on $\mathbf{Z}^{l+1}$, the probability of $z_{l+1} \notin \Gamma^\epsilon(z_1, \ldots, z_l)$ does not exceed ϵ. The trivial way to achieve this, for any $\epsilon \in [0, 1]$, is to set $\Gamma(z_1, \ldots, z_l) := \mathbf{Z}$ for all $z_1, \ldots, z_l$. A confidence predictor $(\Gamma^\epsilon \mid \epsilon \in [0, 1])$ is (*conservatively*) *valid* if each of its constituent set predictors Γ^ϵ is valid at the significance level ϵ. Conformal predictors will provide nontrivial conservatively, and in some sense almost exactly, valid confidence predictors. In the following chapter we will discuss other notions of validity.

By the efficiency of set and confidence predictors we mean the smallness of the prediction sets they output. This is a vague notion, but in any case it can be meaningful only if we impose some restrictions on the predictors that we consider. Without restrictions, the trivial set predictor $\Gamma(z_1, \ldots, z_l) := \emptyset$, $\forall z_1, \ldots, z_l$, and the trivial confidence predictor $\Gamma^\epsilon(z_1, \ldots, z_l) := \emptyset$, $\forall z_1, \ldots, z_l, \epsilon$, are the most efficient ones. We will be looking for the most efficient confidence predictors in the class of valid confidence predictors; different notions of validity (including "conditional validity" considered in the next chapter) and different formalizations of the notion of efficiency will lead to different solutions to this problem.

---

[1]Only validity and efficiency will be used as technical terms.

1.3 Conformal Prediction

Let $n \in \mathbb{N}$, where $\mathbb{N} := \{1, 2, \ldots\}$ is the set of natural numbers. A *(non)conformity n-measure* is a measurable function A that assigns to every sequence $(z_1, \ldots, z_n)$ of n examples a sequence $(\alpha_1, \ldots, \alpha_n)$ of n real numbers that is equivariant with respect to permutations: for any permutation π of $\{1, \ldots, n\}$,

$$(\alpha_1, \ldots, \alpha_n) = A(z_1, \ldots, z_n) \implies (\alpha_{\pi(1)}, \ldots, \alpha_{\pi(n)}) = A(z_{\pi(1)}, \ldots, z_{\pi(n)}).$$
(1.3)

Let $n = l + 1$. The *conformal predictor* determined by A as a nonconformity measure is defined by

$$\Gamma^\epsilon(z_1, \ldots, z_l) := \{z \mid p^z > \epsilon\},$$
(1.4)

where for each $z \in \mathbf{Z}$ the corresponding *p-value* p^z is defined by

$$p^z := \frac{|\{i = 1, \ldots, l + 1 \mid \alpha_i^z \geq \alpha_{l+1}^z\}|}{l + 1}$$
(1.5)

and the corresponding sequence of *nonconformity scores* is defined by

$$(\alpha_1^z, \ldots, \alpha_{l+1}^z) := A(z_1, \ldots, z_l, z).$$
(1.6)

Similarly, the conformal predictor determined by A as a conformity measure is defined by (1.4)–(1.6) with $\alpha_i^z \geq \alpha_{l+1}^z$ in (1.5) replaced by $\alpha_i^z \leq \alpha_{l+1}^z$ (in which case (1.6) are referred to as *conformity scores*); this is not really a new notion as the conformal predictor determined by A as a conformity measure is the same thing as the conformal predictor determined by $-A$ as a nonconformity measure.

Remark 1.1. It is easy to see that the prediction set (1.4) output by the conformal predictor Γ depends on ϵ only via

$$[\epsilon]_l := \frac{\lfloor \epsilon(l + 1) \rfloor}{l + 1}.$$

In other words, $\Gamma^{\epsilon_1} = \Gamma^{\epsilon_2}$ when ϵ_1 and ϵ_2 are *l-equivalent*, in the sense $[\epsilon_1]_l = [\epsilon_2]_l$. Notice that $[\epsilon]_l$ is the smallest value that is *l*-equivalent to ϵ.

Proposition 1.2. *If examples $z_1, \ldots, z_{l+1}$ are generated from an exchangeable probability distribution on $\mathbf{Z}^{l+1}$, the probability of error, $z_{l+1} \notin \Gamma^\epsilon(z_1, \ldots, z_l)$, will not exceed ϵ for any $\epsilon \in [0, 1]$ and any conformal predictor Γ.*

In view of Remark 1.1, we can replace "will not exceed ϵ" in Proposition 1.2 by "will not exceed $[\epsilon]_l$." This proposition was first proved in [364] and [297]; we reproduce the simple argument under simplifying assumptions.

Proof sketch of Proposition 1.2. Let $(\alpha_1, \ldots, \alpha_{z+1}) := A(z_1, \ldots, z_{l+1})$, where A is the nonconformity measure determining Γ. An error is made if and only if α_{l+1} is among the $\lfloor \epsilon(l + 1) \rfloor$ largest elements in the sequence $(\alpha_1, \ldots, \alpha_{l+1})$. Because of the assumption of exchangeability, the distribution of $(z_1, \ldots, z_{l+1})$, and so the distribution of $(\alpha_1, \ldots, \alpha_{l+1})$, is invariant under permutations; in particular, all permutations of $(\alpha_1, \ldots, \alpha_{l+1})$ are equiprobable. For simplicity we assume that the probability of each permutation is positive and that all αs are different. A random permutation moves one of the $\lfloor \epsilon(l+1) \rfloor$ largest αs to the $(l+1)$th position with probability $[\epsilon]_l$, which is therefore the probability of error. $\qquad\qquad\qquad\qquad\qquad\qquad$ $\Box$

1.3.1 The Binary Case

We first consider a toy conformal predictor assuming that $\mathbf{Z} = \{0, 1\}$. The simplest nontrivial example of a nonconformity measure is $A(z_1, \ldots, z_n) := (z_1, \ldots, z_n)$. The conformal predictor determined by A is

$$\Gamma^\epsilon(z_1, \ldots, z_l) = \begin{cases} \emptyset & \text{if } \epsilon = 1 \\ \{0\} & \text{if } \frac{k+1}{l+1} \leq \epsilon < 1 \\ \{0, 1\} & \text{if } \epsilon < \frac{k+1}{l+1}, \end{cases} \tag{1.7}$$

where l is the size of the training set and k is the number of 1s in it. In other words, we can make a confident prediction that $z_{l+1} = 0$ only if the allowed probability ϵ of error is $\frac{k+1}{l+1}$ or more. For large l this agrees with Laplace's rule of succession, which says that $z_{l+1} = 1$ with probability $\frac{k+1}{l+2}$, and with many other estimates of the probability of success in Bernoulli trials (see Section 2.8 for further details).

The usual justification of Laplace's rule of succession is Bayesian: $\frac{k+1}{l+2}$ is the mean of the posterior distribution of the parameter $p \in [0, 1]$ (the probability of success, represented by 1) of the Bernoulli model with the uniform prior on p after observing k 1s and $n - k$ 0s. Avoiding such assumptions (at least to some degree) can make our conclusions more robust.

1.3.2 The Gaussian Case

Figure 1.1 is an empirical illustration of using conformal prediction to make our conclusions more robust by partially avoiding Bayesian assumptions. (It is similar to Figure 1 in [374], as corrected in [362, Figure 11.1]. For other empirical studies of this kind, see, e.g., [365, Section 10.3].) Four observations z_1, z_2, z_3, z_4 are generated from the statistical model $\{N(\theta, 1) \mid \theta \in \mathbb{R}\}$, where $\mathbb{R}$ is the set of real numbers and $N(\theta, 1)$ is the Gaussian distribution with mean θ and variance 1. In the top plot we take $\theta = 1$, in the middle $\theta = 10$, and in the bottom $\theta = 100$. We consider the Gaussian prior $N(0, 1)$ on the parameter θ, so that the Bayesian assumption can be regarded as satisfied for the top plot, violated for the middle plot, and grossly violated for the bottom plot. We take 80% as the confidence level.

The dashed lines are the Bayes prediction intervals and the solid lines are the prediction intervals output by a conformal predictor based on the Bayesian assumption (for details, see later). The performance of both kinds of prediction intervals depends on the assumption, but in very different ways. When the Bayesian assumption is satisfied (the top plot), both prediction intervals give reasonable results; in particular, they cover the four observations. When it becomes violated (middle plot), the conformal prediction interval becomes wider in order to cover the four observations whereas

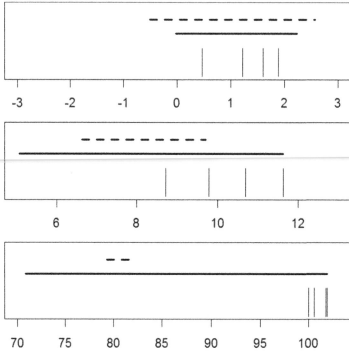

FIGURE 1.1

In the top plot, the four observation are generated from $N(1, 1)$; in the middle plot, from $N(10, 1)$; and in the bottom plot, from $N(100, 1)$. The solid lines are the prediction intervals output by the conformal predictor and the dashed lines are the Bayes prediction intervals.

the Bayes prediction interval ceases to be valid and covers clearly only one observation. And when it becomes grossly violated (bottom plot), the Bayes prediction interval becomes grossly invalid and does not cover any observations; the conformal prediction interval becomes long but still valid (in accordance with Proposition 1.2).

If we measure the efficiency of a prediction interval by its length, we can see that there is a certain symmetry between Bayes and conformal prediction intervals: as the Bayesian assumption becomes less and less satisfied, the Bayes prediction intervals lose their validity while maintaining their efficiency, and the conformal prediction intervals lose their efficiency while maintaining their validity. (In the top plot, the Bayes prediction interval happens to be wider, but for a random seed of the random number generator the Bayes prediction intervals are shorter in approximately 54% of cases.) Validity, however, is more important than efficiency, and efficiency is a meaningful notion only in the presence of validity.

These are the details of the Bayes and conformal predictors used earlier. The conditional distribution of z_5 given $z_1, \ldots, z_4$ under the Bayesian assumption is $N\left(\frac{4}{5}\bar{z}, \frac{6}{5}\right)$, where $\bar{z} := \frac{1}{4}(z_1 + \cdots + z_4)$ is the mean of the given observations. This gives the Bayes prediction interval $[0.8\bar{z} - 1.2c, 0.8\bar{z} + 1.2c]$, where c is the upper 10% quantile of the standard Gaussian distribution. The conformal predictor is based on the nonconformity measure that maps $(z_1, \ldots, z_5) \in \mathbb{R}^5$ to $(\alpha_1, \ldots, \alpha_5)$, where the nonconformity score α_i of z_i is defined as $\alpha_i := |z_i - \frac{5}{6}\bar{z}|$, $\frac{5}{6}\bar{z}$ being the mean of the posterior distribution of θ after observing $z_1, \ldots, z_5$, and $\bar{z} := \frac{1}{5}(z_1 + \cdots + z_5)$ being the mean of the five observations including z_5. This conformal predictor always outputs prediction sets that are intervals; in general, the *prediction interval* output by a conformal predictor is defined to be the convex hull of the prediction set (1.4).

The dependence of the validity of prediction intervals on the Bayesian assumption (which rarely has justifications other than mathematical convenience) is particularly serious in nonparametric statistics. At least in parametric statistics there are several results about the decreasing importance of the prior as the amount of data grows. But in nonparametric statistics, "the prior can swamp the data, no matter how much data you have" ([78, Section 4]), and using Bayes prediction intervals becomes even more problematic.

1.4   Efficiency in the Case of Prediction without Objects

In this section we describe a recent result by Lei, Robins, and Wasserman [200], who propose an asymptotically efficient conformal predictor. The example space $\mathbf{Z}$ is now simply the Euclidean space $\mathbb{R}^d$. We let Λ stand for the Lebesgue measure on $\mathbb{R}^d$.

Let Q be the data-generating distribution on $\mathbf{Z}$; we will assume that the examples $z_1, \ldots, z_{l+1}$ are generated from the power probability distribution Q^{l+1}. Let $\epsilon \in (0, 1)$ be a given significance level. Both Q and ϵ will be fixed throughout this section (except for Remark 1.2).

A natural notion of efficiency of a prediction set is its closeness to the "oracle" prediction set

$$C^{\mathrm{or}} := \arg\min_{C} \Lambda(C), \tag{1.8}$$

where C ranges over the measurable subsets of $\mathbf{Z}$ such that $Q(C) \geq 1 - \epsilon$. We will be interested in the case where the arg min is attained on an essentially unique set C (in particular, this will be implied by the assumptions of Theorem 1.1). Lei et al. [200] construct a conformal predictor Γ such that Γ^ϵ is close to C^{or} for a big training set. The closeness of Γ^ϵ and C^{or} will be measured by the Lebesgue measure $\Lambda(\Gamma^\epsilon \triangle C^{\mathrm{or}})$ of their symmetric difference.

Lei et al.'s conformal predictor enjoys properties of validity and efficiency. As for any conformal predictor, the property of validity does not require any assumptions apart from exchangeability. The property of efficiency, however, will be stated under the following assumptions about the data generating distribution Q:

1. The data-generating distribution has a differentiable density q.
2. The gradient of q is bounded.

3. There exists t such that $Q(\{z \mid q(z) \geq t\}) = 1 - \epsilon$.

4. The gradient of q is bounded away from 0 in a neighbourhood of the set $\{z \mid q(z) = t\}$.

It is clear that under Assumption 2 the arg min in (1.8) is indeed attained at some C; for example, at $\{z \mid q(z) > t\}$ and at $\{z \mid q(z) \geq t\}$, where t is defined in Assumption 3. For concreteness, let us define

$$C^{\mathrm{or}} = \{z \mid q(z) \geq t\};$$

this specific choice does not matter, since $\Lambda(C \bigtriangleup C^{\mathrm{or}}) = 0$ for any C at which the arg min is attained.

Theorem 1.1 ([200, Theorem 3.3]). *Suppose Assumptions 1–4 hold. There exists a conformal predictor Γ (independent of ϵ) such that for any $\lambda > 0$ there exists B such that, as $l \to \infty$,*

$$\mathbb{P}\left(\Lambda(\Gamma^{\epsilon}(z_1, \ldots, z_l) \bigtriangleup C^{\mathrm{or}}) \geq B \left(\frac{\log l}{l}\right)^{\frac{1}{d+2}}\right) = O\left(l^{-\lambda}\right). \tag{1.9}$$

Remark 1.2. It remains an open problem whether the rate $(\log l/l)^{1/(d+2)}$ in (1.9), or its corollary

$$\mathbb{E}\left(\Lambda(\Gamma^{\epsilon}(z_1, \ldots, z_l) \bigtriangleup C^{\mathrm{or}})\right) = O\left(\frac{\log l}{l}\right)^{\frac{1}{d+2}}, \tag{1.10}$$

is optimal. Rigollet and Vert [286] establish a lower bound matching (1.10): for a wide class $\mathcal{P}$ of densities, there exists a constant C such that, for any sample size l and any set predictor Γ (not required to satisfy any conditions of validity),

$$\sup_{q \in \mathcal{P}} \mathbb{E}\left(\Lambda(\Gamma(z_1, \ldots, z_l) \bigtriangleup C^{\mathrm{or}})\right) \geq C \left(\frac{\log l}{l}\right)^{\frac{1}{d+2}}, \tag{1.11}$$

(this is a special case of Rigollet and Vert's Theorem 5.1). However, there are at least two reasons why (1.11) does not prove the optimality of (1.10): first, the class $\mathcal{P}$ in (1.11) consists of data-generating distributions Q satisfying Assumptions 1 and 2 but not necessarily Assumption 4 (and the probability distributions used in the proof do not satisfy Assumption 4); and second, Rigollet and Vert prove (1.11) only in a special symmetric case (that would correspond to $\epsilon = 1/2$ if Assumption 4 were satisfied). It would be ideal to establish an optimal rate for each value ϵ of the significance level.

The conformity measure on which Lei et al.'s conformal predictor is based is easy to describe. Let $K : \mathbf{Z} \to \mathbb{R}$ be a symmetric ($K(z) = K(-z)$ for all z) continuous function that is concentrated on $[-1, 1]^d$ and integrates to 1. (It is interesting that the condition that K be nonnegative is not required.) Choose any sequence $h_1, h_2, \ldots$ of positive numbers satisfying

$$h_n \asymp \left(\frac{\log n}{n} \right)^{\frac{1}{d+2}},$$

where $\asymp$ stands for the asymptotic coincidence to within a constant factor. For a given sequence $(z_1, \ldots, z_n)$ of examples define the function

$$\hat{p}_n(z) := \frac{1}{nh_n^d} \sum_{i=1}^{n} K \left(\frac{z - z_i}{h_n} \right) \tag{1.12}$$

(this is the usual kernel density estimate). The conformity score α_i of each example z_i is defined by $\alpha_i := \hat{p}_n(z_i)$. The conformal predictor Γ determined by this conformity measure will satisfy Theorem 1.1.

One disadvantage of the prediction set $\Gamma^\epsilon(z_1, \ldots, z_l)$ is that it may be difficult to compute. A more computationally efficient version $\Gamma^+(z_1, \ldots, z_l)$ can be defined as follows. For a given training set $(z_1, \ldots, z_l)$ define the function

$$\hat{p}_l(z) := \frac{1}{lh_l^d} \sum_{i=1}^{l} K \left(\frac{z - z_i}{h_l} \right) \tag{1.13}$$

(in analogy with (1.12)) and set

$$\Gamma^+(z_1, \ldots, z_l) := \left\{ z \mid \hat{p}_l(z) \geq \hat{p}_l(z_{(k)}) - (lh_l^d)^{-1} (\sup K - \inf K) \right\}, \tag{1.14}$$

where $z_{(\cdot)}$ refers to the reordering of the z_i such that $\hat{p}_l(z_{(1)}) \leq \cdots \leq \hat{p}_l(z_{(l)})$ and $k := \lfloor \epsilon(l+1) \rfloor$. The set predictor Γ^+ is not a conformal predictor but it is guaranteed to satisfy $\Gamma^\epsilon(z_1, \ldots, z_l) \subseteq \Gamma^+(z_1, \ldots, z_l)$ (and so is conservatively valid) and Theorem 1.1 continues to hold when Γ^ϵ is replaced by Γ^+.

Lei et al.'s paper [200] contains more general results. For example, if we impose strong smoothness conditions on the density q of the data-generating distribution Q, the convergence rate in Theorem 1.1 becomes much faster: namely, we can replace the exponent $1/(d+2)$ by an exponent as close to $1/2$ as we wish. Even faster rates of convergence can be achieved if we replace Assumption 4 by an assumption of a faster change of the density q when moving away from the set $\{q = t\}$.

The material of this section is closely connected to the problem of anomaly detection (see Chapter 4). Now we interpret ϵ as our chosen tolerance level for anomalies and regard a new observation z as anomalous in view of the known observations $z_1, \ldots, z_l$ if $z \notin \Gamma^\epsilon(z_1, \ldots, z_l)$. A more computationally efficient procedure is to regard z as anomalous in view of $z_1, \ldots, z_l$ if $z \notin \Gamma^+(z_1, \ldots, z_l)$, where Γ^+ (depending on ϵ) is as defined earlier. In both cases the probability of a false alarm does not exceed ϵ.

1.5 Universality of Conformal Predictors

In this section we will see that the conformal predictors are universal in the sense of being the only way to achieve validity (in a suitable sense). This notion of universality applies to the whole class of conformal predictors (in Section 1.8 we will discuss individual conformal predictors that are universal in the sense of having the best possible asymptotic efficiency among asymptotically valid set predictors, and Lei et al.'s conformal predictors discussed in the previous section are also universal in a certain sense).

Let us say that a confidence predictor Γ is *invariant* if

$$\Gamma^\epsilon(z_1, \ldots, z_l) = \Gamma^\epsilon(z_{\pi(1)}, \ldots, z_{\pi(l)})$$

for any permutation π of the indices $\{1, \ldots, l\}$. Under the exchangeability assumption, this is a very natural class of confidence predictors (by the sufficiency principle; see, e.g., [63]).

For simplicity we will consider a stronger notion of validity than usual: let us say that a confidence predictor Γ is *(conservatively) valid under (the assumption of) exchangeability* at a significance level $\epsilon \in [0, 1]$ if, under any exchangeable probability distribution P on $\mathbf{Z}^{l+1}$, the probability of error $z_{l+1} \notin \Gamma^\epsilon(z_1, \ldots, z_l)$ does not exceed ϵ.

We will say that a confidence predictor Γ_2 is *at least as good as* another confidence predictor Γ_1 if, for any significance level ϵ,

$$\Gamma_2^\epsilon(z_1, \ldots, z_l) \subseteq \Gamma_1^\epsilon(z_1, \ldots, z_l)$$

holds for almost all $z_1, \ldots, z_l$. It turns out that any invariant confidence predictor that is conservatively valid under exchangeability is a conformal predictor or can be improved to become a conformal predictor.

Proposition 1.3 ([252]). *Let Γ_1 be an invariant confidence predictor that is conservatively valid under exchangeability. Then there is a conformal predictor Γ_2 that is at least as good as Γ_1.*

Proof. The conformity measure that determines Γ_2 is defined as follows. Let $(z_1, \ldots, z_{l+1}) \in \mathbf{Z}^{l+1}$. The conformity score of z_i is defined as

$$\alpha_i := \inf\left\{\epsilon \mid z_i \notin \Gamma_1^\epsilon(z_1, \ldots, z_{i-1}, z_{i+1}, \ldots, z_{l+1})\right\}$$
$$= \sup\left\{\epsilon \mid z_i \in \Gamma_1^\epsilon(z_1, \ldots, z_{i-1}, z_{i+1}, \ldots, z_{l+1})\right\}.$$

Without loss of generality we can assume that the inf is always attained (cf. [365], Proposition 2.11).

Let check that Γ_2 is at least as good as Γ_1. We are required to prove that $z_{l+1} \in \Gamma_1^\epsilon(z_1, \ldots, z_l)$ whenever $z_{l+1} \in \Gamma_2^\epsilon(z_1, \ldots, z_l)$. Fix a data sequence $(z_1, \ldots, z_{l+1})$ and a significance level ϵ, and suppose $z_{l+1} \notin \Gamma_1^\epsilon(z_1, \ldots, z_l)$. Since Γ_1 is conservatively valid under exchangeability,

$$z_i \notin \Gamma_1^\epsilon(z_1, \ldots, z_{i-1}, z_{i+1}, \ldots, z_{l+1})$$

for at most $\lfloor \epsilon(l+1) \rfloor z_i$s (this follows from the definition of conservative validity under exchangeability applied to the uniform distribution on the multiset of all $(l+1)!$

permutations of the data sequence $(z_1, \ldots, z_{l+1})$. We can see that α_{l+1} is among the $\lfloor \epsilon (l+1) \rfloor$ smallest α_is. Therefore, $z_{l+1} \notin \Gamma_2^\epsilon (z_1, \ldots, z_l)$.   □

For more sophisticated versions of Proposition 1.3, see [253] and [365, Section 2.4]. In particular, Theorem 2.6 of [365] is the analogue of Proposition 1.3 for the standard notion of (conservative) validity.

1.6 Structured Case and Classification

Starting from this section we consider the case where each example consists of two components, $z_i = (x_i, y_i)$; the first component x_i is called an *object* and the second component y_i a *label*. The example space $\mathbf{Z}$ is the Cartesian product $\mathbf{Z} = \mathbf{X} \times \mathbf{Y}$ of the *object space* $\mathbf{X}$ and the *label space* $\mathbf{Y}$; we always assume $|\mathbf{Y}| > 1$. This "structured" case covers two fundamental machine learning problems: *classification*, in which $\mathbf{Y}$ is a finite set (with the discrete σ-algebra), and *regression*, in which $\mathbf{Y} = \mathbb{R}$ is the set of real numbers. (Of course, this is a very primitive structure on the examples; both objects and labels can themselves have a nontrivial structure.)

In the structured case $\mathbf{Z} = \mathbf{X} \times \mathbf{Y}$ the prediction algorithm is usually allowed to output its prediction for the label y_{l+1} after being fed with the object x_{l+1}. In this case it is natural to rewrite a confidence predictor $(\Gamma^\epsilon \mid \epsilon \in [0, 1])$ as the function

$$\Gamma^\epsilon (z_1, \ldots, z_l, x_{l+1}) := \{ y \mid (x_{l+1}, y) \in \Gamma^\epsilon (z_1, \ldots, z_l) \}. \qquad (1.15)$$

In the structured case we will usually refer to the right-hand side of (1.15) (rather than $\Gamma^\epsilon (z_1, \ldots, z_l)$) as the *prediction set*. The analogue of (1.4) in the structured case is

$$\Gamma^\epsilon (z_1, \ldots, z_l, x_{l+1}) := \{ y \in \mathbf{Y} \mid p^{(x_{l+1}, y)} > \epsilon \}. \qquad (1.16)$$

In the rest of this section we will concentrate on the problem of classification, $|\mathbf{Y}| < \infty$, starting from two simple examples of nonconformity measures suitable for classification. Given a sequence of examples $z_1, \ldots, z_n$, where $z_i = (x_i, y_i)$ for all i, the corresponding nonconformity scores $(\alpha_1, \ldots, \alpha_n)$ can be computed as follows:

1. In the spirit of the 1-nearest neighbour algorithm, we can set

$$\alpha_i := \frac{\min_{j=1,\ldots,n : j \neq i \ \& \ y_j = y_i} \Delta(x_i, x_j)}{\min_{j=1,\ldots,n : y_j \neq y_i} \Delta(x_i, x_j)}, \qquad (1.17)$$

   where Δ is a metric on $\mathbf{X}$. (Intuitively, an example conforms to the sequence if it is close to the other examples with the same label and far from the examples with a different label.)

2. Suppose, additionally, that $|\mathbf{Y}| = 2$ (our classification problem is *binary*). Train a support vector machine on $z_1, \ldots, z_n$ and use the corresponding Lagrange multipliers $\alpha_1, \ldots, \alpha_n$ as nonconformity scores.

These conformity measures determine conformal predictors by the formula (1.16).

Reporting prediction sets (1.16) at a given significance level ϵ (or, preferably, at several significance levels ϵ) is just one way of presenting the prediction produced by the conformal predictor. Another way is to report the *point prediction* $\hat{y} \in \arg\max_y p^{x_{l+1}, y}$ (let us assume that $\left|\arg\max_y p^{x_{l+1}, y}\right| = 1$ for simplicity), the *credibility* $p^{x_{l+1}, \hat{y}}$, and the *confidence* $1 - \max_{y \neq \hat{y}} p^{x_{l+1}, y}$. A high (i.e., close to 1) confidence means that there is no likely alternative to the point prediction, and a low (i.e., close to 0) credibility means that even the point prediction is unlikely (reflecting the fact that the known data $z_1, \ldots, z_l, x_{l+1}$ are very unusual under the exchangeability assumption, which can happen, albeit with a low probability, even if the data sequence $z_1, \ldots, z_{l+1}$ has been really generated from an exchangeable probability distribution).

A more direct representation of the prediction is as the *p-value function* mapping $y \in \mathbf{Y}$ to $p^{x_{l+1}, y}$. The notion of a p-value function was introduced by Miettinen [230] in the context of confidence intervals (rather than prediction sets). It has been widely used in epidemiology; see, for example, [25, Section 6], for further references and a discussion of several alternative terms to "p-value function." The notion of a p-value function is also applicable in the unstructured case (cf. (1.5) earlier) and in the case of regression discussed in the next section.

1.7 Regression

In regression problems, a very natural nonconformity measure is

$$\alpha_i := \Delta\left(y_i, f(x_i)\right), \tag{1.18}$$

where $\Delta : \mathbf{Y}^2 \to \mathbb{R}$ is a measure of difference between two labels (usually a metric) and $f : \mathbf{X} \to \mathbf{Y}$ is a prediction rule (for predicting the label given the object) found from $((x_1, y_1) \ldots, (x_n, y_n))$ as the training set; to simplify notation, we suppressed the dependence of f on $((x_1, y_1) \ldots, (x_n, y_n))$ in (1.18).

In the case where $\Delta(y, y') := |y - y'|$ and f is found using the ridge regression procedure, the conformal predictor determined by the nonconformity measure (1.18) is called the *ridge regression confidence machine* (RRCM). This assumes that objects are vectors in a Euclidean space, $\mathbf{X} \subseteq \mathbb{R}^d$. The explicit representation of this nonconformity measure is

$$\alpha_i := \left|y_i - x_i'(X'X + aI)^{-1}X'Y\right|, \tag{1.19}$$

where $a \geq 0$ is the parameter of the algorithm (with $a = 0$ corresponding to the least squares algorithm), X is the $n \times d$ object matrix whose rows are $x_1', \ldots, x_n'$, Y is the label vector $(y_1, \ldots, y_n)'$, I is the unit $d \times d$ matrix, and $'$ stands for matrix transposition.

The prediction set output by the RRCM at a given significance level can be computed efficiently; in fact, it is not difficult to show that for a fixed dimension d the RRCM can be implemented with running time $O(l \log l)$.

The definition of the RRCM is somewhat arbitrary: for example, instead of using the *residuals* (1.19) as nonconformity scores we could use *deleted residuals* defined as in (1.19) but with X and Y not including the ith object and label, respectively:

$$X := (x_1, \ldots, x_{i-1}, x_{i+1}, x_n)',$$
$$Y := (y_1, \ldots, y_{i-1}, y_{i+1}, y_n)'.$$

The conformal predictor determined by this nonconformity measure is called the *deleted RRCM*. In the case $a = 0$, an explicit description of the deleted RRCM is given in [365, p. 34]. However, the most natural modification of the RRCM is the "studentized" version, which is in some sense half-way between the RRCM and the deleted RRCM ([365, p. 35], where only the case $a = 0$ is considered). An interesting direction of further research would be to extend the definitions of deleted and studentized RRCM to the case $a \neq 0$ and to study the three versions empirically on benchmark datasets.

The definition of RRCM is ultimately based on fitting linear functions to the data. In nonlinear cases, we can use the kernelized version of the RRCM, in which the nonconformity measure is defined as

$$\alpha_i := \left| y_i - Y'(K + aI)^{-1}k \right|,$$

where Y and a are as in (1.19), K is the $n \times n$ matrix $K_{i,j} := \mathcal{K}(x_i, x_j)$, I is the $n \times n$ unit matrix, k is the vector $k_i := \mathcal{K}(x, x_i)$ in $\mathbb{R}^n$, and $\mathcal{K}$ is a given kernel (another parameter of the algorithm). The kernelized RRCM is also computationally efficient. In the online prediction protocol (discussed in the next section), the computations at step n of the online protocol can be performed in time $O(n^2)$.

For details of the RRCM and its various modifications, see [365, Section 2.3]. The R package `PredictiveRegression` (available from the CRAN web page) includes a program implementing the RRCM.

1.8 Additional Properties of Validity and Efficiency in the Online Framework

The property of validity of conformal predictors can be stated in an especially strong form in the following *online framework*. The examples $z_1, z_2, \ldots$ (which may be structured, $z_i = (x_i, y_i)$) arrive one by one, and before observing z_n (or y_n in the structured case) the prediction algorithm outputs a prediction set; as usual, we say that the algorithm makes an error if the prediction set fails to contain z_n.

The *smoothed conformal predictor* determined by a nonconformity measure A is defined in the same way as the conformal predictor except that the p-values (1.5) are replaced by the *smoothed p-values*

$$p^z := \frac{\left| \{i = 1, \ldots, n \mid \alpha_i^z > \alpha_n^z\} \right| + \tau \left| \{i = 1, \ldots, n \mid \alpha_i^z = \alpha_n^z\} \right|}{n}, \qquad (1.20)$$

where τ is a random variable generated from the uniform distribution on $[0, 1]$ (the same value of τ can be used for all z). In other words, the prediction made by the smoothed conformal predictor determined by A at step n is defined by the right-hand side of (1.4), where p^z are defined by (1.20) and the nonconformity scores α_i^z are defined by (1.6) (with $n - 1$ in place of l). We will sometimes refer to τ as the *tie-breaking random variable*.

For smoothed conformal predictors, the probability of error is exactly ϵ. Moreover, when used in the online mode, smoothed conformal predictors make errors at different steps independently (assuming that the tie-breaking random variables τ at different steps are independent between themselves and of the examples). This is spelled out in the following theorem, where 1_E stands for the indicator function of E.

Theorem 1.2. *Let $N \in \mathbb{N}$ and suppose that examples $z_1, \ldots, z_N$ are generated from an exchangeable distribution on $\mathbf{Z}^N$. For any nonconformity measure A and any significance level ϵ, the smoothed conformal predictor Γ^ϵ determined by A at significance level ϵ makes errors with probability ϵ independently at different steps when applied in the online mode. In other words, the random variables $1_{z_n \notin \Gamma^\epsilon(z_1, \ldots, z_{n-1})}$, $n = 1, \ldots, N$, are independent Bernoulli variables with parameter ϵ.*

Theorem 1.2 is proved in [365] (Theorem 8.2 and Section 8.7) in the general framework of online compression models; for a proof in our current context of exchangeability, see, for example, [359, Theorem 2]. Rényi's "lemme fondamental" ([284, Lemma 2]) is a predecessor of Theorem 1.2 (and in fact implies a version of Theorem 1.2 for nonsmoothed predictors when each nonconformity score α_i depends only on the corresponding example z_i and this dependence is continuous in a suitable sense).

Theorem 1.2 immediately implies that if $z_1, z_2, \ldots$ is an infinite sequence of examples generated from an exchangeable distribution on $\mathbf{Z}^\infty$, at each significance level ϵ any smoothed conformal predictor will still make errors with probability ϵ independently at different steps.

Corollary 1.1. *Suppose examples $z_1, z_2, \ldots$ are generated independently from the same distribution Q on $\mathbf{Z}$. For any nonconformity measure A and any significance level ϵ, the smoothed conformal predictor Γ^ϵ determined by A at significance level ϵ makes errors with probability ϵ independently at different steps when applied in the online mode. In other words, the random variables $1_{z_n \notin \Gamma^\epsilon(z_1, \ldots, z_{n-1})}$, $n = 1, 2, \ldots$, are independent Bernoulli variables with parameter ϵ.*

In this infinite-horizon case, the strong law of large numbers implies that the limiting relative frequency of errors will be ϵ. As a smoothed conformal predictor makes an error whenever the corresponding conformal predictor makes an error, for conformal predictors the limiting relative frequency of errors (in the sense of upper limit) will not exceed ϵ.

In Theorem 1.2 we make the assumption of exchangeability rather than randomness to make it stronger: it is very easy to give examples of exchangeable distributions on $\mathbf{Z}^N$ that are not of the form Q^N (e.g., in the case $\mathbf{Z} = \{0, 1\}$, the uniform probability distribution on the set of all binary sequences of length n containing exactly k 1s, for some $k \in \{1, \ldots, N - 1\}$). On the other hand, in the infinite-horizon case (which is the standard setting for the online mode of prediction) the difference between the exchangeability and randomness assumptions essentially disappears: by de Finetti's theorem, each exchangeable probability distribution is a mixture of power probability distributions Q^∞, provided $\mathbf{Z}$ is a Borel space. In particular, using the assumption of randomness rather than exchangeability in Corollary 1.1 hardly weakens it: the two forms are equivalent when $\mathbf{Z}$ is a Borel space.

1.8.1 Asymptotically Efficient Conformal Predictors

Let us say that a prediction set (1.15) is *multiple* if it contains more than one label. In this subsection we consider randomized set predictors, whose prediction at each step depends on an additional random input that is independent of the examples. If Γ is such a set predictor, we let $\Gamma_n := \Gamma(z_1, \ldots, z_{n-1}, x_n)$ stand for the prediction set output at step n of the online protocol and

$$\mathrm{Mult}_n(\Gamma) := \sum_{i=1}^n 1_{|\Gamma_n| > 1}$$

stand for the cumulative number of multiple predictions over the first n steps. We will also use the notation

$$\mathrm{Err}_n(\Gamma) := \sum_{i=1}^n 1_{y_n \notin \Gamma_n}$$

for the number of errors and

$$\mathrm{Emp}_n(\Gamma) := \sum_{i=1}^n 1_{|\Gamma_n| = 0}$$

for the number of empty predictions made by Γ over the first n steps.

The number of multiple predictions $\mathrm{Mult}_n(\Gamma)$ is a natural measure of efficiency of Γ: the fewer the number of multiple predictions the more efficient the predictor. Of course, we compare only the efficiency of valid set predictors. It turns out (see, e.g., [365, Theorem 3.1]) that there exists a conformal predictor (explicit and computationally efficient) which is at least as asymptotically efficient as any other set predictor that is valid in a weak asymptotic sense. Here we will only state this result; for details, see Chapter 3 of [365].

There is a conformal predictor Γ that is universal in the sense of satisfying the following two conditions. Let us fix a significance level ϵ (Γ will satisfy these conditions for any ϵ).

Let us say that a randomized set predictor Γ' is *asymptotically conservative* at the significance level ϵ for a probability distribution Q on $\mathbf{Z}$ if

$$\limsup_{n\to\infty} \frac{\mathrm{Err}_n(\Gamma')}{n} \leq \epsilon \quad \text{a.s.}$$

under the power distribution Q^∞ on $\mathbf{Z}^\infty$. Since Γ is a conformal predictor, Γ^ϵ is automatically asymptotically conservative for any probability distribution Q on $\mathbf{Z}$.

Let us say that Γ' is *asymptotically optimal* at the significance level ϵ for a probability distribution Q on $\mathbf{Z}$ if, for any randomized set predictor Γ'' that is asymptotically conservative for Q,

$$\limsup_{n\to\infty} \frac{\mathrm{Mult}_n(\Gamma')}{n} \leq \liminf_{n\to\infty} \frac{\mathrm{Mult}_n(\Gamma'')}{n} \quad \text{a.s.} \tag{1.21}$$

under the power distribution Q^∞ on $\mathbf{Z}^\infty$. The first nontrivial condition that Γ^ϵ satisfies is that it is asymptotically optimal for any Q.

The final condition that Γ^ϵ satisfies is that, for any probability distribution Q on $\mathbf{Z}$ and any randomized set predictor Γ' that is asymptotically conservative and asymptotically optimal for Q,

$$\liminf_{n\to\infty} \frac{\mathrm{Emp}_n(\Gamma^\epsilon)}{n} \geq \limsup_{n\to\infty} \frac{\mathrm{Emp}_n(\Gamma')}{n} \quad \text{a.s.} \tag{1.22}$$

under Q^∞.

The condition (1.21) is very natural, but (1.22) might appear less so. Empty predictions (always leading to an error) provide a warning that the object whose label is being predicted is untypical (very different from the previously observed objects), and we would like to be warned as often as possible once we have a guarantee that the long-run frequency of errors will not exceed ϵ.

An asymptotically efficient conformal predictor, satisfying the properties (1.21) and (1.22), is explicitly constructed in [365] using nearest neighbors as the underlying algorithm; the number K_n of nearest neighbors at step n is slowly growing to infinity. The computations at step n take time $O(\log n)$.

Asymptotically efficient conformal predictors discussed in this section have been designed for classification problems, and it would be very interesting to carry out a similar construction in the case of regression. This construction would be different from the one given in [201] (and discussed in Section 2.6); for a further discussion, see Remark 2.3 in Chapter 2.

The criterion of efficiency stated earlier (beating any other predictor in the sense of (1.21) and, if (1.21) holds as an equality, (1.22)) is only one of several natural criteria of efficiency. For a detailed discussion, see [363], which also defines an important class of criteria of efficiency called proper (the criterion (1.21)–(1.22) does not belong to this class). Constructing asymptotically efficient conformal predictors under such criteria is another interesting direction of research. Both for the criterion (1.21)–(1.22) and for proper criteria of efficiency, the rates of convergence in (1.21)–(1.22) or their analogues are of great interest.

Acknowledgments

I am grateful to Sasha Tsybakov for his advice. The empirical studies described in this chapter used the R language and the R package `PredictiveRegression`; I am grateful to Ilia Nouretdinov for cowriting (and writing the first version of) the package. This work was supported in part by the Cyprus Research Promotion Foundation (TPE/ORIZO/0609(BIE)/24) and EPSRC (EP/K033344/1).

Beyond the Basic Conformal Prediction Framework

2

Vladimir Vovk

*Computer Learning Research Centre, Department of Computer Science,
Royal Holloway, University of London, United Kingdom*

CHAPTER OUTLINE HEAD

An appealing property of conformal predictors is their automatic validity under the exchangeability assumption: They make an error with probability not exceeding the prespecified significance level. A major focus of this chapter will be on "conditional" versions of the notion of validity. This requirement will be introduced in Section 2.1 and studied further in Sections 2.2, 2.4, 2.6, and 2.7. Other extensions that we consider are a computationally efficient version of conformal prediction (Section 2.3) and probabilistic prediction (Section 2.8). In Section 2.5 we will discuss classical tolerance regions, which can be regarded as a special case of conformal predictors and as a generalization of inductive conformal predictors; their importance in the context of this chapter lies in the possibility of extending to them certain properties of conditional validity enjoyed by inductive conformal predictors.

2.1 Conditional Validity

The idea of conditional inference in statistics is that we want our conclusions to be conditional as much as possible on the available information. Full conditionality is usually not attainable unless we know the true probability distribution generating the data (or are willing to use a subjective or postulated probability distribution, as in Bayesian theory). The requirement of conditional validity is a special case: for "important" events E we do not want the conditional probability of error given E to be very different from the given significance level ϵ. For example, if our set predictor is valid at the significance level 5% but makes an error with probability 10% for men and 0% for women, both men and women (especially men) can be unhappy with calling 5% the probability of error. It is clear that whenever the size of the training set is sufficient for making conditional claims, we should aim for this.

Of course, we cannot achieve conditional validity for all events E, and so we need to decide which events are "important." If we are interested in very few events E whose probability is not small, we can achieve conservative conditional validity by decreasing the significance level: the conditional probability of error given E will not exceed $\epsilon/\mathbb{P}(E)$, where $\mathbb{P}(E)$ is the probability of E. (But of course, the true conditional probability of error can be much smaller than this upper bound; besides, we might not know the probability of E, even approximately.) The requirement of conditional validity goes more and more beyond unconditional validity as we become interested in more events E and as the probability of some of them becomes smaller.

It will be convenient to give a crude classification of the conditioning events E that we might be interested in. Figure 2.1 (taken from [360]) is one possibility. At its center we have the unconditional notion of validity, which is achieved by conformal predictors automatically. The vertex O corresponds to *object conditional validity*, where E is a property of the test object. Our example at the beginning of this section is of this type: there are two kinds of objects, men and women, and we want validity

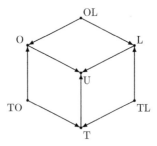

FIGURE 2.1

Eight notions of conditional validity. The visible vertices of the cube are U (unconditional), T (training conditional), O (object conditional), L (label conditional), OL (example conditional), TL (training and label conditional), TO (training and object conditional). The invisible vertex is TOL (and corresponds to conditioning on everything).

conditional of the kind of the test object. The vertex L corresponds to *label conditional validity*, where E is a property of the label of the test object. The vertex T corresponds to *training conditional validity*, where E is a property of the training set. We also have various combinations: for example, OL (*example conditional validity*) allows E that are properties of both the test object and its label (i.e., of the test example).

Each vertex of the cube in Figure 2.1 can stand for different notions. For example, object conditional validity can mean:

- Precise object conditional validity, where we allow E to be any property of the test example. In Section 2.6 we will see that precise object conditional validity is impossible to achieve in a useful way unless the test object is an atom of the data-generating distribution.
- Partial object conditional validity, where E can be any property of the test example in a given set of properties deemed important. We will often omit "partial." Partial example conditional validity (including object conditional validity) will be considered in detail in the next section.
- PAC-type object conditional validity: The conditional probability of error given the test object does not exceed a prespecified level with a high probability. In fact, we do not discuss PAC-type object conditional validity in this book. However, PAC-type training conditional validity will be discussed in Section 2.4.
- Asymptotic object conditional validity, where E can be any property of the test example but the conditional probability of error is required to converge to the significance level only as the sample size goes to infinity. In Section 2.6 we will see that in an important class of regression problems asymptotic object conditional validity can be achieved by an asymptotically efficient conditional conformal predictor.

Combining this list with the vertices of the cube, we can see that the potential number of different notions of conditional validity is very large; only few of them have been studied.

2.2 Conditional Conformal Predictors

For $n \in \mathbb{N}$, an *n-taxonomy* is a measurable function $K : \mathbf{Z}^n \to \mathbf{K}^n$, where $\mathbf{K}$ is a measurable space, that is equivariant with respect to permutations in the sense of

$$(\kappa_1, \ldots, \kappa_n) = K(z_1, \ldots, z_n) \implies (\kappa_{\pi(1)}, \ldots, \kappa_{\pi(n)}) = K(z_{\pi(1)}, \ldots, z_{\pi(n)}) \quad (2.1)$$

(cf. (1.3)). The set $\mathbf{K}$ is usually finite (with the discrete σ-algebra); we will refer to its elements as *categories*. Usually the *category* κ_i of an example z_i is a kind of classification of z_i, which may depend on the other examples in the dataset $(z_1, \ldots, z_n)$. A *K-conditional (non)conformity n-measure* is a measurable function A that assigns to every sequence $(z_1, \ldots, z_n) \in \mathbf{Z}^n$ a sequence $(\alpha_1, \ldots, \alpha_n) \in \mathbb{R}^n$ and that is equivariant with respect to permutations leaving the categories intact: For any sequence

$(z_1, \ldots, z_n) \in \mathbf{Z}^n$ and any permutation π of $\{1, \ldots, n\}$ preserving the categories, $K(z_{\pi(1)}, \ldots, z_{\pi(n)}) = K(z_1, \ldots, z_n)$, it is required that (1.3) hold.

Let $n = l + 1$. The *K-conditional conformal predictor* determined by A (as a K-conditional nonconformity measure) is defined by (1.4), where for each $z \in \mathbf{Z}$ the corresponding *K-conditional p-value* p^z is defined by

$$p^z := \frac{\left|\{i = 1, \ldots, l + 1 \,|\, \kappa_i^z = \kappa_{l+1}^z \ \& \ \alpha_i^z \geq \alpha_{l+1}^z\}\right|}{\left|\{i = 1, \ldots, l + 1 \,|\, \kappa_i^z = \kappa_{l+1}^z\}\right|}, \tag{2.2}$$

where

$$\left(\kappa_1^z, \ldots, \kappa_{l+1}^z\right) := K(z_1, \ldots, z_l, z) \tag{2.3}$$

and the nonconformity scores α_i^z are defined by (1.6). The term "K-conditional conformity measure" (as well as "inductive conformity measure" in the next section) will be used in the same way as for conformal predictors.

Conditional conformal predictors automatically satisfy the following property of conditional validity.

Proposition 2.1. *Let K be an $(l + 1)$-taxonomy. If examples $z_1, \ldots, z_{l+1}$ are generated from an exchangeable probability distribution on $\mathbf{Z}^{l+1}$, the conditional probability of error, $z_{l+1} \notin \Gamma^\epsilon(z_1, \ldots, z_l)$, given $\kappa_{l+1}^z = \kappa$ will not exceed ϵ for any ϵ, any K-conditional conformal predictor Γ, and any category $\kappa \in \mathbf{K}$.*

Proposition 2.1 will remain true if the requirement that $z_1, \ldots, z_{l+1}$ be exchangeable is replaced by the following requirement of conditional exchangeability: the sequence of categories $\kappa_1, \ldots, \kappa_{l+1}$ is generated arbitrarily, for each category κ the multiset of examples z_i with category $\kappa_i = \kappa$ is also generated arbitrarily but the order of these examples is chosen randomly (with each order having the same probability). To see that this assumption (which is an example of an online compression model, discussed in [365], pp. 198–199) can be significantly less restrictive than the exchangeability assumption, consider the following example [294]. In the problem of recognizing hand-written characters produced by a person writing a letter, the assumption of exchangeability is grossly violated: for example, a "q" is almost invariably followed by a "u." However, if we define the category of an example to be its label, the exchangeability assumption becomes satisfied or almost satisfied; for example, the instances of the letter "q" might well be exchangeable.

The most important special case is where

$$K(z_1, \ldots, z_n) = (K_1(z_1), \ldots, K_1(z_n)) \tag{2.4}$$

for some function $K_1 : \mathbf{Z} \to \mathbf{K}$ and all $(z_1, \ldots, z_n) \in \mathbf{Z}^n$ (the category of an example depends only on the example itself). We will often be interested in even more specialized taxonomies. One such interesting special case of (2.4) is where $K_1(z) = y$ coincides with the label y in the problem of classification. The corresponding conditional conformal predictors are called *label conditional conformal predictors*. On the other hand, both in classification and regression problems we can consider functions

$K_1(z) = K_1((x, y))$ that depend only on the object x. The corresponding conditional conformal predictors are called *object conditional conformal predictors*. We will usually drop the lower index 1 in the notation K_1; this will never lead to an ambiguity as the domains of K and K_1 are disjoint (and when a sequence of length 1 is identified with its only element, K becomes an extension of K_1).

Let $n \in \mathbb{N}$. We can generalize n-taxonomies giving rise to object conditional conformal predictors as follows: a *label independent n-taxonomy* is a function K that assigns to every sequence $(x_1, \ldots, x_n) \in \mathbf{X}^n$ of objects a sequence $(\kappa_1, \ldots, \kappa_n) \in \mathbb{N}^n$ of natural numbers and that is equivariant with respect to permutations: for any permutation π of $\{1, \ldots, n\}$,

$$(\kappa_1, \ldots, \kappa_n) = K(x_1, \ldots, x_n) \implies (\kappa_{\pi(1)}, \ldots, \kappa_{\pi(n)}) = K(x_{\pi(1)}, \ldots, x_{\pi(n)}).$$

Intuitively, K clusters $x_1, \ldots, x_n$, and κ_i is the cluster assigned to x_i.

2.2.1 Venn's Dilemma

In his classic book [355] on the foundations of frequentist probability, John Venn discusses the problem of choosing the right reference class for an object (see, e.g., [365], p. 159). We have a similar problem here. On one hand, we want the categories to be large enough so that we have enough statistical data for our inferences. On the other hand, we want them to be sufficiently narrow to make our inferences as specific as possible.

This is a possible strategy for conditional conformal predictors in the problem of classification with a small number of labels:

- At first the conformal predictor should not be conditional at all.
- Then, as the number of examples grows, it should be label conditional.
- As the number of examples grows further, we could split the objects into clusters (using a label independent taxonomy) and make our prediction sets conditional on them as well.

For the last item, a reasonable rule of thumb would be to ensure that the size of a cluster be no less than 100, to have a reasonable chance of getting confident predictions.

2.3 Inductive Conformal Predictors

The method of conformal prediction is relatively computationally inefficient. For example, in the case of using the support vector method for classification (as explained in Section 1.6), for each potential label y of the test object x_{l+1} we need to find the $l + 1$ nonconformity scores (1.6), which involves solving a quadratic optimization problem. And if we want to classify k different test objects, the number of optimization problems to solve becomes $k|\mathbf{Y}| = 2k$.

In the method of inductive conformal prediction, the training set $(z_1, \ldots, z_l)$ is split into two parts, the *proper training set* $(z_1, \ldots, z_m)$ of size $m < l$ and the *calibration set* $(z_{m+1}, \ldots, z_l)$ of size $l - m$. An *inductive (non)conformity m-measure* is a measurable function $A : \mathbf{Z}^m \times \mathbf{Z} \to \mathbb{R}$, with the intuition behind the *inductive (non)conformity score* $A((z_1, \ldots, z_m), z)$ being a measure of how well (or poorly) z conforms to the proper training set $(z_1, \ldots, z_m)$. The *inductive conformal predictor* determined by A as an inductive nonconformity measure is defined by (1.4), where for each $z \in \mathbf{Z}$ the corresponding p-value p^z is defined by

$$p^z := \frac{|\{i = m + 1, \ldots, l \mid \alpha_i \geq \alpha^z\}| + 1}{l - m + 1} \qquad (2.5)$$

and the corresponding inductive nonconformity scores are defined by

$$\alpha_i := A((z_1, \ldots, z_m), z_i), \quad i = m + 1, \ldots, l, \quad \alpha^z := A((z_1, \ldots, z_m), z). \quad (2.6)$$

Inductive conformal predictors can be "smoothed" in exactly the same way as conformal predictors. Namely, the *smoothed inductive conformal predictor* determined by A as an inductive nonconformity measure is defined by (1.4), where the p-values p^z are now defined by

$$p^z := \frac{|\{i = m + 1, \ldots, l \mid \alpha_i > \alpha^z\}| + \tau \left(|\{i = m + 1, \ldots, l \mid \alpha_i = \alpha^z\}| + 1\right)}{l - m + 1},$$

the inductive nonconformity scores are defined as before, by (2.6), and the *tie-breaking random variable* τ is distributed uniformly on $[0, 1]$.

In the case of structured examples, $\mathbf{Z} = \mathbf{X} \times \mathbf{Y}$ (such as in the problems of classification and regression), a natural choice of an inductive nonconformity m-measure is

$$A\big((z_1, \ldots, z_m), (x, y)\big) := \Delta(y, f(x)), \qquad (2.7)$$

where, similarly to (1.18), $f : \mathbf{X} \to \mathbf{Y}'$ is a prediction rule found from $(z_1, \ldots, z_m)$ as the training set and $\Delta : \mathbf{Y} \times \mathbf{Y}' \to \mathbb{R}$ is a measure of difference between a label and a prediction. Allowing the prediction space $\mathbf{Y}'$ to be different from the label space $\mathbf{Y}$ (namely, $\mathbf{Y}' \supset \mathbf{Y}$) may be useful when the underlying prediction method gives additional information as compared to the predicted label; for example, in the support vector method the predicted label is 1 when a certain expression is positive and -1 otherwise, and we can define $f(x)$ as the value of this expression.

Proposition 2.2. *If examples $z_{m+1}, \ldots, z_{l+1}$ are generated from an exchangeable probability distribution on $\mathbf{Z}^{l-m+1}$, the probability of error, $z_{l+1} \notin \Gamma^\epsilon(z_1, \ldots, z_l)$, will not exceed ϵ for any inductive conformal predictor Γ and any significance level ϵ; it will be equal to ϵ for any smoothed inductive conformal predictor whose tie-breaking random variables τ are independent of $z_{m+1}, \ldots, z_{l+1}$.*

A greater computational efficiency of inductive conformal predictors, for reasonable choices of the prediction rule f and the difference measure Δ, is now evident: For example, when applying the support vector method (in the form (2.7)), we need to solve a quadratic optimization problem only once.

A disadvantage of inductive conformal predictors is their potential prediction inefficiency. For example, in the case of the inductive conformal predictors based on (2.7) as compared to the conformal predictors based on (1.18) we waste the calibration set when developing the prediction rule f, and we waste the proper training set when computing the p-values. An attempt to cure this disadvantage is made in [361].

For a general discussion of transductive and inductive inference in the context of conformal prediction, see, for example, [365], p. 6.

2.3.1 Conditional Inductive Conformal Predictors

It is easy to combine the ideas of conditional conformal predictors and inductive conformal predictors. An *inductive m-taxonomy* is a measurable function $K : \mathbf{Z}^m \times \mathbf{Z} \to \mathbf{K}$, where $\mathbf{K}$ is a measurable space. As in the case of conditional conformal predictors, the *category* $K((z_1, \ldots, z_m), z)$ of an example z is a classification of z, which may depend on the proper training set $(z_1, \ldots, z_m)$.

The *conditional inductive conformal predictor* (conditional ICP) corresponding to K and an inductive conformity measure A is defined as the set predictor (1.15), where the p-values $p^{x_{l+1} \cdot y} = p^y$ are now defined by

$$p^y := \frac{|\{i = m + 1, \ldots, l \mid \kappa_i = \kappa^y \,\&\, \alpha_i \leq \alpha^y\}| + 1}{|\{i = m + 1, \ldots, l \mid \kappa_i = \kappa^y\}| + 1}, \tag{2.8}$$

the categories κ are defined by

$$\kappa_i := K((z_1, \ldots, z_m), z_i), \quad i = m + 1, \ldots, l, \qquad \kappa^y := K((z_1, \ldots, z_m), (x, y)),$$

and the conformity scores α are defined as before by (2.6) (where $\alpha^y := \alpha^z$). A *label conditional ICP* is a conditional ICP with the inductive m-taxonomy $K(\cdot, (x, y)) := y$.

The following proposition shows that in classification problems label conditional ICPs achieve label conditional validity.

Proposition 2.3. *If random examples* $z_{m+1}, \ldots, z_l, z_{l+1} = (x_{l+1}, y_{l+1})$ *are exchangeable, the probability of error* $y_{l+1} \notin \Gamma^\epsilon(z_1, \ldots, z_l, x_{l+1})$ *given the category* $K((z_1, \ldots, z_m), z_{l+1})$ *of* z_{l+1} *does not exceed* ϵ *for any significance level* ϵ *and any conditional inductive conformal predictor* Γ *corresponding to* K.

2.4 Training Conditional Validity of Inductive Conformal Predictors

In Section 2.2 we saw that the notion of conformal predictor can be modified in a natural way to improve its example conditional validity. In this section we take up training conditional validity. It is clear that the 1-parameter definitions of validity given in Sections 1.3 and 2.2 will not work for precise training conditional validity: the coverage probability (i.e., the probability of the event $z_{l+1} \in \Gamma(z_1, \ldots, z_l)$) conditional on the training set $(z_1, \ldots, z_l)$ of a set predictor Γ under the randomness assumption is $Q(\Gamma(z_1, \ldots, z_l))$, where Q is the data generating distribution on $\mathbf{Z}$, and the probability of error $Q(\mathbf{Z} \backslash \Gamma(z_1, \ldots, z_l))$ does not have a useful upper bound:

$$\sup_Q Q(\mathbf{Z} \backslash \Gamma(z_1, \ldots, z_l)) = 1$$

unless $\Gamma(z_1, \ldots, z_l)$ covers all of $\mathbf{Z}$. However, some of the Qs are very unlikely once we know the training set, and the following two-parameter definition captures this intuition. A set predictor Γ is (ϵ, δ)-*valid* if, for any probability distribution Q on $\mathbf{Z}$,

$$Q^l \left\{ (z_1, \ldots, z_l) \mid Q\{z_{l+1} \mid z_{l+1} \notin \Gamma(z_1, \ldots, z_l)\} \leq \epsilon \right\} \geq 1 - \delta. \qquad (2.9)$$

In words, (ϵ, δ)-validity means that with probability at least $1 - \delta$ the probability of the prediction set will be at least $1 - \epsilon$. The following proposition shows that inductive conformal predictors satisfy this property for some ϵ and δ (see Corollaries 2.1 and 2.2 for stronger but easier to understand conditions).

Proposition 2.4. *Let $\epsilon, \delta, E \in (0, 1)$. If Γ is an inductive conformal predictor, the set predictor Γ^ϵ is (E, δ)-valid provided*

$$\mathrm{bin}_{h,E}(\lfloor \epsilon(h+1) \rfloor - 1) \leq \delta, \qquad (2.10)$$

where $h := l - m$ is the size of the calibration set and $\mathrm{bin}_{h,E}$ is the cumulative binomial distribution function with h trials and probability of success E (except that $\mathrm{bin}_{h,E}(-1) := 0$).

Proof sketch. Suppose, without loss of generality, that $k := \epsilon(h + 1)$ is an integer. Fix a proper training set $(z_1, \ldots, z_m)$. In this proof sketch we will only check that (2.9) holds for a given data-generating distribution Q if Γ is based on an inductive nonconformity m-measure A such that $A((z_1, \ldots, z_m), Z)$ has a continuous distribution when Z is distributed as Q. Moreover, we will see that in this case the condition (2.10) is necessary and sufficient.

Define α^* as the largest value such that $A((z_1, \ldots, z_m), Z) \geq \alpha^*$ with Q-probability E. The probability of error $Q(\mathbf{Z} \backslash \Gamma(z_1, \ldots, z_l))$ exceeds E if and only if at most $k - 1$ of the α_i, $i = m+1, \ldots, l$, are in the interval $[\alpha^*, \infty)$. The probability of the last event is $\mathrm{bin}_{h,E}(k - 1)$. □

For a full self-contained proof of Proposition 2.4, see [360], proof of Theorem 1; and for further references, see the following section.

In combination with Hoeffding's inequality (see, e.g., [365], p. 287), Proposition 2.4 gives:

Corollary 2.1. *Let $\epsilon, \delta \in (0, 1)$. If Γ is an inductive conformal predictor, the set predictor Γ^ϵ is (E, δ)-valid, where*

$$E := \epsilon + \sqrt{\frac{\ln \frac{1}{\delta}}{2h}} \qquad (2.11)$$

and $h := l - m$ is the size of the calibration set.

The corollary allows us to construct (ϵ, δ)-valid set predictors when the training set is sufficiently large: for any inductive conformal predictor Γ with the size h of the calibration set, the set predictor

$$\Gamma^{\epsilon - \sqrt{\frac{\ln \frac{1}{\delta}}{2h}}} \qquad (2.12)$$

will be (ϵ, δ)-valid (this assumes that the difference in (2.12) is positive).

Applying inequality 2. in [194] (p. 278) instead of Hoeffding's inequality to Proposition 2.4 we obtain:

Corollary 2.2. *Let $\epsilon, \delta \in (0, 1)$. If Γ is an inductive conformal predictor, the set predictor Γ^ϵ is (E, δ)-valid, where*

$$E := \epsilon + \sqrt{\frac{2\epsilon \ln \frac{1}{\delta}}{h}} + \frac{2 \ln \frac{1}{\delta}}{h}. \qquad (2.13)$$

Figure 2.2 gives an idea of the relative accuracy of the bounds in Proposition 2.4 and Corollaries 2.1 and 2.2; remember that (as we saw in the proof) the bound in Proposition 2.4 is optimal.

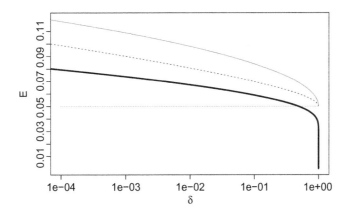

FIGURE 2.2

The probability of error E vs δ from Proposition 2.4 (the thick solid line), Corollary 2.1 (the thin solid line), and Corollary 2.2 (the thin dashed line), where $\epsilon = 0.05$ and $h = 999$.

Proposition 2.4 and Corollaries 2.1 and 2.2 are particularly relevant in the batch mode of prediction: If a set predictor is (ϵ, δ)-valid, the percentage of errors on the test set will be bounded above by ϵ up to statistical fluctuations (whose typical size is the square root of the number of test examples) unless we are unlucky with the training set (which can happen with probability at most δ).

There is a striking similarity between the guarantee (2.10) and a standard hold-out bound on the error probability of classifiers (see, e.g., [194]). In our terminology, the idea of the hold-out estimate can be described as follows. In a classification problem, find a prediction rule from the proper training set. Let the number of errors it makes on a calibration set of size h be k. Then the prediction rule's probability of error on a random test example does not exceed

$$\overline{\mathrm{bin}}_{h,\delta}(k) \tag{2.14}$$

with probability at least $1 - \delta$ over the training set, where $\overline{\mathrm{bin}}$ is the inverse function to bin:

$$\overline{\mathrm{bin}}_{h,\delta}(k) := \max\{p \mid \mathrm{bin}_{h,p}(k) \geq \delta\}.$$

In terms of the function $\overline{\mathrm{bin}}$, the condition (2.10) can be replaced by the definition

$$E := \overline{\mathrm{bin}}_{h,\delta}\left(\lfloor \epsilon(h+1) - 1\rfloor\right) \leq \overline{\mathrm{bin}}_{h,\delta}(\epsilon h). \tag{2.15}$$

The difference between the expressions (2.14) and (2.15) for the guaranteed probability of error at the confidence level $1 - \delta$ is that in one case we have the actual number of errors k in h trials and in the other case essentially the expected number of errors in h trials.

In conclusion of this section we will discuss training conditional validity of smoothed inductive conformal predictors (when defining training conditional validity for randomized set predictors, the outermost probability in (2.9) also involves the generator of random numbers). Unfortunately, there are no guarantees of training conditional validity for them unless we make some extra assumptions, and the next proposition will make a continuity assumption under the data-generating distribution. This can be seen from the following example. Consider the trivial smoothed inductive conformal predictor based on the inductive nonconformity m-measure identically equal to 0. At significance level ϵ it has coverage probability 1 with probability $1 - \epsilon$ and coverage probability 0 with probability ϵ. Therefore, it cannot be (E, δ)-valid for $E < 1$ unless $\delta \geq \epsilon$. This contrasts with the case of unsmoothed ICPs where very small δ are achievable (see, e.g., Figure 2.2). Another natural way to define smoothed ICPs is to use different random variables τ when computing the smoothed p-values p^y for different labels $y \in \mathbf{Y}$; however, without continuity assumptions this version also encounters similar problems with training conditional validity.

Under a continuity assumption we can still prove the following analogue of Proposition 2.4 for smoothed ICPs.

Proposition 2.5. *Let $\epsilon, \delta, E \in (0, 1)$. If Γ is a smoothed inductive conformal predictor based on an inductive nonconformity m-measure A such that $A(z_1, \ldots, z_m, Z)$,*

$Z \sim Q$, is a continuous random variable for Q^m-almost all $(z_1, \ldots, z_m)$, the set predictor Γ^ϵ is (E, δ)-valid under Q provided

$$\mathrm{bin}_{h,E}\left(\lfloor \epsilon(h+1) \rfloor\right) \leq \delta.$$

Proof sketch. We can set $\tau := 0$ in the definition of a smoothed inductive conformal predictor and then use the same argument as in the proof of Proposition 2.4. (See the proof of Theorem 1(b) in [360] for details.) □

2.5   **Classical Tolerance Regions**

So far we have discussed training conditional validity for inductive conformal predictors. However, a large class of conformal predictors—classical tolerance predictors—satisfy the same property of training conditional validity (and this is not accidental, as we will see later).

The first tolerance predictor was introduced by Wilks [379] in 1941. Wilks's tolerance predictor was one-dimensional, $\mathbf{Z} = \mathbb{R}$, but Wald [370] in 1943 extended Wilks's procedure to the multidimensional case, $\mathbf{Z} = \mathbb{R}^d$. The procedure was further generalized first by Tukey [347] in 1947, then by, among others, Fraser [101–102] in 1951 and 1953, and Kemperman [172] in 1956.

We will describe Tukey's procedure as a special case of conformal prediction and indicate the generalizations made by Fraser and Kemperman. *Tukey's nonconformity n-measure* starts from a sequence of measurable functions $(\phi_1, \ldots, \phi_n)$ on $\mathbf{Z}$ and a sequence of numbers $(\beta_1, \ldots, \beta_n)$; these two sequences are the parameters of the procedure. Suppose we are given a sequence of examples $(z_1, \ldots, z_n)$ and want to find the corresponding sequence of nonconformity scores (satisfying (1.3)). Assign nonconformity score β_1 to all z_i at which max $\phi_1(z_i)$ is attained and discard those z_i. Then assign nonconformity score β_2 to all z_i at which max $\phi_2(z_i)$ is attained and discard those z_i. Continue doing this until all z_i are assigned nonconformity scores and discarded (it is clear that this will happen at step n at the latest). Notice that the last function ϕ_n does not play any useful role. The conformal predictor determined by this nonconformity measure will be called *Tukey's (conformal) predictor*; its input is a training set of size $l = n - 1$.

A standard assumption in the theory of tolerance predictors is continuity; in particular, Tukey assumes that the cumulative distribution function of each random variable $\phi_i(Z), i = 1, \ldots, l$, where $Z \sim Q$ and Q is the data-generating distribution on $\mathbf{Z}$, is continuous (which greatly weakened Wald's continuity assumption).

Remark 2.1.   This description of Tukey's [347] procedure essentially follows [365]. Tukey's description, however, is quite different; of course, Tukey defines his tolerance predictor directly, not via a nonconformity measure. The parameters of his predictor are a sequence of measurable functions $(\phi_1, \ldots, \phi_l)$ on $\mathbf{Z}$ and a nonempty set $\lambda \subset \{1, \ldots, l, l + 1\}$. Let $(z_1, \ldots, z_l)$ be a sequence of examples (what we call a training set). Tukey splits a subset of $\mathbf{Z}$ of Q-measure 1 into a sequence of "statistically equivalent blocks" $S_1, \ldots, S_{l+1}$ as follows:

$$S_1 := \{z \mid \phi_1(z) > a_1\},$$

where $a_1 := \max_i \phi_1(z_i) = \phi_1(z_{i(1)})$, which defines $i(1)$,

$$S_2 := \{z \mid \phi_1(z) < a_1, \phi_2(z) > a_2\},$$

where $a_2 := \max_{i \neq i(1)} \phi_2(z_i) = \phi_2(z_{i(2)})$, which defines $i(2)$; continue until

$$S_l := \{z \mid \phi_1(z) < a_1, \ldots, \phi_{l-1}(z) < a_{l-1}, \phi_l(z) > a_l\},$$

where $a_l := \max_{i \notin \{i(1), \ldots, i(l-1)\}} \phi_l(z_i) = \phi_l(z_{i(l)})$, which defines $i(l)$, and finally set

$$S_{l+1} := \{z \mid \phi_1(z) < a_1, \ldots, \phi_l(z) < a_l\}.$$

The prediction set output by Tukey's tolerance predictor is $\cup_{k \in \lambda} S_k$.

Let us check that this definition is equivalent, under Tukey's assumption, to the one given earlier. Define $\beta_1, \ldots, \beta_n$, where $n := l + 1$, in any way such that every $\beta_i, i \notin \gamma$, is greater than every $\beta_j, j \in \gamma$. Let us check that $\cup_{k \in \lambda} S_k$ coincides, to within a set of Q-measure 0, with $\Gamma^\epsilon(z_1, \ldots, z_l)$, where Γ is Tukey's conformal predictor and $\epsilon := (n - |\lambda|)/n$. First suppose $z \notin \cup_{k \in \lambda} S_k$. Let k^* be the $k \notin \lambda$ such that $z \in S_k$ (such a k will exist with probability one, and here and in the rest of this paragraph we ignore events of probability zero). When applied to the sequence $(z_1, \ldots, z_l, z)$, Tukey's nonconformity measure produces

$$\alpha_{i(1)} = \beta_1, \ldots, \alpha_{i(k^*-1)} = \beta_{k^*-1}, \alpha_{l+1} = \beta_{k^*}, \tag{2.16}$$

where α_{l+1} is the nonconformity score of z. The only thing we can say about $(\alpha_{i(k^*)}, \ldots, \alpha_{i(l)})$ is that this sequence is some permutation of $\beta_{k^*+1}, \ldots, \beta_n$. We can see that z's nonconformity score is among the ϵn largest, and so $z \notin \Gamma^\epsilon(z_1, \ldots, z_l)$. Now suppose $z \in \cup_{k \in \lambda} S_k$. Let k^* be the $k \in \lambda$ such that $z \in S_k$ (such a k always exists). When applied to the sequence $(z_1, \ldots, z_l, z)$, Tukey's nonconformity measure again produces (2.16). Since now z's nonconformity score is not among the ϵn largest, we have $z \in \Gamma^\epsilon(z_1, \ldots, z_l)$.

Tukey shows that the coverage probability $Q(\Gamma^\epsilon(z_1, \ldots, z_l))$ of his set predictor has beta distribution with parameters $((1-\epsilon)n, \epsilon n)$, which we will denote $\text{Bet}_{(1-\epsilon)n, \epsilon n}$ (see also [347] or [133], Theorems 2.2 and 2.3). In particular, its expected coverage probability is $1 - \epsilon$ (which we already know as Tukey's predictor is a conformal predictor). This can be stated as a result about (ϵ, δ)-validity of Tukey's predictor. Formally, we say that a set predictor Γ is (ϵ, δ)-*valid for* Q, where Q is a probability distribution on $\mathbf{Z}$, if (2.9) holds. We can see that Tukey's predictor is (E, δ)-valid for a probability distribution Q on $\mathbf{Z}$ satisfying Tukey's assumptions if and only if

$$\delta \geq \text{Bet}_{(1-\epsilon)n, \epsilon n}(1 - E) = 1 - \text{Bet}_{\epsilon n, (1-\epsilon)n}(E), \tag{2.17}$$

where Bet now stands for the cumulative beta distribution function with the parameters given as subscripts.

There is a close connection between beta distributions and binomial distributions: for all $l \in \{1, 2, \ldots\}$, all $k \in \{1, \ldots, l\}$, and all $E \in (0, 1)$,

$$\text{bin}_{l,E}(k - 1) = \text{Bet}_{l+1-k,k}(1 - E). \tag{2.18}$$

(see, e.g., http://dlmf.nist.gov/8.17.E5). Therefore, we can reword (2.17) as follows: Tukey's predictor is (E, δ)-valid for Q if and only if

$$\delta \geq \text{bin}_{l,E}(\epsilon(l + 1) - 1). \tag{2.19}$$

This is identical to (2.10) except that the size h of the calibration set is replaced by the full size l of the training set.

The assumption of continuity was removed by Tukey [348] in 1948, and some of Tukey's mistakes were corrected by Fraser and Wormleighton [103]; this, of course, required a generalization of Tukey's procedures treating the ties carefully. These results show that under (2.19) the generalized version of Tukey's predictor is (ϵ, δ)-valid; no assumptions on the data-generating distribution are needed.

It is an interesting problem to characterize the class of conformal predictors that are (ϵ, δ)-valid under the condition (2.19). A related problem is whether nontrivial guarantees of training conditional validity can be obtained for conformal predictors different from classical tolerance predictors. See [360], Appendix B, for an empirical study of the training conditional validity of conformal predictors and for a corrected version of Nouretdinov's ([254], Theorem 1) theoretical result about training conditional efficiency of conformal predictors based on the nearest neighbors algorithm.

It would also be interesting to develop object and label conditional versions of Tukey's predictors.

Among the developments of Tukey's procedure in other directions are Fraser's [101], who noticed that we can allow ϕ_k to depend on the maxima reached by $\phi_1, \ldots, \phi_{k-1}$ in Tukey's procedure described earlier, and Kemperman's [172], who further noticed that we can allow dependence on the examples were the maxima were reached rather than on the maxima themselves.

Wilks's [379] procedure is a special case of Tukey's procedure in which $\mathbf{Z} = \mathbb{R}$ and $\phi_1 = \cdots = \phi_l$ are the identity functions $\phi_i(z) = z$. For two numbers $L \leq U$ in the set $\{0, \ldots, l, l + 1\}$ Wilks's predictor outputs $[z_{(L)}, z_{(U)}]$, where $z_{(i)}$ is the ith order statistics (the ith smallest value in the training set $(z_1, \ldots, z_l)$, except that $z_{(0)} := -\infty$ and $z_{(l+1)} := \infty$). (This is a slightly generalized version: Wilks considered the symmetric case $L + U = l + 1$.) In 1945 Scheffé and Tukey ([299], p. 192) showed that this set predictor is (E, δ)-valid provided we have (2.17) with $(1 - \epsilon)n$ replaced by $U - L$ and ϵn replaced by $l + 1 + L - U$, removing a continuity assumption in Wilks's result.

Proposition 2.4 can be deduced from Scheffé and Tukey's result (which is a special case of Tukey, Fraser, and Wormleighton's results). This follows from the interpretation of inductive conformal predictors as a "conditional" version of Wilks's predictors corresponding to $L := \epsilon(l+1)$ and $U := l+1$. After observing the proper training set we apply Wilks's predictors to the conformity scores α_i of the calibration examples to predict the conformity score of a test example; the set prediction for the conformity score for the test object is then transformed into the prediction set consisting of the labels leading to a score in the predicted range.

2.6 Object Conditional Validity and Efficiency

In this section we will be concerned with object conditional validity (the vertex O in Figure 2.1) and ways of achieving efficiency under constraints of object conditional validity.

2.6.1 Negative Result

We start from a negative result (a version of Lemma 1 in [201]) which says that the requirement of precise object conditional validity cannot be satisfied in a nontrivial way for rich object spaces (such as $\mathbf{X} = \mathbb{R}$). If Q is a probability distribution on $\mathbf{Z}$, we let $Q_{\mathbf{X}}$ stand for its marginal distribution on $\mathbf{X}$: $Q_{\mathbf{X}}(A) := Q(A \times \mathbf{Y})$. We will consider randomized set predictors that depend, additionally, on a random input $\omega \in \Omega$ whose distribution (characterizing the generator of random numbers used by the predictor) will be denoted R.

Let us say that a set predictor Γ *has $1 - \epsilon$ object conditional validity*, where $\epsilon \in (0, 1)$, if, for all probability distributions Q on $\mathbf{Z}$ and $Q_{\mathbf{X}}$-almost all $x \in \mathbf{X}$, the conditional $(Q^{l+1} \times R)$-probability of error

$$\{(z_1, \ldots, z_l, (x_{l+1}, y_{l+1}), \omega) \in \mathbf{Z}^{l+1} \times \Omega \mid y_{l+1} \notin \Gamma(z_1, \ldots, z_l, x_{l+1}, \omega)\}$$

given $x_{l+1} = x$ is at most ϵ.

If P is a probability distribution on $\mathbf{X}$, we say that a property F of elements of $\mathbf{X}$ holds for *P-almost all* elements of a measurable set $E \subseteq \mathbf{X}$ if $P(E \backslash F) = 0$; a *P-non-atom* is an element $x \in \mathbf{X}$ such that $P(\{x\}) = 0$. We will use the notation Λ for the Lebesgue measure on $\mathbb{R}$ (this agrees with the notation used in Section 1.4). If $E \subseteq \mathbb{R}$, $\mathrm{co}E$ stands for the convex closure of E.

Proposition 2.6 ([360]). *Suppose $\mathbf{X}$ is a separable metric space equipped with the Borel σ-algebra. Let $\epsilon \in (0, 1)$. Suppose that a set predictor Γ has $1 - \epsilon$ object conditional validity. In the case of regression, we have, for all probability distributions Q on $\mathbf{Z}$ and for $Q_{\mathbf{X}}$-almost all $Q_{\mathbf{X}}$-non-atoms $x \in \mathbf{X}$,*

$$(Q^l \times R)(\{(z_1, \ldots, z_l, \omega) \in \mathbf{Z}^l \times \Omega \mid \Lambda(\Gamma(z_1, \ldots, z_l, x, \omega)) = \infty\}) \geq 1 - \epsilon \quad (2.20)$$

and

$$(Q^l \times R)(\{(z_1, \ldots, z_l, \omega) \in \mathbf{Z}^l \times \Omega \mid \mathrm{co}\,\Gamma(z_1, \ldots, z_l, x, \omega)\} = \mathbb{R}) \geq 1 - 2\epsilon. \quad (2.21)$$

In the case of classification, we have, for all Q, all $y \in \mathbf{Y}$, and $Q_{\mathbf{X}}$-almost all $Q_{\mathbf{X}}$-non-atoms x,

$$(Q^l \times R)(\{(z_1, \ldots, z_l, \omega) \in \mathbf{Z}^l \times \Omega \mid y \in \Gamma(z_1, \ldots, z_l, x, \omega)\}) \geq 1 - \epsilon. \quad (2.22)$$

The constant ϵ in each of (2.20)–(2.22) is optimal, in the sense that it cannot be replaced by a smaller constant (unless $\epsilon > 1/2$ in (2.21), in which case we can, of course, set $\epsilon := 1/2$).

We are mainly interested in the case of a small ϵ (corresponding to high confidence). In this case (2.20) implies that, in the case of regression, the prediction interval (i.e., the convex hull of the prediction set) can be expected to be infinitely long unless the test object is an atom. Even an infinitely long prediction interval can be somewhat informative in that it can provide an upper or lower bound on the label of the test object. According to (2.21), the prediction interval can be also expected (with a slightly lower level of confidence) to be completely uninformative unless the test object is an atom.

In the case of classification, (2.22) says that each particular $y \in \mathbf{Y}$ is likely to be included in the prediction set, and so the prediction set is likely to be large. In particular, (2.22) implies that the expected size of the prediction set is a least $(1 - \epsilon)|\mathbf{Y}|$.

Of course, the condition that the test object x be a nonatom is essential: if $Q_{\mathbf{X}}(\{x\}) > 0$, an inductive conformal predictor that ignores all examples with objects different from the current test object can have $1 - \epsilon$ object conditional validity and still produce a small prediction set for a test object x if the training set is big enough to contain many examples with x as their object.

It is very easy to see that the constant ϵ in (2.20) and (2.22) indeed cannot be replaced by a smaller constant. This follows from the fact that the trivial set predictor predicting $\mathbf{Y}$ with probability $1 - \epsilon$ and $\emptyset$ with probability ϵ has $1 - \epsilon$ object conditional validity. Therefore, Proposition 2.6 demonstrates an interesting all-or-nothing phenomenon for set predictors having $1 - \epsilon$ object conditional validity: such predictors produce hopelessly large prediction sets with probability at least $1 - \epsilon$; on the other hand, already a trivial predictor of this kind produces the smallest possible prediction sets with probability ϵ.

To see that the constant ϵ is optimal in (2.21), consider the set predictor predicting $\mathbb{R}$ with probability $1 - 2\epsilon$, $[0, \infty)$ with probability ϵ, and $(-\infty, 0]$ with probability ϵ (this assumes $\epsilon < 1/2$). This predictor's conditional probability of error given all $l + 1$ examples is at most ϵ (0 if $y_{l+1} = 0$ and ϵ otherwise); therefore, the conditional probability of error will be at most ϵ given the test object.

For the full proof of Proposition 2.6, see [360], Theorem 2. Here we will only explain the simple intuition behind the proof. The following naive (but formalizable) argument ignores all subtleties caused by conditional probabilities being defined only almost surely. Let us see why, for example, (2.22) is plausible. Suppose that (2.22) is false. Let P be the same as Q except that the conditional probability of the label given that the object is x is replaced by the probability measure concentrated at y. Since x is a $P_{\mathbf{X}} = Q_{\mathbf{X}}$-nonatom, P and Q are close in the sense of total variation distance. Therefore, (2.22) will remain false if Q is replaced by P: the conditional $(P^l \times R)$-probability of the event

$$y \in \Gamma(z_1, \ldots, z_l, x, \omega)$$

is less than $1 - \epsilon$. By the definition of P this means that the conditional $(P^{l+1} \times R)$-probability of the event

$$y_{l+1} \in \Gamma(z_1, \ldots, z_l, x_{l+1}, \omega)$$

given $x_{l+1} = x$ is less than $1 - \epsilon$, which contradicts Γ having $1 - \epsilon$ object conditional validity.

To formalize this heuristic argument, x has to be replaced by its "neighborhood" (in a suitable sense). The well-known fact that closeness, in total variation distance, of P and Q implies closeness of P^l and Q^l follows from connections between total variation distance and Hellinger distance (see, e.g., [345], Section 2.4). See [360] for further details.

Remark 2.2. Nontrivial set predictors having $1 - \epsilon$ object conditional validity are well known in statistics: see, e.g., [306], Section 5.3.1. The settings in which such predictors are known are very different from the standard setting of machine learning: instead of the assumption of randomness, nothing is assumed about the objects but the labels are assumed, for example, to follow the Gauss linear model given the objects. The Gaussian assumption can be relaxed: for example, nontrivial set predictors having $1 - \epsilon$ object conditional validity are constructed in [225] in the case of non-Gaussian noise. However, the model for the labels remains parametric and nothing at all is assumed about the objects. Since there are no assumptions about the objects, all valid predictions must be automatically object conditionally valid: we cannot use averaging over the objects. On the other hand, the standard results of machine learning are not object conditionally valid, since they use the assumption of randomness (including the assumption of randomness for the objects) in an essential way. (We have already remarked in the discussion following Proposition 2.1 that the assumption of exchangeability can be weakened in the case of conditional conformal predictors.)

2.6.2 Positive Results

Proposition 2.6 does not prevent the existence of set predictors that are object conditionally valid in a partial and asymptotic sense and simultaneously asymptotically efficient. We will now discuss them following Lei and Wasserman [201]. The rest of this section is closely related to Section 1.4. Let the object space $\mathbf{X}$ be $[0, 1]^d$, for simplicity; we consider the problem of regression, $\mathbf{Y} = \mathbb{R}$. Until the end of this section we fix the data-generating distribution Q on $\mathbf{Z}$; as before, the data are generated from Q^{l+1} (l, however, will not be fixed; in particular, we will be interested in asymptotics as $l \to \infty$). Let us also fix a significance level $\epsilon > 0$. We will use the same notation Λ for the Lebesgue measure on $\mathbb{R}$ and on $\mathbb{R}^d$.

The *conditional oracle band* C^{or} is now defined as the set (the assumptions to be made momentarily will ensure that it is essentially unique) $C \subseteq \mathbf{Z}$

- with the conditional Q-probability of coverage $\{(x, y) \in \mathbf{Z} \mid y \in C_x\}$ given x at least $1 - \epsilon$ for $Q_{\mathbf{X}}$-almost all x
- and minimizing $\Lambda(C_x)$ for $Q_{\mathbf{X}}$-almost all x

where C_x stands for the x-cut of C: $C_x := \{y \in \mathbf{Y} \mid (x, y) \in C\}$. We will be interested in set predictors whose prediction for a new object x is asymptotically close to C_x^{or}.

Lei and Wasserman construct a conditional conformal predictor Γ (independent of ϵ) that is asymptotically efficient in the following object conditional sense:

$$\sup_{x \in \mathbf{X}} \Lambda\left(\Gamma^\epsilon(z_1, \ldots, z_l, x) \bigtriangleup C_x^{\mathrm{or}}\right) \to 0 \tag{2.23}$$

in probability, and even almost surely. They also establish the optimal rate of convergence in (2.23). Notice that (2.23) implies that Γ is object conditionally valid in an asymptotic sense.

For the additional properties of efficiency and validity (on top of what is guaranteed for all conditional conformal predictors) established by Lei and Wasserman for their predictor the following regularity conditions are sufficient:

1. The marginal distribution $Q_\mathbf{X}$ of Q has a differentiable density that is bounded above and bounded away from 0.
2. The conditional Q-probability distribution Q_x of the label y given any object x has a differentiable density q_x.
3. Both q_x and q'_x are continuous and bounded uniformly in x.
4. As a function of x, $q_x(y)$ is Lipschitz uniformly in y.
5. For each $x \in \mathbf{X}$ there exists t_x such that $Q_x(\{y \mid q_x(y) \geq t_x\}) = 1 - \epsilon$.
6. For some $\delta > 0$, the gradient of q_x is bounded above and bounded away from 0 uniformly in $x \in \mathbf{X}$ and $y \in \mathbb{R}$ satisfying $|q_x(y) - t_x| < \delta$.
7. Finally, $\inf_{x \in \mathbf{X}} t_x > 0$.

For concreteness, let us set

$$C^{\mathrm{or}} = \{(x, y) \mid q_x(y) \geq t_x\}.$$

The following is a special case of Lei and Wasserman's result.

Theorem 2.1 ([201], Theorem 9). *Suppose Assumptions 1–7 hold. There exists a conditional conformal predictor Γ (independent of ϵ) such that for any $\lambda > 0$ there exists B such that, as $l \to \infty$,*

$$\mathbb{P}\left(\sup_{x \in \mathbf{X}} \Lambda\left(\Gamma^\epsilon(z_1, \ldots, z_l, x) \triangle C^{\mathrm{or}}_x\right) \geq B\left(\frac{\log l}{l}\right)^{\frac{1}{d+3}}\right) = O\left(l^{-\lambda}\right). \quad (2.24)$$

Lei and Wasserman also show that the convergence rate in (2.24) is optimal (see [201], Theorem 12).

The proof of Theorem 2.1 given in [201] is constructive: the authors define explicitly a conditional conformal predictor satisfying (2.24). It is determined by the following taxonomy and conditional conformity measure. Let $z_1, \ldots, z_n$ be a sequence of examples $z_i = (x_i, y_i)$; the corresponding categories and conformity scores are defined as follows. Partition $\mathbf{X} = [0, 1]^d$ into $(1/h_n)^d$ axis-parallel cubes with sides of length

$$h_n \asymp \left(\frac{\log n}{n}\right)^{\frac{1}{d+3}}.$$

Define the category κ_i of z_i as the cell of the partition containing x_i. Let A be a cell of the partition. Define the "conditional" kernel density estimate

$$\hat{p}(y \mid A) := \frac{1}{n_A h_n} \sum_{i:x_i \in A} K\left(\frac{y - y_i}{h_n}\right),$$

where K is a fixed kernel satisfying the same conditions as in Section 1.4 (cf. (1.12)) and $n_A := |\{i \mid x_i \in A\}|$ (if $n_A = 0$, define $\hat{p}(y \mid A)$ arbitrarily). Finally, set the conformity scores to $\alpha_i := \hat{p}(y_i \mid A_i)$, where A_i is the cell of the partition that contains x_i. This defines Lei and Wasserman's conditional conformal predictor Γ.

To make the predictor Γ more computationally efficient (and to facilitate proofs), Lei and Wasserman use again the idea of approximating the density estimate based on the training set augmented by the new object with a postulated label by the density estimate based on the training set alone (cf. (1.13) and (1.14)). See [201], Section 4.2, for details.

It is an interesting direction of further research to construct conformal predictors that are object conditionally valid and efficient in an asymptotic sense in the case of classification. Another direction is to explore the training conditional validity of Lei and Wasserman's object conditional predictors.

Remark 2.3. In Section 1.8 we discussed asymptotically efficient conformal predictors in the case of classification and stated constructing asymptotically efficient conformal predictors in the case of regression as an open problem. Such asymptotically efficient conformal predictors would not be object conditionally valid, even in an approximate or asymptotic sense, unlike the asymptotically efficient conformal predictors of this section. From the point of view of traditional statistics, object conditional validity is a natural ideal goal, even if in its pure form it is not achievable under the randomness assumption (see Proposition 2.6). However, there are cases where this ideal goal has to be abandoned. One example is using (1.21)–(1.22) as the criterion of efficiency (or even using proper criteria of efficiency, in the terminology of [363]). Another example is perhaps even more important. As explained in the next section, in the case of classification we sometimes also want label conditional validity; a typical problem where label conditional validity is desirable is spam detection. We might sometimes want label conditional validity, approximate or asymptotic, in the case of regression as well. However, the ideal goals of object conditional validity and label conditional validity are incompatible, even if we know the data-generating distribution: conditioning on the whole test example does not leave us any probabilities that we could use in predicting the label. At least one of the two goals has to be abandoned, at least partially.

2.7 Label Conditional Validity and ROC Curves

A useful representation of an important class of label conditional inductive conformal predictors in terms of ROC curves is given in [360], Section 7. (Connections between conformal prediction and ROC curves had been studied earlier by Vanderlooy and Sprinkhuizen-Kuyper [350].) In this section we discuss this representation considering a binary classification problem; the possible labels will be denoted 0 and 1.

Let us say that an inductive nonconformity m-measure is *of scoring type* if it is of type (2.7) with $f : \mathbf{X} \to \mathbb{R}$ and the following restrictions on the function Δ:

- $\Delta(0, u)$ is a strictly increasing function of its second argument $u \in \mathbb{R}$;
- $\Delta(1, u)$ is a strictly decreasing function of its second argument $u \in \mathbb{R}$.

The intuition behind the *score* is that it reflects the likelihood of the label of x being 1. Many machine learning algorithms provide scores; for example, when using the support vector machine, we can take as the score the distance to the separating hyperplane (with the negative sign if the object is on the negative side of the hyperplane). A label conditional ICP is *of scoring type* if it is based on an inductive nonconformity m-measure of scoring type.

For illustration in this section we will use the well-known Spambase dataset contributed by George Forman to the UCI Machine Learning Repository [100]. Its overall size is 4601 examples and it contains examples of two classes: email (identified with 0) and spam (identified with 1). Hastie et al. [140] report results of several machine-learning algorithms on this dataset split randomly into a training set of size 3065 and test set of size 1536. The best result is achieved by MART (multiple additive regression tree; 4.5% error rate according to the second edition of [140]).

All our figures are for unsmoothed ICPs. We randomly permute the dataset and divide it into 2602 examples for the proper training set, 999 for the calibration set, and 1000 for the test set. We consider the label conditional ICP whose nonconformity measure is of scoring type with f output by MART and

$$\Delta(y, f(x)) := \begin{cases} f(x) & \text{if } y = 0 \\ -f(x) & \text{if } y = 1. \end{cases} \tag{2.25}$$

MART's output $f(x)$ is intended to model the log-odds of spam vs email,

$$f(x) = \log \frac{Q(1 \mid x)}{Q(0 \mid x)},$$

which makes the interpretation of (2.25) as nonconformity score very natural.

The left plot in Figure 2.3 is the scatter plot of the pairs $(p^{\text{email}}, p^{\text{spam}})$ produced by the label conditional ICP for all examples in the test set. Email is shown as noughts and spam as crosses (and it is noticeable, at least in color, that the noughts were drawn after the crosses). The other two plots are for email and spam separately. Ideally, email should be close to the horizontal axis and spam to the vertical axis; we can see that this is often true, with a few exceptions.

The reader may have noticed that the leftmost plot in Figure 2.3 looks similar to a ROC curve. This is not coincidental; but before we can discuss this we need a few definitions. Choose two nonnegative constants a and b such that $a \le b$. For a threshold $c \in \mathbb{R}$, the type I error on the calibration set will be estimated as

$$\alpha(c) := \frac{|\{i = m + 1, \ldots, l \mid f(x_i) \ge c \ \& \ y_i = 0\}| + a}{|\{i = m + 1, \ldots, l \mid y_i = 0\}| + b} \tag{2.26}$$

and the type II error will be estimated as

$$\beta(c) := \frac{|\{i = m + 1, \ldots, l \mid f(x_i) \le c \ \& \ y_i = 1\}| + a}{|\{i = m + 1, \ldots, l \mid y_i = 1\}| + b} \tag{2.27}$$

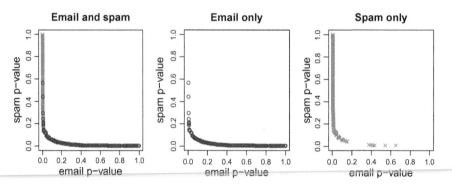

FIGURE 2.3

Scatter plots of the pairs $(p^{\text{email}}, p^{\text{spam}})$ for all examples in the test set (left plot), for email only (middle), and for spam only (right). Email is shown as noughts and spam as crosses.

(with $0/0$ set, e.g., to $1/2$). Intuitively, when $a = b = 0$, these are the error rates for the classifier that predicts 1 when $f(x) > c$ and predicts 0 when $f(x) < c$; our definition is conservative in that it counts the prediction as error whenever $f(x) = c$.

We allow $a > 0$ and $b > 0$ for regularization. The purpose of (2.26) and (2.27) is to provide good estimates of the true probabilities of the errors of type I and type II. The expressions (2.26) and (2.27) correspond to using the estimate $(k + a)/(n + b)$ of the parameter of the binomial distribution based on observing k successes out of n. The most popular estimates are:

- The *empirical estimate* corresponding to $a = b = 0$
- The *minimax estimate* corresponding to $a = 1/2$ and $b = 1$
- The *Laplace estimate* corresponding to $a = 1$ and $b = 2$

We will also be interested in two further estimates:

- The *lower Venn estimate* corresponding to $a = 0$ and $b = 1$
- The *upper Venn estimate* corresponding to $a = 1$ and $b = 1$

All these estimates will be discussed in detail at the end of Section 2.8.

By a *ROC curve* we will mean the parametric curve

$$\{(\alpha(c), \beta(c)) \mid c \in \mathbb{R}\} \subseteq [0, 1]^2, \tag{2.28}$$

and we will use one of the adjectives "empirical," "minimax," "Laplace," "lower Venn," or "upper Venn" to specify the values of a and b used in (2.26) and (2.27). Since $\alpha(c)$ and $\beta(c)$ take only finitely many values, all these ROC curves are not continuous but consist of discrete points.

The Venn estimates $k/(n+1)$ and $(k+1)/(n+1)$ of the parameter of the binomial distribution are nonstandard, and unusual in that the estimate of the probability of an

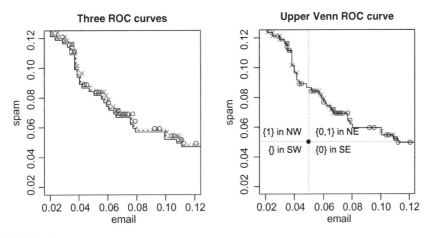

FIGURE 2.4

Left panel: the lower left corner of the left plot of Figure 2.3 with the empirical (solid), minimax (dashed), and Laplace (dotted) ROC curves. Right panel: the lower left corner of the left plot of Figure 2.3 with the upper Venn ROC curve and the partition of the plane corresponding to the label conditional ICP with significance level 5%.

event plus the estimate of the probability of its complement is different from 1. The origin of the name will be discussed in Section 2.8.

The empirical, minimax, and Laplace curve always lie between the lower and upper Venn curves: the lower Venn ROC curve lies southwest of those three curves and the upper Venn ROC curve northeast of them. In the square $[0, 0.5] \times [0, 0.5]$ the order of the ROC curves from southwest to northeast is: lower Venn, empirical, minimax, Laplace, and upper Venn. The first two and the last two are much closer to each other than to the other ROC curves for large n^0 and n^1, where n^y is the number of examples in the calibration set labelled as y, and small $\alpha(c)$ and $\beta(c)$, as in Figure 2.4. The left panel of that figure shows the lower left corner of the left plot of Figure 2.3 with three ROC curves added to it.

All five ROC curves are fairly close to each other: it is easy to check that the Hausdorff distance even between the two extreme curves, lower and upper Venn ROC curves, never exceeds

$$\sqrt{\frac{1}{(n^0 + 1)^2} + \frac{1}{(n^1 + 1)^2}}. \tag{2.29}$$

(Remember that the Hausdorff distance between sets A and B in a metric space is $\max(\sup_{x \in A} \inf_{y \in B} d(x, y), \sup_{y \in B} \inf_{x \in A} d(x, y))$, where d is the metric, which we take to be the Euclidean metric in $\mathbb{R}^2$.)

In the rest of this section we will discuss the upper Venn ROC curve. Notice that the pair (p^0, p^1) of label conditional p-values for any test example belongs to the upper

Venn ROC curve; therefore, this curve passes through all test examples in Figure 2.4. The curve can serve as a convenient classification of all possible test objects: each of them corresponds to a point on the curve.

The label conditional ICP can also be conveniently described in terms of the upper Venn ROC curve. An example is given as the right panel of Figure 2.4. Each test object is represented by a point (p^0, p^1). Let ϵ be the significance level; it is 5% in Figure 2.4 (although there is no need to have the same significance level for email and spam, since there is a clear asymmetry between the labels as we will discuss shortly). If the point (ϵ, ϵ) lies southwest of the curve, the label conditional ICP can produce multiple predictions but never produces empty predictions. If it lies northeast of the curve, the predictor can produce empty predictions but never produces multiple predictions. In particular, it is impossible to produce both multiple and empty predictions for the same calibration set. (Lying on the curve is regarded as a special case of lying southwest of it. Because of the discreteness of the upper Venn ROC curve it is also possible that (ϵ, ϵ) lies neither northeast nor southwest of it; in this case predictions are always singletons.)

If the test object is in the northeast region NE with respect to (ϵ, ϵ) (i.e., $p^0 > \epsilon$ and $p^1 > \epsilon$), the prediction set is multiple, $\{0, 1\}$. If it is in the region SW (i.e., $p^0 \le \epsilon$ and $p^1 \le \epsilon$), the prediction set is empty. Otherwise the prediction set is a singleton: 1 if it is in NW ($p^0 \le \epsilon$ and $p^1 > \epsilon$) and 0 if it is in SE ($p^0 > \epsilon$ and $p^1 \le \epsilon$).

However, a one-sided approach may be more appropriate in the case of the Spambase dataset. There is a clear asymmetry between the two kinds of error in spam detection: classifying email as spam is much more harmful than letting occasional spam in. A reasonable approach is to start from a small number $\epsilon > 0$, the maximum tolerable percentage of email classified as spam, and then to try to minimize the percentage of spam classified as email under this constraint. For example, we can use the "one-sided label conditional ICP" classifying x as spam if and only if $p^0 \le \epsilon$ for x; otherwise, x is classified as email. In the case of $\epsilon = 0.05$, this means classifying a test object as spam if and only if it lands to the left of (or onto) the vertical dotted line in the right panel of Figure 2.4.

Both our procedures, two-sided and one-sided, look very similar to the standard uses of ROC curves. However, the standard justification of these uses presupposes that we know the true ROC curve. In practice, we only have access to an estimate of the true ROC curve, and the error of estimation is usually very significant. The upper Venn ROC curve is defined in terms of the data rather than the unknown true distribution. Despite this, we still have guarantees of validity. For example, our one-sided procedure guarantees that the (unconditional) probability of mistaking email for spam is at most ϵ (see Proposition 2.3).

This section of the paper raises a large number of questions. Not all inductive conformity measures are of scoring type; can other types of label conditional ICPs be analyzed using the notion of ROC curves? Even in the case of probability-type label conditional ICPs their property of training conditional validity (i.e., the version of Proposition 2.4 for label conditional ICPs) remains to be proved. Analyzing smoothed ICPs and ensuring a degree of object conditional validity raise further questions.

2.8 **Venn Predictors**

Conformal predictors and their modifications discussed so far tell us something about the likelihood of various labels for test objects, but they do not give us their probabilities (they only give us p-values associated with various labels). We can, however, use similar ideas for probabilistic prediction.

In this section we consider the problem of classification, $\mathbf{Z} = \mathbf{X} \times \mathbf{Y}$ with $|\mathbf{Y}| < \infty$, and use the notion of n-taxonomy introduced in Section 2.2. Let $n = l + 1$. Given a training set $(z_1, \ldots, z_l) \in \mathbf{Z}^l$ and a test object $x_{l+1} \in \mathbf{X}$, the *Venn predictor* determined by an n-taxonomy K outputs as its probability forecast for y_{l+1} the following set $\{P_y \mid y \in \mathbf{Y}\}$ of probability distributions on $\mathbf{Y}$: for each $y \in \mathbf{Y}$ and $E \subseteq \mathbf{Y}$,

$$P_y(E) := \frac{\left|\{i = 1, \ldots, l+1 \mid \kappa_i^y = \kappa_{l+1}^y \ \& \ y_i \in E\}\right|}{\left|\{i = 1, \ldots, l+1 \mid \kappa_i^y = \kappa_{l+1}^y\}\right|}, \tag{2.30}$$

where

$$(\kappa_1^y, \ldots, \kappa_{l+1}^y) := K(z_1, \ldots, z_l, (x_{l+1}, y)). \tag{2.31}$$

Interesting Venn predictors output probability distributions P_y, $y \in \mathbf{Y}$ that are close to each other (and, therefore, may be said to output one slightly fuzzy probability distribution on $\mathbf{Y}$). We will refer to the set $\{P_y \mid y \in \mathbf{Y}\}$ as the *multiprobability prediction* output by the Venn predictor.

It is shown in [365], Chapter 6, that the multiprobability predictions output by Venn predictors are automatically valid for a somewhat complicated notion of validity (being "well-calibrated"). A weaker but easier to define notion of validity (under the assumption of randomness) is to say that the Venn prediction is guaranteed to contain a conditional probability of the event $y_{l+1} = 1$ with regard to the true probability distribution Q^{l+1} generating the data. In the next few paragraphs we will spell out this definition. (See [367] for yet another notion of validity for Venn predictors.)

The ideal probability prediction for y_{l+1} would be the conditional Q-probability distribution of y_{l+1} given all the available information, $z_1, \ldots, z_l, x_{l+1}$. Since the examples are generated independently, this is the same thing as the conditional Q-probability distribution of y_{l+1} given the object x_{l+1}. Unfortunately, it is not difficult to show (see [365], Proposition 5.1 and Theorem 5.2) that in nontrivial cases it is impossible to estimate this conditional probability. The best we can hope for is to estimate *some* conditional probability. For example, instead of conditioning on x_{l+1} we might want to condition on a neighborhood of x_{l+1} in the hope that the conditional distribution Q_x (in the notation of Section 2.6) is not too sensitive to x; if it is, meaningful probabilistic prediction may be impossible.

This notion of validity of Venn predictors says that their multiprobability predictions contain the conditional probability distribution of y_{l+1} with regard to some σ-algebra on $\mathbf{Z}^{l+1}$, and so are not completely arbitrary. And it is a matter of their efficiency to ensure that σ-algebra is similar enough to the σ-algebra corresponding to the observed data $z_1, \ldots, z_l, x_{l+1}$.

The σ-algebra $\mathcal{F}_K$ corresponding to the Venn predictor determined by a taxonomy K is generated by the following function: $(z_1, \ldots, z_{l+1}) \in \mathbf{Z}^{l+1}$ is mapped to the corresponding categories

$$(\kappa_1, \ldots, \kappa_{l+1}) := K(z_1, \ldots, z_{l+1})$$

(cf. (2.31)) and, for each category κ in the range of K, the bag of examples z_i, $i = 1, \ldots, l + 1$, such that $\kappa_i = \kappa$. In other words, $\mathcal{F}_K$ only carries the following information about the data sequence $z_1, \ldots, z_{l+1}$: the category of each example and, for each category, the bag of examples in this category. It is easy to see that the multiprobability prediction output by this Venn predictor will almost surely contain the $\mathcal{F}_K$-conditional probability distribution of y_{l+1}.

2.8.1 Inductive Venn Predictors

An inductive version of Venn predictors has been introduced recently by Lambrou et al. [193]. As in the case of inductive conformal predictors (Section 2.3), the training set $(z_1, \ldots, z_l)$ is split into two parts, the proper training set $(z_1, \ldots, z_m)$ and the calibration set $(z_{m+1}, \ldots, z_l)$. An *inductive m-taxonomy* is a measurable function $K : \mathbf{Z}^m \times \mathbf{Z} \to \mathbf{K}$, where $\mathbf{K}$ consists of the allowed categories (we allow $\mathbf{K}$ to be any measurable space, although it is usually finite). The *inductive Venn predictor* determined by K outputs $\{P_y \mid y \in \mathbf{Y}\}$, where P_y are now defined by

$$P_y(E) := \frac{|\{i = m + 1, \ldots, l \mid \kappa_i = \kappa^y \ \& \ y_i \in E\}| + 1}{|\{i = m + 1, \ldots, l \mid \kappa_i = \kappa^y\}| + 1},$$

and the categories κ are defined by

$$\kappa_i := K((z_1, \ldots, z_m), z_i), \quad i = m + 1, \ldots, l,$$
$$\kappa^y := K((z_1, \ldots, z_m), (x_{l+1}, y)). \tag{2.32}$$

In many applications inductive Venn predictors are much more computationally efficient than Venn predictors: since the same proper training set is used in calculating the categories in (2.32), preprocessing it often drastically reduces computation time; besides, we can precompute the categories $\kappa_{m+1}, \ldots, \kappa_l$.

2.8.2 Venn Prediction without Objects

In this subsection we will discuss a particularly simple special case of Venn prediction that was used in the previous section (and is also discussed in [365], pp. 159–160). Suppose that there are no objects (equivalently, $|\mathbf{X}| = 1$, and so the object does not carry any information and can be omitted) and that the label space is binary: $\mathbf{Y} = \{0, 1\}$. In other words, we have the *Bernoulli problem*: having observed a sequence of bits $y_1, \ldots, y_l$ we are to predict the probability $p \in [0, 1]$ that $y_{l+1} = 1$. (Formally, Venn predictors output probability distributions on $\mathbf{Y}$, but in the binary case a probability distribution P on $\{0, 1\}$ carries the same information as the number $p := P(\{1\}) \in [0, 1]$.)

Let k be the number of 1s among $y_1, \ldots, y_l$. Standard point estimates of the probability that $y_{l+1} = 1$ are the empirical estimate k/l, the minimax estimate $(k + 1/2)/(l + 1)$, and the Laplace estimate $(k + 1)/(l + 2)$. They were introduced in the previous section.

Another estimate, which we may call the *conformal estimate*, is $(k + 1)/(l + 1)$. According to (1.7), it is the borderline significance level between those producing the multiple prediction $\{0, 1\}$ and those producing the singleton prediction $\{0\}$.

Since we do not have objects in the Bernoulli problem, the most natural Venn predictor V corresponds to the taxonomy assigning all examples to the same category. This Venn predictor outputs

$$\left\{ \frac{k}{l+1}, \frac{k+1}{l+1} \right\}$$

as its multiprobability prediction. The convex hull $[k/(l+1), (k+1)/(l+1)]$ of this set contains the three standard estimates of the probability that $y_{l+1} = 1$ and also contains (as one of its endpoints) the conformal estimate. In the previous section we called $(k+1)/(l+1)$ the upper Venn estimate and $k/(l+1)$ the lower Venn estimate, the former being identical to the conformal estimate. These two estimates are dual in the sense that the lower Venn estimate of the probability that $y_{l+1} = 1$ is equal to 1 minus the upper Venn estimate of the probability of the complementary event $y_{l+1} = 0$ (cf., e.g., [314], (1.7)).

Even in the simple Bernoulli case there are several open problems about Venn predictors. Let $\{0, 1\}_k^n$ be the set of all 0-1-sequences of length n containing k 1s. An *imprecise probability predictor* (IPP) is a pair of functions $\overline{F} : \{0, 1\}^l \to [0, 1]$ and $\underline{F} : \{0, 1\}^l \to [0, 1]$ such that $\underline{F}(x) \leq \overline{F}(x)$ for all $x \in \{0, 1\}^l$. We say that an IPP F is *valid* if there is a σ-algebra $\mathcal{F}$ on $\{0, 1\}^{l+1}$ such that, for all $(z_1, \ldots, z_{l+1}) \in \{0, 1\}^{l+1}$ and all $p \in [0, 1]$,

$$B_p(\{(y_1, \ldots, y_{l+1}) \in \{0, 1\}^{l+1} \mid y_{l+1} = 1\} \mid \mathcal{F})(z_1, \ldots, z_{l+1})$$
$$\in [\underline{F}(z_1, \ldots, z_l), \overline{F}(z_1, \ldots, z_l)],$$

where B_p is the Bernoulli measure on $\{0, 1\}^{l+1}$ with parameter p (assigning probability $p^k(1 - p)^{l+1-k}$ to a sequence with k 1s). There is a natural bijection between σ-algebras and partitions in this case, of course, and we do not always distinguish between partitions and the σ-algebras they generate. The validity of the Venn predictor V considered earlier can be restated by saying that we can take as $\mathcal{F}$ the partition of $\{0, 1\}^{l+1}$ into the cells $\{0, 1\}_0^{l+1}, \{0, 1\}_1^{l+1}, \ldots, \{0, 1\}_{l+1}^{l+1}$. Let $\mathbb{E}_p$ stand for expectation with respect to B_p. A natural question is whether $\mathbb{E}_{1/2}\left(\overline{F} - \underline{F}\right) \geq 1/(l + 1)$ holds for each imprecise probability predictor $(\underline{F}, \overline{F})$. (This inequality holds as an equality for V, and so it can be interpreted as a kind of optimality for V.) If not, the next question is whether $\sup_{p \in [0,1]} \mathbb{E}_p\left(\overline{F} - \underline{F}\right) \geq 1/(l + 1)$. If not, we can still ask whether $\sup_{x \in \{0,1\}^l}\left(\overline{F}(x) - \underline{F}(x)\right) \geq 1/(l + 1)$.

Acknowledgments

I am grateful to Sasha Tsybakov and Bob Williamson for useful discussions. The empirical studies in this chapter used the R language, the gbm package for R written by Greg Ridgeway (based on the work of Freund and Schapire [106] and Friedman [108–109]), the MATLAB language, and the C program for computing tangent distance written by Daniel Keysers and adapted to MATLAB by Aditi Krishn. This work was supported in part by the Cyprus Research Promotion Foundation (TPE/ORIZO/0609(BIE)/24) and EPSRC (EP/K033344/1).

Adaptations

Active Learning

3

Vineeth N. Balasubramanian[*], **Shayok Chakraborty**[†], **Shen-Shyang Ho**[‡],
Harry Wechsler[§], **and Sethuraman Panchanathan**[†]

[*]*Department of Computer Science and Engineering, Indian Institute of Technology,
Hyderabad, India*
[†]*Center for Cognitive Ubiquitous Computing, Arizona State University, AZ, USA*
[‡]*School of Computer Engineering, Nanyang Technological University, Singapore*
[§]*Department of Computer Science, George Mason University, VA, USA*

CHAPTER OUTLINE HEAD

In this chapter, we describe how the p-values derived from the conformal predictions
framework can be used for active learning; that is, to select the informative examples
from a data collection that can be used to train a classifier for best performance.
We show the connection of this approach to information-theoretic methods, as well
as show how the methodology can be generalized to multiple classifier models and
information fusion settings.

3.1 Introduction

The primary goal in any classification problem is to learn a function $f : X \rightarrow C$, which maps input feature vectors X into the corresponding output classes C. To develop a robust recognition engine, it is indispensable to have a large amount of labeled data in the form of a training set. Usually, this data is sampled at random from the underlying distribution and is then used to induce the classifier. This methodology is called *passive learning*. A passive learner receives a randomly selected dataset from the world and outputs a classifier [340] (as depicted in Figure 3.1).

The rapid proliferation of technology and the widespread emergence of modern technological equipments have resulted in the generation of humongous amounts of digital data (in the form of images, videos and text among others). These data are typically unlabeled and need substantial human effort for annotation. For example, in speech recognition applications, accurate labeling of speech utterances is extremely time consuming and requires trained linguists. However, annotation at the word level can take 10 times longer than the actual audio (e.g., one minute of speech takes 10 minutes to label) and annotating phonemes can take 400 times as long (nearly seven hours) [395]. Similarly, labeling entities or relations of interest in text documents can take a half-hour or more for even simple newswire stories [312], and annotating gene data for biomedical knowledge analysis requires highly trained biologists, whose time can be very expensive.

Thus, while gathering a large amount of unlabeled data is cheap and easy, annotating them with class labels involves significant human effort. This poses a serious challenge in the design and development of classification models for automated data analysis. To alleviate this problem, *active learning* strategies have been proposed over the last two decades in machine learning literature. Instead of randomly selecting data points for manual labeling, active learners gather information about the world by querying the class labels of certain specific unlabeled samples and receiving responses from an oracle (e.g., a human annotator). The queries are not pre-defined, but are selected dynamically based on the responses to the previous queries. This tremendously reduces the human annotation effort as only a few samples, which are identified by the algorithm, need to be labeled manually. Moreover, the ability of the active learner to adaptively query the world based on past experience endows it with greater generalization capability, which makes it better than the standard passive learner. Figure 3.2 depicts the general schema of an active learner.

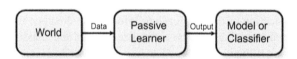

FIGURE 3.1

General schema of a passive learner.

FIGURE 3.2

General schema of an active learner.

The remainder of the chapter is organized as follows. Section 3.2 presents a background of active learning and a survey of the different active learning methods proposed so far. In Section 3.3, we describe how conformal prediction has been used in the design of query functions for active learning in the online setting. In particular, we describe three methods proposed so far: Query by Transduction (QBT), Generalized Query by Transduction (GQBT), and a multi-criteria extension of QBT. Section 3.4 presents the experimental results for each of these three methods, as compared to existing online active learning methods. Finally, Section 3.5 concludes the chapter with a discussion of theoretical connection between QBT, GQBT, and the popularly used Query-by-Committee active learning method.

3.2 **Background and Related Work**

The concept of active learning was initially developed in the domain of education, where students are involved in dialog, debate, writing, and problem solving, as well as higher-order thinking (such as analysis, synthesis, and evaluation) to create an environment in which knowledge retention is significantly increased [34]. In machine learning literature, a student corresponds to a classification model whereas a teacher corresponds to the universe of data samples the model is supposed to learn from. In the passive learning setting, data points are selected at random from the universe to train the model. This is equivalent to the scenario when the students merely listen to the instructor without actively participating in the learning process. In contrast, in active learning, similar to the classroom environment, the learner actively learns from the universe by asking intelligent queries and receiving responses. This has the potential to produce a better model as it gets trained on salient and exemplar data instances from a given population.

Active learning can be categorized broadly as shown in Figure 3.3. At the highest level, we can divide such methods into two types—*pool-based* and *online*. In a pool-based setting, the learner is exposed to a pool of unlabeled instances and iteratively selects one point at a time from the pool to be labeled manually. This is continued until the pool gets exhausted or some stopping criterion is satisfied. In contrast, in an online setting, the learner does not have access to the entire unlabeled pool at once, but encounters the points sequentially over a period of time. At each instant, the model has to decide whether to query the given point and update the hypothesis. Pool-based active learning is further divided into *Serial Query-based Active Learning* and *Batch Mode Active Learning*. We present a brief review of the pool-based and

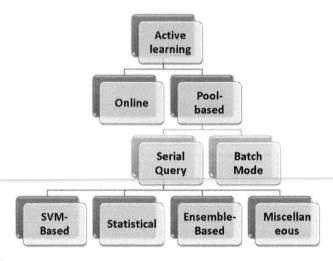

FIGURE 3.3

Categories of active learning.

online active learning algorithms in the rest of this section. Active learning methods have also been extended to newer problem settings such as active feature acquisition [295], active class selection [216], active clustering [152], and for regression [335]. A comprehensive review of these methods can be found in Settles's work [310,309].

3.2.1 Pool-based Active Learning with Serial Query

Most existing active learning approaches have been applied in the pool-based setting. These methods can further be broadly categorized as: (1) SVM-based methods; (2) statistical methods; (3) ensemble-based methods; and (4) other miscellaneous approaches.

SVM-based methods

A sizable number of the pool-based active learning methods are based on the Support Vector Machines (SVM) algorithm. Tong and Koller [342,340,341] designed the query function to select the unlabeled point that is closest to the SVM decision boundary in the feature space. Osugi et al. [256] proposed a probabilistic method of active learning, which decided between labeling examples near the decision boundary and exploring the input data space for unknown pockets of points. Schohn and Cohn [302] applied active learning with SVMs in the document classification task and concluded that the classifier trained through active learning often outperforms those that were trained on all the available data. Mitra et al. [232] assigned a confidence c to examples within the current decision boundary indicating whether or not they were true support vectors. Points were then queried probabilistically according to this confidence factor.

Another active learning scheme using SVMs was proposed by Campbell et al. [46], where the next point to be queried was the one that minimized a predetermined risk function. Cheng and Wang [54] used Co-SVMs in the image retrieval problem where two SVMs trained separately on color and texture features were used to classify unlabeled data—the points that were differently classified by the two SVMs were chosen to be labeled.

Statistical methods

Statistical approaches quantify the informativeness of a data instance based on statistical properties of the learner. We have categorized such methods further as follows:

- **Uncertainty Sampling:** The most commonly used query framework is uncertainty sampling, where a learner queries instances about which it is maximally uncertain. Uncertainty can be quantified in various ways: the expected 0/1 loss, which is computed as 1 minus the maximum posterior probability under the current model, margin sampling [300], and the most popular Shannon's entropy [317]. Holub et al. [156] proposed an active learning framework that attempted to minimize the expected entropy of the labels of the data points in the unlabeled pool. MacKay [218] introduced information-theoretic approaches to active learning by measuring the informativeness of each data point within a Bayesian learning framework. Cohn et al. [58] described a rudimentary form of active learning, which they called selective sampling. Here, the learner proceeded by examining the information already provided and then deriving a "region of uncertainty" where it believed misclassification was still possible. Li and Sethi [207] proposed an algorithm that identified samples that had more uncertainty associated with them, as measured by the conditional error. Lewis and Gale [203] also applied a probabilistic framework to active learning where the most uncertain point was chosen for manual annotation.
- **Expected Model Change:** An active learning framework based on expected model change uses a decision-theoretic approach and selects the instance that would impart the greatest change to the current model if its label was known. An example query strategy in this framework is the expected gradient length (EGL) approach where the change imparted to the model is measured by the length of the training gradient. The learner queries the instance which, if queried and added to the training set, would result in the new training gradient of largest magnitude. This strategy was introduced by Settles et al. [313] and has also been applied to probabilistic sequence models like CRFs [311].
- **Expected Error Reduction:** This type of active learning algorithms aim to quantify the amount of reduction of the generalization error. The idea is to estimate the expected future error of a model trained using $L \cup \{x, y\}$ (where L is the labeled training set and x is the current unlabeled sample under consideration) on the remaining unlabeled instances in the unlabeled pool and query the instance with minimum expected future error (sometimes called the risk). Roy and McCallum [290] first proposed the expected error reduction framework for text classification

using naive Bayes. The authors adopted a sampling approach to estimate the expected reduction in error due to the labeling of a query, and the future error rate was estimated by log-loss using the entropy of the posterior class distribution on a sample of the unlabeled examples. Zhu et al. [396] combined this framework with a semisupervised learning approach resulting in a dramatic improvement over random or uncertainty sampling. Guo and Greiner [130] employed an optimistic variant that biased the expectation toward the most likely label for computational convenience.

- **Variance Reduction:** Minimizing the expectation of a loss function directly is expensive, and in general, cannot be done in closed form. However, we can still reduce generalization error indirectly by minimizing output variance, which sometimes has a closed-form solution. Consider a regression problem, where the learning objective is to minimize the standard error (i.e., squared-loss). The learner's expected future error can be decomposed as: $E_T[(\hat{y}-y)^2|x] = E[(y-E[y|x])^2]+ (E_L[\hat{y}] - E[y|x])^2 + E_L[(\hat{y} - E_L[\hat{y}])^2]$, where E_L is an expectation over the labeled set L; $E[.]$ is an expectation over the conditional density $P(y|x)$, and E_T is an expectation over both; $\hat{y}$ is the model's predicted output for a given instance x; and y indicates the true label for that instance. The first term represents the noise, the second term captures the bias, and the third term depicts the model variance. Therefore, minimizing the variance is guaranteed to minimize the future generalization error of the model (since the learner can do nothing about the bias or noise components). Cohn [57,59] presented the first statistical analyses of active learning for regression using the estimated distribution of the model's output. They showed that this can be done in closed form for neural networks, Gaussian mixture models, and locally\weighted linear regression.

Ensemble-based methods

In ensemble-based approaches, the Query by Committee (QBC) algorithm is most popular. Freund et al. [104], as well as Liere and Tadepalli [214], used the disagreement measure among a committee of classifiers to select points from an unlabeled pool. McCallum and Nigam [224] modified the QBC method for estimating the document density while applying active learning to the text classification problem. They also combined active learning with Expectation Maximization to take advantage of the word co-occurrence information among the documents in the unlabeled pool. Melville and Mooney [227] proposed an ensemble-based active learning method that encouraged diversity among committee members. Abe and Mamitsuka [1] combined QBC with boosting and bagging, where the point to be queried was the one on which the weighted majority voting by the current hypothesis had the least margin. Another form of QBC was proposed with the nearest neighbor classifier [110,215], where each neighbor was allowed to vote on the class label of an unlabeled point, with the proportion of these votes representing the posterior label probability used as a disagreement measure for instance selection.

Other methods

In other pool-based methods with serial query mode, Baram et al. [13] proposed a master algorithm that estimated the progress of each active learner in an ensemble during a learning session and then dynamically switched over to the best performing one at each stage. Using three active learning algorithms (Simple, Kernel Farthest First, and Self-Conf) to construct an ensemble, the authors empirically established that combining them online resulted in a better performance than using any one of them. Blum and Chawla [29] developed an algorithm based on graph-cuts to learn from both labeled and unlabeled data. Nigam et al. [244] combined the Expectation Maximization (EM) algorithm with naive Bayes classifier to learn from labeled and unlabeled text documents. Clustering techniques have also been used to boost the performance of pool-based active learning [64,339]. There have also been efforts in incorporating contextual information in active learning. Very recently, Kapoor et al. [169] incorporated *match* and *nonmatch* constraints in active learning for face recognition. Qi et al. [281] presented a 2D active learning scheme where sampling was done along both sample and label dimensions. The authors proposed to select sample-label pairs to minimize a multilabel Bayesian classification error bound. Kothari and Jain [182] proposed a genetic algorithm-based active learning strategy to iteratively refine the class membership of the unlabeled patterns so that the maximum a posteriori (MAP) based predicted labels of the points in the labeled dataset were in agreement with the known labels. Joshi et al. [165] proposed an active learning algorithm, where two data points were selected in each iteration, one from the training set and one from the unlabeled set and the user had to give feedback regarding whether or not the two samples belonged to the same class. This was the first effort in designing an active learning framework where the user feedback was binary (yes/no) type.

3.2.2 **Batch Mode Active Learning**

Batch mode active learning (BMAL) algorithms are effective in utilizing the presence of multiple labeling oracles and avoiding frequent classifier training, as they select a batch of points simultaneously for manual annotation. Existing approaches for BMAL have largely been based on extending pool-based active learning methods to select multiple instances simultaneously. Brinker [45] extended the version space concept proposed in [342] to query a diverse batch of points using SVMs, where diversity was measured as the angle induced by the hyperplane of the currently selected point to the hyperplanes of the already selected points. Zhang et al. [394] proposed a BMAL scheme that selected a diverse batch of points using the farthest-first traversal strategy. Schohn and Cohn [302] proposed to query a batch of points based on their distance from the separating hyperplane for a linear SVM. Xu et al. [384] proposed an SVM-based BMAL strategy that combined representativeness and diversity measures for batch selection. Shi et al. [323] proposed three criteria (minimum redundancy, maximum uncertainty, and maximum impact) to exploit the link-based dependencies in a network and actively select a batch of instances for user query.

However, extending the pool-based setting to the batch setting by considering the top k instances does not account for other factors such as information overlap between the selected points in a batch. More recently, this has led to newer efforts that are specifically intended to select batches of points using appropriate optimization strategies. Hoi et al. [153, 154] used the Fisher information matrix as a measure of model uncertainty and proposed to query the set of points that maximally reduced the Fisher information. The same authors [155] proposed a BMAL scheme based on SVMs where a kernel function was first learned from a mixture of labeled and unlabeled samples, which was then used to identify the informative and diverse examples through a min-max framework. Joshi et al. [166] introduced a BMAL framework using submodular functions for multiclass image classification. Shi and Zhao [322] proposed a unified framework integrating sparse representation and batch mode active learning. Guo and Schuurmans [131] proposed a discriminative strategy that selected a batch of points that maximized the log-likelihoods of the selected points with respect to their optimistically assigned class labels and minimized the entropy of the unselected points in the unlabeled pool. Very recently, Guo [129] proposed a BMAL scheme that maximized the mutual information between the labeled and unlabeled sets and was independent of the classification model used. The methods described in [131,129] have been shown to be the best performing BMAL schemes to date [129].

3.2.3 Online Active Learning

Sculley [305] proposed an online active learning framework to develop an automated spam email filter system. The author used three online active learning techniques—label efficient b-sampling, logistic margin sampling, and fixed margin sampling and concluded that they can dramatically reduce the labeling cost to design a spam filter. Monteleoni and Kaariainen [234] analyzed the performances of two online active learning algorithms in the optical character recognition problem. The algorithms—DKM and CBGZ and their combined variants were seen to consistently outperform random sampling. The query by committee (QBC) algorithm is popularly used to query points in an online setting based on the level of disagreement among a group of classifiers. If the disagreement is above a certain threshold, the point is queried for its label. Melville et al. [228] used the Jensen Shannon divergence as a disagreement measure to select query points in such a setting. Considering the nature of the online active learning problem, all of these techniques can however be considered to be "serial"; that is, the query function is implemented on each data instance as it arrives.

3.3 Active Learning Using Conformal Prediction

In this section, we describe the active learning methods proposed so far based on conformal prediction. We first describe Query by Transduction (QBT) proposed by Ho and Wechsler [150], then show this was extended to the Generalized Query by Transduction (GQBT) algorithm proposed by Balasubramanian et al. [11], and finally describe how Makili et al. [221] extended QBT to add a multicriteria-based flavor to quantify the information content of an unlabeled example. We begin with the QBT method.

3.3.1 Query by Transduction (QBT)

The Conformal Prediction framework, based on principles of algorithmic randomness, hypothesis testing, and transductive inference, provides rigorous theoretical guarantees on the error frequencies of predictions on unseen data samples in the online setting. Tong and Koller [342] proposed a transductive active learning framework in the pool-based setting. However, using transduction to search through a pool of unlabeled samples is an expensive process in terms of computation. Transductive active learning is much cheaper in a stream-based setting (especially with the use of incremental classifiers) where data samples are observed sequentially. It is therefore intuitive to use the p-values obtained from the transductive learning procedure in conformal predictors, to design query functions for active learning in the stream-based (online) setting. Using this idea, Ho and Wechsler [150] used the theory of conformal prediction to select query points in an online setting. The points were queried based on the difference between the top two p-values computed using the conformal predictions framework. Balasubramanian et al. [11] proposed a generalized version of this approach based on eigen-decomposition of matrices, where the p-values corresponding to all class labels of a given point were incorporated to decide whether or not to query the particular point. We now discuss how the p-values obtained from the Conformal Prediction framework have been used in the design of query functions for active learning in the online setting.

Algorithmic formulation

The Query by Transduction (QBT) algorithm proposed by Ho and Wechsler [150,146] expands the scope of transductive inference to active learning in the stream-based setting. It quantifies the information content of an unlabeled sample using the p-values obtained using transduction. Using the relations between transduction, Bayesian statistical testing, Kullback-Leibler divergence, and Shannon information, QBT was shown to be closely related to the Query-by-Committee (QBC) algorithm for active learning. We now describe the mathematical formulation of the QBT algorithm.

Let p_i be the p-values obtained for a particular sample x_{n+1} using all the possible class labels $i = 1, \ldots M$ and let p_j and p_k be the two highest p-values when sorted in descending order. The absolute difference between p_j and p_k provides a degree of informativeness of the unlabeled sample, with a smaller value of the difference denoting larger ambiguity regarding the proposed label. To quantify the information possessed by the sample, "closeness" was defined as:

$$I(x_{n+1}) = p_j - p_k \qquad (3.1)$$

As $I(x_{n+1})$ approaches 0, the uncertainty in classifying the unlabeled point increases. Thus, addition of this unlabeled point with its actual label (obtained from a human oracle) to the training set provides substantial information regarding the structure of the data model. Such an unlabeled example therefore represents a promising point from an active learning perspective. When using an SVM for a binary classification problem, if a new unlabeled example x_{n+1} has Lagrangian multiplier (the nonconformity measure for an SVM) 0 for its two possible class labels, then $I(x_{n+1}) = 0$. However, to include an unlabeled example for which the corresponding Lagrangian multipliers are close in value for the two possible labels, the threshold for $I(x_{n+1})$ can be relaxed:

$$I(x_{n+1}) < \epsilon \tag{3.2}$$

with $0 < \epsilon << 1$. For a multiclass problem, only the top two p-values need to be considered to quantify the information content. This forms the basis of the Query by Transduction algorithm (outlined in Algorithm 1), which iteratively queries informative samples for their true labels until some stopping criterion (for instance, a budget constraint on the number of instances that can be labeled) is satisfied.

For a binary classification task, a single SVM can be used to compute the nonconformity scores of all the training data points. For a multiclass problem with M classes, M one-versus-all SVMs can be used. To ensure the computational efficiency, incremental SVMs [48] can be used in steps 3 through 7 of the QBT algorithm instead of training an SVM from scratch each time a new data point is observed.

Algorithm 1 The Query by Transduction (QBT) Algorithm

Input: Training set $T = \{(x_1, y_1), \ldots (x_n, y_n)\}$, selection threshold ϵ, stopping threshold γ and the number of classes M

1: **repeat**
2:    A new unlabeled example x_{n+1} is observed
3:    **for** $i = 1 \rightarrow M$ **do**
4:        Assign label i to x_{n+1}
5:        Construct an SVM using $T \cup \{(x_{n+1}, i)\}$
6:        Use the Lagrangian multipliers $\{\alpha_1, \ldots, \alpha_n, \alpha'_{n+1}\}$ to compute the p-value p_i for (x_{n+1}, i) (using Eq. 1.5)
7:    **end for**
8:    Let p_j and p_k be the two highest p-values from $\{p_1, \ldots, p_M\}$
9:    **if** $I(x_{n+1}) < \epsilon$ **then**
10:        $T := T \cup \{(x_{n+1}, y_{n+1})\}$, where y_{n+1} is the true label of x_{n+1}
11:        $n := n + 1$
12:    **end if**
13: **until** No example is included in T after γ consecutive examples are observed

---

3.3.2 **Generalized Query by Transduction**

The Generalized Query by Transduction (GQBT) algorithm was proposed by Balasubramanian et al. [11] for active learning in the online setting. Similar to QBT, this framework also uses the p-values of an unlabeled sample in the online setting to quantify its degree of informativeness. GQBT can be used with any existing pattern classification algorithm and can also be used to combine multiple criteria in selecting an unlabeled example appropriately in the active learning process (as described later in this chapter). The mathematical formulation of the GQBT algorithm is described next.

Algorithmic formulation

The aforementioned QBT algorithm uses the top two p-values to measure the quality of information in an unlabeled example in the active learning process. In the GQBT framework, the query function is generalized to use all (or as many required) p-values that are obtained using the Conformal Predictions framework. The GQBT approach defines a matrix C, which contains the absolute values of the pairwise differences between all the p-values of the current unlabeled example under consideration:

$$C_{ij}(P) = |p_i - p_j| \tag{3.3}$$

where $i, j = 1, \ldots, M$, M being the total number of classes. Since the matrix C is symmetric with diagonal elements 0, its eigen-decomposition provides a naturally useful measure with interesting properties. By the Perron-Frobenius theorem, the largest eigenvalue of C, say $\eta(C)$, assumes values that are directly proportional to the maximum of the pairwise differences between the p-values. When all the p-values are equal, $\eta(C)$ is trivially zero. As the pairwise differences between the p-values increase, $\eta(C)$ increases proportionately. This statement can be trivially shown to be true and is illustrated using the average pairwise difference of the C matrix. The eigen-decomposition of C is given by the characteristic equation:

$$|C - \lambda I| = 0 \tag{3.4}$$

where $|.|$ is the matrix determinant. When the pairwise differences are multiplied by a constant factor, say d, the new C, say C^*, is equal to dC. The characteristic equation for C^* is given by:

$$|C^* - \lambda^* I| = 0 \tag{3.5}$$

where λ^* are the eigenvalues of C^*. Substituting $C^* = dC$, we get:

$$|dC - \lambda^* I| = 0$$
$$\Rightarrow |d\left(C - \frac{\lambda^*}{d}I\right)| = 0$$
$$\Rightarrow |dI|.|C - \frac{\lambda^*}{d}I| = 0$$
$$\Rightarrow |C - \frac{\lambda^*}{d}I| = 0 (since|dI| \neq 0)$$

Comparing with Eq. (3.4), we get:

$$\lambda = \frac{\lambda^*}{d} \tag{3.6}$$

That is, the eigenvalues λ^* are also multiplied by the same constant factor d. For another matrix C, say $\widehat{C}$, whose average pairwise difference lies between the original average pairwise difference in C and that is C^*, the corresponding eigenvalues $\widehat{\lambda}$ can be shown to lie between λ and λ^*. This ordering of the eigenvalues was exploited as a natural measure of the extent of disagreement among the p-values obtained.

Since the p-values lie in the interval [0, 1], the largest eigenvalue $\eta(C)$ tends to have low numeric values. For convenience of implementation, the inverse of C was computed and the largest eigenvalue of C^{-1} was used in the experiments. The largest eigenvalue $\eta(C^{-1})$ will be inversely proportional to the average difference among the p-values and hence, the lower the average pairwise difference, the higher the value of $\eta(C^{-1})$ will be. The pseudocode of the GQBT algorithm is presented in Algorithm 2.

Contrary to most other online active learning algorithms, which depend on empirically obtained thresholds to decide whether an unlabeled example needs to be queried, the largest eigenvalue in the GQBT framework has a straightforward mathematical

---

Algorithm 2 Generalized Query by Transduction (GQBT) for Online Active Learning

---

Input: Training set $T = \{(x_1, y_1), \ldots (x_n, y_n)\}$, classifier Ξ, selection threshold δ, stopping threshold γ, number of classes M, number of queried points p, budget constraint β (maximum number of points that can be queried)

1: $p := 0$
2: **repeat**
3:    A new unlabeled example x_{n+1} is observed
4:    **for** $i = 1 \rightarrow M$ **do**
5:       Assign label y_i to x_{n+1}
6:       Update the classifier Ξ using $T \cup \{(x_{n+1}, y_i)\}$
7:       Compute the nonconformity measure value $\alpha_{n+1}^{y_i}$ to compute the p-value p_i w.r.t class y_i (using Eqs. 1.4 and 1.5)
8:    **end for**
9:    Construct the matrix C such that $C_{ij}(P) = |p_i - p_j|$ (Eq. (3.3))
10:    Compute $\eta(C^{-1})$ as the largest eigenvalue of C^{-1}
11:    **if** $\eta(C^{-1}) > \delta$ **then**
12:       $T := T \cup \{(x_{n+1}, y_{n+1})\}$, where y_{n+1} is the true label of x_{n+1}
13:       $p := p + 1$
14:    **end if**
15: **until** $\eta(C^{-1}) > \gamma$ or $p < \beta$

---

interpretation, which can be exploited. In the empirical evaluations, the selection threshold δ was initialized to the largest eigenvalue of C^{-1} that was constructed assuming the pairwise differences among the p-values are equal to a unit percentage (i.e., 0.01) each. According to Eq. (3.6), the eigenvalues of C^{-1} are divided by a factor of d, when C is multiplied by d. Hence, when the pairwise differences are equal to 0.02 each, the largest eigenvalue of C^{-1} will equal $\frac{\delta}{2}$. In the implementation of the algorithm, if no instances were queried after r examples were observed, the selection threshold was changed to $\delta = \frac{\delta}{2}$, thus allowing for a more accommodative threshold. Depending on the particular dataset, this can be progressively continued at periodic intervals to $\delta = \frac{\delta}{3}$, $\delta = \frac{\delta}{4}$ and so on. This provides for an automatic methodology to set and update the threshold values, where the query condition becomes lenient with time.

Combining multiple criteria in GQBT

In machine learning problems, often multiple sources of information are available, such as the audio and video modalities for person recognition, multiple image features for image classification, and so on. It may thus be essential to combine multiple criteria to decide whether a particular example needs to be queried for its class label in the online active learning setting. In addition to the Lagrangian multipliers, it may thus be useful to consider another nonconformity measure that estimates the density of examples in the neighborhood of a given unlabeled example. This can be defined using the k-NN classifier (a non-parametric density estimator), as explained in the previous chapters. The CP framework can be used in conjunction with this nonconformity measure to obtain another set of p-values of a given unlabeled sample. Results from statistical hypotheses can be used to combine the two sets of p-values. Given the p-value is a uniformly distributed random variable in the interval [0, 1], the combined significance level or the p-value of n individual p-values can be given as [167]:

$$k \sum_{i=0}^{n-1} \frac{(-\log k)^i}{i!} \tag{3.7}$$

where $k = (p_1 \times p_2 \ldots \times p_n)$, the product of the given set of p-values. Besides this, other techniques from hypothesis testing can be used to combine the p-values [217].

3.3.3 Multicriteria Extension to QBT

Makili et al. [221] recently developed an active learning technique, based on conformal prediction, to identify the exemplar and representative training instances for classifying TJ-II Thomson Scattering images. The active learning criterion used was uncertainty sampling, where the degree of uncertainty of the current classifier on an unlabeled image quantified the level of uncertainty (informativeness) of that image. SVM was used as the underlying classification model, similar to the QBT and GQBT frameworks. The uncertainty condition was derived based on the p-values of an unlabeled sample, obtained from the CP framework. Let p_1 and p_2 be the top two p-values of an unlabeled example x. By the CP framework, the credibility ($I_{cr}(x)$) of the

---

Algorithm 3 Active learning using multiplecriteria in conformal prediction

---

Input: Training set $T = (x_1, y_1), \ldots (x_n, y_n)$, unlabeled pool of samples U, calibration set C, selection threshold τ, batch size β

1: Train an initial classifier on T
2: **repeat**
3:    Apply the current classifier to the unlabeled pool of samples
4:    Rank the samples in the pool by the uncertainty criterion using Eq. 3.8
5:    Select the top β examples whose certainty levels fall under the selection threshold τ
6:    Obtain the labels of the selected samples from an oracle and append them to the training set
7:    Train a new classifier on the expanded training set
8: **until** budget constraint is not satisfied

---

example is p_1 and the confidence $(I_{cf}(x))$ is defined as $1 - p_2$. As mentioned earlier, the QBT framework quantifies the informativeness of an example as the difference between the top two p-values:

$$I_{qbt}(x) = p_1 - p_2$$
$$= cred - (1 - conf)$$

Makili et al. extended the QBT method to a multicriteria approach that quantifies the information content of an unlabeled example:

$$I(x) = \mu I_1(x) + (1 - \mu)I_2(x) \tag{3.8}$$

where $I_1(x)$ was taken as $I_{qbt}(x)$ and $I_2(x)$ was taken as $I_{cf}(x)$. The weight parameter μ was set at 0.78 (combination 1) and 0.5 (combination 2), leading to two different active learning criteria. The pseudocode of the framework is given in Algorithm 3.

3.4 Experimental Results

Balasubramanian et al. [11] compared the GQBT and QBT methods against two other online active learning techniques and random sampling. These are detailed below:

Random Sampling: In this method when a new unlabeled example arrives, the decision to query the class label of that point was taken at random; that is, each point was queried with a probability of 0.5.

Margin-based SVM: An SVM classifier was constructed from the given set of training examples. For an unlabeled example x_{n+1}, its decision value $f(x) = w.\phi(x) + b$ was computed and if the value was below a threshold, the point was queried. If a certain number of unlabeled points were not queried in succession, the threshold was updated as the average of the SVM decision values of the unqueried examples.

Query by Committee: A committee consisting of two classifiers SVM and k-NN (with $k = 10$) was used. For a given unlabeled example, the SVM output values were converted into posterior probabilities Platt's method [277]. For k-NN, the class probability of an unlabeled example was defined as the fraction of the number of points of a given class occurring in its k nearest neighbors. The Kullback-Leibler divergence of the two sets of probability values was computed and a high divergence implied that the point was informative and should be queried. The threshold for the KL divergence value was updated as described for the margin-based SVM.

SVM is used as the underlying classifier considering the popularity of SVMs in active learning [150,342]. Besides, there have been recent efforts toward the development of incremental SVM models to effectively train newer examples in an online setting [81]. A limitation of every transductive learning algorithm is the computational overhead associated with retraining newer examples with each possible class label—the use of incremental SVMs substantially offsets this limitation. The Lagrangian multipliers obtained while training an SVM were used as nonconformity scores [365]. The Lagrangian multipliers have values 0 for examples outside the margin and lie between 0 and C for examples on and within the margin, thereby providing a natural measure of nonconformity with respect to the corresponding class.

3.4.1 Benchmark Datasets

The performances were compared on five datasets from the UCI Machine Learning Repository. The datasets and their details are given in Table 3.1. For each dataset, the training, testing, and the unlabeled sets were randomly permuted three times and the results were averaged over these three runs. In each of the runs, the unlabeled pool was randomly permuted 10 different times to remove any bias on the order in which the points are observed, and the results of these 10 trials were averaged for

Table 3.1 Datasets from the UCI Machine Learning repository used in the experiments. An equal number of examples from each class was used in the initial training set. For example, for the Breast Cancer dataset, five examples from each class were used to form the initial training set of 10 examples.

Dataset	Classes	Size of dataset	Dim	Initial training set	Size of unlabeled pool	Size of test set
Breast Cancer	2	569	30	10	259	300
Musk	2	1000	166	2	498	500
Wine	3	178	13	3	88	87
Waveform	3	5000	21	15	2485	2500
Image Segmentation	7	2310	19	35	175	2100

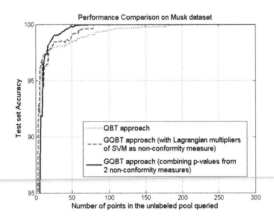

FIGURE 3.4

Performance comparison on the Musk dataset (as in Figure 3.9). The label complexity is further reduced by combining the p-values from the two nonconformity measures. The p-value fusion approach needs only ≈50 examples to reach the peak accuracy [11].

each run. A polynomial kernel SVM was used in the empirical studies as it was found to demonstrate good performance on the datasets.

The results of the experiments are presented in Figure 3.5 and Table 3.2. For each dataset, the formulation of the GQBT approach where the nonconformity measures from the SVM and the k-NN are combined was used, since this provided better performance than a single nonconformity measure. Figure 3.4 depicts the improvement in performance obtained on the same dataset as in Figure 3.9 by combining the p-values obtained using the nonconformity measures from the SVM and k-NN classifiers.

Table 3.2 shows the label complexity values (percentage of the unlabeled pool that was queried to reach the peak accuracy in the active learning process) for each of the methods. The results corroborate the improvement in performance achieved using the GQBT approach, where all the p-values (obtained from the CP framework) of an unlabeled example are used to quantify the information content of the sample.

3.4.2 Application to Face Recognition

In addition to the benchmark datasets, Balasubramanian et al. [11] validated the GQBT approach on a face recognition task, where the high redundancy among the video frames necessitate an active learning approach to decide the frames that need to be queried for annotation. The VidTIMIT biometric dataset [296], containing video recordings of subjects reciting short sentences, was used in this experiment. The videos were sliced into frames and the face regions of 25 subjects were cropped automatically. Each image was subdivided into 8×8 nonoverlapping blocks, and the DCT coefficients of each block were then ordered according to the zigzag scan pattern. The DC coefficient was discarded for illumination normalization, and the first 10 AC coefficients of each block were selected to form compact local feature vectors. Each

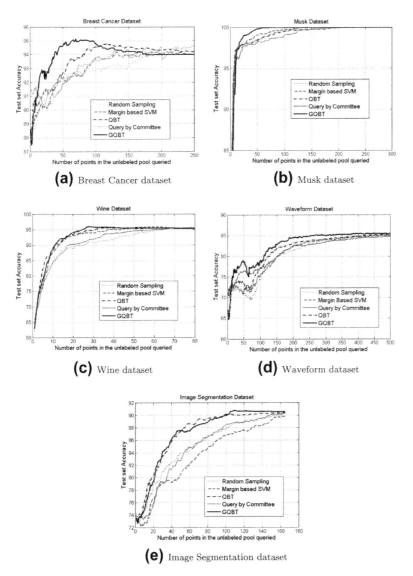

(a) Breast Cancer dataset

(b) Musk dataset

(c) Wine dataset

(d) Waveform dataset

(e) Image Segmentation dataset

FIGURE 3.5

Results with datasets from the UCI Machine Learning repository. In the Musk dataset, the results started with an accuracy of ≈70%, but since all methods had similar initial accuracies, the graph is shown from 85% accuracy onward, where the differences in performance are clearly seen [11].

local feature vector was normalized to unit norm. Concatenating the features from the individual blocks yielded the global feature vector for the entire image. The cropped

Table 3.2 Label complexities of each of the methods for all the datasets. Label complexity is defined as the percentage of the unlabeled pool that is queried to reach the peak accuracy in the active learning process. The GQBT method has low label complexity in all the cases. The label complexities for the other methods on datasets like Waveform and Image Segmentation are very high, although the accuracy did increase at a reasonable rate in the active learning process in Figure 3.5. This only implies that these methods reached their peak accuracy when the unlabeled pool was almost exhausted.

Dataset	Random sampling	Margin-based SVM	Query by committee	QBT	GQBT
Breast Cancer	92.8%	83.6%	80%	46.8%	28%
Musk	77%	55%	72.33%	86.67%	24.33%
Wine	87.5%	78.75%	97.5%	47.5%	35%
Waveform	99.6%	100%	98.2%	98.6%	89.2%
Image Segmentation	100%	100%	100%	98.18%	66.06%

face image had a resolution of 128 × 128 and thus the dimensionality of the extracted feature vector was 2560. Principal Component Analysis (PCA) was then applied to reduce the dimension to 100, retaining about 99% of the variance. 50 images of each subject were randomly picked, and divided into the initial training set (10), unlabeled pool (20), and the test set (20). A polynomial kernel was used for the SVM classifier. Similar to the previous set of experiments, the unlabeled pool was randomly permuted three different times to remove any bias on the order in which the points are observed, and the results of these three trials were averaged. Figure 3.6 shows the results of the online active learning algorithms on this dataset. The GQBT approach once again demonstrated significantly improved performance over the other datasets.

3.4.3 Multicriteria Extension to QBT

As mentioned in Section 3.3.3, Makili et al. [221] developed a multicriteria extension to QBT to identify the exemplar and representative training instances for classifying TJ-II Thomson Scattering images. The image features used for this problem were the vertical detail coefficients of the Haar wavelet transform at level 4, which diminishes the sample dimensionality by reducing the spatial redundancy of the images. There were five classes of images, as shown in Figure 3.7.

Eleven hundred and forty-nine images were used and were divided into an initial training set (5 samples), an unlabeled pool (794 samples), a calibration set (150 samples), and a test set (200 samples). The batch size was taken as 25 and the selection threshold as 0.4. This value was used with QBT, comb1 and comb2 (as described in Section 3.3.3). The success rate, confidence, and credibility were used as the performance metrics. The results are presented in Figure 3.8, which depict the

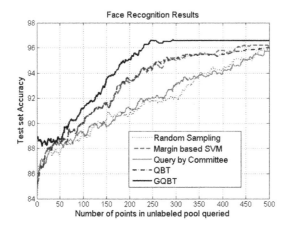

FIGURE 3.6

Results obtained on the VidTIMIT dataset. The GQBT approach led to a significantly higher peak accuracy, and had a lower label complexity of 58.8% to reach the peak accuracy. Label complexities of the other methods: Ho and Wechsler's QBT—98.2%; Query by Committee—100%; Margin-based SVM—89%; Random sampling—99.6% [11].

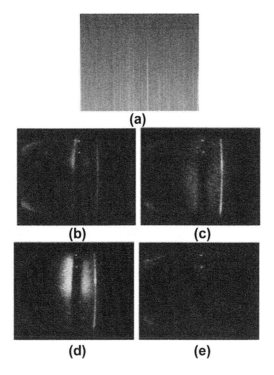

FIGURE 3.7

Patterns of TSD images: (a) BKGND, (b) COFF, (c) ECRH, (d) NBI, and (e) STRAY [221].

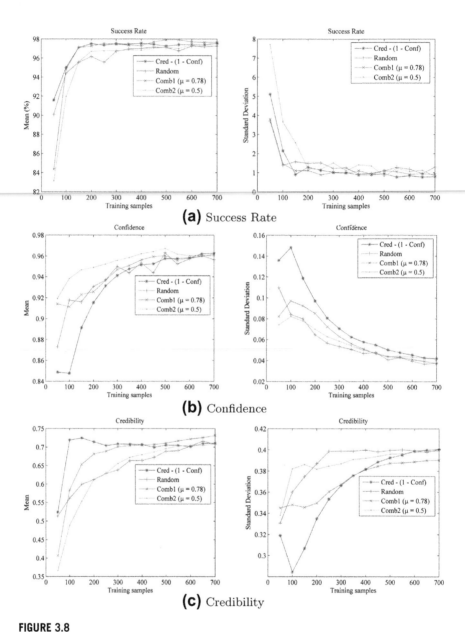

FIGURE 3.8

Performance of multicriteria extension to QBT on image classification task [221].

mean and the standard deviation of each metric. These empirical results portray the potential of active instance selection using multicriteria QBT over random sampling in classification problems.

3.5 **Discussion and Conclusions**

In this chapter, the adaptation of the theory of conformal prediction to the problem of active learning was described. The CP framework is based on the concepts of algorithmic randomness, transductive inference, and hypothesis testing and provides calibration of the error frequencies in an online learning setting. It is therefore intuitive to use the framework for online active learning to decide whether the currently observed unlabeled data sample needs to be queried for annotation.

The Query by Transduction (QBT) framework was detailed, which uses the difference between the top two p-values of an unlabeled sample as a criterion for active learning. We then presented the Generalized Query by Transduction (GQBT) framework, which uses all (or a desired number of) p-values to quantify the informativeness of a data instance, instead of just the top two p-values. We also presented a multi-criteria extension to QBT that was developed for an image classification task. The empirical evaluations on several benchmark datasets corroborated the fact that active learning using conformal prediction in the online setting significantly outperforms other heuristic active learning methods; it was also observed that combining multiple criteria in these strategies tends to perform better than a single criterion.

Ho and Wechsler [150] showed that it is possible to establish a connection between the p-values obtained using conformal prediction and Kullback-Leibler divergence, which is typically used in active learning methods. They also extended this analysis to show that QBT can be shown to be a variant of the Query-by-Committee (QBC) active learning strategy.

Balasubramanian et al. [11] showed that the GQBT method is actually a generalization of QBT. The QBT approach defined the quantity of information of a new unlabeled example as $I(x_{n+1}) = p_j - p_k$, where p_j and p_k are the two highest

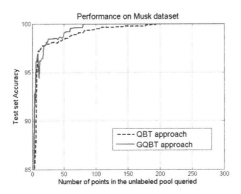

FIGURE 3.9

Comparison of GQBT with QBT on the Musk dataset from the UCI Machine Learning repository [11]. GQBT reaches peak accuracy by querying $\approx$80 examples, while the latter needs $\approx$160 examples.

p-values obtained using the CP framework. The GQBT approach uses the largest eigenvalue of the C matrix containing the pairwise differences among the p-values, to quantify the information content of an unlabeled example. In a binary classification problem (or, if only the top two p-values are used in a multiclass setting), the C matrix becomes:

$$\begin{bmatrix} 0 & |p_1 - p_2| \\ |p_1 - p_2| & 0 \end{bmatrix}$$

whose largest eigenvalue is $|p_1 - p_2|$, which was the measure used in QBT. Thus in case of a binary classification problem, the GQBT approach simplifies to the QBT approach; it is therefore a generalization of QBT, which offers the flexibility to decide the number of p-values that need to be considered while quantifying the information content of an example. They showed that it is possible to obtain a lower label complexity using GQBT as compared to QBT (see Figure 3.9).

Acknowledgments

We thank Lazaro Makili at Instituto Superior Politécnico da Universidade Katyavala Bwila, Benguela, Angola for the kind permission to reproduce images from their article "Active Learning Using Conformal Predictors: Application to Image Classification" (Fusion Science and Technology, American Nuclear Society, 62:347, 2012) in this chapter. This chapter is based upon work supported by the US National Science Foundation under Grant No. 1116360. Any opinions, findings, and conclusions or recommendations expressed in this material are those of the author(s) and do not necessarily reflect the views of the US National Science Foundation.

Anomaly Detection

4

Rikard Laxhammar
Saab AB, Järfälla, Sweden

CHAPTER OUTLINE HEAD

This chapter presents an extension of conformal prediction for anomaly detection applications. It includes the presentation and discussion of the Conformal Anomaly Detector (CAD) and the computationally more efficient Inductive Conformal Anomaly Detector (ICAD), which are general algorithms for unsupervised or semi-supervised and offline or online anomaly detection. One of the key properties of CAD and ICAD is that the rate of detected anomalies is well-calibrated in the online setting under the randomness assumption. Similar to conformal prediction, the choice of nonconformity measure (NCM) is of central importance for the classification performance of CAD and ICAD. A novel NCM for examples that are represented as sets of points is presented. One of the key properties of this NCM, which is known as the directed Hausdorff k-nearest neighbors (DH-kNN) NCM, is that the p-value for an incomplete test example monotonically decreases as more data points are observed. An instance of CAD based on DH-kNN NCM, known as the sequential Hausdorff nearest neighbor conformal anomaly detector (SHNN-CAD), is presented and discussed for sequential anomaly detection applications. We also investigate classification performance results for the unsupervised online SHNN-CAD on a public dataset of labeled trajectories.

4.1 Introduction

The framework of conformal prediction was originally developed for the problem of supervised learning and prediction with valid confidence. However, some of the main theoretical results from conformal prediction are also highly relevant for the problem of *anomaly detection*, which we introduce in Section 4.2. The key observations are two-fold: The first is that the p-value (1.5) for an observed example is a general and useful anomaly measure, and that the significance level ϵ can be interpreted as an anomaly threshold and an upper bound of the probability of detecting an anomaly. The second key observation is that the smoothed p-values (1.20) for a sequence of observed examples are independent in the online framework under the randomness assumption (1.1), which implies that the rate of detected anomalies can be directly controlled by the setting of ϵ.

In Section 4.3, which is based on previous work published by Laxhammar [195] and Laxhammar and Falkman [196], we first discuss informally how a conformal predictor for supervised classification can be used for anomaly detection. This includes the presentation of a nonconformity measure (NCM) that is specifically designed for this setting. In Section 4.4, which is based on further work by Laxhammar and Falkman [197,198], we formalize the *conformal anomaly detector* (CAD). The main idea of CAD is to estimate the p-value for a test example relative to a training set based on a specified NCM. If the p-value is below the predefined *anomaly threshold* ϵ, the example is classified as a conformal anomaly. We present different settings, such as offline versus online and unsupervised versus semi-supervised conformal anomaly detection, and discuss properties related to the anomaly detection rate and classification performance in the different settings. One of the main drawbacks of CAD is that it is computationally inefficient. In response to this, Laxhammar and Falkman [198] proposed the *inductive conformal anomaly detector* (ICAD), which is presented in Section 4.5. Similar to inductive conformal predictors [365], ICAD is computationally more efficient and has a similar notion of offline, semi-offline and online anomaly detection.

Analogously to conformal prediction, the performance of CAD and ICAD depends on the specified NCM, which should accurately discriminate between examples that are considered to belong to the normal or abnormal class. Various NCMs based on modern machine learning algorithms have previously been proposed for supervised conformal prediction [365]. Nevertheless, they all assume that each object is represented as a point in a fixed-dimensional feature space. This may be a limitation in applications where input examples are naturally represented as sets or sequences of points of varying size or length, respectively. Moreover, it may be desirable or necessary to be able to classify an *incomplete* example (i.e., when all the features or points have not yet been observed). One such application is *sequential anomaly detection*, where examples correspond to trajectories of moving objects [195]. In Section 4.6, the *directed Hausdorff k-nearest neighbor* (DH-kNN) NCM is presented, which is a novel NCM designed for comparing complete or incomplete examples represented as sets of points [197,199]. This NCM was designed for sequential anomaly detection in trajectories using CAD, which is described in Section 4.7. This section includes a description and discussion of the *Sequential Hausdorff Nearest Neighbors Conformal Anomaly Detector* (SHNN-CAD) and some empirical results regarding the classification performance on two public datasets of labeled trajectories.

4.2 Background

According to Chandola et al. [50], "anomalies are patterns in data that do not conform to a well-defined notion of normal behavior." These patterns, also known as *outliers*, typically correspond to new, rare, unknown, or otherwise extreme data and may therefore be of particular interest. Indeed, anomaly detection, which is sometimes referred to as *outlier detection* or *novelty detection*, has been identified as an important technique for detecting critical events in a wide range of domains where a majority of the data is considered "normal" and uninteresting. In the statistical community, the concepts of outliers and outlier detection have been known for quite a long time. A commonly cited definition of an outlier was given by Hawkins [142]:

> [An outlier is] an observation that deviates so much from other observations as to arouse suspicion that it was generated by a different mechanism.

The mechanism is usually assumed to follow a stationary probability distribution. Hence, outlier detection essentially involves determining whether or not a particular example has been generated by the same distribution as the rest of the examples.

From an application owner's point of view, anomaly detection may be considered as a classification problem where each example either belongs to a *normal class* or an *abnormal class*. Due to the rarity and diversity of abnormal data, definition of abnormal class models based on expert knowledge, or collection and annotation of labeled training data for supervised learning are usually not applicable. Nevertheless, often large amounts of *unlabeled data* are available, which is assumed to only include a minority, if any, abnormal examples. Thus, many anomaly detection algorithms adopt unsupervised learningtechniques, such as density estimation or clustering, for finding the most anomalous examples in a set of unlabeled examples. These approaches are referred to as *unsupervised anomaly detection* [50]. In some cases, there are normal training data available that can be used for learning *one-class anomaly detectors* or *multi-class anomaly detectors,* depending on whether the training dataset includes labeled examples from a single normal class or multiple normal classes, respectively [50]. One-class anomaly detectors (e.g., the one-class support vector machine (SVM) [304]) classify unlabeled examples as either normal or anomalous. Multiclass anomaly detectors also can, in addition to discriminating between normal and abnormal examples, discriminate between the different normal classes. Approaches that assume training data labeled normal are sometimes referred to as *semi-supervised anomaly detection* [50].

4.3 Conformal Prediction for Multiclass Anomaly Detection

Let us consider the general supervised classification setting (Section 1.6) where each example z_i consists of the object x_i and the label y_i and the task is to predict the unknown label y_{l+1} based on the observed object x_{l+1} and the training set $(z_1, \ldots, z_l)$. A conformal predictor outputs a prediction set $\Gamma^\epsilon (z_1, \ldots, z_l, x_{l+1}) \subseteq \mathbf{Y}$ for the label y_{n+1} at the specified significance level ϵ. Now, assuming that the significance level is low, say 1% or less, an interesting situation arises if the prediction set is empty; this happens if all p-values (one for each possible class) are below ϵ and it indicates that the new object x_{l+1} is a novelty that does not match any of the previous objects $x_i : i = 1, \ldots, l$. An empty prediction set at significance level ϵ is equivalent to the case of a single label prediction that has *credibility* less than ϵ [114]. As discussed by Gammerman and Vovk [114], "low credibility means that either the training set is non-random or the test object is not representative of the training set." As an example, the authors discuss an optical character recognition (OCR) application, where an empty prediction set may arise if the new image corresponds to a letter while the training set consists of images of digits. Another interesting situation arises if a nonempty prediction set does not include the true label. This means that the object was recognized but the (later observed) class label was unexpected. An example of such situation would be a badly written "7" that resembles a "1" (or vice versa). In both situations, the prediction set is incorrect but we may suspect that the corresponding example is an outlier according to Hawkins's definition. That is, it is not a random sample from the same distribution as the training set. In general, if the new example and the training set are IID or exchangeable, we know from Proposition 1.2 that the probability of error is bounded by ϵ. Thus, if we classify examples as anomalous when the corresponding prediction set is incorrect, we know that the specified significance level ϵ corresponds to an upper bound of the probability of an anomaly detection.

4.3.1 **A Nonconformity Measure for Multiclass Anomaly Detection**

Gammerman and Vovk [114] proposed the following k-nearest neighbor NCM for classification applications:

$$\alpha_i := \frac{\sum_{j=1}^{k} d_{ij}^{+}}{\sum_{j=1}^{k} d_{ij}^{-}}, \tag{4.1}$$

where d_{ij}^{+} is the jth shortest distance in the object space from z_i to other examples with the same label and d_{ij}^{-} is the jth shortest distance from z_i to examples labeled differently. The intuition is rather simple: It is assumed that examples of the same (normal) class are close to each other in feature space, while examples of different (normal) classes are further away from each other. Nevertheless, it was argued by Laxhammar and Falkman [196] that this NCM is suboptimal in multi-class anomaly detection applications if there are reasons to believe that normal classes overlap in the object space. The authors showed this point with the following intuitive example illustrated by Figure 4.1: Assume a binary label space where the two class distributions (circles and solid gray points) overlap in a high-density region in the object space. Considering an example that is located in the overlapping high-density region (left solid black point), we expect that the sum of the distances to its nearest neighbors will be approximately the same for the two classes. Thus, the nonconformity score according to (4.1) would be close to 1, regardless of which class the example actually belongs to. Moving away from both class distributions and considering another example that is located far to the right (right solid black point), the ratio of the sum of the nearest neighbor distances for the two classes will approach 1. Hence, the p-value of a normal point located in the overlapping high density area will be close to the p-value of an obviously anomalous point located far away from both class distributions. In response to this problem, Laxhammar and Falkman [196] proposed a modified NCM for the case of partially overlapping class distributions, which simply omits the distances to other classes:

$$\alpha_i := \sum_{j=1}^{k} d_{ij}^{+}. \tag{4.2}$$

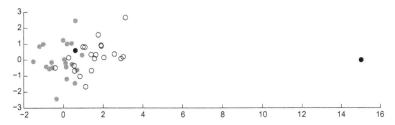

FIGURE 4.1

Illustration of the problem with the NCM based on distances to nearest neighbors of the same class and nearest neighbors of other classes discussed in Section 4.3.1.

This NCM is expected to be more sensitive to anomalous points located far away from all known classes.

Remark 4.1. The problem with using (4.1) for detecting outliers was in fact first identified by Barbará et al. [14] (and later independently rediscovered by Laxhammar and Falkman [196]). In their work, Barbará et al. proposed a cluster-based outlier detection algorithm based on ideas from *Transductive confidence machines* [280], which is a precursor to conformal predictors. Given a cluster model and a new example, they proposed the use of (4.2) for estimating the p-values for the new example belonging to each of the corresponding clusters. If all p-values are below a specified threshold, the example is considered to be an outlier.

4.4 Conformal Anomaly Detection

In many applications, we are interested only in detecting anomalies and not determining which, if any, of the normal classes that the example belongs to. In this case it makes more sense to estimate the p-value only for the *observed* label, rather than calculating p-values for *all* possible labels $y \in \mathbf{Y}$. Moreover, the structured prediction discussed in Section 4.3.1 may be considered as a special case of the more general problem of predicting the example z_{l+1} based on the training set $(z_1, \ldots, z_l)$ (Section 1.1). Hence, in the remainder of this chapter, we will consider the general problem of classifying an unlabeled example z_{l+1} as normal or anomalous based on the training set $(z_1, \ldots, z_l)$.

CAD (Algorithm 4), which was proposed by Laxhammar and Falkman [197], is a general algorithm for classifying an unlabeled test example z_{l+1} based on a NCM A, a specified anomaly threshold ϵ and a training set $(z_1, \ldots, z_l)$. The idea is to estimate the p-value p_{l+1} for z_{l+1} relative $(z_1, \ldots, z_l)$ using the specified NCM A according

---

Algorithm 4 The conformal anomaly detector (CAD)

Input: NCM A, anomaly threshold ϵ, training set $(z_1, \ldots, z_l)$ and test example z_{l+1}.

Output: Indicator variable $\mathrm{Anom}_{l+1}^{\epsilon} \in \{0, 1\}$.

1: **for** $i \leftarrow 1$ to $l + 1$ **do**
2:    $\alpha_i \leftarrow A\left(\{z_1, \ldots, z_{l+1}\} \backslash z_i, z_i\right)$
3: **end for**
4: $p_{l+1} \leftarrow \frac{|\{i=1,\ldots,l+1 : \alpha_i \geq \alpha_{l+1}\}|}{l+1}$
5: **if** $p_{l+1} < \epsilon$ **then**
6:    $\mathrm{Anom}_{l+1}^{\epsilon} \leftarrow 1$
7: **else**
8:    $\mathrm{Anom}_{l+1}^{\epsilon} \leftarrow 0$
9: **end if**

---

to (1.5). If $p_{l+1} < \epsilon$, then z_{l+1} is classified as a *conformal anomaly*:

$$\text{Anom}^{\epsilon}_{l+1} = 1. \tag{4.3}$$

Otherwise, z_{l+1} is considered to be *normal*:

$$\text{Anom}^{\epsilon}_{l+1} = 0. \tag{4.4}$$

4.4.1 Conformal Anomalies

The definition of a conformal anomaly is consistent with the statistical definition of an outlier given by Hawkins (Section 4.2). That is, a conformal anomaly corresponds to a test example z_{l+1} that deviates so much from $(z_1, \ldots, z_l)$ as to arouse suspicion that it was not generated according to the same mechanism as $(z_1, \ldots, z_l)$. Analogously to statistical hypothesis testing, ϵ can be interpreted as an upper bound of the probability of erroneously rejecting the null hypothesis that z_{l+1} and $(z_1, \ldots, z_l)$ are independent and random samples from the same probability distribution [315]. Hence, we state the following proposition regarding the probability of a conformal anomaly:

Proposition 4.1. *Assume that $z_1, \ldots, z_{l+1}$ are independent and identically distributed (IID). For any choice of NCM A, the specified anomaly threshold ϵ corresponds to an upper bound of the probability of the event that z_{l+1} is classified as a conformal anomaly by CAD:*

$$Pr\left(\text{Anom}^{\epsilon}_{l+1} = 1\right) \leq \epsilon. \tag{4.5}$$

The larger the value of ϵ, the higher the expected rate of detected conformal anomalies.

From an application perspective, there are at least three different explanations for a conformal anomaly. First, it may correspond to a relatively rare or previously unseen example generated from the same probability distribution as $(z_1, \ldots, z_l)$. Second and third, it may be a "true" anomaly in the sense that it was not generated according to the same probability distribution as $(z_1, \ldots, z_l)$; either z_{l+1} is a true novelty, or $(z_1, \ldots, z_l)$ itself is in fact not IID. A non-IID training set may be explained by incomplete or biased data collection. In a public video surveillance application, for example, observed behavior during early morning or late afternoon may appear anomalous if the training set is based on data recorded during a limited time of the day (e.g., 10 a.m. to 2 p.m). Another possible reason for a non-IID training set is that the underlying probability distribution has actually changed. In maritime surveillance, for example, new vessel trajectories may arise as a result of new traffic regulations. If the rate of detected conformal anomalies suddenly starts to deteriorate from ϵ in an online application, there may be reasons to suspect that the underlying probability distribution has changed recently.

4.4.2 Offline versus Online Conformal Anomaly Detection

Assume an initial training set $(z_1, \ldots, z_l)$ and a sequence of new test examples $z_{l+1}, \ldots, z_N$. The *offline CAD* classifies each $z_n : n = l + 1, \ldots, N$ based on the initial training set $(z_1, \ldots, z_l)$. In contrast, the *online CAD* classifies each z_n based on the *updated* training set $(z_1, \ldots, z_{n-1})$. That is, z_{n-1} is appended to the training set $(z_1, \ldots, z_{n-2})$ before the classification of z_n. If $z_1, \ldots, z_n$ are IID, we know from Proposition 4.1 that the *unconditional* probability that z_n is classified as a conformal anomaly is bounded by ϵ. Nevertheless, the actual rate of detected anomalies for the offline CAD may be significantly higher than ϵ since the sequence of random variables $\text{Anom}_{l+1}^{\epsilon}, \ldots, \text{Anom}_N^{\epsilon}$ are *not* independent. In the online framework, though, the rate of detected anomalies will, with very high probability, be less or approximately equal to ϵ. This nonasymptotic property, which we refer to as *well-calibrated alarm rate*, is formalized by Theorem 4.1.

Theorem 4.1. *Assume that the sequence of examples $z_1, \ldots, z_N$ are IID and that $N - l$ is large. For any choice of NCM A and anomaly threshold ϵ, the rate of detected conformal anomalies will, with very high probability, be less or approximately equal to ϵ for the online CAD:*

$$\frac{\left| \text{Anom}_n^{\epsilon} = 1 : n = l + 1, \ldots, N \right|}{N - l} \lesssim \epsilon. \qquad (4.6)$$

Proof. Let us temporarily assume that the determinstic p-value (1.5) for each test example $z_n : n = l + 1, \ldots, N$ is replaced by the corresponding *smoothed* p-value (1.20). This would imply that $Pr\left(\text{Anom}_n^{\epsilon} = 1\right) = \epsilon$; that is, that the probability of the event that z_n is classified as a conformal anomaly is exactly equal ϵ. Since the smoothed p-values $p_{l+1}, \ldots, p_N$ are independent in the online framework [365, Theorem 8.2], the random variables $\text{Anom}_{l+1}^{\epsilon}, \ldots, \text{Anom}_N^{\epsilon}$ are also independent. Therefore, if $N - l$ is large, it follows from the law of large numbers that the rate of detected conformal anomalies will, with very high probability, be approximately equal to ϵ. Now, since the probability of a conformal anomaly is less than or equal to ϵ in the case of determinstic p-values (Proposition 4.1), the rate of detected conformal anomalies for the online CAD must be less or approximately equal to ϵ. $\qquad \square$

4.4.3 Unsupervised and Semi-supervised Conformal Anomaly Detection

The conformal anomaly detection framework is essentially based on an unsupervised learning paradigm where there is no explicit notion of normal and abnormal classes. However, from an application owner's or domain expert's point of view, each example is often considered to belong to either a normal or an abnormal class (Section 4.2). Hence, when classifying an unlabeled example using CAD, there are generally two types of possible errors: The first error is when a normal example is classified as a conformal anomaly, which is known as a *false alarm*. The second error is when an abnormal example is *not* classified as a conformal anomaly.

Analogously to Eskin [94], let us assume that examples of the normal and abnormal classes are generated according to the unknown probability distributions P_{Normal} and $P_{Abnormal}$ and that the unknown prior probability of the abnormal class is equal to λ.

The generative distribution for *unlabeled* examples can then be modeled as a *mixture model*:

$$P_{Data} = (1 - \lambda) P_{Normal} + \lambda P_{Abnormal}. \tag{4.7}$$

Depending on whether the training set is assumed to be unlabeled or labeled normal, CAD can be considered to operate in an unsupervised or semi-supervised anomaly detection mode, respectively (Section 4.2). The unsupervised online CAD is perhaps the most interesting from both a theoretical and practical point of view; it does not require any label feedback and the overall rate of detected conformal anomalies is well-calibrated, regardless of P_{Normal}, $P_{Abnormal}$, and λ. The only assumption is that $(z_1, \ldots, z_N)$ constitutes an IID sample from P_{Data}, which does not seem to be an impractical or otherwise unrealistic assumption in an anomaly detection application.

The semi-supervised online CAD utilizes a similar notion of well-calibrated alarm rate: Assume that $\left(z'_{l+1}, \ldots, z'_Q : Q \leq N\right)$ corresponds to the subsequence of normal test examples of the full sequence $(z_{l+1}, \ldots, z_N)$ and that each $z'_n : n = l+2, \ldots, Q$ is classified based on the updated training set $(z_1, \ldots, z_l, z'_{l+1}, \ldots, z'_{n-1})$. Further, assume that $Q - l$ is large and that $\left(z_1, \ldots, z_l, z'_{l+1}, \ldots, z'_Q\right)$ constitutes an IID sample from P_{Normal}. Then, the rate of the normal test examples $\left(z'_{l+1}, \ldots, z'_Q\right)$ that are erroneously classified as anomalous (i.e., the *false alarm rate*) is well-calibrated. The semi-supervised approach is, however, less practical in the online mode since it requires label feedback for each $z_n : n = l+1, \ldots, N$ in order to know whether z_n is part of $\left(z'_{l+1}, \ldots, z'_Q\right)$ and, hence, should be added to the training set before the classification of z_{n+1}. The semi-supervised offline CAD mitigates this practical problem at the cost of losing the theoretical guarantee of a well-calibrated false alarm rate.

4.4.4 Classification Performance and Tuning of the Anomaly Threshold

Regardless of whether CAD operates in the unsupervised or semi-supervised mode, classification performance is obviously dependent on the chosen NCM and how well it discriminates between examples from $P_{Abnormal}$ and P_{Normal}. In the unsupervised mode, classification performance is further dependent on the character of $P_{Abnormal}$; intuitively, if the abnormal examples vary greatly (i.e., $P_{Abnormal}$ has high entropy), then performance in the unsupervised mode should not be worse than in the semi-supervised mode. However, if abnormal examples vary relatively little from each other (i.e., $P_{Abnormal}$ has very small entropy), then performance in the unsupervised mode may suffer as new abnormal examples might not differ significantly from the abnormal examples in the training set.

The parameter ϵ regulates the *sensitivity* [96] to abnormal examples; that is, the proportion of abnormal examples that are detected as conformal anomalies. It also affects the *precision* [96], or the proportion of abnormal examples among the detected conformal anomalies. A higher value of ϵ may increase sensitivity but at the same time reduce precision due to increased false alarm rate. Although achieving high sensitivity is important, it has been argued that the limiting factor in anomaly detection applications is in fact low precision [287,10]. The problem, which was referred to as the base-rate fallacy by Axelsson [10], is that precision becomes dominated by the false alarm rate due to the low frequency of abnormal examples. Hence, ϵ should be tuned depending on the level of precision that is acceptable in the current application.

In the case of the unsupervised CAD, it may be argued that ϵ should be set close to λ (4.7) in order to achieve a good balance between the sensitivity and precision. Indeed, assuming an ideal NCM such that $\alpha_i > \alpha_j$ for any examples z_i and z_j belonging to the abnormal and normal classes, respectively, it is intuitively clear that setting $\epsilon = \lambda$ will result in sensitivity and precision both being close to 1. Considering the semi-supervised CAD, ϵ corresponds the expected false alarm rate (Section 4.4.3) and should therefore be set as low as possible while still maintaining reasonable sensitivity. Nevertheless, setting $\epsilon < \frac{1}{l+1}$ should always be avoided for both the unsupervised and semi-supervised CAD and regardless of the NCM, since the sensitivity to abnormal examples will then be zero. To see this, assume we observe an abnormal example z_{l+1} such that $\alpha_{l+1} \gg \alpha_i : i = 1, \ldots, l$. From (1.5), it is clear that $p_{l+1} = \frac{1}{l+1}$. Hence, if $\epsilon < \frac{1}{l+1}$, z_{l+1} will not be classified as anomalous, even though it appears to be very extreme.

4.5 Inductive Conformal Anomaly Detection

One of the main drawbacks of CAD is that it is computationally inefficient; in addition to calculating the nonconformity score α_{l+1} for the test example z_{l+1}, CAD has to calculate the nonconformity scores for each example $z_1, \ldots, z_l$ in the training set. When l is large, CAD may therefore become computationally infeasible, especially when the computational complexity of the underlying NCM is relatively high. In response to this problem, Laxhammar and Falkman [198] introduced ICAD (Algorithm 5),

---

Algorithm 5 The inductive conformal anomaly detector (ICAD)

Input: Nonconformity measure A, anomaly threshold ϵ, proper training set $(z_1, \ldots, z_m)$, precomputed nonconformity scores $(\alpha_{m+1}, \ldots, \alpha_l)$, test example z_{l+1}.

Output: Indicator variable $\text{Anom}_{l+1}^\epsilon \in \{0, 1\}$.

1: $\alpha_{l+1} \leftarrow A\left(\{z_1, \ldots, z_m\}, z_{l+1}\right)$
2: $p_{l+1} \leftarrow \frac{|\{i = m+1, \ldots, l+1 : \alpha_i \geq \alpha_{l+1}\}|}{l - m + 1}$
3: **if** $p_{l+1} < \epsilon$ **then**
4:     $\text{Anom}_{l+1}^\epsilon \leftarrow 1$
5: **else**
6:     $\text{Anom}_{l+1}^\epsilon \leftarrow 0$
7: **end if**

---

which is an extension of CAD based on the concept of inductive conformal prediction (ICP) (2.3).

Similar to ICP, the idea is to use precomputed nonconformity scores for previous examples when estimating the p-value for a new test example. More specifically, the training set is split into the proper training set $(z_1, \ldots, z_m)$ of size $m < l$ and the calibration set $(z_{m+1}, \ldots, z_l)$ of size $l - m$. Further, the nonconformity score α_i is precomputed for each example $z_i : i = m + 1, \ldots, l$ of the calibration set relative the proper training set. Given a test example z_{l+1}, ICAD calculates the corresponding nonconformity score α_{l+1} for z_{l+1} relative the proper training set and estimates the p-value p_{l+1} similar to (2.5). Thus, the computational complexity of ICAD is reduced by a factor l as compared to CAD. Similar to CAD, the probability of a conformal anomaly is bounded by ϵ:

Proposition 4.2. *Assume that $z_{m+1}, \ldots, z_{l+1}$ are IID. For any choice of NCM A, the specified anomaly threshold ϵ corresponds to an upper bound of the probability of the event that z_{l+1} is classified as a conformal anomaly by ICAD:*

$$Pr\left(\text{Anom}_{l+1}^{\epsilon} = 1\right) \leq \epsilon. \tag{4.8}$$

4.5.1 Offline and Semi-Offline Inductive Conformal Anomaly Detection

Analogously to ICP [365], ICAD can run in an offline, semi-offline, or online mode, depending on whether the set of precomputed nonconformity scores and the proper training set are updated or not. For each test example $z_n : n = l + 1, \ldots, N$, the *offline ICAD* reuses the same proper training set $(z_1, \ldots, z_m)$ and the same sequence of precomputed nonconformity scores $(\alpha_{m+1}, \ldots, \alpha_l)$. Similar to the offline CAD, the unconditional probability that z_n is classified as a conformal anomaly is bounded by ϵ under the assumption that $z_{m+1}, \ldots, z_l$ and z_n are IID (Proposition 4.2). Yet, the actual rate of detected anomalies for the offline ICAD may still be significantly higher than ϵ since the sequence of random variables $\text{Anom}_{l+1}^{\epsilon}, \ldots, \text{Anom}_N^{\epsilon}$ are not independent.

In contrast, the *semi-offline ICAD* uses the *updated* sequence of nonconformity scores $(\alpha_{m+1}, \ldots, \alpha_l, \ldots, \alpha_{n-1}) : n = l + 1, \ldots, N$ when classifying the test example z_n. That is, the nonconformity score α_{n-1} for the previous example z_{n-1} is added to the sequence of precomputed nonconformity scores before classifying z_n. From Theorem 4.2, it follows that the rate of detected conformal anomalies of the semi-offline ICAD is well calibrated.

Theorem 4.2. *Assume that the sequence of examples $z_{l+1}, \ldots, z_N$ are IID and that $N - l$ is large. For any NCM A, the rate of detected conformal anomalies will, with very high probability, be less or approximately equal to the specified anomaly threshold ϵ for the semi-offline ICAD:*

$$\frac{\left|\text{Anom}_n^{\epsilon} = 1 : n = l + 1, \ldots, N\right|}{N - l} \lessapprox \epsilon. \tag{4.9}$$

Proof. This theorem can be proved based on the same logic as the proof of Theorem 4.1. That is, let us temporarily assume that the deterministic p-value for each test example $z_n : n = l + 1, \ldots, N$ is replaced by the corresponding *smoothed* p-value. This would imply that $Pr\left(\text{Anom}_n^\epsilon = 1\right) = \epsilon$ and that $p_{l+1}, \ldots, p_N$ are independent [365, Theorem 8.2]. Hence, $\text{Anom}_{l+1}^\epsilon, \ldots, \text{Anom}_N^\epsilon$ are also independent. If $N - l$ is large, it follows from the law of large numbers that the rate of detected conformal anomalies will, with very high probability, be approximately equal to ϵ. Since the probability of a conformal anomaly is less than or equal to ϵ in the case of deterministic p-values (Proposition 4.2), the rate of detected conformal anomalies for the semi-offline ICAD must be less than or approximately equal to ϵ. □

4.5.2 Online Inductive Conformal Anomaly Detection

In addition to updating the sequence of precomputed nonconformity scores, the *online ICAD* involves updating the training set at the predefined *update trials* $m_1, m_2, \ldots$: $l < m_1 < m_2 < \cdots$ similar to online ICP [365, Section 4.1]. Assume an initial proper training set $\left(z_1, \ldots, z_{m_0}\right)$, a calibration set $\left(z_{m_0+1}, \ldots z_l\right))$ and the corresponding precomputed nonconformity scores $\left(\alpha_{m_0+1}, \ldots, \alpha_l\right)$ where $m_0 < l$. For each test example $z_n : n = l + 1, \ldots, m_1$, the fixed proper training set $\left(z_1, \ldots, z_{m_0}\right)$ and the updated sequence of nonconformity scores $\left(\alpha_{m_0+1}, \ldots, \alpha_{n-1}\right)$ are used for the classification, similar to the semi-offline ICAD earlier. However, prior to the classification of the next test example z_{m_1+1}, which corresponds to the first update trial, the proper training set is updated to $\left(z_1, \ldots, z_{m_1}\right)$ and the sequence of nonconformity scores is reset. For each subsequent example $z_n : n = m_1 + 2, \ldots, m_2$, the fixed proper training set $\left(z_1, \ldots, z_{m_1}\right)$ and updated sequence of nonconformity score $\left(\alpha_{m_1+1}, \ldots, \alpha_{n-1}\right)$ are used. Generally, for each test example $z_{m_j+1} : j = 1, 2, \ldots$, the proper training set is updated to $\left(z_1, \ldots, z_{m_j}\right)$ and the sequence of precomputed nonconformity scores is reset.

A drawback of this online approach is that the initial sequence of p-values after each update trial is not very useful. The reason for this is that the size of the calibration set is yet too small in order to provide any significant p-values for new examples; note that even if $\alpha_n \gg \alpha_i : i = m_j + 1, \ldots, n - 1$, the p-value for z_n can never be less than $(n - m_j)^{-1}$, where m_j corresponds to the most recent update trial. If $\epsilon < (n - m_j)^{-1}$, which is typically the case after an update trial, sensitivity to abnormal examples will suffer severely since no conformal anomalies will be detected. Of course, this problem can be mitigated by temporarily increasing the value of ϵ, but this will disrupt the well-calibrated alarm rate and likely result in more false alarms.

A more practical online approach

In order to address the practical problem discussed earlier, Laxhammar and Falkman [198] proposed the following alternative update strategy for the online ICAD: For each test example $z_{m_j+1} : j = 1, 2, \ldots$, only the subsequence

$\left(z_{m_{j-1}+1}, \ldots, z_{m_j-\lceil \epsilon^{-1}\rceil}\right)$ of the calibration set is removed and added to the training set. For each $z_i : i = m_j - \lceil \epsilon^{-1}\rceil + 1, \ldots, m_j$ that remains in the calibration set, we recalculate α_i relative the updated proper training set $\left(z_1, \ldots, z_{m_j-\lceil \epsilon^{-1}\rceil}\right)$. The sequence of examples $z_n : n = m_j + 2, \ldots, m_{j+1}$ until the next update trial m_{j+1} are classified using the fixed proper training set $\left(z_1, \ldots, z_{m_j-\lceil \epsilon^{-1}\rceil}\right)$ and the updated sequence of nonconformity scores $\left(\alpha_{m_j-\lceil \epsilon^{-1}\rceil+1}, \ldots, \alpha_{n-1}\right)$. This strategy ensures that sensitivity to abnormal examples will not suffer from a too small calibration set; the number of calibration nonconformity scores is never less than $\lceil \epsilon^{-1}\rceil$. Nevertheless, the property of well-calibrated alarm rate across different update trials is now lost; the corresponding smoothed p-values (cf. the proof of Theorem 4.2) from different update trails are no longer independent, since some of the examples are used for calibration across two or more update trails. Hence, in contrast to the standard online inductive approach, the overall alarm rate is not guaranteed to be well-calibrated when considering a sequence of test examples over multiple update trails. In practice, however, this seems to have little impact on the empirical alarm rate, which was investigated by Laxhammar and Falkman [198].

Tuning of the update frequency

For simplicity, the sequence of update trails can be chosen so that $m_j = m_{j-1} + \eta$: $j = 1, 2, \ldots$ where the parameter $\eta \in \mathbb{N}^+$ regulates the frequency of the update trails. Setting $\eta = \infty$ is equivalent to the semi-offline ICAD and is obviously computational efficient since the training set is never updated. Nevertheless, this setting may result in reduced sensitivity to abnormal examples, especially if the initial training set is small. Conversely, setting $\eta = 1$ implies that every iteration is an update trail and that maximum sensitivity is achieved. The drawback of setting $\eta = 1$ is of course increased computational complexity and that the guarantee of well-calibrated alarm rate is completely lost.

4.6 Nonconformity Measures for Examples Represented as Sets of Points

Previously proposed NCMs [365] assume that examples are represented as fixed-dimensional feature vectors. This may be a limitation in applications where the examples (or objects in case of structured prediction) are naturally represented as sequences or sets of data points of varying length or size, respectively. In a video surveillance application, for example, we may need to compare two trajectories of different lengths. Moreover, in applications where data points or features of the new example z_{l+1} are sequentially observed, such as surveillance of moving objects, we need to sequentially update the *preliminary* nonconformity score $\hat{\alpha}_{l+1}$ until z_{l+1} is completely observed. In this setting, it is important that the *preliminary* p-value $\hat{p}_{l+1}$ for the new example monotonically decreases as more data points or features are observed; if this is not true, the property of well-calibrated alarm rate of CAD or ICAD will no longer be valid. In order to address these issues, Laxhammar and Falkman [197,199] proposed DH-kNN NCM, which is a novel NCM designed for examples that are represented as sets of points. This NCM is based on the *directed Hausdorff distance* (DHD) [5].

4.6.1 The Directed Hausdorff Distance

Generally speaking, the DHD is a dissimilarity measure for two sets of points in a metric space. It is a well-known distance measure in the field of computational geometry and image processing, where it has been applied for shape matching and shape recognition [5]. Given two sets of points $A, B \subseteq \mathbb{R}^d$, the DHD from A to B is defined as:

$$\vec{\delta}_H (A, B) = \max_{a \in A} \left\{ \min_{b \in B} \{ dist (a, b) \} \right\}, \tag{4.10}$$

where distance between points is measured by some metric $dist (a, b)$, typically Euclidean distance. That is, $\vec{\delta}_H (A, B)$ corresponds to the maximum distance from a point in A to the closest point in B. In applications where the point sets represent different shapes, the DHD captures the degree to which the shape A resembles some part of the shape B. The DHD between two polygonal curves are illustrated in Figure 4.2. Note that the DHD is not a metric since it is not symmetric; $\vec{\delta}_H (B, A)$ is in general different from $\vec{\delta}_H (A, B)$.

4.6.2 The Directed Hausdorff k-Nearest Neighbors Nonconformity Measure

Assume a bag of examples $\{z_1, \ldots, z_n\}$ where each example $z_i \subset \mathbb{R}^d : i = 1, \ldots, n$ is represented by a nonempty set of points in a d-dimensional space. DH-kNN NCM for z_i relative $\{z_1, \ldots, z_n\} \setminus z_i$ is defined as:

$$\alpha_i := \sum_{j=1}^{k} \vec{\delta}_H \left(z_i, NN \left(z_i, \{z_1, \ldots, z_n\} \setminus z_i, j \right) \right), \tag{4.11}$$

where $NN \left(z_i, \{z_1, \ldots, z_n\} \setminus z_i, j \right) \in \{z_1, \ldots, z_n\} \setminus z_i$ corresponds to the jth nearest neighbor to z_i according to (4.10).

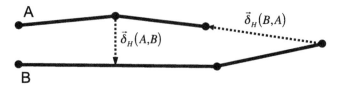

FIGURE 4.2

Illustration of the directed Hausdorff distance $\vec{\delta}_H$ between two polygonal curves A and B.

One of the key properties of (4.11) is that the preliminary p-value $\hat{p}_{l+1}$ for an incomplete example $z_{l+1}^* \subset z_{l+1}$ monotonically decreases as more points are included from z_{l+1}; this property is formalized by Theorem 4.3, which is proved based on Lemmas 4.1 and 4.2.

Lemma 4.1. *Assume that z_i^* and z_i^{**} are nonempty subsets of z_i such that $z_i^* \subset z_i^{**} \subset z_i$. Then the preliminary DH-kNN nonconformity scores $\hat{\alpha}_i$ and $\hat{\alpha}_i'$ for z_i^* and z_i^{**}, respectively, and the final DH-kNN nonconformity score α_i, calculated according to (4.11), must satisfy $\hat{\alpha}_i \leq \hat{\alpha}_i' \leq \alpha_i$. That is, the nonconformity score for a subset of z_i monotonically increases as more data points are included in the subset.*

Proof. From (4.10) it is clear that $\overrightarrow{\delta_H}\left(z_i^*, z\right) \leq \overrightarrow{\delta_H}\left(z_i^{**}, z\right) \leq \overrightarrow{\delta_H}\left(z_i, z\right)$ for any $z \in \{z_1, \ldots, z_n\}$; the maximum distance from any point $a \in A$ to the closest point in B monotonically increases as more points are added to A. Thus, the sum in (4.11) also monotonically increases as more points are considered from z_i; that is, $\hat{\alpha}_i \leq \hat{\alpha}_i' \leq \alpha_i$ when $z_i^* \subset z_i^{**} \subset z_i$. $\square$

Lemma 4.2. *Assume that z_i^* and z_i^{**} are nonempty subsets of z_i such that $z_i^* \subset z_i^{**} \subset z_i$. Then, the corresponding preliminary DH-kNN nonconformity scores $\hat{\alpha}_j$ and $\hat{\alpha}_j'$ and the final nonconformity score α_j for any other example $z_j \in \{z_1, \ldots, z_n\} \setminus z_i$, calculated according to (4.11) must satisfy $\hat{\alpha}_j \geq \hat{\alpha}_j' \geq \alpha_j$. That is, the nonconformity score for any other example z_j monotonically decreases as more data points are included in the subset of z_i.*

Proof. Considering (4.10), we see that the distance from each point a from a fixed set A to the closest point in B monotonically decreases as more points are added to B. Hence, it follows that $\overrightarrow{\delta_H}\left(z_j, z_i^*\right) \geq \overrightarrow{\delta_H}\left(z_j, z_i^{**}\right) \geq \overrightarrow{\delta_H}\left(z_j, z_i\right)$ for any $z_j \in \{z_1, \ldots, z_n\} \setminus z_i$. Consequently, the sum in (4.11) also monotonically decreases as more points are considered from z_i, which proves that $\hat{\alpha}_j \geq \hat{\alpha}_j' \geq \alpha_j$ when $z_i^* \subset z_i^{**} \subset z_i$. $\square$

Theorem 4.3. *Assume that z_i^* and z_i^{**} are nonempty subsets of z_i such that $z_i^* \subset z_i^{**} \subset z_i$. Then, the corresponding preliminary p-values $\hat{p}_i$ and $\hat{p}_i'$ and the final p-value p_i, estimated according to (4.11), must satisfy $\hat{p}_i \geq \hat{p}_i' \geq p_i$. That is, the p-value for a subset of z_i monotonically decreases as more points are included into the subset.*

Proof. From Lemmas 4.1 and 4.2, it follows that:

$$\left|\left\{j = 1, \ldots, n : \hat{\alpha}_j \geq \hat{\alpha}_i\right\}\right| \geq$$
$$\geq \left|\left\{j = 1, \ldots, n : \hat{\alpha}_j' \geq \hat{\alpha}_i'\right\}\right| \geq$$
$$\geq \left|\left\{j = 1, \ldots, n : \alpha_j \geq \alpha_i\right\}\right|.$$

Therefore, the corresponding p-values must also satisfy $\hat{p}_i \geq \hat{p}_i' \geq p_i$. $\square$

As a consequence of Theorem 4.3, a well-calibrated alarm rate is maintained for any conformal anomaly detector based on DH-kNN NCM when the new example is sequentially updated with new points. Note that this would not be the case if we used another NCM based on, for example, on the *average* (instead of maximum) distance to the closest point of the other set.

4.7   Sequential Anomaly Detection in Trajectories

One important application domain for anomaly detection is public surveillance [195]. Indeed, there is a clear trend toward more and more advanced sensor systems, producing huge amounts of trajectory data from moving objects such as people, vehicles, vessels, and aircraft. In the maritime domain, anomalous trajectories may indicate threats and dangers related to smuggling, sea drunkenness, collisions, grounding, terrorism, hijacking, piracy, and so on. In video surveillance of ground activities, anomalous trajectories may be indicative of illegal and adverse activity related to personal assault, robbery, burglary, infrastructural sabotage, and such. Timely detection of these relatively infrequent events, which is critical for enabling proactive measures, requires careful analysis of all moving objects at all times. But this is typically a great challenge to human analysts due to information overload, fatigue, and inattention. Thus, various anomaly detection algorithms based on learning normal trajectory patterns from historical data have been proposed for assisting analysts in identifying the important objects [195].

Technically speaking, a trajectory Tr is modeled by a finite sequence of data points:

$$Tr = (\chi_1, t_1), \ldots, (\chi_L, t_L) : t_1 = 0, t_i < t_{i+1}, i = 1, \ldots, L - 1, \qquad (4.12)$$

where each $\chi_i \in \mathbb{R}^d$ is a multidimensional feature vector at time point t_i and where the total length in time of the trajectory is t_L [239]. In the simple case, $\chi_i \in \mathbb{R}^2$ represents an object's (estimated) location in the two-dimensional plane at time point t_i. Depending on the application, the feature space may be extended, for example, by a third spatial dimension or a velocity vector. In the remainder of this chapter, we assume that all trajectories have been uniformly sampled in time; that is, $t_{i+1} - t_i = t_i - t_{i-1} : i = 2, \ldots, L - 1$. This allows us to drop t_i from each data point without loss of information.

In general, anomaly algorithms assume that the whole sequence $\chi_1, \ldots, \chi_L$ has been observed before the corresponding trajectory is classified as normal or abnormal. In contrast, algorithms for *sequential* anomaly detection [197] incrementally updates the classification of the *incomplete* trajectory $\chi_1, \ldots, \chi_{L^*} : 1 \leq L^* < L$.

4.7.1   The Sequential Hausdorff Nearest Neighbors Conformal Anomaly Detector

SHNN-CAD (Algorithm 6) was proposed by Laxhammar and Falkman [199] for sequential anomaly detection in trajectories. It is essentially a sequential version of CAD where the nonconformity scores are calculated using (4.11). Given:

- The anomaly threshold ϵ
- The number of nearest neighbors k

Algorithm 6 The sequential Hausdorff nearest neighbors conformal anomaly detector (SHNN-CAD)

Input: Anomaly threshold ϵ, number of nearest neighbors k, training set $(z_1, \ldots, z_l)$, distance matrix H, empty priority queue Q, sequence of updates $x_1, \ldots, x_L$ of test example z_{l+1}

Output: Sequence of indicator variables $\text{Anom}_{l+1,1}^\epsilon, \ldots, \text{Anom}_{l+1,L}^\epsilon$, distance vectors $(h_1, \ldots, h_l)$ and $(h'_1, \ldots, h'_l)$.

1: **for** $i \leftarrow 1$ to l **do**
2: $\quad v_i \leftarrow \text{sum}\{H_{i,1}, \ldots, H_{i,k-1}\}$
3: $\quad h_i \leftarrow 0$
4: **end for**
5: **for** $j \leftarrow 1$ to L **do**
6: $\quad$ **for** $i \leftarrow 1$ to l **do**
7: $\quad\quad h_i \leftarrow \max\left\{\overrightarrow{\delta_H}\left(x_j, z_i\right), h_i\right\}$
8: $\quad\quad$ **if** $i \leq k$ **then**
9: $\quad\quad\quad Q.\text{insertElement}(h_i)$
10: $\quad\quad$ **else**
11: $\quad\quad\quad$ **if** $Q.\text{maxElement}() > h_i$ **then**
12: $\quad\quad\quad\quad Q.\text{removeMaxElement}()$
13: $\quad\quad\quad\quad Q.\text{insertElement}(h_i)$
14: $\quad\quad\quad$ **end if**
15: $\quad\quad$ **end if**
16: $\quad\quad h'_i \leftarrow \overrightarrow{\delta_H}\left(z_i, \{x_1 \cup \cdots \cup x_j\}\right)$
17: $\quad\quad$ **if** $h'_i < H_{i,k}$ **then**
18: $\quad\quad\quad \hat{\alpha}_i \leftarrow v_i + h'_i$
19: $\quad\quad$ **else**
20: $\quad\quad\quad \hat{\alpha}_i \leftarrow v_i + H_{i,k}$
21: $\quad\quad$ **end if**
22: $\quad$ **end for**
23: $\quad (h_1^*, \ldots, h_k^*) \leftarrow Q.\text{removeAllElements}()$
24: $\quad \hat{\alpha}_{l+1} \leftarrow \text{sum}\{h_1^*, \ldots, h_k^*\}$
25: $\quad \hat{p}_{l+1} \leftarrow \frac{|\{i=1,\ldots,l+1 : \hat{\alpha}_i \geq \hat{\alpha}_{l+1}\}|}{l+1}$
26: $\quad$ **if** $\hat{p}_{l+1} < \epsilon$ **then**
27: $\quad\quad \text{Anom}_{l+1,j}^\epsilon \leftarrow 1$
28: $\quad$ **else**
29: $\quad\quad \text{Anom}_{l+1,j}^\epsilon \leftarrow 0$
30: $\quad$ **end if**
31: **end for**

- The training set $(z_1, \ldots, z_l)$
- The distance matrix H, where each element $H_{i,j} : i = 1, \ldots, l, j = 1, \ldots, k$ corresponds to the DHD from z_i to its jth-nearest neighbor among $(z_1, \ldots, z_{i-1}, z_{i+1}, \ldots, z_l)$
- The empty priority queue Q [124]
- The test example $z_{l+1} = \{x_1 \cup x_2 \cup \cdots \cup x_L\}$ observed as a sequence of disjunct subsets $x_1, \ldots, x_L$ such that $x_i \cap x_j = \emptyset : i, j = 1, \ldots, L \ \& \ j \neq i$

SHNN-CAD sequentially updates the classification of z_{l+1} and outputs:

- The sequence of indicator variables $\text{Anom}_{l+1,1}^{\epsilon}, \ldots, \text{Anom}_{l+1,L}^{\epsilon}$, where each $\text{Anom}_{l+1,i}^{\epsilon} : i = 1, \ldots, L - 1$ corresponds the preliminary classification of z_{l+1} (anomalous or not) based on the subset $\{x_1 \cup \cdots \cup x_i\} \subset z_{l+1}$, and $\text{Anom}_{l+1,L}^{\epsilon}$ corresponds to the final classification of z_{l+1}
- The vector $(h_1, \ldots, h_l)$ where $h_i : i = 1, \ldots, l$ corresponds to the DHD from z_{l+1} to z_i
- The vector $(h'_1, \ldots, h'_l)$ where $h'_i : i = 1, \ldots, l$ corresponds to the DHD from z_i to z_{l+1}

The algorithm works as follows: For each $z_i : i = 1, \ldots, l$, the DHD from z_{l+1} to z_i, h_i, is initialized to zero and the sum of the distances to the $(k - 1)$-nearest neighbors of z_i is precomputed (lines 1–4 of Algorithm 6). The following nested loops (lines 5–31) are then repeated for each $x_j : j = 1, \ldots, L$ and $z_i : i = 1, \ldots, l$: First, h_i is updated as the DHD from $\{x_1 \cup \cdots \cup x_j\}$ to z_i, which is calculated in an incremental manner based on the distance from $\{x_1 \cup \cdots \cup x_{j-1}\}$ to z_i calculated in the previous iteration (line 7). If Q, which stores the current k-nearest neighbor distances to $\{x_1 \cup \cdots \cup x_j\}$, contains less than k distance values, h_i is simply inserted into Q (line 9). If Q contains k distance values and h_i is less than the current k-nearest neighbor distance, the maximum distance value in Q is removed and h_i is inserted into Q (lines 12–13). The DHD from z_i to z_{l+1}, h'_i, is updated as the distance from z_i to $\{x_1 \cup \cdots \cup x_j\}$. The preliminary nonconformity score $\hat{\alpha}_i$ for z_i is then updated depending on whether h'_i is smaller than the DHD from z_i to its kth-nearest neighbor in the training set (lines 16–21). Next, the k distance values are extracted from Q and $\hat{\alpha}_{l+1}$ is updated as the sum of these distances (lines 23–24). Finally, the preliminary p-value and the classification of the test example are updated (lines 25–30).

In the case of the unsupervised online SHNN-CAD, the test example z_{l+1} is added to the training set when all $x_1, \ldots, x_L$ have been observed. This is also true for the semi-supervised online SHNN-CAD if z_{l+1} is assumed to belong to the normal class. If z_{l+1} is added to the training set, then:

1. The sorted distances to the k-nearest neighbors of each $z_i : i = 1, \ldots, l$—that is, rows 1–l of H—are updated based on h'.
2. The sorted distances to the k-nearest neighbors of z_{l+1} are determined based on h and appended as the last row of H.

The updated training set $(z_1, \ldots, z_{l+1})$ and the updated distance matrix H are then provided as input to SHNN-CAD when classifying the next test example z_{l+2}. More details, including a complexity analysis, of Algorithm 6 can be found in [199].

Discussion

A natural approach to applying SHNN-CAD for sequential anomaly detection in trajectories is to adopt a polyline representation; each trajectory (4.12) is represented by an example $z = \{x_1 \cup x_2 \cup \cdots \cup x_L\}$ where $x_1 = \chi_1$ and $x_j = \left\{\chi_{j-1} + s \cdot (\chi_j - \chi_{j-1}) : s \in (0, 1]\right\}$ for $j = 2, \ldots, L$. That is, the first subset x_1 represents the first trajectory point and each remaining subset x_j represent the set of all points along the line segment that connects χ_{j-1} and χ_j. The exact DHD between two trajectories can then be calculated using algorithms from computational geometry [5]. An alternative approach is to consider only the endpoints of the line segments (i.e., assume that $x_j = \left\{\chi_j\right\} : j = 1, \ldots, L$). This representation corresponds to a less detailed model of the actual trajectory but allows for a more simple implementation of the DHD [197].

As discussed by Laxhammar and Falkman [197], SHNN-CAD has some principal advantages compared to other algorithms for anomalous trajectory detection. One of the main advantages is that it is parameter-light and has well-calibrated alarm rate during sequential anomaly detection under relatively weak statistical assumptions.

The DHD is by definition insensitive to the ordering of the data points. Thus, if only position is included in the point feature model, this may result in contra-intuitive matching. An example is two objects that follow the same path but travel in opposite directions. This could be addressed by simply extending the point feature model to also include the current course or velocity vector. Another approach would be to include relative time as an explicit feature.

4.7.2 **Empirical Investigations**

The classification performance of SHNN-CAD has been investigated on public datasets with synthetic and recorded video trajectories [197,199]. In this section, we present the results from two experiments on two different public datasets of synthetic trajectories. In the first experiment, which was first published by Piciarelli et al. [276] and later reproduced by Laxhammar and Falkman [197], the accuracy of DH-kNN NCM is compared to the accuracy of two other trajectory outlier measures. The second experiment, which was published by Laxhammar and Falkman [199], is concerned with investigating the classification performance of the unsupervised online SHNN-CAD.

Datasets

The first dataset of synthetic trajectories[1] was created by Piciarelli et al. [276] and consists of 1000 randomly generated trajectory subsets. Each subset contains 260

---

[1] http://avires.dimi.uniud.it/papers/trclust/dataset2.zip.

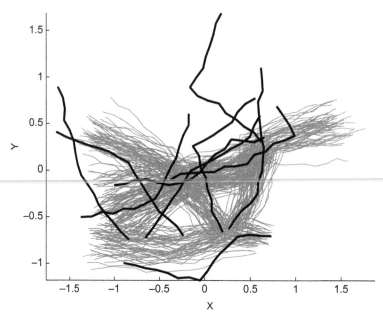

FIGURE 4.3

Plot of 260 trajectories from one of the 1000 trajectory subsets of the first experimental dataset (Section 4.7.2). Gray trajectories are labeled normal and black trajectories are labeled abnormal. All abnormal trajectories in this particular dataset are discriminated by DH-kNN NCM with perfect accuracy.

two-dimensional trajectories of length 16 without any time information; that is, $T_i = (\chi_1^i, \ldots, \chi_{16}^i)$, $\chi_j^i \in \mathbb{R}^2$ for $i = 1, \ldots, 260$ and $j = 1, \ldots, 16$. Of the 260 trajectories, 250 belong to five different clusters and are labeled as normal. The remaining 10 are stray trajectories that do not belong to any cluster and are labeled as abnormal (see Figure 4.3 for a plot of one of the subsets).

The second dataset of synthetic trajectories[2] was generated by Laxhammar using the publicly available trajectory generator software[3] written by Piciarelli. The dataset contains 100 random trajectory sequences, each sequence consisting of 2000 two-dimensional trajectories of length 16 that are labeled normal or abnormal. Each sequence, which is independent of the other 99 sequences, was created as follows: First, a set of 2000 normal trajectories from 10 different trajectory clusters and another set of 1000 abnormal trajectories from 1000 different clusters were created using the trajectory generator with the randomness parameter set to the default value (0.7). Next, a sequence of 2000 trajectories was created by random sampling without replacement from the set of normal trajectories. Finally, each normal trajectory in the sequence was

[2] http://www.researchgate.net/profile/Rikard_Laxhammar/.
[3] http://avires.dimi.uniud.it/papers/trclust/create_ts2.m.

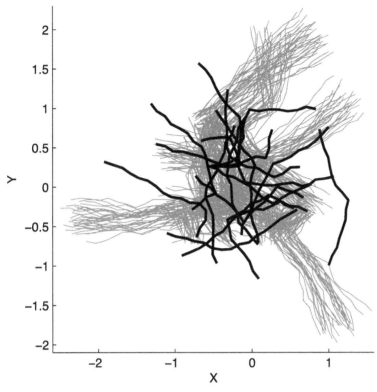

FIGURE 4.4

Plot of trajectories from the first random sequence of 2000 synthetic trajectories of the second experimental dataset (Section 4.7.2). Gray trajectories are labeled normal and black trajectories (17) are labeled abnormal. Note that for clarity, only 300 of the 1983 normal trajectories are plotted.

independently and with probability 1% replaced by an abnormal trajectory, which was randomly sampled without replacement from the set of abnormal trajectories. Hence, the trajectory generation process is consistent with (4.7) where $\lambda = 0.01$. A subset of the normal trajectories and all abnormal trajectories from the first sequence are shown in Figure 4.4.

Accuracy of trajectory outlier measures

The first experiment was originally published by Piciarelli et al. [276], who evaluated two outlier measures for complete trajectories based on a one-class SVM [276] and time-series *discords* [173], respectively. Given a set of complete trajectories, each outlier measure produces an outlier score for each trajectory relative to the rest (i.e., equivalent to a NCM). For each of the 1000 synthetic datasets (Section 4.7.2), the author calculated outlier scores for each of the 260 trajectories and checked if the

Table 4.1   Average accuracy for different outlier measures on the first public set of synthetic trajectories (Section 4.7.2). Note that accuracy results for one-class SVM and discords are 1 minus the corresponding error rate reported by Piciarelli et al. [276].

Outlier measure	# of most similar neighbors considered				
	$k = 1$	$k = 2$	$k = 3$	$k = 4$	$k = 5$
DH-kNN	96.51%	97.09%	97.05%	96.95%	96.77%
NCM [197]	[197]	[197]	[197]	[197]	[197]
One-class SVM [276]			96.30% [276]		
Discords [173]			97.04% [276]		

10 trajectories with highest outlier scores correspond to the 10 trajectories labeled abnormal. The *error rate*, which is equivalent to 1 minus accuracy, was calculated for each measure by averaging the number of normal trajectories among the 10 trajectories with highest outlier scores. Since DH-kNN nonconformity scores correspond to the outlier scores of the two other outlier measures, comparison is straightforward. Laxhammar and Falkman reproduced this experiment for DH-kNN NCM based on a simple implementation of the DHD that considers only the set of 16 points of a trajectory (cf. Section 4.7.1). Accuracy results for DH-kNN NCM, reported by Laxhammar and Falkman [197], and the corresponding accuracy results for the one-class SVM and discords, reported by Piciarelli et al. [276], are summarized in Table 4.1.

It is clear from Table 4.1 that DH-kNN NCM is an accurate outlier measure, regardless of the parameter value k. It should be stressed that competitive accuracy was achieved without any parameter tuning. Nevertheless, it may be argued that the generally high accuracy indicates that the dataset is too simplistic. Hence, future work should investigate accuracy on more challenging datasets in order to gain deeper insights into the strengths and weaknesses of DH-kNN NCM.

Unsupervised online learning and sequential anomaly detection

In this experiment, which is similar to the experiment presented in [199], the sequential anomaly detection performance of the unsupervised online SHNN-CAD is investigated on the second dataset of synthetic trajectories. The main objectives of this experiment are to:

1. Investigate how different values of k affect the overall classification performance and the average *detection delay* (i.e., the average number of observed trajectory points prior to the detection of an abnormal trajectory). As pointed out by Laxhammar and Falkman [197], a low detection delay is advantageous since it enables earlier response in a real-time surveillance application.
2. Investigate how the sensitivity, precision, and detection delay depend on the size of the training set and the value of ϵ.

3. Validate that the rate of detected anomalies (both normal and abnormal trajectories) is indeed well calibrated.

The design of the experiment is as follows: For each of the 100 sequences, we allocate the first six trajectories as initial training set and calculate the corresponding distance matrix M of size 6×6 (Section 4.7.1); note that six is the minimum size of the training set for which (4.11) is defined when $k = 5$. The remaining 1994 trajectories are sequentially classified by the unsupervised online SHNN-CAD (Algorithm 6). The whole process is repeated for each pairwise combination of $k = 1, \ldots, 5$ and $\epsilon = 0.005, 0.01, 0.02$. The choice of $\epsilon = 0.01$ is motivated by the discussion in Section 4.4.4, that the anomaly threshold should be set close to λ. Nevertheless, the exact value of λ may be unknown and, hence, we also investigate the performance for $\epsilon = 0.005$ and $\epsilon = 0.02$. Moreover, in order to avoid the problem of zero sensitivity when the size of training set is relatively small (Section 4.4.4), the anomaly threshold is dynamically re-tuned to $(l + 1)^{-1}$ as long as $l < \epsilon^{-1}$.

In order to address objective 1, we calculate the average F_1-score and the average detection delay for each combination of the previous parameters (see Table 4.2). The F_1-score corresponds to an evenly weighted combination of precision and recall:

$$F_1 = \frac{2 \cdot precision \cdot recall}{precision + recall}, \tag{4.13}$$

and it is therefore useful for comparing the overall classification performance for different parameter values. In order to address objective 2, we estimate logistic

Table 4.2 Average F_1-score and mean detection delay for the unsupervised online learning and sequential anomaly detection experiments (Section 4.7.2). Note that the maximum possible detection delay is 16, since this is the length of each trajectory.

ϵ	k	F_1	Detection delay
0.005	1	0.54	12.7
	2	0.54	12.7
	3	0.54	12.8
	4	0.54	12.8
	5	0.54	12.8
0.01	1	0.76	10.2
	2	0.76	10.3
	3	0.76	10.3
	4	0.77	10.4
	5	0.76	10.4
0.02	1	0.63	8.1
	2	0.63	8.0
	3	0.63	8.0
	4	0.63	8.1
	5	0.63	8.1

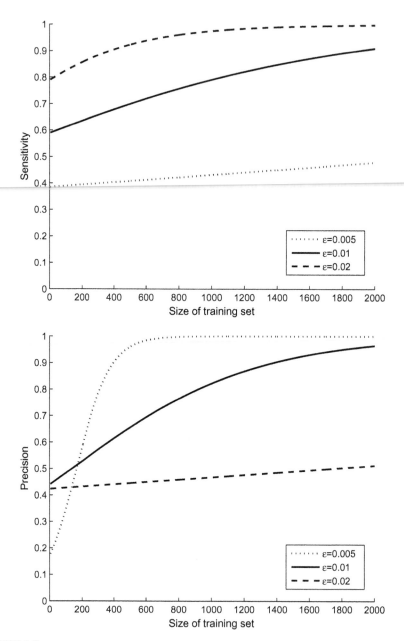

FIGURE 4.5

Plots of the sensitivity (upper plot) and the precision (lower plot) dependent on the size of the training set, according to the estimated logistic regression models (Section 4.7.2).

regression models for the sensitivity and precision, respectively, dependent on the size of the training set for the different values of the anomaly threshold. The coefficients of the logistic regression models for the sensitivity are estimated based on the final classification results for the subset of trajectories that are labeled abnormal. In case of the precision, the coefficients are estimated based on the true label for those trajectories that are detected as anomalous. Plots of the sensitivity and precision dependent on the size of the training set are illustrated in Figure 4.5 for the different anomaly thresholds. Further, we estimate linear regression models for the detection delay dependent on the current size of the training set (see Figure 4.6). Finally, a histogram of the overall alarm rate for $\epsilon = 0.01$ is shown in Figure 4.7 (objective 4).

Discussion

It is clear from Table 4.2 that the best overall classification performance is achieved for $\epsilon = 0.01$, regardless of the value of k. This confirms the hypothesis that ϵ should be close to λ (Section 4.4.4). Nevertheless, the detection delay is less for $\epsilon = 0.02$, which suggests that setting the anomaly threshold slightly higher than λ might be appropriate if low detection delay is critical. The value of k, however, does not seem

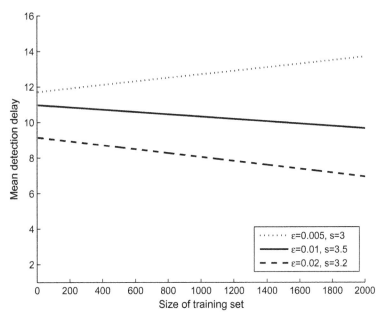

FIGURE 4.6

Plot of the mean detection delay dependent on the size of the training set according to the linear regression models, which are estimated based on the online learning sequential anomaly detection results (Section 2). The variable s in the legend is an unbiased estimate of the standard deviation of the error term of the linear regression model.

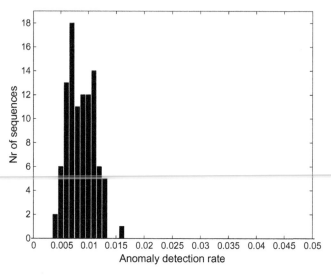

FIGURE 4.7

Histogram of the overall alarm rate (normal and abnormal trajectories detected as anomalous) for $\epsilon = 0.01$. Each data point of the histograms corresponds to the average anomaly detection rate on one of the 100 random sequences of trajectories (Section 2).

to have any significant impact on either the classification performance or the detection delay. For clarity and brevity, we therefore have included the results only for $k = 2$ in Figures 4.5 and 4.6.

Examining Figure 4.5, it is clear that the sensitivity and precision generally improve as more unlabeled training data is accumulated. In particular, there is a large increase in precision when $\epsilon = 0.005$ and $\epsilon = 0.01$. Furthermore, for $\epsilon = 0.01$ and $\epsilon = 0.02$, the expected detection delay decreases as the size of the training increases (Figure 4.6). However, for $\epsilon = 0.005$, the detection delay actually *increases* with the size of the training set. The explanation for this result does not seem obvious, but the same pattern was observed for the other values of k, which suggests that for low anomaly thresholds, the detection delay generally increases as the training set grows. Considering the end of the curves, at the point where the size of the training set approaches 2000, we see that either sensitivity or precision, or both of them, are still increasing, albeit at a slower rate. This indicates that the anomaly detectors may still benefit from more training data but are approaching the point where they may be considered fully "trained."

It is obvious that the choice of ϵ, in contrast to k, has a significant impact on the balance between the sensitivity, precision, and detection delay. Generally, the best balance between the three is achieved for $\epsilon = 0.01$. However, if high sensitivity and low detection delay is critical, it may be more appropriate to set $\epsilon > \lambda$ at the expense of reduced precision. Conversely, if high precision is critical, even when the training set is relatively small (less than 400 in Figure 4.5), it may be appropriate to set $\epsilon < \lambda$ at the cost of reduced sensitivity and increases detection delay.

Finally, considering the histogram of the anomaly detection rate for $\epsilon = 0.01$ (Figure 4.7), we see that there is a clear peak around 0.01. Hence, alarm rate of the online unsupervised SHNN-CAD is indeed well calibrated in practice.

4.8 Conclusions

In this chapter, we have presented the conformal anomaly detection framework, which is based on results from conformal prediction. Assuming that an appropriate NCM is defined, CAD and ICAD are applicable in virtually any unsupervised or semi-supervised, online or offline, anomaly detection problem. In fact, any existing anomaly or outlier detection algorithm, which has shown to have good accuracy in the current application domain, may potentially be adopted as a NCM and used by CAD or ICAD. One of the main benefits of such "wrapper" strategy is the additional property of well-calibrated alarm rate. We have also presented DH-kNN NCM, which is a novel NCM designed for examples represented as sets of points. A key property of DH-kNN NCM is that the p-value for an incomplete test example monotonically decreases as more points are observed. An instance of CAD based on DH-kNN NCM, known as SHNN-CAD, has been presented and discussed for sequential anomaly detection applications. Empirical results on public trajectory datasets show that DH-kNN NCM accurately discriminates normal and abnormal trajectories without any parameter tuning. Moreover, empirical results for the unsupervised online SHNN-CAD demonstrates that classification performance increases as more unlabeled training data accumulated and that the best classification performance is achieved when the anomaly threshold ϵ is close to the rate of abnormal trajectories.

From the perspective of supervised conformal prediction, DH-kNN NCM may also be useful for classification applications. For example, DH-kNN NCM may potentially be used for predicting the vessel class (cargo vessel, passenger ship, fishing boat, etc.) based on the observed trajectory.

One of the main challenges when adopting CAD or ICAD for an anomaly detection application is how to design an appropriate NCM. Hence, future research should investigate appropriate NCMs for different anomaly detection applications.

Online Change Detection

5

Shen-Shyang Ho[*] and Harry Wechsler[†]

[*]*School of Computer Engineering, Nanyang Technological University, Singapore*
[†]*Department of Computer Science, George Mason University, VA, USA*

CHAPTER OUTLINE HEAD

In this chapter, we provide an overview of the recent development of online change detection approach for multidimensional data sequences based on testing exchangeability using martingale. We first review previous work on change detection in both machine learning/data mining and statistical field. Then, we provide some background knowledge not covered in other chapters in the book. We point the reader to relevant background information if it is available in earlier chapters. Next, we provide an overview of the martingale-based change detection approach. After that, we summarize and discuss (1) the effectiveness of the change detection method on different scenarios and (2) implementation issues related to the martingale-based change detection method. Finally, we conclude with a discussion on possible future work.

5.1 Introduction

Change is the process of transition (moving) from one state (or form) to another [151]. Many decision-making tasks rely on the timely and accurate pattern extraction and prediction from observed data; the changing nature of the data model creates tremendous challenges for many learning algorithms and data mining techniques. On the other hand, changes in the models may convey interesting time-dependent information and knowledge. Hence, detecting changes in the data generating process is a very important problem.

Intuitively, we assume that a sequence of data points with a change consists of two concatenated data segments, S_1 and S_2, such that S_1 is generated from one source and S_2 is generated from another source. Switching some data points from S_2 to positions in S_1 will make the data points stand out in S_1, and vice versa. The exchangeability assumption (5.4) is thus violated. Exchangeability is a necessary condition for a data stream generated from a fixed source (i.e., data points are identically distributed). The absence of exchangeability suggests a change in the data-generating process.

A logical and natural change detection approach is to test the existence or absence of exchangeability condition for the data sequence as data points are observed one by one. Vovk et al. [366] first proposed a martingale approach to test the exchangeability assumption for data sequences based on p-values (1.5) derived from the nonconformity scores (1.6). Our change detection approach is motivated by this martingale approach for testing exchangeability.

5.2 **Related Work**

The problem of detecting changes in the characteristics of sequential data was extensively studied by statisticians and mathematicians. In the online data streaming setting, data are observed sequentially from a source. The disruption of "stochastic homogeneity" of the data might signal a change in the data-generating process such that timely identification of this change is required. This problem is generally known as "change-point detection" [17]. The change-detection problem in the 1920s was mostly concerned with quality control of continuous manufacturing process. Shewhart [320,321] introduced the Shewhart control charts to monitor the production process and to detect any significant deviation from a chosen quality characteristic of the products. At each regular time interval a sample of some fixed size is used to compute a statistic. The sequence of statistics are presented graphically in the form of a control chart. When a statistic falls outside the control limit(s) drawn on the chart, a warning is signaled that a production process has deviated from the desirable state.

In the 1940s, Wald [369] proposed the sequential probability ratio test (SPRT) used during the manufacturing process of military and naval equipment during World War II. Later, Page [259] introduced the cumulative sum method (CUSUM). Girshik and Rubin [119], and Shiryaev [324] independently proposed an optimal sequential change-point detection procedure (GRSh) using the Bayesian framework. A summary of these three procedures are as follows:

1. Sequential Probability Ratio Test (SPRT): Let $H_0 : \theta = \theta_0$ and $H_1 : \theta = \theta_1$ be two simple hypotheses on the parameter θ of some distribution f, and t_a and $t_b \in \mathbb{R}, t_a < t_b$. When we observe the sequence $(x_1, x_2, \ldots)$, the SPRT is

as follows:

$$\phi_1(x_i) = \begin{cases} \text{accept } H_0, & S_n \leq t_a; \\ \text{accept } H_1, & S_n \geq t_b; \\ \text{continue test}, & t_a < S_n < t_b, \end{cases} \tag{5.1}$$

where $S_n = \log \frac{f_1(x_n)}{f_0(x_n)}$ and f_i is the density function with θ_i, $i = 0, 1$.

2. Cumulative sum (CUSUM) procedure: Let $H_0 : \theta = \theta_0$ and $H_1 : \theta = \theta_1$ be two simple hypotheses on the parameter θ of some distribution f and $t_c \in \mathbb{R}$. Assume that the initial parameter is $\theta = \theta_0$ and we observe the sequence $\{x_1, x_2, \ldots\}$. The CUSUM procedure is as follows:

$$\phi_2(x_i) = \begin{cases} \text{reject } H_0 \text{ and accept } H_1, & S_n \geq t_c; \\ \text{continue procedure}, & S_n < t_c, \end{cases} \tag{5.2}$$

where $S_n = \sum_{i=k}^{n} \log \frac{f_1(x_i)}{f_0(x_i)}$, $S_0 = 0$. CUSUM procedure is a repeated SPRT.

3. Girshick-Rubin-Shirayev (GRSh) Procedure: Similar to CUSUM procedure with $t_d \in \mathbb{R}$, GRSh procedure is as follows:

$$\phi_3(x_i) = \begin{cases} \text{reject } H_0 \text{ and accept } H_1, & S_n \geq t_d; \\ \text{continue procedure}, & S_n < t_d, \end{cases} \tag{5.3}$$

where $S_n = \frac{f_1(x_n)}{f_0(x_n)} \left(1 + W_{n-1}\right) = \sum_{i=1}^{n} \prod_{j=1}^{n} \frac{f_1(x_j)}{f_0(x_j)}$, $W_0 = 0$.

While the Shewhart control chart is a heuristic method that requires the sample (or window) size to be chosen, the other three methods are likelihood techniques that attempt to detect changes in the parameter value, such as the Gaussian mean.

The concept drift problem studied by (data mining or machine learning) computer scientists is also about the changes in data distribution. Instead of detecting the changes, we are interested in handling the changes (or concept drift). The concept drift problem is about maintaining the performance of learner or predictor as data distribution evolves in an online setting. Hence, it is of no surprise that change detection techniques have been utilized to handle the concept drift problem [56]. Other popular methods for the concept drift problem include using (1) a sliding window (instance selection) [178,378], (2) instance weighting [177], and (3) ensemble learning [55,179,373]. For the instance selection method, a sliding window is used to select the data points used to build a classifier. The instance weighting method assumes that more recent data points in a sliding window are more important than those further back in time. These two methods ensure that the predictor evolves based on data models built using recent data that are considered more relevant. However, the two methods require proper window size selection and instance weighting. For the ensemble method, multiple predictors with different window sizes or weighting models are constructed. Prediction is based on a vote by the predictors. New problems on the optimal number of predictors needed in the ensemble and their parameter settings arise.

Change detection techniques have also been proposed for data stream change profiling and visualization such as velocity density estimation [4], nonparametric

Kolmogorov-Smirnov (KS) type of change detection procedure with statistical guarantees of the reliability of detected changes [174], and the use of sketch, a probabilistic summary technique for analyzing large streaming datasets, to detect changes [183]. The first procedure visualizes the flow in data stream and the user decides on whether change occurs based on the visualization. The change detection method related to KS test determines whether the two probability distributions of the data points in two different windows differs. This change detection method is impractical for high dimensional data streams. The last procedure is evaluated in an offline setting and does not have any statistical guarantees on the false detection rate. The latter two techniques require proper window size selection.

5.3 Background

Let $\{Z_i : 1 \leq i < \infty\}$ be a sequence of random variables. A finite sequence of random variables $Z_1, \ldots, Z_n$ is *exchangeable* if the joint distribution $p(Z_1, \ldots, Z_n)$ is invariant under any permutation of the indices of the random variables; that is,

$$p(Z_1, Z_2, \ldots, Z_n) = p(Z_{\pi(1)}, Z_{\pi(2)}, \ldots, Z_{\pi(n)}) \tag{5.4}$$

for all permutations π defined on the set $\{1, \ldots, n\}$. Notes that this property (5.4) holds for every finite subset of the sequence of random variables.

Exchangeable random variables are identically distributed, and i.i.d. random variables are exchangeable. Exchangeability allows random variables to be dependent. Hence, the exchangeable assumption is weaker (i.e., more general) than i.i.d. assumption on random variables.

A sequence of random variables $\{M_i : 0 \leq i < \infty\}$ is a *martingale* with respect to the sequence of random variables $\{Z_1 : 0 \leq i < \infty\}$ (in particular M_0 is a constant value) if, for all $i \geq 0$, the following conditions hold:

1. M_i is a measurable function of $Z_0, Z_1, \ldots, Z_i$.
2. $E(|M_i|) < \infty$.
3. $E(M_{n+1}|Z_0, \ldots, Z_n) = M_n$.

Vovk et al. [366] introduced the idea of testing exchangeability online using the martingale. A family of martingales, indexed by $\epsilon \in [0, 1]$ and referred to as the *power martingale*, is defined as

$$M_n^{(\epsilon)} = \prod_{i=1}^{n} \left(\epsilon p_i^{\epsilon-1} \right) \tag{5.5}$$

where the p_is are defined by (1.5) derived from a particular conformal predictor, with the initial martingale $M_0^{(\epsilon)} = 1$. We note that $M_n^{(\epsilon)} = \epsilon p_n^{\epsilon-1} M_{n-1}^{(\epsilon)}$. Hence, it is not necessary to store the previous p-values. After each new data point is received, an observer outputs a positive martingale value reflecting the strength of evidence found against the null hypothesis of data exchangeability.

5.4 A Martingale Approach for Change Detection

The martingale-based change detection method first introduced in [145,148] is summarized as the following theorem.

Theorem 5.1. *Let $\{M_i^{(\epsilon)} : 0 \le i < \infty\}$ be a martingale sequence of the form (5.5) constructed from p-values $\{p_i : 1 \le i < \infty\}$ computed using (1.5) and the nonconformity scores (1.6) for a given data sequence. If no change occurs in the given data sequence, then*

$$P\left(\max_k M_k^{(\epsilon)} \ge \lambda\right) \le \frac{1}{\lambda}, \tag{5.6}$$

where λ is a positive number.

Notes that the Doob's Maximal Inequality [333] is general enough for (5.6) to be true when k is any positive integer. This means that (5.6) is true as long as the data-generating model remains stable. Based on (5.6), we construct the change detection algorithm shown in Algorithm 7.

Let α be the size of the test deciding in favor of the alternative hypothesis "change occurs in the data sequence" when the null hypothesis "no change occurs in the data

---

Algorithm 7 : Martingale Test (MT)

Initialize: $M(0) = 1$; $i = 1$; $T = \{\}$.
Set: λ.

 1: **loop**
 2:    A new example $\mathbf{x}_i$ is observed.
 3:    **if** $T = \{\}$ **then**
 4:       Set nonconformity score of $\mathbf{x}_i := 0$
 5:    **else**
 6:       Compute the nonconformity scores of $\mathbf{x}_i$ and data points in T.
 7:    **end if**
 8:    Compute the p-value p_i using (1.5).
 9:    Compute $M(i)$ using (5.5).
10:    **if** $M(i) > \lambda$ **then**
11:       **CHANGE DETECTED**
12:       Set $M(i) = 1$;
13:       Re-initialize T to an empty set.
14:    **else**
15:       Add $\mathbf{x}_i$ into T.
16:    **end if**
17:    $i := i + 1$;
18: **end loop**

---

sequence" is true, and $1 - \beta$ be the power of the test deciding in favor of the alternative hypothesis when it is true. If the martingale test according to (5.6) is an approximation of the sequential probability ratio test (SPRT) with

$$\lambda \leq \frac{1 - \beta}{\alpha}, \tag{5.7}$$

then the mean delay time $E(m)$ (i.e., the expected number of data points, m) observed before a change is detected is approximated from the SPRT as follows:

$$E(m) \approx \frac{(1 - \beta) \log \lambda}{E(\mathcal{L})} \tag{5.8}$$

where $\mathcal{L} = \log \epsilon p_i^{\epsilon - 1}$.

Earlier work [148,145] focused on detecting changes in data sequence consisting of labeled data from a classification task perspective. Recently, the martingale-based change detection approach (MT) was shown to be feasible for data sequence consisting of unlabeled examples from a clustering task perspective and labeled examples from a regression task perspective [151]. Instead of using the nonconformity measure based on support vector machine or nearest neighbor rule [365], we use the nonconformity measure for an example $\mathbf{x}_i$ for

- **Cluster model**

$$s(T, \mathbf{x}_i) = ||\mathbf{x}_i - c|| \tag{5.9}$$

where c is the cluster center and $|| \cdot ||$ is a distance metric, given the unlabeled data sequence $T = \{\mathbf{x}_1, \mathbf{x}_2, \ldots, \mathbf{x}_n\}$; or
- **Regression model**

$$s(T, (\mathbf{x}_i, y_i)) = \frac{|y_i - f(\mathbf{x}_i)|}{\exp(g(\mathbf{x}_i))} \tag{5.10}$$

where $y_i \in \mathcal{R}$, f is the regression function, and g is the error estimation function for f at $\mathbf{x}_i$ [266]. In our case, the estimation function g is based on a regression model of the values $\ln(|y_i - f(\mathbf{x}_i)|)$ for $\mathbf{x}_i$ where $i = 1, \ldots, n$, given the data sequence $T = \{(\mathbf{x}_1, y_1), (\mathbf{x}_2, y_2), \ldots, (\mathbf{x}_n, y_n)\}$.

To improve the performance of the martingale change detection approach (MT), we consider the multiview setting such that an example $\mathbf{x}_i$ is represented by a number of feature subsets. Each feature subset describes a view of the examples in the data sequence. A multiple-martingale test is implemented such that each constructed martingale attempts to identify changes with respect to the particular feature subset. The feature representation used does not affect the probability bound (5.6). Moreover, we have

Corollary 5.1. *When the multiple martingale test with K views is used for change detection, the expected number of data points, m, observed before a change point is detected,*

$$E_M^*(m) \leq E(m). \tag{5.11}$$

For a change detection task on a particular domain, the number of miss detection using the multiple-martingale test is upper-bounded by the maximum number of miss detection using MT on all possible views considered. Moreover, the number of false alarm using the multiple martingale test is lower-bounded by the minimum number of false alarm using MT on all possible views considered. The multiple-martingale test is first introduced in [149].

To construct the multiple-martingale test with multiple views, we modify Algorithm 7 as follows. Assume that the K views are derived from the original data sequence. Line 6 is modified to compute K sets of nonconformity scores for the K views of $\mathbf{x}_i$ and data points in T. Lines 8 and 9 are modified to compute K p-values and K martingale values, $M_\kappa(i)$ for $\kappa = 1, \ldots, K$, respectively. Line 10 is modified such that the sentence

$$M_1(i) > \lambda \, \text{OR} \cdots \text{OR} M_\kappa(i) > \lambda \, \text{OR} \cdots \text{OR} M_K(i) > \lambda \qquad (5.12)$$

on the K martingale values is satisfiable; that is, it is true for at least one of the MT tests in (5.12).

Empirical results demonstrating the feasibility and performance for the martingale-based change detection are presented in [145,148,149,151] and are not repeated in this chapter. Readers can refer to these papers for detailed empirical results.

In the next two sections, the effectiveness of the martingale-based change detection approaches some implementation issues and are discussed from the classification task perspective using some empirical results from [148] and [151].

5.5 Experimental Results

Using some empirical results from [148], we examine the effectiveness of the martingale-based change detection method based on the retrieval performance indicators, recall and precision, and the delay time for change detections for various λ values on five different scenarios. The retrieval performance indicators, recall and precision, is defined in our context as:

$$\text{Precision} = \frac{\text{Number of Correct Detections}}{\text{Number of Detections}}$$

Probability that a detection is actually correct, detecting a true change.

$$\text{Recall} = \frac{\text{Number of Correct Detections}}{\text{Number of True Changes}}$$

Probability that the change detection system recognizes a true change.

The delay time for a detected change is the number of time units from the true change point to the detected change point, if any. One time unit is equivalent to one data point entering the change detection system.

Empirical results on data streams simulated using a two-dimensional rotating hyperplane [158] are used to show the effectiveness of the martingale method in scenarios where the data streams contain (A) gradual changes, (B) arbitrary changes (gradual and abrupt changes), (C) arbitrary changes in a noisy environment. We also show its feasibility for (D) high dimensional, noisy data stream with arbitrary changes. Data streams simulated using normally distributed clusters (NDC) data generator [240] are used to show the effectiveness of the martingale criteria on (E) high-dimensional, noisy, linearly nonseparable binary-class data stream with arbitrary changes. The SVM, needed to compute the p-values, uses $C = 10$ and the Gaussian kernel.

5.5.1 Simulated Data Stream Using Rotating Hyperplane

Using a rotating hyperplane, we generate a sequence of 100,000 data points consisting of changes occurring at points $(1,000 \times i) + 1$, for $i = 1, 2, \ldots, 99$. First we randomly generate 1,000 data points with each component value ranged in $[-1, 1]$. These data points are labeled positive and negative based on the following equation:

$$\sum_{i=1}^{m} w_i x_i = \begin{cases} < c & : \text{ negative} \\ \geq c & : \text{ positive} \end{cases} \tag{5.13}$$

where c is an arbitrary fixed constant, x_i is the component of a data point, x, and the fixed components, w_1 and w_2, of a weight vector are randomly generated between -1 and 1. Similarly, the next 1,000 random data points are labeled using Equation (5.13) with a new randomly generated fixed weight vector. This process continues until we get a data stream consisting of 100 segments of 1,000 data points each. For scenarios (A), (B) and (C), $m = 2$.

- **Scenario (A)—Gradual Changes:** We control the rotation of the hyperplane about the origin by using the weights $w = [cos(r)sin(r)]$ restricting $r \in [-\frac{\pi}{3}, \frac{\pi}{3}]$. Hence, the maximum angle difference between two consecutive hyperplanes is $\frac{2\pi}{3}$ rad.
- **Scenario (B)—Arbitrary Changes (Gradual and Abrupt Changes):** We allow the weight $w = [cos(r)sin(r)]$ to change using $r \in [-\pi, \pi]$. In this case, any rotating hyperplane about the origin is possible.
- **Scenario (C)—Arbitrary Changes with Noisy Data Stream:** Noise is added by randomly switching the class labels of $p\%$ of the data points. In our experiment, $p = 5$.
- **Scenario (D)—Arbitrary Changes in a High Dimensional, Noisy Data Stream:** Setting $m = 10$, we repeat Scenario (C).

5.5.2 Simulated Data Streams Using NDC

The NDC linearly nonseparable binary-class data stream is generated as clusters of normally distributed points in R^{10} with randomly generated means and variances. The values for each dimension are scaled to range in $[-1, 1]$. The generating process for the NDC data stream is similar to that used for the rotating hyperplane data stream described earlier.

- **Scenario (E) : Arbitrary Changes in a High-Dimensional, Noisy, Linearly Nonseparable Data Stream**

For the previous scenarios, we vary λ^{-1} from 0.01 to 0.25. The performance of Scenarios (A), (B), (C), (D), and (E) are shown in Figures 5.1–5.5, respectively (with λ^{-1} scaled by a factor of 100 for easier visualization). The mean delay time is shown as it is a measure of performance in the study of change detection [17]. However, the median delay time, which is also shown, is a more meaningful performance measure as the delay time distribution for our method, independent of the λ value, deviates from normality. The distribution skews toward large values; small values are pack tightly together and large values stretch out and cover a wider range.

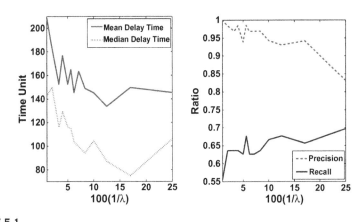

FIGURE 5.1

Scenario (A): Gradual changes.

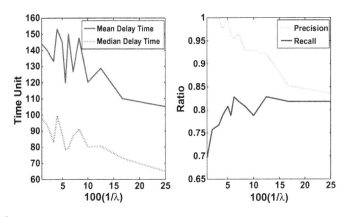

FIGURE 5.2

Scenario (B): Arbitrary changes (gradual and abrupt changes).

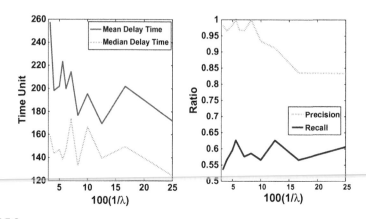

FIGURE 5.3

Scenario (C): Arbitrary changes with noise.

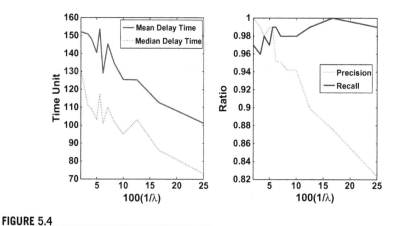

FIGURE 5.4

Scenario (D): Arbitrary changes on a high-dimensional noisy data stream.

The probability of the martingale value greater than some fixed λ value is inversely proportional to λ (i.e., λ^{-1}). As this probability decreases, we are rejecting the null hypothesis—"no change detected in the data stream"—with higher confidence. This comes at the expense of lower recall (see Figures 5.1–5.5). Surprisingly, the choice of λ does not significantly affect the delay time if we were to slightly deviate from a chosen λ value.

T-tests are performed to determine whether after log transformation, the delay time of changes detected using two different λ could have the same (log) mean delay time. High p-values are obtained for most pairs of λ values—their means are likely to be equal. When the difference between the two λ values are significant, for example, 4 and 25 (i.e., $\lambda^{-1} = 0.25$ and 0.04), the mean delay times are unlikely to be equal.

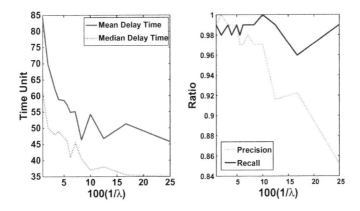

FIGURE 5.5

Scenario (E): Arbitrary changes on a high-dimensional noisy linearly non-separable binary data stream.

We observe this from Table 5.1 for Scenario (B) as an example. Hence, attempting to find an optimal λ with a minimal (log) mean delay time may not be worth the effort.

We perform t-tests, again, on the log transformed delay time of changes detected to determine if at a specific λ value, say 10, two different scenarios could have the same (log) mean delay time. We observe that at more sensitive λ (i.e., lower λ values), the means are likely to be equal. However, when noise is added, the mean delay time is affected. But if the data stream is high-dimensional, noise has limited effects. For higher λ, say 30, the method is less sensitive but more conservative in detecting changes. The mean delay time varies for different scenarios. For Scenario (E), it is not surprising to see that its mean delay time is different from the other scenarios as the dataset used is different. We observe the significantly small p-values of the t-tests in Table 5.2 for $\lambda = 10, 20,$ and 30. Hence, if the high-dimensional data stream comes from the same source, a fixed λ has similar performance in both a noiseless and a noisy environment. This may not be true for lower dimensional data streams.

Some observations (see Figures 5.1–5.5) on the recall and precision for the martingale-based change detection method for the different scenarios are as follows:

1. Precision decreases with decreasing λ value. The precision shows similar decreasing trends (from 1.0 to around 0.8) as λ^{-1} increases, independent of the different scenarios.
2. The recall of a data stream with restricted gradual changes (Scenario (A)) is lower than the recall of a data stream with unrestricted gradual changes (Scenario (B)).
3. Both a noisy data stream (Scenario (C)) and a data stream with restricted gradual changes (Scenario (A)) have low recall.
4. Higher dimension data streams (Scenarios (D) and (E)) with arbitrary changes have high recall.
5. Despite Remark 3, noise in the high-dimension data streams has limited effect on the recall.

Table 5.1 P-values associated with the t-test to determine whether the log transformed delay time of changes detected using two different λ could have the same mean, when the standard deviations are assumed equal in Scenario (B). The distributions of log delay time for all λ values are shown to be normal using the Kolmogorov-Smirnov Test at the 0.05 significance level. The bold values are two-sample comparison where we can reject the null hypothesis that the means are equal at the 0.05 significance level.

	6	8	10	12	14	16	18	20	25	30	50	100
4	0.54082	0.16393	0.32245	**0.03676**	0.15971	0.10278	0.17299	**0.04350**	**0.00349**	0.10260	**0.02416**	**0.00702**
6	–	0.42207	0.69828	0.12542	0.40758	0.27528	0.45158	0.14279	**0.01834**	0.29161	0.09124	**0.03277**
8	–	–	0.67639	0.45370	0.96814	0.72827	0.93736	0.49091	0.12653	0.79833	0.37874	0.19209
10	–	–	–	0.24729	0.65296	0.46377	0.72331	0.27450	**0.04921**	0.50146	0.19200	0.08061
12	–	–	–	–	0.48560	0.72008	0.39602	0.95754	0.47194	0.62101	0.91445	0.61345
14	–	–	–	–	–	0.76062	0.90584	0.52323	0.14476	0.83277	0.41008	0.21598
16	–	–	–	–	–	–	0.66851	0.76034	0.29083	0.91463	0.64050	0.39845
18	–	–	–	–	–	–	–	0.43233	0.09524	0.73135	0.32058	0.14775
20	–	–	–	–	–	–	–	–	0.44180	0.66265	0.87204	0.57834
25	–	–	–	–	–	–	–	–	–	0.20821	0.52901	0.82399
30	–	–	–	–	–	–	–	–	–	–	0.53545	0.29765
50	–	–	–	–	–	–	–	–	–	–	–	0.68005

Table 5.2 P-values associated with the t-test to determine whether the log transformed delay time of changes detected of two different scenarios at $\lambda = 10$ (top table), $\lambda = 20$ (middle table), and $\lambda = 30$ (bottom table) could have the same mean, when the standard deviations are assumed equal. The distributions of log delay time for all scenarios are shown to be normal using the Kolmogorov-Smirnov Test at the 0.05 significance level. The bold values are two-sample comparison where we can reject the null hypothesis that the means are equal at the 0.05 significance level.

Scenario	B	C	D	E
		$\lambda = 10$		
A	0.1547	**0.0072**	0.8367	**3.9068e-11**
B	–	**2.6277e-05**	0.1335	**1.8834e-08**
C	–	–	**0.0006**	**2.7475e-19**
D	–	–	–	**1.5633e-14**
		$\lambda = 20$		
A	0.47444	**0.040521**	0.91357	**2.1516e-09**
B	–	**0.006136**	0.32866	**8.4013e-08**
C	–	–	**0.01873**	**1.5486e-15**
D	–	–	–	**3.8321e-13**
		$\lambda = 30$		
A	**9.9537e-05**	0.1387	**0.0291**	**1.9040e-17**
B	–	**2.6277e-05**	**0.0063**	**3.3158e-06**
C	–	–	**0.0002**	**1.2310e-19**
D	–	–	–	**8.4090e-17**

We see that the martingale-based change detection method works well on noisy high-dimensional data streams. From Figures 5.1 through 5.5, we can choose $\lambda \in [8, 20]$ (i.e., λ^{-1} between 0.05 and 0.125). The chosen λ should ensure that the change detection system has (1) a reasonable high precision, (2) the mean (or median) delay time between a true change point and its detection be minimal and (3) the number of miss detections be minimal (maximal recall).

5.6 Implementation Issues

Two implementation aspects of the martingale-based change detection method are: (1) the type of nonconformity measure used for constructing the p-value (1.5) and (2) the ϵ parameter for the martingale (5.5). [145,148,149] utilized the Lagrange multipliers from SVM as the nonconformity measure and ϵ is set to 0.92 according to Figure 2 in [366].

We investigate the effect of different nonconformity measures on the performance of the martingale-based change detection method. In particular, we compare the martingale-based change detection methods when Lagrange multipliers from Gaussian SVM and Linear SVM are used as nonconformity measures and using nonconformity measures based on K-nearest neighbor with $K = 1, 3$ and 5. We study the effect of various $\epsilon \in [0.82, 1.00)$ on the performance of the martingale-based change detection method.

Here, we use an additional performance measure

$$F_1 = \frac{2 \times \text{Recall} \times \text{Precision}}{\text{Recall} + \text{Precision}}$$

F_1 measure represents a harmonic mean between recall and precision. A high value of F_1 measure ensures that the precision and recall are reasonably high.

5.6.1 **Effect of Various Nonconformity Measures**

From Table 5.3, we observe that MT using various nonconformity measures detects all the changes in the 25 noisy linearly separable RHP data streams (since Recall is 1). However, MT using K-NN-based nonconformity measure (precision range from 0.89 to 0.78) has a higher number of false positives than MT using Lagrange multipliers from SVM (precision is 0.96). For noisy linearly separable data stream, MT using nonconformity measures from SVM should be used to minimize false positive. To ensure a reasonable mean delay time, a Gaussian SVM should be used. One interesting observation from the empirical result from RHP data streams is the lower mean delay time when K-NN-based nonconformity measure is used.

For linearly nonseparable NDC data stream, the performance of MT using K-NN strangeness measure is better than the performance of MT using Lagrange multipliers from SVM based on the F_1 measure in Table 5.3. This is a surprising result as there is a general understanding that nonlinear SVM works well for nonseparable data. From Table 5.3, we also observe that the mean delay time for change detection when K-NN-based nonconformity measure is used is much lower than when Lagrange multipliers from SVM are used. From Table 5.3, a 1-NN-based nonconformity measure can be used to achieve high recall and precision with reasonable mean delay time for online change detection for linearly nonseparable data stream. In fact, if we were to look at the empirical results for both RHP and NDC data streams, a 1-NN nonconformity measure could be used in general for any situation with a reasonably good performance for the martingale-based change detection method!

5.6.2 **Effect of Parameter ϵ**

Next, we analyze the effect of various $\epsilon \in [0.82, 1.00)$ on the performance of the martingale-based change detection method. We use the nonconformity measure based on the Lagrange multiples from Gaussian SVM with $C = 10$ and $\lambda = 10$ for MT.

From Table 5.4, we observe that to achieve a reasonable performance for the martingale-based change detection method based on both F_1 measure and mean

Table 5.3 Empirical comparison for the performance of the martingale-based change detection method (MT) with various nonconformity measures based on SVM and K-NN (MDT: Mean Delay Time).

Classifier	Recall	Precision	F_1	MDT
		RHP Data Stream		
SVM (Gaussian)	**1.00**	**0.96**	**0.98**	112.80
Linear SVM	**1.00**	**0.96**	**0.98**	234.44
1-NN	**1.00**	0.89	0.94	135.92
3-NN	**1.00**	0.86	0.92	98.44
5-NN	**1.00**	0.78	0.88	**79.44**
		NDC Data Stream		
SVM (Gaussian)	0.80	0.77	0.78	195.30
Linear SVM	0.56	0.54	0.55	292.71
1-NN	0.96	**0.92**	**0.94**	92.08
3-NN	**1.00**	0.74	0.85	71.48
5-NN	**1.00**	0.83	0.91	**64.36**

Table 5.4 Empirical comparison for the performance of the martingale-based change detection method (MT) with $\epsilon \in [0.82, 1)$ using the Gaussian SVM.

ϵ	RHP Data Stream			
	Recall	Precision	F_1	Mean Delay Time
0.82	0.84	0.84	0.84	204.48
0.90	**1.00**	0.86	0.92	120.56
0.92	**1.00**	0.96	0.98	112.80
0.94	**1.00**	0.96	0.98	101.60
0.96	**1.00**	**1.00**	**1.00**	**99.32**
0.98	**1.00**	**1.00**	**1.00**	245.44
0.99	0.76	**1.00**	0.86	505.16

delay time, we can select $\epsilon \in [0.92, 0.96]$. This empirical result on the performance of martingale-based change detection method corresponds to the result on the exchangeability martingale in [366] (Figure 2) where the martingale (5.5) is shown to be most sensitive when $\epsilon \in [0.88, 0.96]$. From Table 5.4, MT has the best performance when $\epsilon = 0.96$.

5.7 Conclusions

The online change detection task can be effectively handled by testing exchangeability. The change detection solution is based on martingale computed using p-values derived from a nonconformity predictor. Theoretically, the martingale-based change detection method has small false positive. The incremental change detection method (1) does not require a sliding window on the data stream, (2) does not require monitoring the explicit performance (e.g., classification, regression, clustering error) as data points are streaming, and (3) works well for high-dimensional data streams.

The martingale-based change detection method has successfully applied to implement (1) an online adaptive learning algorithm for labeled data streams, which compares favorably against a sliding window method [147]; and (2) a single-pass video-shot change detector for unlabeled video streams, which compares favorably to some standard offline methods [149].

The martingale-based change detection method is based on the idea that the lack of exchangeability leads to newly observed data to look strange compared to the previously observed ones and therefore small p-values are computed at the new instances. Fedorova et al. [97] have observed that there are situations where a lack of exchangeability makes the p-values cluster around one (i.e., high p-values) due to consistent decreasing random noise in the data stream. In such situations, the existing martingale-based change detection method will not be able to detect a change in the data stream. To overcome this problem, the martingale used in the change detection method needs to be replaced by a martingale that requires no assumption about the p-values generated by the conformal prediction and adapts to the unknown p-values distribution by "estimating a good betting function from the past data" as proposed by Fedorova et al. [97].

Some other future research directions include:

1. Change detection for data streams that contain both labeled and unlabeled (missing label) data points.
2. Current research does not take into account what should be done when a change is not detected. A generic change detection system that includes some error correcting mechanism will be the next stage in the implementation of a more robust and autonomous system.
3. The application of the martingale method to additional real-life problems such as surveillance, Internet security, and fraud detection.

CHAPTER

Feature Selection

6

Tony Bellotti[*], Ilia Nouretdinov[†], Meng Yang[†], and Alexander Gammerman[†]

[*]*Mathematics Department, Imperial College, London, United Kingdom*
[†]*Computer Learning Research Centre, Department of Computer Science, Royal Holloway,*
University of London, United Kingdom

In this chapter, we consider the implementation of feature selection approaches within the Conformal Predictor framework. We begin with a review of feature selection, and then consider several approaches to implementation. The first approach uses existing feature selection methods within conformal predictors, which raises some computational issues. Second, we use techniques specifically designed for conformal predictors: (1) the strangeness minimization feature selection (SMFS) method and (2) the average confidence maximization (ACM) method. SMFS minimizes the overall nonconformity values of a sequence of examples, whereas ACM maximizes the average confidence output by the conformal predictor using a subset of features.

6.1 **Introduction**

Feature selection is the process of selecting a subset of features from a given space of features with the intention of meeting one or more of the following goals.

1. Choose the feature subset that maximises the performance of a learning algorithm.
2. Reduce the requirement for computer storage and/or computational time to classify data without significantly reducing the performance of a learning algorithm on a learning problem.
3. Detect a subset of features that are related to the natural problem being studied.

Feature selection is of most value when only a small number of significantly different features are expected to be relevant. Sometimes, reduction of features can improve the quality of prediction and even be a necessary, embedded step of the prediction algorithm. Several algorithms, related to the first goal, are mentioned in Chapter 11. In this chapter, we mostly consider the second goal as prior: selection of a feature subset either of a fixed size or of a size as small as possible without an essential decrease of performance. The third goal is partially taken into account in the structure of the method.

Some example application areas for which feature selection has proved valuable are gene expression analysis and document classification. In the first example, we may want to model a disease or biological effect based on data containing thousands of gene expression measurements, of which we may expect less than 100 to be relevant. In the second, classification is often conducted on lists of counts of words in a document. Clearly, many words will not be relevant (e.g., "the" and "a"). These will need to be filtered out. The goals listed earlier can be in conflict, since the feature subset that gives optimal performance is not necessarily the smallest that still gives good performance, or may not be computationally efficient. The decision regarding which is the most important goal depends on the outcome required by the user of the learning algorithm. Sometimes a small set of most important features is sought to facilitate better understanding or visualisation of the problem. This may direct further research within the problem domain. This is often the case in gene expression analysis where the particular set of genes selected through analysis is important to direct further biological research. Gene expression analysis is also an example where the third goal is actually a biological task. On the other hand, if the user is primarily interested in achieving the best learning performance then the first goal is more important [134].

For most learning problems there is an implicit feature selection process that is undertaken by researchers. For example, for document classification, researchers will choose features that are expected to be pertinent to the problem, such as the language and words in documents or the structure of the document. Researchers would not suppose the source of the paper or the kind of ink the documents are printed with as useful indicators of the document class, so these would not be included as features in the learning problem. However, in this work, we are interested in the task of explicit automated feature selection. Both [30] and [134] provide reviews of feature selection methods. Feature selection remains an open area of research within the machine learning community. Since the first review of these methods in [30], there have been many developments. Not least is the fact that the number of features in a typical machine learning problem has leapt from tens to tens or hundreds of thousands. Hence, the problem of feature selection has become acute.

6.2 Feature Selection Methods

Typically a feature selection algorithm will use a given training dataset in order to make a decision about which features to select. There are three general methods for feature selection: filters, wrappers, and embedded feature selection. These are discussed in the following sections.

6.2.1 Filters

The filter method employs a feature ranking function to choose the best features. The ranking function gives a relevance score based on a sequence of examples. Intuitively, the more relevant the feature, the higher its rank. Either a fixed number of features with the highest rank are selected, or a variable number of features above a preset threshold value of the rank are selected.

When the outcome variable is binary and the features are numeric, typical ranking functions are the signal-to-noise ratio (SNR) and the Fisher discriminant ratio (FDR) given for each feature as:

$$\text{SNR} = \frac{|\mu_1 - \mu_2|}{\sigma_1 + \sigma_2} \quad \text{and} \quad \text{FDR} = \frac{(\mu_1 - \mu_2)^2}{\sigma_1^2 + \sigma_2^2}$$

where μ_i and σ_i are the sample mean and standard deviation, respectively, of the feature for each class label i.

Figure 6.1 illustrates the use of this approach for classification of childhood leukaemia using data sourced from [387]. For small numbers of features (say, 5), performance is poor, but as the number of selected features increases, the performance improves. However, the performance peaks at about 600 features. When more features are included, the performance gets worse. If all features are included then performance deteriorates markedly. This demonstrates that including too many irrelevant features can actually worsen the performance of a learning algorithm, and hence shows the need for feature selection.

Other ranking functions can be constructed based on the t and χ^2 statistics. If the features are categorical, then criteria related to information gain can be used. If the learning problem involves a multiclass outcome variable, then FDR can be generalized or the ANOVA (ANalysis Of VAriance) test can be used. If a linear classifier is used, the magnitude of weights can also be used as ranks for filter feature selection [22]. Recursive feature elimination (RFE) is an iterative method using this approach and has been shown to give optimal results when applied to microarray data [135].

Filter methods have been successful in a number of problem domains and are very efficient. Nevertheless, the disadvantage of this method is that each feature is assessed

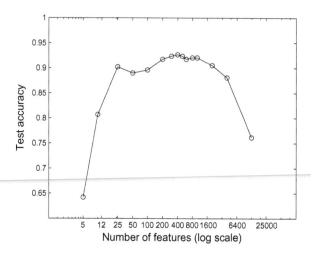

FIGURE 6.1

Feature selection: Accuracy on an independent test dataset against the number of features selected using SNR (log width). Classification of childhood leukemia using a naive Bayes classifier, based on 12,600 gene expression measures.

independently. Correlations between features are not taken into consideration. It is possible that two features are individually useless in classification, but taken together become useful [134, Section 3.3].

6.2.2 Wrappers

Wrapper methods are general-purpose algorithms that search the space of feature subsets, testing performance of each subset using a learning algorithm. The feature subset that gives the best performance is selected for final use. Clearly, if there are m features in total, then there are 2^m possible subsets to search. Such an exhaustive search is impractical, so most wrapper algorithms incorporate a heuristic to narrow the search space. For example, one simple method is *backward elimination* that starts the search with the full set of features and eliminates them one at a time using some form of feature scoring, until an optimal subset is found. This search is linear on the number of features.

Wrapper methods have a long history in statistical modeling, in the form of *stepwise variable selection* [88]. This approach involves either forward selection, adding features one at a time, or backward selection, removing features one at a time until some criterion is reached. Additionally, a bidirectional selection method is available that involves adding *or* removing a feature at each step. A common wrapper criterion is to use the Akaike information criterion (AIC) of model fit. The application of wrappers in machine learning is relatively recent [30, Section 2.5].

The disadvantage of the wrapper technique is that it tends to be computationally intensive and the use of a heuristic to refine the search space can be ad hoc. There has been much research into improving the performance of wrappers. For example, [377] proposed a principled approach for optimal feature selection specifically for Support Vector Machines (SVM), based on the goal of reducing risk of generalization error.

6.2.3 Embedded Feature Selection

Some learning algorithms include an embedded feature selection method. Selecting features is then an implicit part of the learning process. This is the case, for example, with decision tree learners such as CART [44] that use an information measure or loss function to choose the best features. Other learning algorithms have been developed with embedded feature selection in mind. For example, Littlestone's WINNOW algorithm is an adaptation of the Perceptron algorithm that uses multiplicative weight updates instead of additive. This has the effect of rapidly degrading the weights on irrelevant features quickly, leaving only a relatively few features with nonzero weights [30, Section 2.6].

6.3 Issues in Feature Selection

We have already discussed computational issues with wrapper methods and the need for multiclass feature selection methods. However, there are three key issues for feature selection: the problem of selection bias, which is about the correct use of feature selection, false discovery rates, and questions about relevance and redundancy. We discuss each of these issues next.

6.3.1 Selection Bias

It is important that feature selection is applied correctly. Some published research, using feature selection for microarray classification, has been criticized for using the entire dataset for feature selection prior to dividing the data into training and test sets. Presumably, the researchers supposed that the involvement of the test data in the derivation of the feature selection would not have a great impact on their results. However, [6] have shown that a significant *selection bias* does occur as a consequence of this approach. For two published datasets, for which no errors are reported, errors emerge when the feature subset is constructed on the training set alone. They conclude that "the test set must play no role in the feature-selection process for an unbiased estimate to be obtained." They recommend that feature selection is conducted only on the training dataset. Or, if that is not possible, perhaps due to a small sample size, then a procedure involving cross-validation should be used.

6.3.2 False Discovery Rate

When selecting relevant features from a large pool of possible features based on sample data, it may be that some of those features are only *apparently* relevant, in the sense that their relevance in the sample is only the result of chance. These are known as *false discoveries*. The larger the pool of features to choose from, the more likely false discoveries will be. In order for the selected feature subset to be relevant to the population and more importantly, future examples, it is important to reduce the number of false discoveries. We define the *False Discovery Rate* (FDR) as the percentage of false discoveries among the features selected [26]. Controlling FDR is an important area of feature selection research, for problems with large feature spaces such as analysis of bioinformatics data [283].

Using the t-statistic filter, we can readily compute an expected FDR based on the p-value. If we set a significance level α as a threshold and select only features with a p-value less than α, then we can expect that the FDR will be approximately $\alpha/2$, assuming distribution of p-values is approximately uniform. Even for low values of α, we can expect a large number of features to be false discoveries. For example, if we have 10,000 features, $\alpha = 0.01$ will still give an expected 50 false discoveries [349].

Significance analysis of microarrays (SAM) is a popular method developed to overcome this problem. It was designed with microarrays in mind, but could be used with other problem domains. Feature selection is conducted using a variation of the SNR for different permutations of the data. The number of false discoveries is then estimated as the average number of falsely significant features corresponding to each permutation based on a user-defined threshold of significance. This then yields an estimate of FDR. As the threshold decreases, the number of significant features discovered increases, but at the cost of increasing FDR. Experiments show that SAM works well in controlling FDR compared to conventional methods [349].

6.3.3 Relevance and Redundancy

Feature selection was first considered as a search for the most *relevant* features where, broadly, a relevant feature is one that provides some information about the target label [30]. In contrast, [134] takes a more pragmatic approach to feature selection, considering the goal of feature selection to discover a feature subset that is most *useful* to build a good predictor.[1] Being relevant is not necessarily the same as being useful in this sense.

Some researchers have argued that the inclusion of *all* relevant features may not be necessary and may actually reduce performance. This is particularly the case for features that represent the same *factor*, or are correlated and so are *redundant*. The inclusion of a large number of redundant features will over-represent that factor in the classification algorithm and may mean other factors that are just as important but underrepresented and have less weight. This will skew the decision process. Therefore, feature selection algorithms have been developed that have the dual optimization goal of maximizing relevance and minimizing redundancy (MRMR) by measuring information content [82,99] or by analysis of correlation coefficients between features [161]. These all show improvements in performance over other methods that do not consider redundancy. However, these results are not conclusive. Guyon and

---

[1] They quite deliberately focus on the first feature selection goal to maximize performance.

Elisseeff [134] suggested that removing redundant features may not always improve performance and provide artificial data to demonstrate this assertion.

> *"Noise reduction and consequently better class separation may be obtained by adding variables that are presumably redundant. Variables that are independently and identically distributed are not truly redundant"* [134].

Hence, for data sets that include much noise, the removal of redundant features may actually be a disadvantage.

6.4 Feature Selection for Conformal Predictors

In this section we first consider feature selection in the context of conformal predictors. In particular, we address the following three problems:

1. Ensure we do not incur a selection bias, as discussed in Section 6.3.1.
2. Ensure that the nonconformity measure is *exchangeable* as required by Equation 1.3.
3. Ensure reasonable computation time.

To meet the first condition, feature selection should be independent of the test data. Therefore, as a first attempt to implement feature selection, we might design the feature selection process on only the training examples. Consider examples of the form $z = (x, y)$ where x is a vector of features and y is a class label. Let $(z_1, \ldots, z_{n-1})$ be a sequence of $n - 1$ labeled examples given to the conformal predictor to make a prediction for a new unlabeled example x_n. Then feature selection is based only on the first $n - 1$ examples. However, this will not work for standard (transductive) conformal predictors (as described in Chapter 1.3) since this procedure breaks the exchangeability requirement. Recall that the value of the NCM does not change with different ordering of the sequence (Equation 1.3). The intuitive meaning of the NCM is that it measures how unusual example i is relative to the whole sequence of n examples. We then see that a feature selection procedure on just the first $n - 1$ examples would, in general, lead to a different feature space for different sequences of examples, which in turn would, in general, mean that the NCM is not well defined. However, this is not a problem for inductive conformal predictors (Chapter 2.3) since in the inductive setting, feature selection would be restricted to the training data, therefore giving the same feature subset for the sequence of examples, regardless of ordering.

  To implement feature selection in a standard conformal predictor, it is necessary to build the feature selection into the NCM. To do this, an auxiliary nonconformity measure $\tilde{A}$ is introduced, which includes a function f that performs feature selection on a sequence of examples and returns a subset of features:

$$\alpha_i = \tilde{A}\left(z_i, (z_1, \ldots, z_n), f(z_1, \ldots, z_n)\right)$$

To ensure exchangeability of $\tilde{A}$, it is therefore necessary that f is exchangeable. That is, the feature subset output by f should be the same for any ordering of the sequence of example. Most feature selection methods are exchangeable in this sense. For example, this is the case for the filter methods described in Section 6.2.1 using means and variances in computing ranks for each feature, such as SNR and FDR. The use of the entire sequence, including the unlabeled nth example, for feature selection does not lead to selection bias, since in TCM the last example is $z_n = (x_n, y)$ where the label y is a conjecture made by a standard conformal predictor to compute p-values for all possible class labels and the feature selection process is never informed of the true label for example n.

This procedure unfortunately increases computational time since it requires the feature selection procedure to be called every time the NCM is used. For large problems, in the online setting, using a computationally intensive feature selection method such as a wrapper, this may make it impractical to implement. In such cases, it may be better to use an inductive conformal predictor. Nevertheless, for simple feature selection methods, such as filter or embedded approaches, the added computational requirement may be small. In the online setting, some feature selection methods allow the selection to be updated iteratively with each new example. For example, filter methods that use summary statistics, such as SNR and FDR, simply need an iterative update to in-class sample means and standard deviations.

We have so far looked at how to implement existing feature selection methods within the context of conformal predictors. However, it is possible to derive feature selection by taking advantage of properties of conformal predictors. In the next two sections, we describe two such approaches: the Strangeness Minimization Feature Selection and Average Confidence Maximization methods.

6.4.1 Strangeness Minimization Feature Selection

Strangeness Minimization Feature Selection (SMFS) selects the subset of features that minimizes the overall nonconformity value of a sequence of examples. The intuition for this approach is that reducing overall strangeness implies an increase in conformity among the examples in the sequence. Therefore, the set of features minimizing overall strangeness are most relevant to maximizing measured conformity between training examples.

The SMFS goal is defined in relation to any underlying NCM. In common with wrapper feature selection methods, it requires a search over the space of all feature subsets, although restricted to subsets of some fixed size t. For m features, this search has computational complexity $O(m^t)$. The number of selected features t does not need to be very large for this to become impractical. Fortunately, practical implementations of SMFS are possible if we restrict our attention to a subclass of *linear NCMs*. The problem becomes tractable without the need for ad-hoc heuristics that are often required with wrapper methods and, within this framework, we can still implement useful versions of conformal predictors based on a wide range of learning algorithms. We find that SMFS is a principled, broad, and practical feature selection framework, for which distinct feature selection methods are determined by NCMs. We can also apply the principle in reverse to derive novel NCMs based on existing feature selection methods. Bellotti et al. [23] have shown that it has practical application, with results in classifying leukemia diagnosis based on gene expression data.

Given an auxiliary NCM $\tilde{A}$, SMFS can be defined formally as the feature selection function

$$f_{\text{SMFS}}(z_1, \ldots, z_n) = \arg \min_{S \in G} \sum_{i=1}^{n} \tilde{A}(z_i, (z_1, \ldots, z_n), S) \tag{6.1}$$

where $G = \{R : R \subseteq F, |R| = t\}$ and F is the total feature space available. So long as $\tilde{A}$ is exchangeable for any fixed S, it follows that f_{SMFS} is also exchangeable. Hence a conformal predictor using the auxiliary NCM $\tilde{A}(z_i, (z_1, \ldots, z_n), f_{\text{SMFS}}(z_1, \ldots, z_n))$ will be well calibrated.

Example

Simulated data is shown in Figure 6.2, forming a simple classification problem. The large cross (+) is clearly far from the clustering of other crosses and so we would expect it to have a relatively high strangeness value in relation to all the others.

We use an auxiliary NCM based on the Euclidean distance from a centroid restricted to a feature subset S,

$$\alpha_i^S = \sqrt{\sum_{j \in S} \left(x_{ij} - \mu_{(y_i)j}\right)^2 \sigma_j^{-2}},$$

where the index j refers to the jth feature in a feature vector x_i and σ_j is the sample standard deviation of feature j. Using this auxiliary NCM, we find that all examples have a nonconformity value less than 1.5, except the large cross, which has the relatively high nonconformity value 4.5 as we had expected, since it is so different from

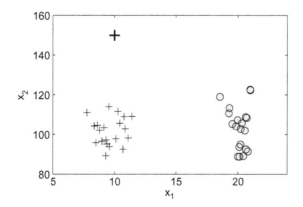

FIGURE 6.2

Simulated data to illustrate SMFS.

all the others. We can compute the sum of nonconformity values restricted to feature subsets of size $t = 1$:

$$\sum_{i=1}^{n} \alpha_i^{\{1\}} = 1.0, \quad \sum_{i=1}^{n} \alpha_i^{\{2\}} = 6.4$$

Therefore, using the SMFS method, the first feature would be chosen as most relevant since it minimizes the total nonconformity value. By observation, it is clear from Figure 6.2 that this is the correct choice since the first feature (x_1-axis) has more discriminatory power than the second (x_2-axis).

β-nonconformity values

The use of linear NCMs is central to implementing SMFS efficiently. In conformal predictors, nonconformity is computed as α-nonconformity values for each example. By using linear NCMs, nonconformity values are computed for each feature instead. We call them β-*nonconformity values* and the SMFS function is reformulated in terms of them.

An auxiliary NCM is defined as a *linear NCM* if

$$\tilde{A}(z, (z_1, \ldots, z_n), S) = \sum_{j \in S} \phi(z, j, (z_1, \ldots, z_n))$$

for all examples z, sequences $(z_1, \ldots, z_n)$ and $S \subseteq F$, for some exchangeable transformation function ϕ. The β-nonconformity value for feature j is defined as

$$\beta_j = \sum_{i=1}^{n} \phi(z_i, j, (z_1, \ldots, z_n)).$$

It follows that

$$f_{\text{SMFS}}(z_1, \ldots, z_n) = \arg \min_{S \in G} \sum_{j \in S} \beta_j.$$

Hence, the SMFS optimization problem is solved by (1) computing β-nonconformity values for each feature, (2) sorting the β-nonconformity values in ascending order, and (3) choosing the top t features in this sorted list. This algorithm is $O(m \log m)$ in the number of features m.

Although the SMFS goal is defined in a way similar to a wrapper feature selection method as a search to minimize the nonconformity value across all possible feature subsets, the implementation for linear NCM involves searching for the subset of features with smallest β-nonconformity values. As such, the implementation is like filter feature selection. In fact, $-\beta_j$ can be used as a feature ranking function. We can also reverse this relationship and build new NCMs based on existing ranking functions. In the next three sections we explore these approaches for different underlying learning methods: the nearest centroid (NC) and support vector machine (SVM) classifiers, and the ranking function SNR.

Nearest centroid linear NCM

The NC classifier computes centroids for each class and for a new example will predict the class with the nearest centroid based on a given distance metric. Using Euclidean distance, a plausible NCM is given by

$$\tilde{A}_{NC}((x_0, y_0), (z_1, \ldots, z_n), S) = \sum_{j \in S} (x_{0j} - \mu_{(y_0)j})^2 \sigma_j^{-2}$$

with μ_{yj} and σ_j computed on the sample sequence $(z_1, \ldots, z_n)$. Then

$$\phi_{NC}((x_0, y_0), j, (z_1, \ldots, z_n)) = (x_{0j} - \mu_{(y_0)j})^2 \sigma_j^{-2}.$$

and, where Y is the set of all class labels and $C_y = \{i : z_i = (x_i, y)\}$,

$$\beta_j = \sum_{i=1}^{n} (x_{0j} - \mu_{(y_0)j})^2 \sigma_j^{-2} = \sigma_j^{-2} \sum_{y \in Y} \left[(|C_y| - 1) \sigma_{(y)j}^2 \right]. \qquad (6.2)$$

The negation of this β-NCM forms a natural ranking function for feature filtering since it measures the ratio of the weighted sum of within-class variances and total variance. A low ratio implies greater variance between classes than noise within classes.

Linear classifier NCM

A linear classifier can be characterized by a score, linear on weighted features, giving a prediction of outcome:

$$\hat{y} = g(w \cdot x)$$

where w is a vector of feature weights and g is a monotonically increasing function. For example, in logistic regression, g is the logit function, and in SVM, it is the sign function with label space $Y = \{-1, +1\}$. A plausible NCM is based on the distance of an example i from the separating hyperplane:

$$\tilde{A}_{LC}((x_i, y_i), (z_1, \ldots, z_n), S) = -y_i \sum_{j \in S} w_j x_{ij}$$

where the weight vector w has been computed using an inductive learner l, such as SVM. That is, $w = l(z_1, \ldots, z_n)$. A version of this NCM was originally derived for logistic regression by [365]. This NCM then yields

$$\beta_j = -w_j \sum_{i=1}^{n} y_i x_{ij}$$

SNR linear NCM

We can use feature ranking functions, such as SNR, to form a β-NCM that can be used to build a new implementation of NCM.

Consider a learning environment with binary label space $Y = \{-1, +1\}$, and transformation functions with the general form

$$\phi_F((x_i, y_i), j, (z_1, \ldots, z_n)) = -\frac{y_i}{|C_{y_i}|} w_j x_{ij} \tag{6.3}$$

This gives the NCM

$$\alpha_i^S = -\frac{y_i}{|C_{y_i}|} \sum_{j \in S} w_j x_{ij}$$

and

$$\beta_j = -w_j(\mu_{(+1)j} - \mu_{(-1)j}).$$

Taking

$$w_j = \frac{\text{sgn}(\mu_{(+1)j} - \mu_{(-1)j})}{\sigma_{(+1)j} + \sigma_{(-1)j}}$$

gives $-\beta_j$ as SNR. Other forms of w give the FDR and t-statistic ranking functions. Therefore, we find that the general form of transformation function (6.3) is versatile. It is interesting that it has the same form as the linear classifier NCM, except for normalizing each example by the number of training examples in its class.

Results for microarray classification

NCM with feature selection was used to classify microarray data [21,19]. In this section we give results using NCM to classify different forms of childhood leukemia based on microarray data. The two major forms of acute leukemia are ALL (acute lymphoblastic leukemia) and AML (acute myeloblastic leukemia). A dataset of 132 children with ALL and 130 with AML was available for analysis [289,288]. Each observation had 22,283 gene probe features. Classification was performed using different implementations of NCM to compare predictive performance. Offline learning was used with 10-fold cross-validation. The same division of data into folds was used for each algorithm to ensure fair comparison. Results are given in Table 6.1. Accuracy (Acc.) measures the fraction of predictions that are correct. In all cases, the accuracy is greater than the confidence level demonstrating the results are well calibrated, as we expect. The NCM classifier works by allowing region predictions. That is, the prediction is a *set* of possible outcomes [365]. In this way, accuracy can be controlled. A prediction is called *certain* if it is a single class label and is called *uncertain* otherwise. In Table 6.1, efficiency (Eff.) measures the fraction of certain predictions. Therefore, larger values represent more efficient algorithms. Table 6.1 shows that using no feature selection yields poor efficiency at all confidence levels. Although using SNR for feature selection improves efficiency, SMFS gives the best results with efficiency close to 1 even at a 97.5% confidence level (both methods were

Table 6.1 Performance of NCM classifiers for childhood leukemia classification.

Classifier	FS method	Confidence level					
		97.5%		95%		90%	
		Acc.	Eff.	Acc.	Eff.	Acc.	Eff.
SVM	None	0.989	0.034	0.966	0.065	0.939	0.160
SVM	SNR	0.989	0.496	0.977	0.710	0.973	0.966
SVM	SMFS	0.989	0.996	0.989	1	0.989	1
NC	SMFS	0.992	0.992	0.992	0.992	0.992	0.992

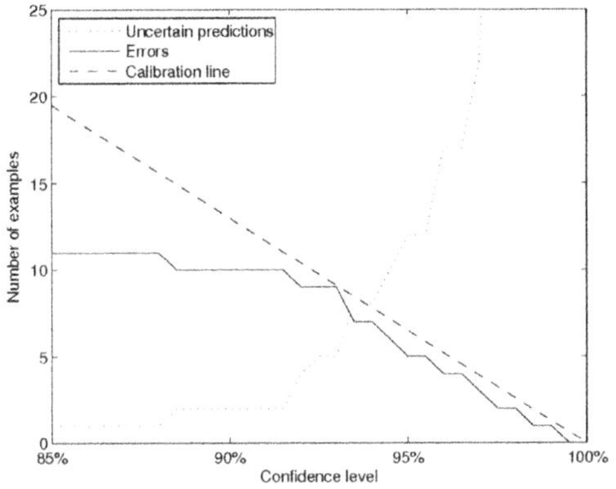

FIGURE 6.3

NCM-NC results classifying AML subtypes.

used to select the top 40 features). The choice of underlying classifier (SVM or NC) makes little difference to the results.

The same data was also used for the more difficult task of subclassifying AML. There are six subtypes of AML in the data with small sample sizes: MLL (23), AML1-ETO (21), FAB-M7 (10), PML-RARα (15), CBFβ-MYH11 (14), and Other (47). Figure 6.3 shows results using NCM-NC with SNR feature selection. Changing confidence level is shown on the horizontal axis. The calibration line shows the maximum number of errors expected at each confidence level. We see that the actual number of prediction errors is always less than this and for higher confidence levels is close to the calibration line. This is a clear demonstration of the calibration property of NCM, and that this property is preserved with feature selection. The figure also shows that with rising confidence level, beyond a 90% level, although number of errors are controlled, the number of uncertain predictions rises quite sharply.

6.4.2 **Average Confidence Maximization (ACM)**

As we can see, SMFS combined ideas of filters and wrappers in the feature selection: the features were sorted by β-nonconformity values (like filtering) but the calculation of these values was based on the whole feature set, which makes the method a wrapper. An alternative approach based on conformal prediction (Algorithm 8) was originally presented in [386]. It also uses elements of the embedded feature selection methodology because the process of selection is connected with the process of confident prediction. It is a stepwise method of increasing feature set size with average confidence as the optimization goal, which can be also used as the stopping criterion.

Suppose we try to separate the two classes just by one feature. We take all examples from the dataset that belong to one of these two classes and process them in the online mode in order to average the results over different sizes of the training set. This is done for each feature, so the feature with the largest average confidence will be the first important feature of the set of useful features. We then continue in the same way with a new question: What is the second feature that can be added to this one in order to maximize average confidence? On answering this question, we will have a list of two features; we then look for the third feature, and so on. Adding new features can be stopped when we reach either a desired number of features or at a selected confidence level when it is reached. If it is never reached, it might be reasonable to stop when it stabilizes and stops growing.

Algorithm 8 ACM Feature Selection by Conformal Predictor

Input: feature subset U, candidate feature $\overline{U}$, $z_1 = (x_1, y_1)$, $z_2 = (x_2, y_2)$, ..., $z_l = (x_l, y_l)$

Input: a set of new object $\{x_{l+1}, x_{l+2}, ..., x_{l+n}\}$

Input: nonconformity measure A

  for $U = U \bigcup \overline{u}, \overline{u} \in \overline{U}$ **do**

    for i=1:n **do**

      for $y \in Y$ **do**

        $z_{l+i} = (x_{l+i}, y)$

        $(\alpha_1, \ldots, \alpha_{l+1}) = A(\{z_1, z_2......z_{l+i}\}/z_j, z_j)$

        $p(y) = \frac{\#\{j=1,....,l+i:\alpha_j \geq \alpha_{l+i}\}}{l+i}$

      end for

      confidence(i) $= 1-$ the second largest p

      $z_{l+i} = (x_{l+i}, y_{true})$

      $Z = Z \bigcup z_{l+i}$

    end for

  end for

  $U = U \bigcup \overline{u}$ which achieve highest average confidence

---

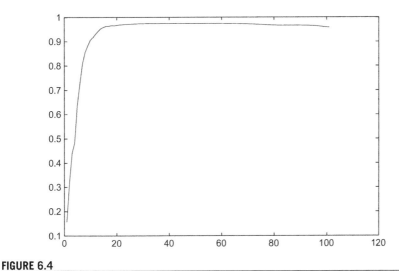

FIGURE 6.4

Average level of individual confidence for different number of features (APP vs DYS).

A typical result follows in Figure 6.4 [386]. The sample dataset was part of the Abdominal Pain dataset [262] containing 126 Appendicitis (APP) and 173 Dyspepsia (DYS) patients with 33 features that are clinical symptoms. The figure shows the dependence of the average confidence level on the number of selected features as it increases according to the method. Based on this figure, a user can decide at what number of features to stop, depending on the desired level of confidence: 10 features are enough for 90% confidence, 20 are needed for 95%. Alternatively, we can stop when the confidence stabilizes and stops increasing: this is at about 25 features.

6.5 Discussion and Conclusions

We presented two feature selection methods, SMFS and ACM, based on conformal prediction in the previous sections. Our experience has revealed that SMFS is usually better in the sense that it agrees with the selection of features given by human experts. On the other hand ACM has some advantages from a theoretical point of view. It is based, not on an NCM directly as SMFS is, but on the conformal prediction output (confidence). This means that a bad choice of NCM will be better reflected in the results (low average confidence), giving a warning to the user before the results of feature selection are assessed. Another advantage of ACM is the flexibility of the stopping criterion: instead of fixing the number of selected features, we can select a level of confidence to be achieved. This was illustrated in the earlier example.

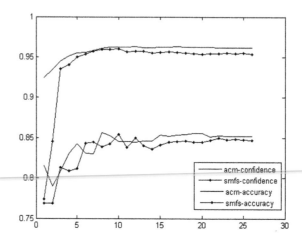

FIGURE 6.5

Accuracy and average confidence for APP.

In order to have a direct comparison between the two algorithms, we applied both of them to the same dataset using the NC (Nearest Centroid) method. The Nearest Centroid for an example x_i classified as y_i is

$$\alpha_i = \frac{d(\mu_{y_i}, x_i)}{min_{y \neq y_i} d(\mu_y, x_i)}.$$

The two methods are applied to the problem of classification of appendicitis in the abdominal pain dataset (Section 6.4.2). The comparison shows that both methods have about the same quality in accuracy and average confidence (Figure 6.5). Although further empirical work is required, results so far suggest that in the context of conformal predictors, good results are obtained using both SMFS and ACM, in comparison to standard methods.

Model Selection

7

David R. Hardoon[*], **Zakria Hussain**[†], **and John Shawe-Taylor**[†]

[*]*Ernst & Young, Singapore*
[†]*Department of Computer Science, University College London, United Kingdom*

CHAPTER OUTLINE HEAD

In this chapter, we investigate the issue of model selection and the use of the nonconformity (strangeness) measure in batch learning. Using the nonconformity measure, we propose a new training algorithm that helps avoid the need for Cross-Validation or Leave-One-Out model selection strategies. We provide a new generalization error bound using the notion of nonconformity to upper bound the loss of each test example and show that our proposed approach is comparable to standard model selection methods, but with theoretical guarantees of success and faster convergence. We demonstrate our novel model selection technique using the Support Vector Machine algorithm.

7.1 Introduction

Model Selection is the task of choosing the best model for a particular data analysis task. It generally makes a compromise between fit with the data and the complexity of the model. Furthermore, the chosen model is used in subsequent analysis of test data. Currently the most popular techniques used by practitioners are Cross-Validation (CV) and Leave-One-Out (LOO).

In this chapter, the model we concentrate on is the Support Vector Machine (SVM) [35]. Considering the popularity, CV and LOO will form our modus operandi despite there being a number of alternative approaches proposed in SVM literature. For instance, Chapelle and Vapnik [53] explore model selection using the span of the support vectors and rescaling of the feature space, whereas Momma and Bennett [233], motivated by an application in drug design, propose a fully automated search methodology for model selection in SVMs for regression and classification. Gold and Sollich [120] give an in-depth review of a number of model selection alternatives for tuning the kernel parameters and penalty coefficient C for SVMs, and although they find a model selection technique that performs well (at high computational cost), the authors conclude that "the hunt is still on for a model selection criterion for SVM classification which is both simple and gives consistent generalization performance." More recent attempts at model selection have been given by Hastie et al. [139], who derive an algorithm that fits the entire path of SVM solutions for every value of the cost parameter, while Li et al. [206] propose to use the Vapnik-Chervonenkis (VC) bound; they put forward an algorithm that employs a coarse-to-fine search strategy to obtain the best parameters in some predefined ranges for a given problem. Furthermore, Ambroladze et al. [7] propose a tighter PAC-Bayes bound to measure the performance of SVM classifiers, which in turn can be used as a way of estimating the hyperparameters. Finally, de Souza et al. [71] have addressed model selection for multiclass SVMs using Particle Swarm Optimization.

Recently, Özöğür-Akyüz et al. [258], following on work by Özöğür-Akyüz et al. [257], show that selecting a model whose hyperplane achieves the maximum separation from a test point obtains comparable error rates to those found by selecting the SVM model through CV. In other words, while methods such as CV involve finding one SVM model (together with its optimal parameters) that minimizes the CV error, Özöğür-Akyüz et al. [258] keep all the models generated during the model selection stage and make predictions according to the model whose hyperplane achieves the maximum separation from a test point. The main advantage of this approach is the computational saving when compared to CV or LOO. However, their method is only applicable to large margin classifiers like SVMs.

In this chapter, we continue this line of research, but rather than using the distance of each test point from the hyperplane, we explore the idea of using the *nonconformity measure* (see Eq. 1.6) [365,315] of a test sample to a particular label set. The nonconformity measure is a function that evaluates how "strange" a prediction is according to the different possibilities available. As explained in Chapter 1, the notion of nonconformity has been proposed in the online learning framework of conformal prediction [315], and is a way of scoring how different a new sample is from a bag[1] of old samples. The premise is that if the observed samples are well-sampled then we should have high confidence on correct prediction of new samples, given that they *conform* to the observations.

We take the nonconformity measure and apply it to the SVM algorithm during testing in order to gain a time advantage over CV and to generalize the algorithm of Özöğür-Akyüz et al. [258]. Hence, we are not restricted to SVMs (or a measure of

---

[1]A *bag* is a more general formalism of a mathematical *set* that allows repeated elements.

the margin for prediction) and can apply our method to a broader class of learning algorithms. However, due to space constraints we only address the SVM technique and leave the application to other algorithms (and other nonconformity measures not using the margin) as a future research study. Furthermore we also derive a novel learning theory bound that uses nonconformity as a measure of complexity. To our knowledge this is the first attempt at using this type of measure to upper bound the loss of learning algorithms.

The paper is laid out as follows. In Section 7.2, we present the definitions used throughout the paper. Our main algorithmic contributions are given in Section 7.3 where we present our nonconformity measure and its novel use in prediction. Section 7.4 presents a novel generalization error bound for our proposed algorithm. Finally, we present experiments in Section 7.5 and conclude in Section 7.6.

7.2 Background

The following definitions pertaining to conformal prediction are mainly taken from Chapter 1 and [315].

Let (x_i, y_i) be the ith input-output pair from an input space $\mathbf{X}$ and output space $\mathbf{Y}$. Let $z_i = (x_i, y_i)$ denote shorthand notation for each pair taken from the joint space $\mathbf{Z} := \mathbf{X} \times \mathbf{Y}$. We define a *nonconformity measure* as a real valued function $A(S, z)$ that measures how different a sample z is from a set of observed samples $S = \{z_1, \ldots, z_m\}$. A nonconformity measure must be fixed *a priori* before any data has been observed.

Conformal predictions work by making predictions according to the nonconformity measure outlined earlier. Given a set $S = \{z_1, \ldots, z_m\}$ of training samples observed over $t = 1, \ldots, m$ time steps and a new sample x, a conformal prediction algorithm will predict y from a set containing the correct output with probability $1 - \epsilon$. For example, if $\epsilon = 0.05$ then the prediction is within the so-called *prediction region*—a set containing the correct y, with 95% probability. In this paper, we extend this framework to the batch learning model to make predictions using confidence estimates, where for example we are 95% confident that our prediction is correct.

In the batch learning setting, rather than observing samples incrementally such as $x_1, y_1, \ldots, x_m, y_m$, we have a training set $S = \{(x_1, y_1), \ldots, (x_m, y_m)\}$ containing all the samples for training that are assumed to be distributed i.i.d. from a fixed (but unknown) distribution $\mathcal{D}$. Given a function (hypothesis) space $\mathcal{H}$ the batch algorithm takes training sample S and outputs a hypothesis $f : \mathbf{X} \mapsto \mathbf{Y}$ that maps samples to labels.

For the SVM, let $\phi : \mathbf{X} \mapsto \mathbf{F}$ map the training samples to a higher dimensional feature space $\mathbf{F}$. The primal SVM optimization problem can be defined as:

$$\min_{w,b} \quad \|w\|_2^2 + C \sum_{i=1}^{n} \xi_i$$
$$\text{subject to} \quad y_i \left(\langle w, \phi(x_i) \rangle + b \right) \geq 1 - \xi_i$$
$$i = 1, \ldots, n,$$

where b is the bias term, $\xi \in \mathbb{R}^n$ is the vector of slack variables and $w \in \mathbb{R}^n$ is the primal weight vector, whose 2-norm minimization corresponds to the maximization of the margin between the set of positive and negative samples. The notation $\langle \cdot, \cdot \rangle$ denotes the inner product.

The dual optimization problem gives us the flexibility of using *kernels* to solve nonlinear problems [303,319]. The dual SVM optimization problem can be formulated as:

$$\max_\alpha \quad \sum_i^m \alpha_i - \frac{1}{2} \sum_{i=1}^m y_i y_j \alpha_i \alpha_j \kappa(x_i, x_j),$$
$$\text{subject to} \quad \sum_{i=1}^m y_i \alpha_i = 0,$$
$$0 \le \alpha_i \le C,$$

where $\kappa(\cdot, \cdot)$ is the kernel function and $\alpha \in \mathbb{R}^m$ is the dual (Lagrangian) variables. Throughout the paper we will use the dual optimization formulation of the SVM as we attempt to find the optimal regularization parameter for the SVM together with the optimal kernel parameters.

7.3 SVM Model Selection Using Nonconformity Measure

We now discuss the main focus of the paper. Let $S = S_{\text{trn}} \cup S_{\text{val}}$ be composed of a training set S_{trn} and a validation set S_{val}. We assume without loss of generality that,

$$S = \{z_1^t, \ldots, z_m^t, z_1^v, \ldots, z_n^v\}$$

where $S_{\text{trn}} = \{z_1^t, \ldots, z_m^t\}$ and $S_{\text{val}} = \{z_1^v, \ldots, z_n^v\}$.

We start by defining our nonconformity measure $A(S_{\text{val}}, z)$ for a function f over the validation set S_{val} and $j = 1, \ldots, n$ as,

$$A(S_{\text{val}}, z) = yf(x). \tag{7.1}$$

Note that this does not depend on the whole sample but just the test point. In itself it does not characterize how different the point is. To do this, we need the so-called *p-value* $p_A(S_{\text{val}}, z)$ that computes the fraction of points in S_{val} with "stranger" values:

$$p_A(S_{\text{val}}, z) = \frac{\left| \left\{ 1 \le j \le n : A(S_{\text{val}}, z_j^v) \le A(S_{\text{val}}, z) \right\} \right|}{n},$$

which, in this case, measures the number of samples from the validation set that have smaller functional margin than the test point functional margin. The larger the margin obtained, the more confidence we have in our prediction. The p-value of z is between 1 and $1/n$. If it is small (tends to $1/n$) then sample z is nonconforming and if it is large (tends to 1) then it is conforming.

In order to better illustrate this idea, we show a simple pictorial example in Figure 7.1. We are given six validation samples ordered around 0 (solid line) in terms of their correct/incorrect classification; that is, the value $y^v f(x^v)$ for an $(x^v, y^v) = z^v$

Validation samples ●
Test sample ◆

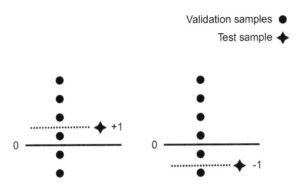

FIGURE 7.1
A simple illustrative example of conformal prediction using a validation set of six samples
(two are misclassifications, four are correctly classified) on a single test sample with a
positive functional value and its two label possibilities of +1 (left) and −1 (right).

pair will be correctly classified by f iff $y^v f(x^v) > 0$. In our example, two are incorrectly classified (below the threshold) and four are correct. The picture on the left also
includes $yf(x)$ for a test sample x when its label is considered to be positive ($y = +1$).
In this case, there remain three validation samples below its value of $yf(x)$ giving us a
nonconformity measure-based p-value using Eq. (7.2) as $p_A(S_{\text{val}}, (x, y = +1)) = \frac{3}{6}$.
A similar calculation can be made for the picture on the right when we consider the
label $y = -1$ for test point x, $(x, y = -1)$. We are able to conclude, for this sample, that assigning x a label of $y = +1$ gives a p-value of $p_A(S_{\text{val}}, (x, +1)) = \frac{1}{2}$
while assigning a label of $y = -1$ gives a p-value of $p_A(S_{\text{val}}, (x, -1)) = \frac{1}{6}$. Therefore, with a higher probability, our test sample x is conforming to +1 (or equally
nonconforming to −1) and should be predicted positive. We state the standard result
for nonconformity measures, but first define a nonconformity prediction scheme and
its associated error.

Definition 7.1. For a fixed nonconformity measure $A(S, z)$, its associated p-value,
and $\epsilon > 0$, the confidence predictor Γ^ϵ predicts the label set

$$\Gamma^\epsilon(S, x) = \{y : p_A(S, (x, y)) \geq \epsilon\}$$

The confidence predictor Γ^ϵ makes an error on sample $z = (x, y)$ if $y \notin \Gamma^\epsilon(S, x)$.

Proposition 7.1. *For exchangeable distributions we have that*

$$P^{n+1}\left\{(S, z) : y \notin \Gamma^\epsilon(S, x)\right\} \leq \epsilon.$$

Proof. By exchangeability, all permutations of a training set are equally likely. Denote
with $\tilde{S}$ the set S extended with the sample z_{n+1} and for σ a permutation of $n + 1$
objects. Let $\tilde{S}_\sigma$ be the sequence of samples permuted by σ. Consider the permutations

for which the corresponding prediction of the final element of the sequence is not an error. This implies that the value $A(\tilde{S}_\sigma, z_{\sigma(n+1)})$ is in the upper $1 - \epsilon$ fraction of the values $A(\tilde{S}_\sigma, z_{\sigma(i)})$, $i = 1, \ldots, n + 1$. This will happen at least $1 - \epsilon$ of the time under the permutations, hence upper bounding the probability of error over all possible sequences by ϵ as required.   □

Following the theoretical motivation from Shawe-Taylor [318], we proceed by computing all the SVM models and applying them throughout the prediction stage. A fixed validation set, withheld from training, is used to calculate the nonconformity measures. We start by constructing K SVM models so that each decision function $f_k \in F$ is in the set F of decision functions with $k = 1, \ldots, K$. The different set of SVM models can be characterized by different regularization parameters for C (or ν in ν-SVM) and the width parameter γ in the Gaussian kernel case. For instance, given 10 $C = \{C_1, \ldots, C_{10}\}$ values and 10 $\gamma = \{\gamma_1, \ldots, \gamma_{10}\}$ values for a Gaussian kernel, we would have a total of $|C| \times |\gamma| = 100$ SVM models, where $|\cdot|$ denotes the cardinality of a set.

We now describe our new model selection algorithm for the SVM using nonconformity. If the following

$$\frac{\left|\{\forall j : y_j\, f_k(x_j) \le y f_k(x)\}\right|}{n} > \epsilon$$

statement holds, then we include $y \in \Gamma_k^\epsilon$ where Γ is the prediction region (set of labels conforming). For classification, the set Γ can take the following values:

$$\{\emptyset\}, \{-1\}, \{+1\}, \{-1, +1\}.$$

Clearly finding the prediction region $\Gamma = \{-1\}$ or $\Gamma = \{+1\}$ is useful in the classification scenario as it gives higher confidence of the prediction being correct, while the sets $\Gamma = \{\emptyset\}$ and $\Gamma = \{-1, +1\}$ are useless as the first abstains from making a prediction and the second is unbiased toward a label.

Let ϵ_{crit} be the critical ϵ that creates one label in the set Γ_k^ϵ for at least one of the K models:

$$\epsilon_{crit} = \min_{k \in K}\ \min_{y \in \{-1, +1\}} \frac{\left|\{\forall j : y_j^v\, f_k\left(x_j^v\right) \le y f_k(x)\}\right|}{n}. \tag{7.2}$$

Furthermore, let k_{crit}, y_{crit} be arguments that realize the minimum ϵ_{crit}, chosen randomly in the event of a tie. This now gives the prediction of x as $y = -y_{crit}$. This is because y_{crit} is nonconforming (strange) and we wish to select the *opposite* (conforming) label. In the experiments section, we refer to the prediction strategy outlined earlier and the model selection strategy given by Eq. (7.2) as the nonconformity model selection strategy. We set out the pseudocode for this procedure in Algorithm 9.

Before proceeding, we would like to clarify some aspects of the algorithm. The data is split into a training and validation set *once* and therefore all K models are computed on the training data—after this procedure we only require to calculate the

---

Algorithm 9 Nonconformity Model Selection

Input: Sample $S = \{(x_i, y_i)\}_{i=1}^{\ell}$, SVM parameters C and γ (for Gaussian kernel) where $K = |C| \times |\gamma|$

Output: Predictions of test points $x_{\ell+1}, x_{\ell+2}, \ldots$

1: Take training data S and randomly split into training set $S_{\text{trn}} = \{(x_1^t, y_1^t), \ldots, (x_m^t, y_m^t)\}$ and validation set $S_{\text{val}} = \{(x_1^v, y_1^v), \ldots, (x_n^v, y_n^v)\}$ where $m + n = \ell$ {This split is only done *once*}.

2: Train K SVM models on training data S_{trn} to find $f_1(\cdot), \ldots, f_K(\cdot)$.

3: **Prediction Procedure**: For a test point x compute:

$$\epsilon_{crit} = \min_{k \in K} \min_{y \in \{-1, +1\}} \left\{ \frac{\left| \left\{ \forall j : y_j^v f_k\left(x_j^v\right) \leq y f_k(x) \right\} \right|}{n} \right\},$$

realised by $k = k_{crit}$ and $y = y_{crit}$.

4: Predict label $-y_{crit}$ for x.

---

nonconformity measure-based p-value for all test points in order to make predictions. However, in b-fold Cross-Validation we require to train, for each C and γ parameter, a further b times. Hence CV will be at most b times more computationally expensive.

7.4 Nonconformity Generalization Error Bound

The problem with Proposition 7.1 is that it requires the validation set to be generated afresh for each test point, specifies just one value of ϵ, and only applies to a single test function. In our application, we would like to reuse the validation set for all of our test data and use an empirically determined value of ϵ. Furthermore we would like to use the computed errors for different functions in order to select one for classifying the test point.

We therefore need to have uniform convergence of empirical estimates to true values for all values of ϵ and all functions K. We first consider the question of uniform convergence for all values of ϵ.

If we consider the cumulative distribution function $F(\gamma)$ defined by

$$F(\gamma) = P\left((x, y) : y f(x) \leq \gamma\right),$$

we need to bound the difference between empirical estimates of this function and its true value. This corresponds to bounding the difference between true and empirical probabilities over the sets

$$\mathcal{A} = \{(-\infty, a] : a \in \mathbb{R}\}.$$

Observe that we cannot shatter two points of the real line with this set system as the larger cannot be included in a set without the smaller. It follows that this class of functions has Vapnik-Chervonenkis (VC) dimension 1. We can therefore apply the following standard result (see for example Devroye et al. [77]).

Theorem 7.1. *Let $\mathcal{X}$ be a measurable space with a fixed but unknown probability distribution P. Let $\mathcal{A}$ be a set system over $\mathcal{X}$ with VC dimension d and fix $\delta > 0$. With probability at least $1 - \delta$ over the generation of an i.i.d. m-sample $S \subset \mathcal{X}$,*

$$\left| \frac{|S \cap \mathcal{A}|}{m} - P(\mathcal{A}) \right| \leq 5.66 \sqrt{\frac{d \ln \left(\frac{em}{d} \right) + \ln \frac{8}{\delta}}{m}}.$$

We now apply this result to the error estimations derived by our algorithm for the K possible choices of model.

Proposition 7.2. *Fix $\delta > 0$. Suppose that the validation set S_{val} of size n in Algorithm 9 has been chosen i.i.d. according to a fixed but unknown distribution that is also used to generate the test data. Then with probability at least $1 - \delta$ over the generation of S_{val}, if for a test point x the algorithm returns a classification $y^v = -y_{crit}$, using function $f_{k_{crit}}$, $1 \leq k_{crit} \leq K$, realizing a minimum value of ϵ_{crit}, then the probability of misclassification satisfies*

$$P\left((x, y) : y \neq y^v \right) \leq \epsilon_{crit} + 5.66 \sqrt{\frac{\ln (en) + \ln 8K\delta}{n}}.$$

Proof. We apply Theorem 7.1 once for each function f_k, $1 \leq k \leq K$ with δ replaced by δ/K. This implies that with probability $1 - \delta$ the bound holds for all of the functions f_k, including the chosen $f_{k_{crit}}$. For this function the empirical probability of the label y_{crit} being observed is ϵ_{crit}, hence the true probability of this opposite label is bounded as required. □

Remark 7.1. The bound in Proposition 7.2 is applied *using* each test sample, which in turn gives a different bound value for each test point (e.g., see Shawe-Taylor [318]). Therefore, we are unable to compare this bound with existing training set CV bounds [171,393] as they are traditional *a priori* bounds computed over the training data, and which give a uniform value for all test points (i.e., training set bounds [194]).

7.5 **Experimental Results**

In the following experiments we compare SVM model selection using traditional CV to our proposed nonconformity strategy as well as to the model selection using the maximum margin [258] from a test sample. We make use of the Votes, Glass, Haberman, Bupa, Credit, Pima, BreastW, and Ionosphere data sets acquired from the UCI machine learning repository.[2] The datasets were preprocessed such that samples

---

[2] http://archive.ics.uci.edu/ml/.

Table 7.1 Description of datasets: Each row contains the name of the dataset, the number of samples and features (i.e., attributes), as well as the total number of positive and negative samples.

Data set	# Samples	# Features	# Positive Samples	# Negative Samples
Votes	52	16	18	34
Glass	163	9	87	76
Haberman	294	3	219	75
Bupa	345	6	145	200
Credit	653	15	296	357
Pima	768	8	269	499
BreastW	683	9	239	444
Ionosphere	351	34	225	126

Table 7.2 Model selection values for γ and C for both cross-validation and nonconformity measure.

$$\gamma = \{2^{-15}, 2^{-13}, 2^{-11}, 2^{-9}, 2^{-7}, 2^{-5}, 2^{-3}, 2^{-1}, 2^{1}, 2^{3}\}$$
$$C = \{2^{-5}, 2^{-3}, 2^{-1}, 2^{1}, 2^{3}, 2^{5}, 2^{7}, 2^{9}, 2^{11}, 2^{13}, 2^{15}\}$$

containing unknown values and contradictory labels were removed. Table 7.1 lists the various attributes of each dataset. The LibSVM package 2.85 [51] and the Gaussian kernel were used throughout the experiments. Model selection was carried out for the values listed in Table 7.2.

In the experiments we apply a 10-fold CV routine where the data is split into 10 separate folds, with one used for testing and the remaining nine split into a training and validation set. We then use the following procedures for each of the two model selection strategies:

- *Nonconformity*: Split the samples into a training and validation set of size $\min(\frac{1}{5}\ell, 50)$ where ℓ is the number of samples.[3] Using the training data, we learn all models using C and γ from Table 7.2.
- *Cross-Validation*: Carry out a 10-fold CV *only* on the training data used in the nonconformity procedure to find the optimal C and γ from Table 7.2.

The validation set is excluded from training in both methods, but used for prediction in the nonconformity method. Hence, the samples used for training and testing were identical for both CV and the nonconformity model selection strategy. We feel that this was a fair comparison as both methods were given the same data samples from which to train the models.

---

[3]The size of the validation set was varied without much difference in generalization error.

Table 7.3 presents the results where we report the average error and standard deviation for Cross-Validation and the Nonconformity strategy. We are immediately able to observe that carrying out model selection using the nonconformity measure is, on average, a factor of 7.3 times faster than using CV. The results show that (excluding the Haberman data set) nonconformity seems to perform similarly to CV in terms of generalization error. However, lower values for the standard deviation on Votes, Glass, Bupa, and Credit suggest that on these data sets nonconformity gives more consistent results than CV. Furthermore, when excluding the Haberman data set, the overall error for the model selection using nonconformity is 0.1730 ± 0.0659 and CV is 0.1686 ± 0.0886, constituting a difference of only 0.0044 (less than half a percent) in favor of CV and a standard deviation of 0.0227 in favor of the nonconformity approach. We hypothesize that the inferior results for Haberman are due to the very small numbers of features (only three).

We also compare the nonconformity strategy to the SVM L_∞ maximum margin approach [258]. The SVM L_∞ selects the model with the maximum margin from the test sample in order to make predictions. Once again, the training and testing sets were identical for both methods. Observe that despite the L_∞ method being approximately 7 seconds faster (on average) than our proposed method, we obtain an improvement of 0.0251 ± 0.0108, hence, bringing us closer to the CV error rate (nonconformity is overall only 1.17% worse than CV when including the Haberman dataset and 0.44% worse when excluding). In fact, we obtain lower error rates than SVM L_∞ on all datasets except for Credit (but with a smaller standard deviation).

Since we do not have a single number for the bound on generalization (as traditional bounds) but rather individual values for each test sample, it is not possible to simply compare the bound with the test error. In order to show how the bound performs we plot the generalization error as a function of the bound value. For each value of the bound we take the average error of all test points with predicted error less than or equal to that value. In other words, we create a set[4] B containing the various bound values computed on the test samples. Subsequently, for each element in the set (i.e., $\forall i, b_i \in B$) we compute the average error value for the test samples that have a bound value that is smaller or equal to b_i.

Figure 7.2 shows a plot of this error rate as a function of the bound value. The final value of the function is the overall generalization error, while the lower error rates earlier in the curve are those attainable by filtering at different bound values. As expected, the error increases monotonically as a function of the bound value. Clearly, there is considerable weakness in the bound, but this is partly a result of our using a quite conservative VC bound. Our main aim here is to show that the predictions are correlated with the actual error rates.

We believe these results to be encouraging as our theoretically motivated model selection technique is faster and achieves similar error rates to Cross-Validation, which is generally considered to be the gold standard. We also find that the nonconformity

---

[4]Hence, no repetition of identical bound values are allowed.

Table 7.3 Model selection results: Average error and standard deviation as well as the runtime (in seconds) for model selection using Nonconformity measure, 10-fold Cross Validation, and the SVM-L_∞ margin distance.

Data set	Nonconformity	Runtime	Cross-Validation	Runtime	SVM-L_∞	Runtime
Votes	0.0700 ± 0.1201	0.72s	0.0833 ± 0.2115	5.74s	0.0933 ± 0.0991	0.43s
Glass	0.2167 ± 0.0932	5.25s	0.2085 ± 0.1291	32.58s	0.2328 ± 0.1263	3.08s
Haberman	0.3133 ± 0.0680	58.23s	0.2518 ± 0.0397	455.77s	0.3300 ± 0.0524	49.23s
Bupa	0.2753 ± 0.0620	44.85s	0.2840 ± 0.0604	329.96s	0.3192 ± 0.1085	38.81s
Credit	0.2990 ± 0.0468	86.85s	0.2745 ± 0.1111	592.42s	0.2914 ± 0.0850	72.31s
Pima	0.2562 ± 0.0554	169.05s	0.2473 ± 0.0361	1305.29s	0.3019 ± 0.0516	155.65s
BreastW	0.0378 ± 0.0350	24.80s	0.0335 ± 0.0282	150.36s	0.0408 ± 0.0367	18.29s
Ionosphere	0.0562 ± 0.0493	17.63s	0.0479 ± 0.0440	103.45s	0.1158 ± 0.0565	11.85s
Overall	0.1905 ± 0.0662	50.92s	0.1788 ± 0.0825	371.94s	0.2156 ± 0.0770	43.71s
Overall ex. Haberman	0.1730 ± 0.0659	49.87s	0.1686 ± 0.0886	359.97s	0.1993 ± 0.0805	42.91s

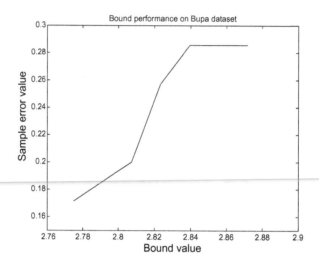

FIGURE 7.2

The generalization error as a function of the bound value for a single train-test split of the Bupa data set. The final value of the function is the overall generalization error.

strategy is slightly slower than the maximum margin approach but performs better in terms of generalization error.

7.6 Conclusions

We have presented a novel approach for model selection and test sample prediction using the nonconformity (strangeness) measure proposed in the conformal prediction framework. Furthermore, we have given a novel generalization error bound on the loss of the learning method. The proposed model selection approach is both simple and gives consistent generalization performance [120].

We find these results encouraging as they constitute a much needed shift from costly model selection based approaches to a faster method that is competitive in terms of generalization error. Furthermore, in relation to the work of Özöğür-Akyüz et al. [258] we have presented a method that is (1) not restricted to SVMs and (2) can use measures other than the margin to make predictions.

Therefore, the nonconformity measure approach gives us a general way of choosing to make predictions, allowing us the flexibility to apply it to algorithms that are not based on large margins. In future work, we aim to investigate the applicability of our proposed model selection technique to other learning methods. Another future research direction is to apply different nonconformity measures to the SVM algorithm presented in this paper such as, for example, a nearest neighbor nonconformity measure [315].

Acknowledgments

The authors would like to acknowledge financial support from the EPSRC project Le Strum,[5] EP-D063612-1, and from the EU project PinView,[6] FP7-216529.

---

[5] http://www.lestrum.org.
[6] http://www.pineview.eu.

Prediction Quality Assessment

Matjaž Kukar

Faculty of Computer and Information Science, University of Ljubljana, Ljubljana, Slovenia

CHAPTER OUTLINE HEAD

In the last decade machine learning and data mining were established as highly valuable data analysis tools. Their pervasive use means that they are used in several risk-sensitive domains, where failed predictions may cause substantial financial, economic, health, reputational, or other damage. For such use, most data mining approaches are less than ideal, since more often than not, they cannot produce reliable and unbiased assessments of their predictions' quality. In last years, several approaches for estimating reliability or confidence of individual classifiers have emerged, many of them building upon the algorithmic theory of randomness, such as (historically ordered) transduction-based confidence estimation, typicalness-based confidence estimation, transductive reliability estimation, and conformal prediction. In the chapter we describe a general approach to estimating quality of data mining predictions, based upon transductive reliability estimation and conformal prediction frameworks. The resulting conformal predictors produce confidence values in the statistical sense (e.g., a confidence level of 95% means that in 95% the predicted class is also a true class), as well as providing a general principle that is independent of the particular underlying data mining method.

8.1 Introduction

In recent years with pervasive use of data mining in various prediction problems, it became clear that it is very important to have some measure of how good a data mining prediction is. Often, data mining methods output only bare predictions (discrete classes for classification, or real-valued point predictions for regression problems) for the new unclassified examples. While there are ways for most data mining methods to at least partially provide quantitative assessment of the particular predictions, this is often difficult to achieve (especially when using commercial closed-source tools). Insofar there exists no general method to assess the quality (confidence, reliability) of single predictions. Thus we focus on quality assessment of data mining method's performance with respect to a *single prediction* and not on predicting the method's expected performance on an independent dataset. Quality assessments of single predictions are very useful, especially in risk-sensitive applications (medical diagnosis, financial and critical control applications) because there it often matters how much we can rely upon a given prediction. This has been made all the more evident in October 2012: seven scientific experts in Italy were convicted of manslaughter and sentenced to six years in prison for failing to give warning before the April 2009 earthquake that killed 309 people [79]. This raises a question of data scientists' responsibility for predictions, including the tools they use [275]. In such cases an overall quality measure of a predictor (e.g., predictive accuracy, mean squared error, ...) with respect to the whole input distribution would not provide the desired value. Another use of quality assessment of single predictions is in ensembles of data mining methods for selecting or combining answers of different predictors [187].

There have been numerous attempts to assign probabilities to data mining predictors (decision trees and rules, Bayesian classifiers, neural networks, nearest neighbor classifiers, etc.) in order to interpret their decision as a probability distribution over all possible classes. In fact, we can trivially convert every machine learning classifier's output to a probability distribution by assigning the predicted class the probability 1, and 0 to all other possible classes. The posterior probability of the predicted class can be viewed as a classifier's confidence (reliability) of its prediction. However, such estimations may in general not be good due to inherent data mining algorithms' biases.[1]

---

[1] An extreme case of inherent bias can be found in a trivial constant classifier that blindly labels any example with a predetermined class with the self-proclaimed confidence of 100%.

In this chapter we present a further development of two reviewed approaches where transductive reliability estimation serves as a generic non-conformity (strangeness) measure in the conformal prediction framework.

The chapter is organized as follows. In Section 8.2 we review several approaches aiming to assess the quality of single predictions in terms of confidence values and intervals, related to both terms of goal and methods. In Section 8.3 we describe the basic ideas of generalized transductive reliability estimation, and outline the process of its integration in conformal prediction framework. We also present some extensions of the original approach used for regression problems. In Section 8.4 we evaluate how our methodology compares to some other approaches in 15 domains with six machine learning algorithms. In Section 8.5 we present some conclusions and directions for future work, and discuss the online/offline dilemma of our approach.

8.2 Related Work

In statistics, estimation for individual predictions is assessed by confidence values and intervals. On the same basis, the reliability estimation was implemented in machine learning methods, where properties of predictive models were utilized to endow predictions with corresponding reliability estimates. Although these approaches are specific for a particular predictive model and cannot be generalized, they provide favorable results to the general approaches. Such reliability estimates were developed for the Support Vector Machines [115,297] the ridge regression model [251], the multilayer perceptron [376], the ensembles of neural networks [143,47], and others.

In contrast to the former group of methods, general (model-independent) methods utilize approaches, such as local modeling of prediction error based on input space properties and local learning [27,117], metapredicting the leave-one-out error of a single example [344], transductive reasoning [280,187], and sensitivity analysis [43,171,176,41,40].

Sensitivity analysis aims at determining how much the variation of input can influence the output of a system. The idea for putting the reliability estimation in the context of the sensitivity analysis framework is, therefore, in observing the changes in model outputs by modifying its inputs. Treating the predictive model as a black box, the sensitivity analysis approach, therefore, indirectly analyzes qualitatively describable aspects of the model, such as generalization ability, bias, resistance to noise, avoidance of overfitting, and so on. The motivation came from the related fields of data perturbation [90] and colearning (using unlabeled examples in supervised learning) [31]. Transductive reliability estimation (Section 8.2.2 and 8.3.2) can be viewed as an intersection of these two fields, as it perturbs the training set with a single unlabeled example.

8.2.1 Conformal Prediction

According to [315], conformal prediction uses past experience to determine precise levels of confidence in predictions. Given a method for making a prediction $\widehat{y}$, conformal prediction produces a $1 - \epsilon$ say, 95% prediction region Γ^ϵ—a set that contains true y with probability at least 95% (and normally also contains the prediction $\widehat{y}$).

$\widehat{y}$ is a point prediction, and Γ is a region prediction (or interval prediction in the case of regression). In the case of classification, where y has a limited number of possible values, Γ may consist of a few of these values, or ideally, of just one.

In conformal prediction we start from the method for point prediction, and construct a nonconformity (also called strangeness) measure, which measures how unusual an example looks relative to previous examples. The conformal algorithm turns this nonconformity measure into prediction regions.

Given a nonconformity measure A, the conformal algorithm (Figure 8.1) produces a prediction region Γ^ϵ for every probability of error ϵ. The region Γ^ϵ a $(1 - \epsilon)$ prediction region; it contains y with probability at least $1 - \epsilon$. In classification, we can also reverse the problem: given the prediction $\widehat{y}$, we may ask how small ϵ can be made before we must enlarge Γ^ϵ by inserting another class label; the corresponding value of $1 - \epsilon$ is the confidence (quality) of the predicted label $\widehat{y}$.

Creating a nonconformity measure for a particular data mining algorithm can be a challenge that also requires an in-depth knowledge of its working. The main focus of our work is leveraging the transduction principle (Sections 8.2.2 and 8.3.2) in order to establish a generic approach for producing nonconformity measure functions.

8.2.2 Confidence Estimation and the Transduction Principle

Several methods for inducing probabilistic descriptions from training data, figuring the use of density estimation algorithms, are emerging as an alternative to more established approaches for machine learning. Frequently kernel density estimation [371] is used for density estimation of input data using diverse machine learning paradigms such as probabilistic neural networks [331], Bayesian networks and classifiers [163], and decision trees [330]. By this approach a chosen paradigm, coupled with kernel density estimation, is used for modeling the probability distribution of input data. Alternatively, stochastically changing class labels in the training dataset is proposed [136] in order to estimate conditionally class probability.

Input: Nonconformity measure $A(\textit{example set, example})$, significance
level ϵ, examples $z_1, \ldots, z_n$, object x_{n+1}, label y
Output: Decision whether to include the label y in $\Gamma^\epsilon(\{z_1, \ldots, z_n\}, x_{n+1})$.

1: Provisionally set $z_{n+1} = (x_{n+1}, y)$.
2: For $i = 1 \ldots n + 1$, set $\alpha_i = A(\{z_1, \ldots, z_{n+1}\} - \{z_i\}, z_i)$
3: Set $p_y = \frac{\#\{i = 1 \ldots n+1 | \alpha_i \geq \alpha_{n+1}\}}{n}$
4: Include y in $\Gamma^\epsilon(\{z_1, ..., z_n\}, x_{n+1})$ if and only if $p_y > \epsilon$.

FIGURE 8.1

The conformal algorithm for a set of examples $z_1, \ldots, z_n$, an object x_{n+1}, and a nonconformity measure A [315].

There is some ongoing work for constructing classifiers that divide the data space into reliable and unreliable regions [18]. Such metalearning approaches have also been used for picking the most reliable prediction from the outputs of an ensemble of classifiers [307].

Metalearning community is partially dealing with predicting the right machine learning algorithm for a particular problem [272] based on performance and characteristics of other, simpler learning algorithms. In our problem of confidence estimation such an approach would result in learning to predict confidence value based on characteristics of single examples.

A lot of work has been done in applications of the transduction methodology [297], in connection with algorithmic theory of randomness. Here, approximations of randomness deficiency for different methods (SVMs, ridge regression) have been constructed in order to estimate confidence of single predictions. The drawback of this approach is that confidence estimations need to be specifically designed for each particular method and cannot be applied to other methods.

Another approach to reliability estimation, similarly based on the transduction principle, has been proposed in [187]. While it is general and independent of the underlying classifier, interpretation of its results isn't always possible in the statistical sense of confidence levels.

Recently, typicalness has emerged as a complementary approach to transduction [226,280,144]. By this approach, a "strangeness" measure of a single example is used to calculate its typicalness, and consequently a confidence in classifier's prediction. The main drawback of this approach is that for each machine learning algorithm it needs an appropriately constructed strangeness measure. The typicalness framework can be considered as a predecessor (with slightly stronger assumptions) to the conformal prediction approach.

8.3 **Generalized Transductive Reliability Estimation**

Reliability (quality) estimation of a classification ($\widehat{y}$) of a single example (x), given its true class (y) should have the following property:

$$\mathrm{Rel}(\widehat{y} \mid x) = t \implies P(\widehat{y} \neq y) \leq 1 - t \tag{8.1}$$

If Eq. (8.1) holds, or even better, if it approaches equality, a reliability measure can be treated as a confidence value [226].

The produced confidence values should be valid in the following sense. Given some possible label space $\mathbf{Y}$, if an algorithm predicts some set of labels $Y \subseteq \mathbf{Y}$ with confidence t for a new example that is truly labeled by $y \in \mathbf{Y}$, then we would expect the following to hold over randomization of the training set and the new example:

$$P(y \notin Y) \leq 1 - t \tag{8.2}$$

Note that Eq. (8.2) is very general and valid for both classification (Y is predicted set of classes) and regression problems (Y is a predicted interval). As we deal only with single predictions in this chapter, Eq. (8.2) can be simplified to a single predicted class value ($Y = \{\hat{y}\}$):

$$P(y \neq \hat{y}) \leq 1 - t \tag{8.3}$$

8.3.1 Typicalness

In the typicalness framework [226,251,297] we consider a sequence of examples $(z_1, \ldots, z_n) = ((x_1, y_1), \ldots, (x_n, y_n))$, together with a new example x_{n+1} with an unknown label $\hat{y}_{n+1}$, all drawn independently from the same distribution over $\mathbf{Z} = \mathbf{X} \times \mathbf{Y}$ where $\mathbf{X}$ is an attribute space and $\mathbf{Y}$ is a label space. Our only assumption is therefore that the training as well as new (unlabeled) examples are independently and identically distributed (i.i.d. assumption).

We can use the typicalness framework to gain confidence information for each possible labeling for a new example x_{n+1}. We postulate some labels $\hat{y}_{n+1}$ and for each one we examine how likely (typical) it is that all elements of the extended sequence $((x_1, y_1), \ldots, (x_{n+1}, \hat{y}_{n+1}))$ might have been drawn independently from the same distribution or how typically i.i.d. the sequence is. The more typical the sequence, the more confident we are in $\hat{y}_{n+1}$. To measure the typicalness of sequences, we define, for every $n \in \mathbb{N}$, a typicalness function $t : \mathbf{Z}^n \rightarrow [0, 1]$ which, for any $\epsilon \in [0, 1]$ has the property

$$P((z_1, \ldots, z_n) : t(z_1, \ldots, z_n) \leq \epsilon) \leq \epsilon \tag{8.4}$$

If a typicalness function returns 0.05 for a given sequence, we know that the sequence is unusual because it will be produced at most 5% of the time by any i.i.d. process. It has been shown [226] that we can construct such functions by considering the "strangeness" of individual examples. If we have some family of functions

$$f : \mathbf{Z}^n \times \{1, 2, \ldots, n\} \rightarrow \mathbb{R}, \quad n \in \mathbb{N} \ldots, \tag{8.5}$$

then we can associate a strangeness value

$$\alpha(z_i) = f(\{z_1, \ldots, z_n\}; i), \quad i = 1, 2, \ldots n \tag{8.6}$$

with each example and define the following typicalness function

$$t((z_1, \ldots, z_n)) = \frac{\#\{\alpha(z_i) : \alpha(z_i) \geq \alpha(z_n)\}}{n} \tag{8.7}$$

We group individual strangeness functions α_i into a family of functions $A_n : n \in \mathbb{N}$, where $A_n : \mathbf{Z}^n \rightarrow \mathbb{R}^n$ for all n. This is called an individual strangeness measure if, for any n, any permutation $\pi : \{1, \ldots, n\} \rightarrow \{1, \ldots, n\}$, any sequence $(z_1, \ldots, z_n) \in \mathbf{Z}^n$, and any $(\alpha_{\pi(1)}, \ldots, \alpha_{\pi(n)}) \in \mathbb{R}^n)$ it satisfies the following criterion [226]:

$$(\alpha_1, \ldots, \alpha_n) = A_n(z_1, \ldots, z_n) \Longrightarrow$$
$$(\alpha_{\pi(1)}, \ldots, \alpha_{\pi(n)}) = A_n(z_{\pi(1)}, \ldots, z_{\pi(n)}) \tag{8.8}$$

The meaning of this criterion is that the same value should be produced for each individual element in sequence, regardless of the order in which their individual strangeness values are calculated. This is a very important criterion, because it can be proven [226] that the constructed typicalness function (8.7) satisfies the condition from (8.4), provided that the individual strangeness measure satisfies the criterion (8.8).

From a practical point of view it is advisable [226] to use positive strangeness measures (ranging between 0 for most typical examples) and some positive upper bound (up to $+\infty$) for most untypical examples.

Typicalness in machine learning

In the machine learning setup, for calculating the typicalness of a new example $z_{n+1} = (x_{n+1}, \widehat{y}_{n+1})$ described with attribute values x_{n+1} and labeled with $\widehat{y}_{n+1}$, given the training set $(z_1, \ldots, z_n)$, Eq. (8.7) changes to

$$t((z_1, \ldots, z_{n+1})) = \frac{\#\{\alpha(z_i) : \alpha(z_i) \geq \alpha(z_{n+1})\}}{n+1} \tag{8.9}$$

Note that on the right-hand side of Eq. (8.9), z_i belongs to the extended sequence, $z_i \in \{z_1, \ldots, z_{n+1}\}$. For a given machine learning algorithm, first we need to construct an appropriate strangeness measure and modify the algorithm accordingly. Then, for each new unlabeled example x, all possible labels $\widehat{y} \in Y$ are considered. For each label $\widehat{y}$ a typicalness of labeled example $t((x, \widehat{y})) = t((z_1, \ldots, z_n, (x, \widehat{y})))$ is calculated. Finally, the example is labeled with "most typical" class, that is the one that maximizes $\{t((x, \widehat{y}))\}$. By Eq. (8.7) the second largest typicalness is an upper bound on the probability that the excluded classifications are correct [280]. Consequently, the confidence is calculated as follows:

$$\text{confidence}((x, \widehat{y})) = 1 - \text{typicalness of second most typical label.} \tag{8.10}$$

8.3.2   **Transductive Reliability Estimation**

Transduction is an inference principle that takes a training sample and aims at estimating the values of a discrete or continuous function only at given unlabeled points of interest from input space, as opposed to the whole input space for induction. In the learning process the unlabeled points are suitably labeled and included into the training sample. The usefulness of unlabeled data has also been advocated in the context of cotraining. It has been shown [31] that for every better-than-random classifier its performance can be significantly boosted by utilizing only additional unlabeled data.

It has been suggested [352] that when solving a given problem we should avoid solving a more general problem as an intermediate step. The reasoning behind this principle is that, in order to solve a more general task, resources may be wasted or compromises made that would not have been necessary for solving only the problem at hand (i.e., function estimation only on given points). This common-sense principle reduces a more general problem of inferring a functional dependency on the whole input space (inductive inference) to the problem of estimating the values of a function only at given points (transductive inference).

A formal background

Let $\mathbf{X}$ be a space of attribute descriptions of points (examples) in a training sample (dataset), and $\mathbf{Y}$ a space of labels (continuous or discrete) assigned to each point. Given a probability distribution $\mathcal{P}$, defined on the input space $\mathbf{X} \times \mathbf{Y}$, a training sample

$$S = \{(x_1, y_1), \ldots, (x_l, y_l)\} \tag{8.11}$$

consisting of l points, is drawn i.i.d. according to $\mathcal{P}$. Additional m data points (working sample)

$$W = \{x_{l+1}, \ldots, x_{l+m}\} \tag{8.12}$$

with unknown labels are drawn in the same manner. The goal of transductive inference is to label all the points from the sample W using a fixed set $\mathcal{H}$ of functions $f : \mathbf{X} \rightarrow \mathbf{Y}$ in order to minimize an error functional both in the training sample S and in the working sample W (effectively, in $S \cup W$). In contrast, inductive inference aims at choosing a single function $f \in \mathcal{H}$ that is best suited to the unknown probability distribution $\mathcal{P}$.

At this point there arises a question on how to calculate labels of points from a working sample. This can be done by labeling every point from a working sample with every possible label value; however given m working points this leads to a combinatorial explosion yielding n^m possible labelings. For each possible labeling, an induction process on $S \cup W$ is run, and an error functional (error rate) is calculated.

By leveraging the i.i.d. sampling assumption and transductive inference, for each labeling we can estimate its reliability (also referred to as confidence, a probability that it is correct). If the i.i.d. assumption holds, the training sample S as well as the joint correctly labeled sample $S \cup W$ should both reflect the same underlying probability distribution $\mathcal{P}$.

If we could measure a degree of similarity between probability distributions $\mathcal{P}(S)$ and $\mathcal{P}(S \cup W)$, this could be used as a measure of reliability of the particular labeling. Unfortunately, this problem in general belongs to the noncomputable class [208], so approximation methods have to be used [364,184].

Evaluation of prediction reliability for single points in data space has many uses. It often matters how much we can rely upon a given prediction of a risk-sensitive application (e.g., medical diagnosis, financial, and critical control applications). In such a case a general reliability measure of a classifier (e.g., classification accuracy, mean, squared error, etc.) with respect to the whole input distribution would not provide the desired warranty. Another use of reliability estimations is in combining answers from different predictors, weighed according to their reliability.

The transductive reliability estimation process and its theoretical foundations originating from Kolmogorov complexity are described in more detail in [187]. Basically, we have a two-step process, featuring an *inductive step* followed by a *transductive step*.

- An *inductive step* is just like an ordinary inductive learning process in machine learning. A machine learning algorithm is run on the training set, *inducing* a

classifier. A selected example is taken from an independent dataset and classified using the induced classifier. An example labeled with the classified class is
temporarily included into the training set.

- A *transductive step* is almost a repetition of an inductive step. A machine learning
  algorithm is run on the changed training set, *transducing* a classifier. The same
  example as before is taken from the independent dataset and classified using
  the transduced classifier. Both classifications of the same example are compared
  and their difference (distance) is calculated, thus approximating the randomness
  deficiency.

- After the reliability is calculated, the example in question is removed from the
  training set.

In practice the inductive step is performed only once, namely on the original
training set. New examples are not permanently included in the training set; this
would be improper since the correct class is at this point still unknown. Although
retraining for each new example seems to be highly time consuming, it is not such
a problem in practice, especially if incremental learners (such as naive Bayesian
classifier) are used.

A brief algorithmic sketch is given in Figure 8.2. An intuitive explanation of
transductive reliability estimation is that we disturb a classifier by inserting a new
example in a training set. A magnitude of this disturbance is an estimation of a
classifier's instability (unreliability) in a given region of its problem space.

Input: Machine learning classifier, a training set, and an unlabeled test
example
Output: Estimation of test example's classification reliability

1: Inductive step:

- train a classifier from the provided training set
- select an unlabeled test example
- classify this example with an induced classifier
- label this example with a predicted class
- temporarily add the newly labeled example to the training set

2: Transductive step:

- train a classifier from the extended training set
- select the same unlabeled test example as above
- classify this example with a transduced classifier

3: Calculate a randomness deficiency approximation as a *normalized difference* $J_N(P, Q)$
between inductive (P) and transductive (Q) classification.

4: Calculate the reliability of classification as $1 - $ *normalized difference*, as in a universal
Martin-Löf's test for randomness

FIGURE 8.2

The algorithm for transductive reliability estimation.

Since a prerequisite for a machine learning algorithm is to represent its classifications as a probability distribution over all possible classes (it may, however, be biased), we need a method to measure the difference between two probability distributions. The difference measure D should ideally satisfy all requirements for a distance (i.e., nonnegativity, triangle nonequality, and symmetry), however in practice nonnegativity suffices. For calculating the difference between probability distributions, a *Kullback-Leibler divergence* is frequently used [118,338]. Kullback-Leibler divergence, sometimes referred to as a relative entropy or I-divergence, is defined between probability distributions P and Q

$$I(P, Q) = -\sum_{i=1}^{n} p_i \log_2 \frac{p_i}{q_i} \tag{8.13}$$

In our experiments we use a symmetric Kullback-Leibler divergence, or J-divergence, which is defined as follows:

$$J(P, Q) = \big(I(P, Q) + I(Q, P)\big) = \sum_{i=1}^{n} (p_i - q_i) \log_2 \frac{p_i}{q_i} \tag{8.14}$$

$J(P, Q)$ is limited to the interval $[0, \infty]$, where $J(P, P) = 0$. Since in this context we require the values to be from the $[0, 1]$ interval we normalize it in the spirit of Martin-Löf's test for randomness.

$$J_N(P, Q) = 1 - 2^{-J(P,Q)} \tag{8.15}$$

However, measuring the difference between probability distributions does not always perform well. There are at least a few exceptional classifiers (albeit trivial ones) where the original approach utterly fails.

Assessing the classifier's quality: the curse of trivial models

So far we have implicitly assumed that the model used by the classifier is good (at the very least better than random). Unsurprisingly, our approach works very well with random classifiers (probability distributions are randomly calculated) by effectively labeling their classifications as unreliable [184,185].

On the other hand, there also exist anomalous *constant* and *majority* classifiers. A *constant classifier* is such that it classifies all examples into the same class C_k with probability 1. In such cases our approach always yields reliability 1 since there is no change in probability distribution. A *majority classifier* is such that it classifies all examples into the same class C_k that is the majority class in the training set. Probability distribution is always the same and corresponds to the distribution of classes in the training set. In such cases our approach yields reliability very close to 1 since there is almost no change in probability distribution (only for the example in question), that is at most for $1/N$, where N is the number of training examples. In large datasets this change is negligible.

Note that such extreme cases do occur in practice and even in real life. For example, a physician who, due to unfortunate past experience, always diagnoses an incoming patient as ill, is a constant classifier. On the other hand, a degenerated—overpruned—decision tree (one leaf only) is a typical majority classifier.

In both cases all classifications are seemingly completely reliable. Obviously we also need to take in account the quality of classifier's underlying model and appropriately change our definition of reliability.

We assume that the learned (induced) data model is good. Our reliability estimations actually estimate the conditional reliability with respect to the model M

$$\text{Rel}(y_i|M) = P(y_i \text{ is a true class of } x_i \mid \text{model M is good}) \qquad (8.16)$$

To calculate the required unconditional reliability, we apply the conditional probability theorem for the whole model

$$\text{Rel}'(y_i) = P(\text{model M is good}) * P(y_i \text{ is true class of } x_i \mid \text{model M is good}) \qquad (8.17)$$

or even better for the partial models for each class y_i

$$\text{Rel}'(y_i) = P(\text{model M is good for } y_i) * \qquad (8.18)$$
$$P(y_i \text{ is true class of } x_i | \text{model M is good for } y_i)$$

Now we only need to estimate the unconditional probabilities

$$P(\text{model is good}) \quad \text{or} \quad \forall i : P(\text{model is good for } y_i) \qquad (8.19)$$

In machine learning we have many methods to estimate the quality of the induced model; for example, a cross-validation computation of classification accuracy is suitable for estimation of Eq. (8.19). However it may be better to calculate it in a less coarse way, since at this point we already know the predicted class value (y_i).

We propose a Bayesian calculation of probability that the classification in a certain class is correct. Our approach is closely related to the calculation of posttest probabilities [80,255]. Required factors can be easily estimated from the confusion matrix (Definition 8.1) with internal testing.

Definition 8.1. A *confusion matrix (CM)* is a matrix of classification errors obtained with an internal cross validation or leave-one-out testing on the training dataset. The ij-th element c_{ij} stands for the number of classifications to the class i that should belong to the class j.

$$CM = \begin{pmatrix} c_{11} & c_{12} & c_{13} & \cdots & c_{1N} \\ c_{21} & c_{22} & c_{23} & \cdots & c_{2N} \\ c_{31} & c_{32} & c_{33} & \cdots & c_{3N} \\ \vdots & \vdots & \vdots & \ddots & \vdots \\ c_{N1} & c_{N2} & c_{N3} & \cdots & c_{NN} \end{pmatrix}$$

$$c_{ij} = \text{number of classifications to class i that belong to class j} \qquad (8.20)$$

Definition 8.2. Class sensitivity and specificity are a generalization of sensitivity (true positives ratio) and specificity (true negatives ratio) values for multiclass problems. Basically, for N classes we have N two-class problems. Let C_p be a correct class in certain case, and C a class, predicted by the classifier in the same case. For each of possible classes $C_i, i \in \{1..N\}$, we define its *class sensitivity* $Se(C_i) = P(C = C_i|C_p = C_i)$ and its *class specificity* $Sp(C_i) = P(C \neq C_i|C_p \neq C_i)$ as follows:

$$Se(C_i) = P(C = C_i|C_p = C_i) = \frac{c_{ii}}{\sum_j c_{ij}} \tag{8.21}$$

$$Sp(C_i) = P(C \neq C_i|C_p \neq C_i) = \frac{\sum_{j \neq i} c_{ji}}{\sum_{j \neq i} \sum_k c_{jk}} \tag{8.22}$$

Class conditional probability is calculated for each class C_i, given its prior probability $P(C_i)$, approximated with the prevalence of C_i in the training set, its class specificity (Sp), and sensitivity (Se):

$$\mathrm{P_{cond}}(C_i) = \frac{P(C_i)\mathrm{Se}(C_i)}{P(C_i)\mathrm{Se}(C_i) + (1 - P(C_i))(1 - \mathrm{Sp}(C_i))} \tag{8.23}$$

To calculate the reliability estimation we therefore need the probability distributions P and Q, and index $i = \mathrm{argmax}\, P$ that determines the class with max. probability (C_i). According to Eq. (8.18) we calculate the reliability estimations by

$$Rel(P, Q; C_i) = P_{cond}(C_i) \times J_N(P, Q) \tag{8.24}$$

Multiplication by class conditional probabilities accounts for basic domain characteristics (prevalence of classes) as well as classifier's performance. This includes class sensitivity and specificity, and it is especially useful in an automatic setting for detecting possible anomalies such as default (either majority or constant classifiers) that, of course, cannot be trusted. It is easy to see that in this case we have one class with sensitivity 1 and specificity 0, whereas for all other classes we have sensitivity 0 and nonzero specificity. In the first case, the class post-test probability is equal to its prior probability, whereas in the second case it is 0.

8.3.3 Merging the Typicalness and Transduction Frameworks

The rationale for merging typicalness and transductive reliability estimation frameworks is as follows. While transduction gives useful reliability estimations (see Figure 8.3a), they are often hard to interpret in the statistical sense. On the other hand, the typicalness framework gives clear confidence values, however in order to achieve this a good strangeness measure $\alpha(z_i)$ needs to be constructed.

Of course, there is a trivial solution to it, namely a uniform strangeness measure $\alpha_i = C$, where C is some constant value. Unfortunately, this does us no good, since it treats all examples as equally strange and can be considered as most conservative strangeness measure. It is therefore necessary to construct a sensible strangeness

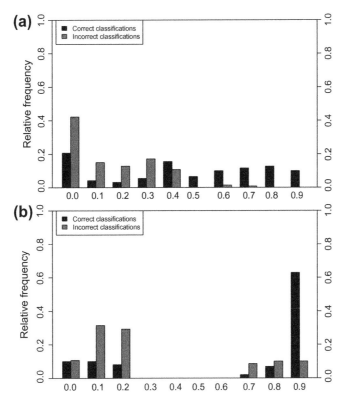

FIGURE 8.3

Relative frequencies of reliability estimation and confidence level values in Soybean dataset using neural networks. Confidence levels are separated much clearly, and are more easily interpretable.

measure. In [226,298,280] some ideas on how to construct strangeness measures for different machine learning algorithms are presented.

On the other hand, as we shall see later, for a strangeness measure we can always use transductive reliability estimation. We may speculate that the most "reliable" example labelings are also least strange (or least nonconformant). Therefore we define the strangeness measure for a new example $z_{n+1} = (x_{n+1}, \widehat{y}_{n+1})$, described with attribute values x_{n+1} and labeled with $\widehat{y}_{n+1}$, given the training set $(z_1, \ldots, z_n)$ as follows:

$$\alpha(z_{n+1}) = f(z_1, \ldots, z_{n+1}; n+1) = 1 - \text{Rel}(z_{n+1}) \in [0, 1] \qquad (8.25)$$

It is easy to see that such a strangeness function satisfies the criterion from Eq. (8.8) and therefore has the property required by Eq. (8.7).

The training set is only temporarily changed by including a suitably labeled new example in a transductive step (Figure 8.2). It is restored back to the initial training set as soon as the reliability estimation is calculated. Therefore the training set remains invariant for all new examples for which the reliability estimation needs to be calculated. It follows that it is irrelevant in which order the examples are presented and the criterion for Eq. (8.8) is therefore satisfied. Note that Eq. (8.8) does not require that examples are ordered in any particular way, but only that any permutation of the order of their evaluations produces the same result for each example.

Consequently we can, for any machine learning classifier, universally use a strangeness measure $\alpha((x, \widehat{y})) = 1 - Rel((x, \widehat{y}))$ (although, as we shall see later, in the typicalness setting this expression can be even more simplified). It is positive, and the "more strange" examples have higher strangeness values, as suggested in [226].

Simplification of transductive reliability estimation for application within the typicalness framework

Alternatively, the calculation of the strangeness measure can, in the context of typicalness and reliability estimation, be much simplified. Simplifications are twofold.

1. Since the only requirement for strangeness measure is that it is positive, no transformations to [0, 1] interval are necessary. The transformation is actually performed by Eq. (8.9).
2. The typicalness framework efficiently deals with extremely deviant classifiers (such as those from Section 8.3.2). As an example, let us consider the most "pathological" case, the constant classifier. Therefore all strangeness values are equal (i.e., all examples are equally (maximally) strange). Note that in this case magnitudes of strangeness values are irrelevant as they are all the same. By Eq. (8.9) it follows that for all possible classifications of every (new) example the typicalness is therefore 1.0. By Eq. (8.10) this yields confidence of 0. Such trivial classifiers are therefore maximally distrusted.

Let $P_{(x,\widehat{y})}$ and $Q_{(x,\widehat{y})}$ be the probability distributions obtained after the inductive step ($P_{(x,\widehat{y})}$) and transductive step ($Q_{(x,\widehat{y})}$) of the algorithm from Figure 8.2. It can easily be shown that the strangeness measure requirement (Eq. (8.8)) holds also for $\alpha((x, \widehat{y})) = J(P_{(x,\widehat{y})}, Q_{(x,\widehat{y})})$ (symmetric Kullback-Leibler divergence) as well as for $\alpha((x, \widehat{y})) = I(P_{(x,\widehat{y})}, Q_{(x,\widehat{y})})$ (asymmetric Kullback-Leibler divergence).

An implementation of transductive reliability estimation in typicalness framework is straightforward. For all training examples, reliability estimation is calculated by leave-one-out testing, and they are labeled as correctly or incorrectly classified. For each new example x with classification $\widehat{y}$ its confidence conf$((x, \widehat{y}))$ is calculated as in Section 8.3.1, Eq. (8.10). Regardless of the number of classes in the original problem, there are only two possibilities (metaclasses) for each classification. It is either correct or incorrect. Therefore we always deal with exactly two metaclasses that represent correct classifications and incorrect classifications. As we want the confidence to reflect the probability of a correct classification, we need to invert the confidence values for incorrect metaclass:

$$\text{confidence}((x, \widehat{y})) = \begin{cases} \text{conf}((x, \widehat{y})) & \text{"correct" metaclass,} \\ 1 - \text{conf}((x, \widehat{y})) & \text{"incorrect" metaclass.} \end{cases} \tag{8.26}$$

Strictly speaking, an efficient implementation can only be made for offline (batch) learning. Consider our definition of a strangeness (nonconformity) measure (8.25). If we want to use precalculated α values in an online setting, they may not be correct, as our strangeness measure changes with every used example. Although these changes may be infinitely small in the limit, they may affect the calculation of typicalness (p-values). Alternatively, we could recalculate α values in every step (as in the basic conformant prediction algorithm on Figure 8.1), but this would in most cases impose a severe performance hit. Therefore, we focus only on offline learning. The conformal prediction framework is basically an evolution of the typicalness framework with weaker assumptions (exchangeability vs i.i.d.) and the ability to use it in an online setting. Because of possible inefficiency (if staying really strict) of our method in an online setting, we therefore use the typicalness framework terminology in order to avoid confusion.

8.3.4 Extension of Transductive Reliability Estimation to Regression by Means of Local Sensitivity Analysis

In the regression the procedure for generating a nonconformity measure is similar except that the predicted label is first slightly corrupted: $\widehat{y} = \widehat{y}_{predicted} + \delta$ and then we insert the newly generated instance $(x, \widehat{y})$ into the learning set and rebuild the predictive model. We define $\delta = \epsilon(l_{\max} - l_{\min})$, where ϵ expresses the proportion of the distance between largest ($l_{\max}$) and smallest ($l_{\min}$) prediction. In this way we obtain a sensitivity model, which computes a sensitivity estimate K_ϵ for the instance $(x, \_)$. To widen the observation window in local problem space and make the measures robust to local anomalies, the reliability measures use estimates from the sensitivity models, gained and averaged across different values of $\epsilon \in E$. For more details see [36]. Let us assume we have a set of nonnegative ϵ values $E = \epsilon_1, \epsilon_2, \ldots, \epsilon_{|E|}$. We define the estimates as follows:

- Estimate $SAvar$
  (Sensitivity Analysis local variance):

$$SAvar = \frac{\sum_{\epsilon \in E} (K_\epsilon - K_{-\epsilon})}{|E|} \tag{8.27}$$

- Estimate $SAbias$
  (Sensitivity Analysis local bias):

$$SAbias = \frac{\sum_{\epsilon \in E} (K_\epsilon - K) + (K_{-\epsilon} - K)}{2 |E|} \tag{8.28}$$

Bagging variance

In related work, the variance of predictions in the bagged aggregate of artificial neural networks has been used to estimate the reliability of the aggregated prediction [143,47]. The proposed reliability estimate is generalized to other models [37].

Let $K_i, i = 1 \ldots m$, be the predictor's class probability distribution for a given unlabeled example $(x, \_)$. Given a bagged aggregate of m predictive models, where each of the models yields a prediction $B_k, k = 1 \ldots m$, the reliability estimator $BAGV$ is defined as the variance of predictions' class probability distribution:

$$BAGV = \frac{1}{m} \sum_{k=1}^{m} \sum_{i} \left(B_{k,i} - K_i \right)^2 . \tag{8.29}$$

The algorithm uses a bagged aggregate of 50 predictive models as default.

Local cross-validation

The LCV (Local Cross-Validation) reliability estimate is computed using the local leave-one-out (L1O) procedure. Focusing on the subspace defined by k nearest neighbors, we generate k (usually one tenth of the size of the learning set) local models, each of them excluding one of the k nearest neighbors. Using the generated models, we compute the L1O predictions $K_i, i = 1 \ldots k$, for each of the k excluded nearest neighbors. Since the labels $C_i, i = 1 \ldots k$, of the nearest neighbors are known, we are able to calculate the local L1O prediction error as the average of the nearest neighbors' local errors:

$$LCV = \frac{1}{k} \sum_{i} |C_i - K_i| . \tag{8.30}$$

Local error modeling

Given a set of k nearest neighbors, where C_i is the true label of the i-th nearest neighbor, the estimate CNK ($C_{Neighbors} - K$) is defined as the difference between average label of the k nearest neighbors and the instance's prediction K:

$$CNK = \frac{\sum_i C_i}{k} - K . \tag{8.31}$$

CNK is not a suitable reliability estimate for the k-nearest neighbors algorithm, as they both work by the same principle. In regression tests, CNK-a denotes the absolute value of the estimate, whereas CNK-s denotes the signed value.

8.3.5 Testing Methodology

To validate the proposed methodology we performed extensive experiments with six different machine learning algorithms: naive and seminaive Bayesian classifier [181], backpropagation neural network [293], K-nearest neighbor, locally naive Bayesian classifier (a combination KNN of and naive Bayesian classifier) [187], two kinds of Assistant (ID3-like decision trees) [180] on 14 well-known benchmark datasets from the UCI repository (Mesh, Breast cancer, Diabetes, Heart, Hepatitis, Iris, Chess endgame (king-rook vs. king), LED, Lymphography, Primary tumor, Rheumatology, Soybean, Voting), and on a real-life problem of nuclear cardiology diagnostics (Nuclear).

For each dataset and algorithm we determined for each training example by internal L1O testing its correctness, whether it was correctly (1) or incorrectly (0) classified. For reliability estimations, confidence values, and density estimations, we calculated their correlation with correctness. In an ideal case (each correct example has value 1, each incorrect 0), the result would be 1.

We also measured how well a method discriminates between correctly and incorrectly classified examples. For each method (reliability estimations, confidence values, and density estimations) we calculated the boundary b that maximizes the purity (information gain) of the discriminated examples. The boundary b is calculated by maximizing Eq. (8.32).

$$H(S) = -\frac{|S_1|}{|S|} \log_2 \frac{|S_1|}{|S|} - \frac{|S_2|}{|S|} \log_2 \frac{|S_2|}{|S|} \quad \text{(entropy before split)}$$

$$H(S; b) = \frac{|S_1|}{|S|} H(S_1) + \frac{|S_2|}{|S|} H(S_2) \quad \text{(entropy after split)}$$

$$\text{Gain}(S, b) = H(S) - H(S; b) \tag{8.32}$$

Here, S is the set consisting of all examples, in the set S_1 there are unreliable examples $\{z_i : \text{Rel}(z_i) < b\}$ whereas in the set S_2 there are reliable examples $\{z_i : \text{Rel}(z_i) \geq b\}$. In an ideal case when both splits are pure, the result would be equal to the entropy of classifications $H(S)$.

All experiments were performed by leave-one-out testing. In this setup, one example was reserved, while learning and preparatory calculations were performed on the rest, in many cases two nested L1O testings were carried out. Final results are averages of L1O experiments on all examples from the dataset.

Finally, we also applied our approach to several real-world problems. For classification, they include estimating quality of medical diagnosed from SPECT images [336] and a real-world application on a large database of 600,000 customers of a large local corporation [185]. Here, due to large quantities of data, testing methodology was slightly different. While L1O testing was still used for obtaining strangeness values for the training set (50%) of data, the remaining data was used as an independent testing set. For regression, experiments were performed for breast cancer recurrence prediction [337], electricity load forecast prediction [38], and predicting maximum artery wall shear stress magnitude and location [39].

8.4 **Experimental Results**

Experimental results were obtained with two different setups. The first one consists of a series of experiments on well-known (UCI) problem domains. These results were used to validate our approach and compare it with existing ones. The second experimental setup consists of applications in a real-life commercial data mining system. It also presents some valuable practical considerations.

8.4.1 Experiments on Benchmark Problems

Results of confidence estimation on KNN (nearest neighbor) algorithm are compared with the TCM-NN nearest neighbor confidence machine [280], where a tailor-made strangeness measure for confidence estimation in typicalness framework was constructed. In Table 8.1, experimental results in 15 domains are shown. Results of TCM-NN are slightly better, as could be expected from the tailor-made method, though the differences are not significant with two-tailed, paired t-test.

Comparing reliability and confidence

The obtained confidence values are compared with transductive reliability estimations and density estimations. Our first goal was to evaluate the performance of confidence values in terms of correlation with correctness, and its ability to separate correct and incorrect classifications in terms of information gain. Our second goal was to see whether confidence values are more easily interpretable than transductive reliability estimations.

Figure 8.3a and b depict how reliability estimations are transformed to confidence levels. This is a typical example and probably the most important result of our work, as it makes them easily statistically interpretable. On average, the best decision boundary for reliability estimations is 0.74; on the other hand, for confidence it is about 0.45.

Table 8.1 Comparison of confidence estimation on KNN with the algorithm-specific TCM-NN, both with 10 nearest neighbors. Accuracy was obtained with standard 10-NN algorithm.

	Accuracy	Correlation with correctness		Information gain (in bit)	
	KNN	TCM-NN	KNN	TCM-NN	KNN
Mesh	64.7%	0.49	0.40	0.26	0.19
Breast cancer	80.2%	0.09	0.14	0.02	0.03
Nuclear	81.0%	0.35	0.28	0.12	0.07
Diabetes	73.7%	0.26	0.19	0.06	0.05
Heart	79.3%	0.34	0.18	0.11	0.09
Hepatitis	85.2%	0.28	0.25	0.07	0.07
Iris	94.7%	0.23	0.36	0.12	0.12
Chess end.	92.0%	0.43	0.33	0.21	0.12
LED	73.2%	0.20	0.19	0.04	0.05
Lymphography	83.1%	0.50	0.22	0.32	0.18
Primary tumor	41.3%	0.10	0.37	0.00	0.19
Rheumatology	61.3%	0.42	0.42	0.17	0.16
Soybean	92.1%	0.32	0.38	0.12	0.12
Voting	94.0%	0.42	0.26	0.18	0.09
Average	78.3%	0.32	0.28	0.13	0.11

Table 8.2 Experimental results with confidence values, reliability and density estimations, with six machine learning algorithm in 15 datasets. Accuracy was calculated as an average of all six base classifiers.

Domain	Accuracy	Correlation with correctness		Information gain (in bit)	
		Reliability	Confidence	Reliability	Confidence
Mesh	65.7%	0.51	0.46	0.25	0.25
Breast cancer	77.4%	0.28	0.22	0.10	0.10
Nuclear	88.0%	0.21	0.21	0.07	0.08
Diabetes	74.3%	0.26	0.33	0.18	0.18
Heart	80.7%	0.26	0.27	0.11	0.11
Hepatitis	86.6%	0.25	0.30	0.12	0.11
Iris	93.8%	0.23	0.42	0.13	0.13
Chess endgame	95.5%	0.09	0.27	0.11	0.11
Chess endgame	71.1%	0.11	0.12	0.10	0.10
LED	73.0%	0.16	0.18	0.05	0.05
Lymphography	81.9%	0.20	0.27	0.13	0.13
Primary tumor	44.8%	0.39	0.38	0.16	0.16
Rheumatology	58.0%	0.47	0.48	0.22	0.22
Soybean	89.4%	0.35	0.37	0.14	0.13
Voting	94.0%	0.17	0.22	0.08	0.08
Average	78.3%	0.26	0.30	0.13	0.13

Also, the mass of correct and incorrect classification has shifted toward 1 and 0, respectively.

In Table 8.2, experimental results are presented. We see that confidence values significantly ($p < 0.05$ with two-tailed, paired t-test) outperform reliability estimations in terms of correlation with correctness. From Figure 8.3 it is clear that this is because of the shift toward 1 and 0. Information gains do not differ significantly.

8.4.2 Practical Applications and Considerations

We also did a practical application of integration of decision support system with data mining methods working with data from extensive customer relationship management (CRM) survey for a large local corporation. It turned out that immense quantities of raw data had been collected and needed to be assessed. Thus the use of data mining methods was called for. The system was implemented in Oracle application framework using Oracle's Data Mining (ODM) database extension. An Adaptive Bayesian Network classifier was used. The database consisted of about 600,000 customers' records consisting of up to 100 attributes. The preparatory calculations (L1O testing on training datasets) were quite lengthy as they took more than a week. However, producing a confidence estimation for a single customer was much more acceptable; depending on system use it took about a minute.

Produced confidence values were much better (on average by 0.2 bit of gained information) than the probability estimations of the applied Adaptive Bayesian Network classifier. There was also improvement of more than 10% of confident classification (confidence $\geq 95\%$). In practice this could save significant amounts of CRM campaign money. The main drawback of our approach in this particular problem is its relative slowness. It needed (back in 2005) more than a week to perform preparatory calculations and it took more than a week to calculate confidence values for all testing examples (customer records from independent set). However, this is what we have to pay when dealing with closed commercial systems. It may therefore not be suitable for quick real-time analysis, but is perfectly acceptable for assessment of individual customers. A great advantage of typicalness/transduction approach over other approaches (such as kernel density estimation) is that it can be easily implemented even with relatively closed (no source code available for modifications) commercial data mining systems.

The described reliability estimation methodology for regression has been implemented in several applications of machine learning and data mining in areas of medicine, financial applications, and economy. In these application domains, the bare regression predictions have been supplemented with a suitable reliability estimator (the best performing among the proposed was chosen after the initial evaluation study), which helped the users of predictive systems gain greater insight and confidence in single predictions. The most interesting of these applications are:

- Breast cancer recurrence prediction problem for the Institute of Oncology, Ljubljana [337]. The collected dataset included data for 1023 patients, for whom the task was to predict potential cancer recurrence for the next 20 years. Given that a predictive timespan is so wide and that it reaches into the far future, the difficulty of the predictive problem was alleviated by implementing reliability estimators.
- Electricity load forecast prediction problem for a particular European country [38]. Two regression models were implemented, the neural network and the k nearest neighbors algorithm and their predictions were corrected using the reliability estimator CNK. The results showed that the accuracy of corrected predictions using CNK is favorable in comparison to accuracy of predictions corrected with the referential Kalman filter method.
- Predicting maximum wall shear stress magnitude and its coordinates in the model of human carotid artery bifurcation [39]. Since one of the most common causes of human death is stroke, a medical expert system could significantly aid medical experts to detect hemodynamic abnormalities. Based on the acquired simulated data, we applied several prediction reliability estimators and the model explanation methodology that provided a useful tool for the given problem domain.

8.5 Discussion and Conclusions

We describe a general approach for constructing strangeness (nonconformity) measures based upon transduction. We use it within the typicalness framework in order to produce a joint confidence machine for almost any data mining algorithm. The resulting values are true confidence levels, and this makes them easy to interpret. Contrary to the other typicalness- and transduction-based confidence estimation methodologies, as well as conformal prediction, the described approach is not bound to a particular underlying classifier. This is an important improvement since this makes it possible to calculate confidence values for almost any classifier, no matter how complex it is.

Experimental comparison on comparable unmodified and modified algorithms (confidence estimation on k-nearest neighbor algorithm and TCM-NN nearest neighbor confidence machine) show that the proposed approach performs similarly to the specially modified algorithm. There is no significant reduction in performance while there is a huge gain in generality. Experimental results performed with different machine learning algorithms in several problem domains show that there is no reduction of discrimination performance with respect to transductive reliability estimation. More important than this, statistical interpretability of confidence values makes it possible for applications in risk-sensitive problems with strict confidence limits.

The main drawback of our approach is computational complexity, as it needs to perform the L1O testing in advance, and requires temporary re-learning of a classifier for each new example. However, this may not be a problem if incremental learners (such as naive Bayesian classifier) are used. On the other hand, the main advantages are its generality and ability to add it to existing data mining methods without requiring any changes (either not wanted or not allowed).

A conformal predictor should, given a method for making a prediction, produce an $1 - \epsilon$ prediction region Γ^ϵ, or, looking from another point of view, given a prediction $\widehat{y}$, produce a confidence level that this prediction is the correct one. In this sense, our approach corresponds nicely to the conformal prediction paradigm. There is, however, a possible caveat. Conformal prediction is designed for an online setting in which labels are predicted successively, each one being revealed before the next is predicted, and the nonconformity measure should produce the same value for each example, regardless of their order. If we strictly follow the conformal algorithm (Figure 8.1), we need to recalculate the nonconformity measure scores for all examples every time the new example is presented. This, however, can be unacceptably slow. If the nonconformity measure does not change with time (incoming examples), we can incrementally calculate nonconformity scores, and there would be no need to recalculate all of them for each incoming example. However, by our approach the nonconformity (strangeness) measure does change with incoming examples for an online setting, so we cannot do this. Therefore, we limit ourselves to using it in an offline setting, where no examples are added in the training set and therefore the nonconformity measure does not change.

We applied our approach in several problems, both for classification and regression problems, and obtained encouraging results. While our approach may be slower and produce slightly less confident predictions as tailor-made nonconformity measures, it is general and can be used even without access to learner's internals and/or source code. This can be a significant advantage, since it makes it possible to assess the quality of commercial, closed-source data mining tools by providing confidence values for their predictions.

Acknowledgments

This work was supported by the Ministry of Education, Science, Culture and Sport, and the Slovenian Research Agency.

Other Adaptations

Vineeth N. Balasubramanian[*], Prasanth Lade[†], Hemanth Venkateswara[†],
Evgueni Smirnov[‡] and Sethuraman Panchanathan[†]

[*]*Department of Computer Science and Engineering, Indian Institute of Technology,*
Hyderabad, India
[†]*Center for Cognitive Ubiquitous Computing, Arizona State University, AZ, USA*
[‡]*Department of Knowledge Engineering, Maastricht University, Maastricht, The Netherlands*

CHAPTER OUTLINE HEAD

9.1 Introduction

The previous chapters demonstrated how the Conformal Predictions (CP) framework has been adapted to traditional machine learning problems including active learning, feature selection, anomaly detection, change detection, model selection, and quality estimation. In this last chapter of the Adaptations section, we describe three other extensions of the CP framework, each of which is nontraditional in its own way. The task of obtaining a reliability value for the classification of a data instance has been the focus of a number of studies [16,60,85,157,315,327,365,391].

In Sections 9.2 and 9.3, we describe two methods that use the idea of a meta classifier to associate reliability values with output predictions from a base classifier. In particular, in Section 9.2, we describe the Metaconformal Predictors proposed by Smirnov et al. [328], where a base classifier is combined with a metaclassifier that is trained on metadata generated from the data instances and the classification results of the base classifier to associate reliability values on the classification of data instances. In Section 9.3, we describe the Single-Stacking Conformal Predictors proposed by Smirnov et al. in [329] where an ensemble classifier consisting of the base classifier and the meta classifier is constructed to compute reliability values on the classification outputs. The difference between the metaconformal and the single-stacking approaches is the manner in which the metadata are constructed and the way in which the reliability values are estimated.

In Section 9.4, we describe the application of conformal predictors to online time series analysis as proposed by Dashevskiy and Luo [70]. As mentioned earlier, the emphvalidity property of the CP framework makes it an attractive prediction tool for real-world applications involving machine learning algorithms (see Chapter 1). However, this property relies on the exchangeability assumption, which is not generally associated with time series data. Dashevskiy and Luo [70] proposed different methods to transform time series data in order to apply the CP framework to derive conformal prediction intervals using regression models. We briefly describe the overall idea, while the details of this methodology have been presented in Chapter 12.

9.2 Metaconformal Predictors

Smirnov et al. [328] noted that there are settings when it may not be possible to define a suitable nonconformity measure for a classifier (for instance, when the algorithmic details of a classifier are not known such as when a human expert is the classifier). For such cases, Smirnov proposed the Metaconformal Predictor. We begin our discussion with a description of classifier performance metrics, as in [328].

9.2.1 Classifier Performance Metrics

In order to construct reliable classifiers, metrics are needed to compare classifier performance. In this section, some of the standard metrics that are used to measure classifier performance are outlined. Given a binary classifier $h \in \mathbf{H}$, and an example space of test instances, a confusion matrix is constructed as defined in Figure 9.1. The matrix gives a count of the classified test instances based on the hypothesized class labels and the real class labels. These counts are true positives (TP), false positives (FP), true negatives (TN), and false negatives (FN). The confusion matrix is extended to include counts for unclassified instances in case of a reliable classifier. It has entries for unclassified positives (UP) and unclassified negatives (UN). These counts are used to derive metrics to measure classifier performance. The basic metrics are: true positive rate (TPr), false positive rate (FPr), true negative rate (TNr), and

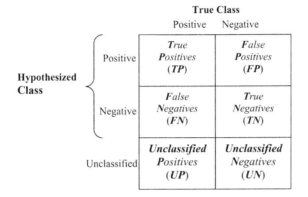

FIGURE 9.1

Confusion matrix for a binary classifier (as in [328]).

false negative rate (FNr).

$$TPr = \frac{TP}{TP+FN} \quad FPr = \frac{FP}{FP+TN}$$

$$FNr = \frac{FN}{TP+FN} \quad TNr = \frac{TN}{FP+TN}$$

The *accuracy rate A*, and *precision P*, are defined for the positive class as:

$$A = \frac{TP+TN}{TP+FP+FN+TN} \quad P = \frac{TP}{TP+FP} \tag{9.1}$$

In addition, the *rejection rate R* is defined as follow. The *coverage rate* is given as one minus rejection rate.

$$R = \frac{UP+UN}{TP+FP+FN+TN+UP+UN} \tag{9.2}$$

9.2.2 **Metaclassifiers and Metaconformal Predictors**

Given the best classifier $h \in \mathbf{H}$ for a problem, p-values need to be calculated for every test instance to estimate the reliability of the label assigned to the test instance. Smirnov et al. [328] pointed out the need for a metaclassifier, when a classifier h, such as a human expert or a decision rule-based system, may not be sufficient to obtain p-values using the conformal prediction framework. In such cases, a metaclassifier $m \in \mathbf{M}$ (where $\mathbf{M}$ is a space of classifiers conducive to use with the conformal prediction framework in our case) is trained, and estimates the correctness of each instance classification of h. The p-values for the test instances obtained using m can be considered as the p-values by h. The combined classifier is denoted as $h : m$. The base classifier is trained using the training data and the metaclassifier is trained using

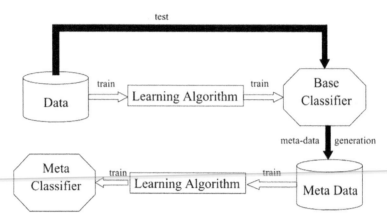

FIGURE 9.2

Combined Classifier($h : m$) which consists of the Base Classifier(h) and Metaclassifier(m).

metadata. Figure 9.2 depicts a combined classifier. Different metaclassifiers differ in the way the metadata is generated.

The base classifier h is trained on data $\mathbf{Z}$. The metaclassifier m is trained on metadata $\mathbf{Z}'$ that is generated from $\mathbf{Z}$ in the following manner. The metadata $\mathbf{Z}'$ is defined on metainstance space $\mathbf{X}'$ and metalabel space $\mathbf{Y}'$. While $\mathbf{X}'$ coincides with $\mathbf{X}$, $\mathbf{Y}'$ consists of two class labels: a "positive metaclass" that indicates reliable classification and a "negative metaclass" that indicates unreliable classification. k-fold cross validation is deployed to estimate $\mathbf{Z}'$ from $\mathbf{Z}$ [86], as described later.

The data $\mathbf{Z}$ is divided into k equally sized folds $\mathbf{F}_i$, $i \in [1, k]$. For every $\mathbf{F}_j$, $j \in [1, k]$, all the folds $\mathbf{F}_i$ with $i \neq j$ are combined into $\mathbf{Z}_j$. The base classifier h is trained on $\mathbf{Z}_j$ and tested with $\mathbf{F}_j$. The metadata is obtained using the test instances in $\mathbf{F}_j$. If an instance $(x_i, y_i) \in \mathbf{F}_j$ was classified correctly, an instance (x_i, y_i') is created to be placed in $\mathbf{Z}'$ where the value of y' is "positive metaclass." If on the other hand (x_i, y_i) was incorrectly classified by the base classifier, y' is "negative metaclass." In this way, all the elements in fold $\mathbf{F}_j$ are placed into $\mathbf{Z}'$. This process is repeated for all the folds $j \in [1, k]$. Once the metadata is complete, the metaclassifier m is trained using the data $\mathbf{Z}'$. The metaclassifier is usually a nonlinear classifier that is adaptable to the CP framework because the metadata is generally not linearly separable.

The combined classifier is denoted as $h : m$. This classifier assigns to an instance $x \in \mathbf{X}$ a class label $y \in \mathbf{Y}$ predicted by the classifier h, if m decides that the classification is reliable (i.e., m predicts a "positive metaclass"); else, the instance x is left unclassified. Hence, it is possible that not all instances $x \in \mathbf{X}$ are classified. The rejection rate is estimated for the combined classifier $h : m$ as $R_{h:m}$, and is equal to the proportion of instances to which m assigns "negative metaclass" (as shown by Smirnov et al. in [328]).

$$\frac{TN_m + FN_m}{TP_m + FP_m + FN_m + TN_m}.$$

The authors also showed that the accuracy $A_{h:m}$ of the combined classifier $h : m$ is equal to the precision P_m of the metaclassifier, measured with respect to the "positive metaclass" (replicated in Theorem 9.1).

Theorem 9.1. *Given a base classifier h, a metaclassifier m, and a combined classifier h : m, the accuracy rate $A_{h:m}$ of the classifier h : m equals the precision rate P_m of the classifier m.*

Proof. Given the combined classifier $h : m$ it follows that:

$$TP_{h:m} + TN_{h:m} = (TP_h + TN_h)\frac{TP_m}{TP_m + FN_m} \tag{9.3}$$

$$FP_{h:m} + FN_{h:m} = (FP_h + FN_h)\frac{FP_m}{FP_m + TN_m} \tag{9.4}$$

From the confusion matrices of the base classifier h and the metaclassifier m, we have:

$$TP_h + TN_h = TP_m + FN_m \tag{9.5}$$

$$FP_h + FN_h = FP_m + TN_m \tag{9.6}$$

Substituting for $TP_h + TN_h$ in Eq. (9.3) and $FP_h + FN_h$ in Eq. (9.4), we get:

$$TP_{h:m} + TN_{h:m} = TP_m \tag{9.7}$$
$$FP_{h:m} + FN_{h:m} = FP_m \tag{9.8}$$

The values for $TP_{h:m} + TN_{h:m}$ and $FP_{h:m} + FN_{h:m}$ as in Eqs. (9.7) and (9.8) are substituted in the formula for accuracy $A_{h:m}$ given in (9.1) to get:

$$A_{h:m} = \frac{TP_{h:m} + TN_{h:m}}{TP_{h:m} + TN_{h:m} + FP_{h:m} + FN_{h:m}} \tag{9.9}$$

$$= \frac{TP_m}{TP_m + FP_m} \tag{9.10}$$

The last expression is the precision rate P_m for the metaclassifier m for the "positive metaclass." It can therefore be concluded that $A_{h:m} = P_m$. □

In Theorem 9.1 it was observed that the accuracy of the base classifier does not influence the accuracy of the combined classifier $h : m$. The accuracy of the combined classifier $h : m$ is equal to the precision of the metaclassifier m. To increase the accuracy of the combined classifier, P_m needs to be maximized.

Interpreting the p-values

Unlike in a standard conformal prediction setting, the p-values of the combined classifier $h : m$ need to be interpreted. It has been assumed that the base classifier h is not based on the conformal prediction framework and is therefore not capable of providing p-values as output for instance classifications. Example classifiers of h are human experts, decision rules, and such [141,231]. On the other hand, the metaclassifier is conducive to use with the conformal prediction framework and is capable of providing p-values as outputs for the "positive metaclass" and the "negative metaclass." Example classifiers include nearest-neighbor classifiers [280], Support Vector Machines [297], and other classifiers listed in earlier chapters. Given this setting, an instance $x \in \mathbf{X}$ is classified by the combined classifier $h : m$ as follows.

The base classifier h assigns a label $y \in \mathbf{Y}$ to the instance x. The meta classifier m acts upon the instance x and estimates the p-value p_p for the "positive metaclass" and the p-value p_n for the "negative meta class." The "positive metaclass" indicates that the assigned label y is correct and the "negative metaclass" indicates that the label y is incorrect. Based upon this understanding, two assumptions are arrived at:

(A1) The p-value p_p of the "positive meta class" can be considered as an approximation of the p-value p_y of the class y assigned to x.

(A2) The p-value p_n of the "negative meta class" can be considered as the sum of the p-values of the all classes $\mathbf{Y} \setminus \{y\}$ when y is assigned to instance x.

These intuitive assumptions (A1) and (A2) are the basis for how the combined classifier $h : m$ is interpreted. The score $\frac{p_p}{p_n}$ is considered to decide if the particular instance should be classified (as in [188]). A reliable threshold T is determined on the score $\frac{p_p}{p_n}$ to decide if a classification made by h on an instance x is reliable. If the score is greater than the threshold, the classification of x is reliable; otherwise x is left unclassified. The threshold T imposes a certain accuracy on the instances that $h : m$ can classify and the rejection of the combined classifier.

Generalized performance

Smirnov et al. [328] further estimated a threshold T such that the combined classifier $h : m$ has a predefined target accuracy rate $At_{h:m}$ on the instances that $h : m$ can classify. We showed earlier that the p-values of the combined classifier $h : m$ equal the p-values of the conformity-based metaclassifier. By Theorem 9.1, the accuracy $A_{h:m}$ of the combined classifier is equal to the precision rate P_m of the metaclassifier m. A threshold T on the p-values of m is obtained such that the precision rate P_m is equal to the target accuracy rate $At_{h:m}$. To build a conformity-based metaclassifier with precision rate Pt_m, the authors in [328] identified a reliability threshold T using the following steps (similar to [351]):

1. Construct the Receiver Operating Characteristic (ROC) convex hull, called ROCCH, for the metaclassifier m using the score ratio $\frac{p_p}{p_n}$. Each threshold value for the score ratio yields a single value on the ROC curve. Use k-fold cross validation as in Section 9.2.2.

2. Construct the iso-precision line with the target precision Pt_M given by the equation relating TP_r and FP_r; $TPr_M = \frac{Pt_M}{1 - Pt_M} \frac{N_M}{P_M} FPr_M$, where N_M is the number of "negative metaclass" instances and P_M is the number of "positive metaclass" instances. This line represents classifiers with precision rate Pt_M.

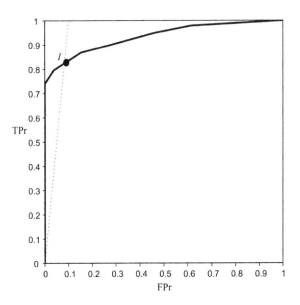

FIGURE 9.3

ROCCH for a conformity-based nearest neighbor classifier [280], trained on metadata from a naive Bayes classifier on the Wisconsin Breast Cancer data [8]. The iso-precision line is for a precision rate of 0.9. Figure as in [328].

3. Find the intersection I of the iso-precision line with the convex hull. The value of the ratio $\frac{p_p}{p_n}$ at the intersection point is the reliability threshold T (see Figure 9.3).

According to [351], the precision rate P_M of the conformity-based metaclassifier will now be equal to the target precision rate Pt_M. From Theorem 9.1, the accuracy $A_{h:m}$ of the combined classifier $h:m$ on the classified instances will be Pt_M, which is equal to $At_{h:m}$, the target accuracy. Also, evidently, the accuracy $A_{h:m}$ is maximized when the precision P_m is maximized. The precision is maximized for the iso-precision line with slope equal to the slope of the line segment of the ROCCH starting from the origin. The highest point of this segment maximizes the number of covered metainstances (see point $(0, 0.74)$ of ROCCH in Figure 9.3). Thus, at this point, by Theorem 2, the accuracy rate of the combined classifier $h:m$ is maximized while the rejection rate is minimized.

9.2.3 **Experiments**

For completeness, we now present the experimental results obtained by Smirnov et al. in [328] using the 12 UCI data multisets [8]. The base classifier was chosen to be naive Bayes (NB) [231]. The metaclassifier was chosen to be a conformity-based nearest neighbor classifier (called the CNN) [280]. The metaclassifier provides the p-values and is nonlinear. The resulting combined classifier is denoted by $NB : CNN$.

Table 9.1   Rejection rates for classifiers $NB : CNN$ and CNN for accuracy rate at 1.0.

Data Set	$R_{NB:CNN}$	$A_{NB:CNN}$
Annealing	0.57*	0.88
Audiology	0.84*	0.99
Wisconsin breast cancer	0.29	0.31
Glass	0.82*	0.88
Hepatitis	0.71	0.65
Heart-Statlog	0.94	0.85*
Ionosphere	0.70	0.55
Iris	0.29	0.13*
Lymphography	0.80*	0.99
Soybean	0.87*	0.90
Vote	0.52	0.47*
Zoo	0.23	0.14*

* Indicates rejection rates that are statistically lower according to a paired-t test on significance level of 0.05 (as presented in [328]).

Ten-fold cross validation was used to create the metadata for $NB : CNN$. The metaconformity approach was used to estimate the p-values of $NB : CNN$.

The combined classifier was experimented on 12 UCI data multisets [8] (listed in Table 9.1). At each value of the reliability threshold T in the range $[0, +\infty)$, the score $\frac{p_p}{p_n}$ was estimated. If the score was greater than the threshold for a particular instance, the classification was considered reliable, otherwise the instance was left unclassified. At each value of T, 10-fold cross validation was used to estimate the accuracy/rejection graphs for the different data sets. The results are presented in Figure 9.4. Each point on the curves represents a $NB : CNN$ classifier with a particular threshold $T \in [0, +\infty)$. The leftmost points refer to $T = 0$, the subsequent points refer to increasing T values with the rightmost points depicting T approaching $+\infty$. The rejection rates for the combined classifier $NB : CNN$ and the metaclassifier CNN for accuracy 1.0 are presented in Table 9.1. From the data in Table 9.1, it is seen that each of these classifiers is significantly better for five data multisets. This indicates that the classifiers are good and different, which validates assumptions (A1) and (A2) that the classifiers approximate the p-values very well.

The ROC procedure was used to construct classifiers with predefined accuracies for all the UCI data multisets. The ROCCH was constructed using 10-fold cross validation similar to the manner in which metadata was generated (see Section 9.2.2). The reliability threshold T was estimated for a target accuracy of $At = 1.0$. The accuracy and rejection rates for the combined classifier $NB : CNN$ for accuracy $At = 1.0$ are depicted in Table 9.2. The deviation in accuracy was 0.3. This was attributed to the instability in the 10-fold cross validation during metadata generation and/or the size of the training (meta) data. The largest deviations were observed

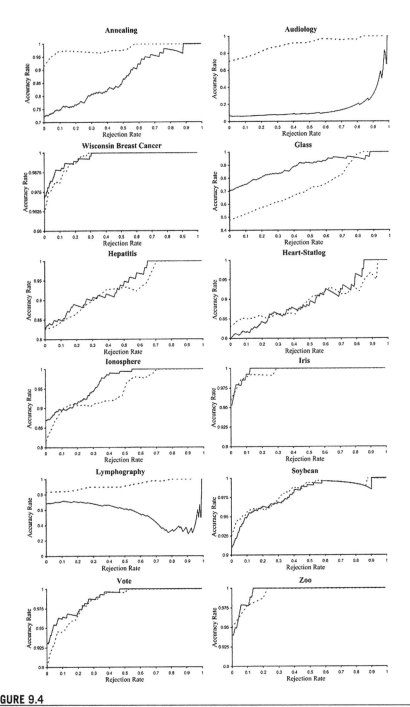

FIGURE 9.4

The accuracy/rejection graphs for *NB:CNN* (dashed line) and *CNN* (bold line) (as presented in [328]).

Table 9.2 Accuracy and Rejection rates for the *NB* : *CNN* classifier generated using the ROC method with target accuracy *At* = 1.0 (as presented in [328]).

Data Set	$R_{NB:CNN}$	$A_{NB:CNN}$
Annealing	0.65	1.00
Audiology	0.83	0.97
Wisconsin. breast cancer	0.29	1.00
Glass	0.87	1.00
Hepatitis	0.71	0.98
Heart-Statlog	0.88	0.97
Ionosphere	0.72	1.00
Iris	0.31	0.99
Lymphography	0.79	0.98
Soybean	0.72	1.00
Vote	0.49	1.00
Zoo	0.18	0.99

for data with size less than 300 instances: Audiology, Hepatitis, Heart-Statlog, Iris, Lymphography, and Zoo. We infer from the results that the ROC-based strategy is applicable in practice and produces accurate results when the data size is reasonably large.

9.3 Single-Stacking Conformal Predictors

The metaconformal approach works well in a binary class setting. For a multi class problem, the meta conformal approach does not provide the p-value estimates for all the class labels $y \in Y$. Smirnov et al. [329] proposed the Single-Stacking Conformal Predictors which employ a stacking ensemble to create a combined classifier to overcome the limitations of metaconformal predictors. In this section, we describe the Single-Stacking Conformal Predictors and illustrate their performance on the MYCAREVENT dataset as in [329]. The MYCAREVENT project seeks to find the reliable estimate on a car status to provide roadside assistance.

9.3.1 Metaconformity versus Single Stacking

In the metaconformal approach, a base classifier $h \in H$ was combined with a meta-classifier $m \in M$ to create a combined classifier $h : m$. The combined classifier is capable of estimating p-values for the classified instances. There is however, one shortcoming with the combined classifier. If the classifier m assigns a class label y to an instance x, the associated p-value of class y is set to p_0, the p-value of the metaclass "correct classification." The sum of the p-values of the remaining classes $Y \backslash \{y\}$ is set to p_1, the p-value of the meta class "incorrect classification." The p-value of every class $y \in Y$ cannot be estimated using the metaconformal approach. If $p_0 < p_1$, the class with the highest p-value cannot be estimated. To overcome this shortcoming, the Single-Stacking Conformal Predictor was introduced in [329]. This approach employs a stacking ensemble consisting of a base classifier h and a metaclassifier m (with a suitable nonconformity measure) and yields p-values for the instance classifications of the base classifier h. While the base classifier h and the metaclassifier m are similar to the base classifier and metaclassifier in the metaconformal approach, the difference lies in the manner in which metadata is created and the way in which the class labels are estimated by the metaclassifier. The single stacking approach also needs the base classifier to output the class probability distribution. We now describe the Single-Stacking Conformal Predictor.

9.3.2 Single-Stacking Conformal Predictor

Like the metaconformal predictor, the single-stacking predictor also consists of a base classifier $h \in \mathbf{H}$ and a metaclassifier $m \in \mathbf{M}$. The key idea of the combined classifier is to employ a stacking ensemble [383] of a base classifier h and a metaclassifier m. Figure 9.5 depicts a single-stacking classifier. The p-values of the metapredictions are considered as the p-values of the instance classifications of the base classifier. The metadata belongs to space $\mathbf{X}'$ defined by the attributes of the input space $\mathbf{X}$ concatenated with $|\mathbf{Y}|$ elements from the class probability distribution as estimated by the base classifier h. The meta class $\mathbf{Y}'$ coincides with the class set $\mathbf{Y}$.

The metadata $\mathbf{Z}'$ are formed in $\mathbf{X}' \times \mathbf{Y}'$ using k-fold cross validation. A labeled instance $(x_i', y_i) \in \mathbf{Z}'$ is formed from the labeled instance $(x_i, y_i) \in \mathbf{Z}$ such that x_i' is the concatenation of x_i and the class probability distribution computed by h on x_i. The metaclassifier m is then trained on this metadata $\mathbf{Z}'$. The single-stacking ensemble

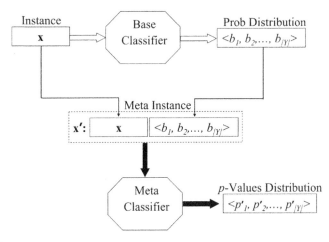

FIGURE 9.5

Single-Stacking Conformity Approach (as in [329]).

classifier consisting of the base classifier h and the meta-classifier m is denoted as $SST_{h:m}$. Given an instance x, the $SST_{h:m}$ classifies it as follows: The base classifier h provides a class probability distribution $\langle b_1, b_2, \ldots, b_{|\mathbf{Y}|}\rangle$ for x. The instance x and the distribution $\langle b_1, b_2, \ldots, b_{|\mathbf{Y}|}\rangle$ are concatenated to form the meta-instance x'. Since the meta-classifier m is associated with a nonconformity score, the class probability distribution of m is a p-values distribution $\langle p'_1, p'_2, \ldots, p'_{|\mathbf{Y}|}\rangle$ consisting of p-values for the classes in $\mathbf{Y}$ obtained using the CP framework. The single-stacking conformity approach approximates for the base classifier h the p-value p_i for each class $y \in \mathbf{Y}$ with the p-value p'_i of the metaclassifier m.

9.3.3 Experiments

Once again, for completeness, we present the results of applying the Single-Stacking Conformal Predictor to the problem of roadside assistance as presented in [329]. These experiments were based on data obtained from the MYCAREVENT project, which has historical patrol car data of previously diagnosed faults and symptoms provided by RAC (Royal Automobile Club, a UK-based motor organization) derived from call center operator conversations. The data consists of four discrete attributes: *Brand* (40 discrete values), *Model* (229 discrete values), *Primary Fault* (35 discrete values), *Secondary Fault* (80 discrete values), and the class attribute *Status*. The class attribute *Status* has three values (class labels):

1. *Fixed*: The problem is solved by roadside assistance and the car can continue its journey safely (3366 instances).
2. *Required Tow*: The car needs to be towed to the workshop (1077 instances).
3. *Other*: Some parts of the problem cannot be solved by roadside assistance but the car is able to get to the workshop on its own (1477 instances).

The experiment employed four standard classifiers: the C4.5 decision tree learner ($C4.5$) [282], the k-nearest neighbor classifier (NN), naive Bayes classifier (NB) [83], and the CP framework-based nearest neighbor classifier (called $TCMNN$) [280]. $C4.5$, NN, and NB were used as independent classifiers and as base classifiers. $TCMNN$ was used as an independent classifier and as a metaclassifier in conformity ensembles. The metaconformal approach was experimented using the following classifiers $MCT(C4.5 : TCMNN)$, $MCT(NN : TCMNN)$, and $MCT(NB : TCMNN)$. The single-stacking ensemble was experimented using the following classifiers $SST(C4.5 : TCMNN)$, $SST(NN : TCMNN)$, and $SST(NB : TCMNN)$. The classifiers' parameters were empirically obtained for maximum classifier performance. The classification probabilities of $C4.5$, NN, and NB were interpreted as the reliability values for the classifiers. For the $TCMNN$ and the ensembles, the p-values that were generated were used as the reliability values.

Many experiments were conducted by varying the reliability threshold r in the range [0,1]. When the reliability value of a classification was above r, the classification was considered reliable, otherwise the instance was left unclassified. For each value

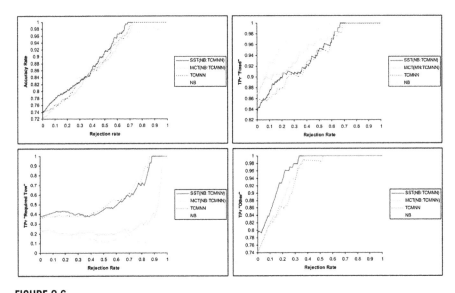

FIGURE 9.6

Accuracy/rejection and *TPr*/rejection graphs for *NB*, *TCMNN*, *SST*(*NB* : *TCMNN*), *MCT* (*NB* : *TCMNN*) (as presented in [329]).

of r, the following were evaluated using 10-fold cross validation: rejection rate (proportion of unclassified instances), accuracy rate (on the classified instances), rejection rate per class (proportion of unclassified instances per class), and true positive rate per class TPr (on the classified instances). Figures 9.6, 9.7, and 9.8 provide the results of the experiments as accuracy/rejection and TPr/rejection graphs for each of the three independent classifiers, NB, NN, and $C4.5$[98]. To enable comparison between the classifiers, the rejection rates for accuracies of 1.0 and TPr of 1.0 per class were extracted from the graph and are presented in Table 9.3.

It can be observed that the accuracy/rejection and TPr/rejection rates of the $TCMNN$, SST ensembles, and the MCT ensembles dominate those of NB, NN, and $C4.5$ classifiers. This leads to the following conclusions:

- The classification probabilities of NB, NN, and $C4.5$ are estimates of the classification reliability values. They fail for the minority classes "Required Tow" and "Other." They can be used for the majority class "Fixed," as the last two columns of Table 9.3 indicate.
- The SST ensembles, MCT ensembles, and the $TCMNN$ provide good classification reliability values for all the classes.

---

[1] The accuracy/rejection (TPr/rejection) graph of the "always right" classifier is determined by the $\langle(0,1),(1,1)\rangle$ segment. If two classifiers have the same accuracy rate, the classifier with lower rejection rate is preferred.

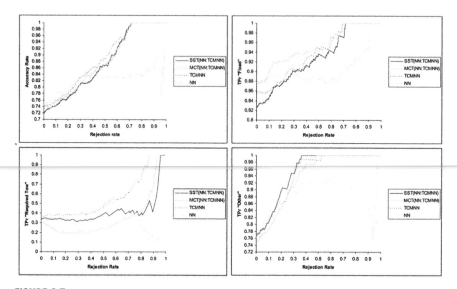

FIGURE 9.7

Accuracy/rejection and *Tpr*/rejection graphs for *NN*, *TCMNN*, *SST*(*NN* : *TCMNN*), *MCT* (*NN* : *TCMNN*) (as presented in [329]).

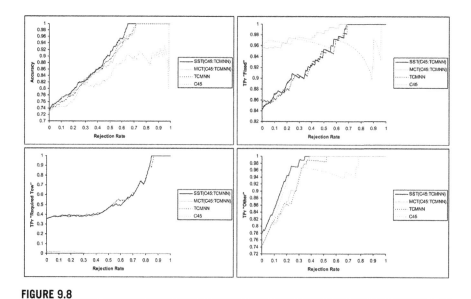

FIGURE 9.8

Accuracy/rejection and *Tpr*/rejection graphs for *C*4.5, *TCMNN*, *SST*(*C*4.5 : *TCMNN*), *MCT*(*C*4.5 : *TCMNN*) (as presented in [329]).

Table 9.3 Rejection rates for accuracy rate 1.0 and *TPr* rate of 1.0. *R* is the rejection rate for accuracy rate 1.0. R_F is the rejection rate for *TPr* rate 1.0 for "Fixed" class. R_R is the rejection rate for *TPr* rate 1.0 for "Required Tow" class. R_O is the rejection rate for *TPr* rate 1.0 for "Other" class. Undefined rejection rates are denoted by "–".

Classifiers	R	R_F	R_R	R_O
NB	0.93	**0.56**	–	0.51
NN	0.98	0.90	–	0.97
C4.5	0.98	0.95	–	0.78
TCMNN	0.72	0.69	0.93	0.52
MCT(NB : TCMNN)	0.72	0.71	0.96	0.37
MCT(NN : TCMNN)	0.71	0.69	0.92	0.48
MCT(C4.5 : TCMNN)	0.71	0.62	–	0.38
SST(NB : TCMNN)	0.68	0.67	0.88	**0.34**
SST(NN : TCMNN)	0.71	0.71	0.95	0.36
SST(C4.5 : TCMNN)	**0.64**	0.68	**0.84**	**0.34**

The *SST* ensembles outperform the *MCT* ensembles and the *TCMNN* on the accuracy graphs as indicated in Table 9.3. For the majority class "Fixed," the *MCT(C4.5 : TCMNN)* outperforms both the *SST* ensembles and the *TCMNN*. For the minority classes, however, the *SST* ensembles perform better than the *MCT* ensembles and the *TCMNN*. The best classifier is the *SST(C4.5 : TCMNN)* ensemble. For an accuracy rate of 1.0, its rejection rate is below those of *MCT* ensembles and *TCMNN*, whose values are at 0.07 and 0.08, respectively. Although the rejection rate of *MCT(C4.5 : TCMNN)* is below that of *SST(C4.5 : TCMNN)* for the "Fixed" class, *SST(C4.5 : TCMNN)* has lower rejection rates for the minority classes "Required Tow" and "Other."

9.4 Conformal Predictors for Time Series Analysis

A time series is a sequence of data points $a_1, \ldots, a_n$ where the indices $1, \ldots, n$ indicate the time or order in which the point has been observed. When applying conformal predictors to time series data, an important consideration is the exchangeability assumption that is necessary for the validity property of the CP framework to be true (see Chapter 1). The observations from a time series are dependent on each other; that is, the order of observations is important and they cannot be assumed to be exchangeable. Hence, in order to apply the CP framework to time series data, the dependency between observations needs to be minimized through suitable data/feature transformations. Dashevskiy and Luo [70] proposed different methods to transform time series data in order to apply the CP framework to derive conformal prediction intervals using regression models. We briefly describe the overall idea of their methodology in this section, while the details of their algorithm and experimental results are substantiated in Chapter 12.

9.4.1 Time Series Analysis Methods

The prediction problem for a time series is defined as the prediction of the current output of a process (that generates the series) using past observations of the process. In addition to typically used methods in machine learning, such as K-Nearest Neighbors (KNN) and Ridge Regression (RR), other stochastic models such as the Auto Regressive Moving Average (ARMA) and Fractional Auto Regressive Integrated Moving Average (FARIMA) models have also been used for time series analysis. In addition, the Aggregating algorithm (AA), which gives a prediction by aggregating the decisions given by various models, has also been used. Since ARMA, FARIMA, and AA models are not familiar models, we briefly describe them next.

Autoregressive moving average (ARMA)

In the Autoregressive Moving Average (ARMA) model [270], the current observation is modeled as a linear combination of the past observations and also as a linear combination of a set of normally distributed random variables. An ARMA process $\{X_t\}$ is defined as:

$$X_t = \phi_1 X_{t-1} + \phi_2 X_{t-2} + \cdots + \phi_p X_{t-p} + W_t + \theta_1 W_{t-1} + \cdots + \theta_q W_{t-q}, \quad (9.11)$$

where $\phi_p \neq 0, \theta \neq 0$ and $\{W_t\} \sim \mathrm{WN}(0, \sigma^2)$ where WN is white noise (i.e., a normal distribution with mean 0 and variance σ^2). An ARMA process is defined by two parameters p and q, where p defines the order of dependency between current and past data and q defines the dependency between the current observation and a set of normally distributed variables. To make a prediction, the parameters θ, ϕ, and σ^2 are updated at each time step and X_t is calculated using a recursive algorithm (see [270] for details).

Fractional auto regressive integrated moving average

Introduced in [126], the Fractional Auto Regressive Integrated Moving Average (FARIMA) method is used to model processes with long-range dependence such as network traffic data. A FARIMA process $\{X_t\}$ is defined as:

$$\phi(B)X_t = \theta(B)(1 - B)^{-d}\epsilon_t, \quad (9.12)$$

where $\phi(B) = 1 + \phi_1 B + \cdots + \phi_p B^p$ and $\theta(B) = 1 + \theta_1 B + \cdots + \phi_q B^q$. p and q exactly correspond to the parameters used in the ARMA model. A FARIMA model is thus parametrized by (p, q, d), where p and q are nonnegative and d is a real number such that $(-1/2) < d < (1/2)$. (For more details of FARIMA, please see [28,126].)

Aggregating algorithm

The Aggregating Algorithm (AA) was first introduced in [358] and is used to aggregate the information given by different experts. When there are multiple experts, we need an algorithm that can utilize all the expert advice and come up with an overall prediction. AA calculates the final outcome such that the error incurred by comparing it with the true value is less than the maximum of the errors given by all experts. In time series analysis, each regression model can be considered as an expert that predicts the current observation using the past ones. At each time step, the errors from each model are calculated by comparing the predictions with the true value and the expert models are weighted accordingly. A model with high error rate will get smaller weight, and a model with a low error rate will be assigned a greater weight. The AA calculates the final outcome using the weights and the predictions of different models (see [358] for more details).

9.4.2 Conformal Predictors for Time Series Analysis: Methodology

As time series data is not inherently exchangeable, we cannot theoretically guarantee that conformal predictors will assure calibrated error rates in time series analysis. Since the dependency between observations limits the exchangeability assumption, we can relax the dependency assumption. Instead of assuming that every observation is dependent on all its previous observations, we assume that it depends only on observations within a given a lag $T \in N$, which we call the *window*. Considering (without any loss of generality) only time series of type $a_1, a_2, a_3, \ldots$ where $a_i \in R^K$ for any finite dimension K, the objective for our analysis is to predict a_i given $a_1, \ldots, a_{i-1}$. In order to apply the CP framework for regression (see Section 1.7, the underlying regression algorithms may require each data point to be of the form $z_i = (x_i, y_i)$, that is, an (object, label) pair. Hence, the data a_i is transformed into z_i in two different ways where one is exchangeable and the other is not.

To create data that is not exchangeable or *dependent* we use the following rule:

$$\forall T + 1 \le i \le n : z_i = (x_i, y_i) := ((a_{i-T}, \ldots, a_{i-1}), a_i),$$

where n is the length of the time series. For example, if $n = 6$ and $T = 2$, the new transformed data will be $\{z_1, z_2, z_3, z_4\} = \{((a_1, a_2), a_3), ((a_2, a_3), a_4), ((a_3, a_4), a_5), ((a_4, a_5), a_6)\}$. We observe that the order of the data is important because there is an overlap of data between z_1 and z_2, and so on. Even though conformal predictors can now be applied to the data, this transformation may not assure theoretical guarantee for validity. Following is another rule that transforms the time series into an exchangeable or *independent* sequence:

$$\forall 0 \le i \le \left[\frac{n}{T+1} \right] - 1 : z_i$$
$$= (x_i, y_i) := ((a_{n-i(T+1)-T}, \ldots, a_{n-i(T+1)-1}), a_{n-i(T+1)}),$$

where $[k]$ denotes the integer part of k. Considering the earlier example where $n = 6$ and $T = 2$, this rule gives $\{z_1, z_2\} = \{((a_4, a_5), a_6), ((a_1, a_2), a_3)\}$. Thus this transformation generates data points that are *independent* and thus, are exchangeable.

Once the data is transformed into (object, label) pairs, regression models are used to predict a new observation. If an ARMA process is used, the data need not be transformed to (object, label) pairs. As in regression, the nonconformity measure $\alpha(y)$, for a new point in the time series is the error of prediction $|\hat{y} - y|$, where $\hat{y}$ is the estimate and y is the actual value of the observation (see Section 1.7. It should be noted that the nonconformity score of a point y, $\alpha(y)$ depends only on the current observation and not on any other observations.

Algorithm 10 Conformal Prediction Interval calculation for Time series data based on one nearest neighbor

---

Input: Parameters ϵ and y_1, y_2

$\quad x_2 := y_1$

$\quad \alpha_2(y) := 0$

$\quad$ **for** n = 3, 4, 5, ... **do**

$\qquad x_n := y_{n-1}$

$\qquad \hat{y}_n := y_{\arg \min_{i,2 \leq i \leq n-1}\{|x_i - x_n|\}}$

$\qquad p := \max\{r \in R : \frac{\#\{\alpha_i \geq r, 2 \leq i \leq n-1\}}{n-2} \geq \epsilon\}$

$\qquad$ Output $\Gamma_n := [\hat{y}_n - p, \hat{y}_n + p]$ as prediction for y_n

$\qquad$ Get y_n

$\qquad \alpha_n(y) := |y_n - \hat{y}_n|$

$\quad$ **end for**

Algorithm 10 shows the steps involved in computing conformal prediction intervals for time series data, as described by Dashevskiy and Luo [70] for the one nearest neighbor regression method. The maximum error r is selected as the range of the prediction interval such that a significant number of points have errors greater than r. The significance level ϵ is given as a parameter to the algorithm. The prediction interval is given by $[\hat{y}_n - p, \hat{y}_n + p]$. The calculation of the estimate $\hat{y}$ changes in Algorithm 10 depending on whether the underlying model is based on ridge regression or ARMA, and the rest of the steps remain the same. More details of the methodology, experimental results, and analysis are presented in Chapter 12.

9.5 Conclusions

In conclusion, the theoretical guarantees on validity provided by the conformal prediction framework (in the online setting), along with its general applicability to all classification and regression methods, render it suitable to be incorporated in various machine learning settings. While the use of conformal prediction in traditional machine learning settings such as active learning, anomaly detection, and change detection were discussed in earlier chapters, this chapter presented its adaptation to other seemingly nontraditional machine learning settings such as reliability estimation and time series analysis. The experimental results presented in this chapter also support the potential use of conformal predictors in varied machine learning settings.

Acknowledgments

This chapter is based upon work supported by the US National Science Foundation under Grant No. 1116360. Any opinions, findings, and conclusions or recommendations expressed in this material are those of the author(s) and do not necessarily reflect the views of the US National Science Foundation.

Applications

Biometrics and Robust Face Recognition

10

Harry Wechsler[*] and Fayin Li[†]

[*]*Department of Computer Science, George Mason University, VA, USA*
[†]*CleverSys Inc., VA, USA*

CHAPTER OUTLINE HEAD

The uses of conformal prediction, in general, and transduction, in particular, are discussed in terms of scope, challenges, and vulnerabilities for biometrics with robust face recognition as application domain of interest. Robustness refers to the ability to cope with uncontrolled settings characteristic of incomplete and/or corrupt (adversarial) biometric information on one side, and varying image quality on the other side. The motivation for the conformal prediction approach comes from the use of discriminative methods such as likelihood ratios, to link biometrics and forensics. The methods and algorithms proposed are realized using transductive inference (transduction for brevity). They leverage nonconfidence measures (NCM), make use of both labeled (annotated) and unlabeled biometric data, address multilayer categorization, and provide measures of reliability in the predictions made, for example, credibility and confidence. Toward that end we describe a novel Transduction Confidence Machine for Detection and Recognition (TCM-DR) that expands on the traditional Transduction Confidence Machine (TCM). The two machines, TCM and TCM-DR, are suitable for closed and open set recognition, respectively, with TCM-DR also suitable for verification. Basic concepts, architectures, and empirical results are presented for open set face recognition and watch list/surveillance using TCM-DR. Recognition-by-parts using transduction and boosting is the adversarial learning solution that addresses vulnerabilities due to occlusion and disguise. Future venues for biometric research are discussed including reidentification using sensitivity analysis and revision for the purpose of metaprediction, in general, and interoperability and identity management, in particular.

10.1 Introduction

Quantifying the uncertainty of the predictions made by classification and regression (e.g., video tracking) is an important problem for machine learning (ML). Conformal Prediction (CP) complements the predictions made by ML algorithms with metrics of reliability (e.g., nonconformity measures (NCM)). The purpose for NCM is to support hedging/punting between accuracy and confidence, when making predictions, according to the costs and risks involved. In particular, the methods developed using the CP framework produce "well-calibrated" reliability measures for individual examples without assuming anything more than that the data are generated independently by the same (but unknown) probability distribution (i.i.d). Transduction, in general, and the Transduction Confidence Machine (TCM) and the Transduction Confidence Machine for Detection and Recognition (TCM-DR), in particular, which are closely related to CP, address categorization as a whole and are the subject of this chapter. In addition, both TCM and TCM-DR yield credibility and confidence as reliability measures using strangeness and p-values to code for NCM. The credibility measure is well calibrated (or conservatively valid) as the frequency of prediction error does not exceed significance level ϵ (between 0 and 1) at a chosen confidence level $1 - \epsilon$ (in the long run). Smaller values of ϵ correspond to greater reliability. The confidence measure, which expresses the extent of ambiguity, becomes efficient as the TCM and TCM-DR prediction sets (regions) shrink (in terms of number of possible outcomes). The basic mode of operation for transduction is incremental in nature as it leverages the complementarity between training and test data for the purpose of robust and stable predictions. TCM and TCM-DR further advance modeling and metaprediction for learning from both labeled (annotated) and unlabeled examples, while employing ranking and sensitivity analysis for the purpose of sequential importance sampling and revisions during online recognition and tracking.

This chapter discusses the role that transduction plays in real-world problems related to biometrics, in general, and face recognition, in particular, for the purpose of biometric authentication. Transduction mediates between randomness deficiency, nonconformity measures, and metaprediction for biometrics authentication. The challenge for face recognition comes from uncontrolled settings affecting image quality, and incomplete or deceiving information characteristic of occlusion and/or disguise. Toward that end, we discuss here biometric tasks and their application to face recognition, the role transduction plays in addressing specific biometric challenges, approaches and methods for tasks such as open set face recognition and surveillance, empirical results, and venues for future research and novel applications.

The outline of the chapter is as follows. The linkage between biometrics and forensics that motivates discriminative methods is discussed in Section 10.2, while basics of face recognition are introduced in Section 10.3. Randomness and complexity, transduction, and nonconformity measures are briefly addressed in Sections 10.4–10.6 and mediate between discriminative methods and face recognition functionalities. Closed and open set face identification/recognition (including verification) and watch list/surveillance using TCM and TCM-DR are discussed in Sections 10.7 through 10.8. Score normalization is discussed in Section 10.9. Recognition-by-parts using TCM-DR and boosting is discussed in Section 10.10, and reidentification using sensitivity analysis and revision is addressed in Section 10.11. The last section, Section 10.12, concludes the chapter.

10.2 **Biometrics and Forensics**

The scope and reach for biometrics are all encompassing. They consider appearance, behavior, and cognitive state or intent for the purpose of digital identification. Forensics, complementary to biometrics [73], addresses data collection and decision-making for legal purposes. Together, biometrics and forensics are mostly concerned with identity (ID), which for all practical purposes is about information rather than data. Raw biometric data (i.e., unprocessed identity data) refers to a mere collection of images. Information, however, expands on data to include implicit or explicit associations. The etymology and semiotics of the word "information" are clear on this aspect. They involve communication and meaning, and their hallmarks are those of entropy and uncertainty. Last but not least "information" has value and establishes context to inform and instruct, and ultimately to control behavior. Identity management (IM) stands for the application of management principles to the acquisition, organization, control, dissemination, and strategic use of biometric information for security and privacy purposes. It is responsible with authentication, like (ATM) verification, identification ("recognition"), and large-scale screening and surveillance. IM is also involved with change detection, deduplication, retention, and/or revision of biometric information as people age and/or experience illness.

Gonzales-Rodriguez et al. [123] provide strong motivation from forensic sciences for the evidential and discriminative use of the likelihood ratio (LR). Classical forensic reporting provides only "identification" or "exclusion/elimination" decisions and requires the use of subjective thresholds. If the forensic scientist is the one choosing the thresholds, he or she will be ignoring the prior probabilities related to the case, disregarding the evidence under analysis, and usurping the role of the Court in taking the decision. The use of biometrics for identification purposes requires context and forensic expertise for making choices, with "... the use of thresholds in essence a qualification of the acceptable level of reasonable doubt adopted by the expert" [49].

The roles of the forensic scientist and the judge/jury are clearly separated using the LR while driven by the Bayesian approach. What the Court wants to know are the posterior odds in favor of the prosecution proposition (P) over the defense (D) [posterior odds = LR × prior odds]. The prior odds concern the Court (background information relative to the case), while the LR, which indicates the strength of support from the evidence, is provided by the forensic scientist. The forensic scientist cannot infer the identity of the probe ("subject") from the analysis of the forensic evidence, but gives the Court the LR for the two competing hypothesis (P and D). The likelihood ratio, an indicator of discriminating power, comparatively assesses recognition performance. This discussion motivates the use of nonconformal measures for addressing authentication using confident predictors.

The discriminative methods link the Bayesian framework, forensics, and likelihood ratios (odds) on one side, and statistical learning, randomness, and complexity on the other side. Additional philosophical and linguistic arguments that support the discriminative approach have to do with practical reasoning and epistemology, when recalling from Hume, that "all kinds of reasoning consist in nothing but a comparison and a discovery of those relations, either constant or inconstant, which two or more objects bear to each other," similar to non-accidental coincidences and sparse but discriminative codes for association [15]. Formally, "the goal of pattern classification can be approached from two points of view: informative [generative]—where the classifier learns the class densities or discriminative—where the focus is on learning the class boundaries without regard to the underlying class densities" [291]. Discriminative methods avoid estimating how the data has been generated and instead focus on estimating their posteriors similar to the use of likelihood ratios (LR) and odds. These "discriminative" considerations further motivate the use of nonconformity measures throughout this chapter and the adoption of the conformal prediction framework for face recognition. Set and nested confidence predictors (see Chapter 1) trade reliability and informativeness, using validity and efficiency as main indicators of the quality of the predictions made. The nested confidence predictors substitute for the use of subjective thresholds.

10.3 Face Recognition

The robust aspect of identity management concerns inference and prediction, for example, authentication for the purpose of classification and discrimination. It is accomplished using incremental evidence accumulation and corresponding disambiguation, learning and adaptation, and closed-loop control. This is characteristic of reidentification, with matching of faces or parts thereof taking place across multiple but possibly disjoint fields of view (FOV) for the purpose of progressive authentication over space and time. It is also characteristic of the search for the most efficient conformal predictors. Biometric ("face") detection and seeding for initialization do not presume known ID and allow for reidentification ("surveillance") of targets, like faces, whose identity might remain unknown.

Face recognition in well-controlled environments is relatively mature and has been heavily studied, but face recognition in uncontrolled or moderately controlled environments is still in its early stages. The challenges that have to be met, characteristic of uncontrolled settings, which bear on interoperability, include coping with incomplete ("occlusion") and corrupt ("disguise") information, image variability like pose, illumination, and expression (PIE), and temporal change. Both recognition-by-parts and reidentification, which are discussed later, cope with uncontrolled settings using the CP framework. Interoperability concerns mass screenings when enrollment and authentication take place at multiple locations, physically and temporally separated. This involves different human operators whose performance varies due to training and fatigue. The capture devices used vary too in terms of their working condition. Proper validation of protocols and results, including the cumulative effect of such varying conditions, hard to estimate and predict, affects interoperability.

Best practices or protocols for biometrics in general, and face recognition in particular, consist of learning the representation basis (face space), gallery enrollment (training), and querying for authentication (testing) (see Figure 10.1). The face processing space can be conceptualized as an $n - D$ space with its axes indexing variability along dimensions related to data acquisition and processing conditions. The axes describe the geometry used during image acquisition, such as pose, illumination, and expression (PIE); motion and/or temporal change; and last but not least the impact of uncooperative subjects (e.g., impostors). Characteristic of uncooperative subjects are occlusion and disguise, or equivalently denial and deception. Disguise can be deliberate and used by impostors for nefarious purposes. Deception is most effective in cluttered environments when it becomes easier to hide, thanks to many distracters. Occlusion and disguise, however, are not always deliberate. Examples for accidental occlusion occur for the crowded environments processed by CCTV, when only parts of faces are visible from time to time and not necessarily in the right 3D sequence. Normal phenomena with deceptive impact include bags under the eyes, which affect eye location and thus face detection and normalization, wrinkles from aging, medical conditions (allergies, injuries, and moles), fatigue, and facial hair. Correspondence using precise alignment required for matching during authentication remains a major challenge for face recognition. Biometrics cannot continue to assume that the personal signatures used for face authentication are complete, constant, and time-invariant. Most clients are indeed legitimate and honest. They have nothing to hide, and have all the incentives to cooperate. The very purpose of biometrics, however, is to provide security from impostors seeking to breach security and/or from uncooperative subjects.

Performance evaluation is an integral part of any serious effort to field reliable face recognition systems [375]. We start by considering target gallery G and query probe Q. The output is a full (distance) similarity matrix $S(q, g)$, which measures the similarity between each query face, $q \in Q$, and each target face, $g \in G$. The nearest neighbor (nn) classifier authenticates (tests) face images (of unknown identity) using the similarity scores recorded by S. The availability of the matrix S allows for different "virtual" experiments to be conducted when we select the specific query Q^* and gallery G^* as subsets of Q and G, respectively. Note that we can expand on this

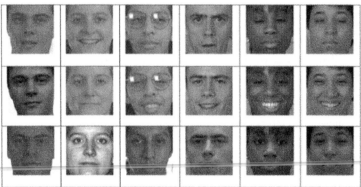

Face Space Basis Derivation

FIGURE 10.1

Face recognition methodology.

model using data fusion when sets rather than singletons are enrolled and/or queried for matching purposes, and/or both the query and the gallery are acquired using multimodal sensors. The use of "set" for terminology here assumes that subjects are distinct from each other in both G and Q and that their examples disregarding their provenance are distinct too. Closed set face recognition corresponds to $1 : N$ identification and employs repeated verification. As each probe has always a mate in the gallery, it is restrictive and does not reflect the true intricacies of positive and negative biometric enrollment and identification. Under positive enrollment, the client is authenticated to become eligible for "admission" or apprehended if on some watch list, while under negative identification the biometric system has to determine that the client does not belong to some most-wanted list. Positive identification can be determined using traditional personal tokens like PIN, but negative identification can only be established using biometrics. More challenging is open set face recognition, which operates under the assumption that not all the probes have mates (counterparts) in the gallery (of known subjects) (see Section 10.7). Open set recognition requires the *a priori* availability of a reject option to provide for the answer "none of the above" for unknown ("unfamiliar") subject ("client") probes. If the probe is found as familiar and it is not rejected, the face recognition engine must subsequently *identify/recognize* the subject.

The operational analog for open set face recognition is the (usually small) watch list or *surveillance* task, which involves (1) negative identification ("rejection") due to the obvious fact that the large majority (almost all) of the people screened at security entry points are law abiding citizens, and (2) correct identification for those who make up the watch list. "Performance for the open set problem is quantified over two populations. First the impostors, those persons who are not present in the gallery, i.e., not on the watch list, are used to compute the false match [acceptance] rate, which is needed to quantify rejection capability. Second, for those persons who are "known" (i.e., previously enrolled) to a system, the open set identification rate is used to quantify user [hit] performance" [127]. Open set recognition supports outlier detection and is characteristic of intrusion detection. Cumulative Matching Curves (CMC) and Receiver Operating Characteristics (ROC) are used to display the results for identification and verification, respectively. Ground truth, however, is not available during real field operation, hence the need for *a priori* setting of decision thresholds (see Section 10.7).

10.4 **Randomness and Complexity**

The Kolmogorov complexity K of a finite string $\mathbf{x}$ is the information in $\mathbf{x}$ defined by the length of the shortest program for a reference Universal Turing Machine (UTM) (encoded in binary bits) that outputs the string $\mathbf{x}$. The information distance $d(\mathbf{x}, \mathbf{y})$ is the length of the shortest program on the reference UTM computing $\mathbf{y}$ from $\mathbf{x}$ and $\mathbf{x}$ from $\mathbf{y}$. Up to an additive logarithmic term, $d(\mathbf{x}, \mathbf{y}) = max\{K(\mathbf{x}|\mathbf{y}), K(\mathbf{y}|\mathbf{x})\}$, where $K(\mathbf{x}|\mathbf{y})$ is the conditional complexity of $\mathbf{x}$ given $\mathbf{y}$. The normalized information distance (NID) between two strings $\mathbf{x}$ and $\mathbf{y}$ is $NID(\mathbf{x}, \mathbf{y}) = d(\mathbf{x}, \mathbf{y})/max\{K(\mathbf{x}), K(\mathbf{y})\}$ with $K(\mathbf{x})$ and $K(\mathbf{y})$ approximated by a real-life compressor C such that $C(\mathbf{x})$ is the length of the compressed version of $\mathbf{x}$.

Let S be the set of binary strings $\mathbf{x}$ of fixed length and Kolmogorov complexity $K(\mathbf{x})$. The randomness deficiency $D(\mathbf{x}|S)$ for string $\mathbf{x}$ is $D(\mathbf{x}|S) = log|S| - K(\mathbf{x}|S)$ with $D(\mathbf{x}|S)$ a measure of how random the binary string $\mathbf{x}$ is. The larger the randomness deficiency, the more regular and more probable the string $\mathbf{x}$ is. Transduction (see Section 10.5) chooses from all the possible labeling ("identities") for test data the one that yields the largest randomness deficiency (i.e., the most probable labeling). The biometric face recognition engine is built around randomness and complexity using NCM and rankings driven by strangeness and p-values, respectively (see Section 10.6). Kolmogorov complexity and randomness are conceptually related through the minimum description length (MDL). This recalls Gottfried Leibniz's 1685 philosophical essay *Discourse on Metaphysics*. The essay discusses how we can distinguish between facts that can be described by some law and those that are lawless or irregular. Leibniz observed that "a theory has to be simpler than the data it explains; otherwise it does not explain anything. The concept of a law becomes vacuous if arbitrarily high mathematical complexity is permitted, because then one can always construct a law no matter how random and patternless the data really are." The corollary for Chaitin is that "a useful theory is a compression of the data; comprehension is compression." Last but not least, modeling for the purpose of prediction rather than mere explanation then should be preferred.

10.5 Transduction

Transductive inference or for brevity transduction is a type of local inference that moves from particular to particular. "In contrast to inductive inference where one uses given empirical data to find the approximation of a functional dependency (the inductive step [that moves from particular to general]) and then uses the obtained approximation to evaluate the values of a function at the points of interest (the deductive step [that moves from general to particular]), one estimates [using transduction] the values of a function [only] at the points of interest in one step" [352]. Transduction incorporates the unlabeled data, characteristic of test point, in the decision-making process responsible for their eventual labeling. This involves some combinatorial optimization process that seeks to maximize the likelihood or fitness for the local model chosen to predict ("label") the combined training and test data. As an example, the transductive SVM (TSVM) maximizes the margin for both labeled and unlabeled examples [162]. Transduction "works because the test set can give you a nontrivial factorization of the [discrimination] function class" [52]. One key concept behind transduction is the symmetrization lemma [352]. The idea is to replace the true risk by an estimate computed on an independent set of data (e.g., unlabeled or test data). The extra data set is referred to as "virtual" or "ghost sample." The simplest mathematical realization for transductive inference is the method of k-nn. The Cover-Hart [62] theorem proves that asymptotically the one nearest neighbor algorithm is bounded above by twice the Bayes' minimum probability of error.

10.6 Nonconformity Measures for Face Recognition

The nonconformity measure A used throughout is that of strangeness. The conformal predictor corresponding to A as a nonconformity measure employs p-values. The particular strangeness and p-values used throughout are defined in the following.

The strangeness measures the lack of typicality (for a face or face component) with respect to its true or putative (assumed) identity label and the labels for all the other faces or parts thereof known to some gallery G. Formally, the k-nn strangeness measure α_i is the (likelihood) ratio of the sum of the k nearest neighbor (k-nn) distances d for sample x_i from the same class y divided by the sum of the k nearest neighbor (k-nn) distances from all the other classes ($\neg y$). The smaller the strangeness, the larger its typicality and the more probable its (putative) label y is. We note here the impact of nearest-neighborhood relations, characteristic of lazy learning, on the computation involved in the derivation of nonconformity measures (NCM).

The strangeness facilitates both feature selection (similar to Markov blankets) and variable selection (dimensionality reduction). We find empirically that the strangeness, classification margin, sample and hypothesis margin, posteriors, and odds are all related via a monotonically nondecreasing function with a small strangeness amounting to a large margin. Note that k-nn error approaches the Bayes error (with factor 1) if $k = O(\log n)$; strangeness α is related to the optimal decision boundary ($\alpha = 1$) and the posterior $P(c_j | x_i)$; and the k-nn strangeness smoothes boundaries and generalizes better than k-nn, particularly for overlapping distributions. An alternative definition for NCM as hypothesis margin, similar to the strangeness, is

$$\Phi(x) = (\|x - nearmiss(x)\| - \|x - nearhit(x)\|) \tag{10.1}$$

with nearhit (x) and nearmiss (x) being the nearest samples of x that carry the same and a different label, respectively. The strangeness can also be defined using the Lagrange multipliers associated with (kernel) SVM classifiers but this requires a significant increase in computation. We note here that the likelihood-like definitions for strangeness are intimately related to discriminative methods. Transduction chooses from all the possible labelings ("identities") for test data the one that yields the largest randomness deficiency (i.e., the most probable labeling). Randomness deficiency is, however, not computable. We must approximate it instead, using a slightly modified Martin-Löf test for randomness, and the values taken by such randomness tests are called p-values. They compare ("rank") the strangeness values to determine the credibility and confidence in the alternative putative classifications ("labelings") made. The p-values bear resemblance to their counterparts from statistics but are not the same [151]. The p-values are determined using the relative strangeness of each of the putative authentications across the identity classes known to the gallery whose number of enrolled subjects is l. The standard p-value construction shown here, where l is the cardinality of the training ("gallery") G, constitutes a valid randomness (deficiency) test approximation for some putative label y hypothesis assigned to a new sample image z of known representation **x** whose label has to be predicted:

$$p^z(y) = \#(i : \alpha_i \geq \alpha_{new}^y)/(l + 1) \tag{10.2}$$

Note that each *new* test example z with putative label y (and strangeness α_{new}^y) requires to recompute, if necessary, the strangeness for all the training examples when the identity of their k nearest neighbors changes due to the location of (the just inserted new example) z. An alternative valid randomness (deficiency) test approximation and the one used here, defines the p-value p^z for the example z (with putative label y) as

$$p^z(y) = \frac{f(\alpha_1) + f(\alpha_2) + \cdots + f(\alpha_l) + f(\alpha_{new}^y)}{(l+1)f(\alpha_{new}^y)} \qquad (10.3)$$

where f is some monotonic nondecreasing function with $f(0) = 0$, for example, $f(\alpha) = \alpha$, and l is the number of training exemplars. Empirical evidence shows that the alternative randomness approximation yields better performance than the standard one, which may suffer from "distortion phenomenon" [364].

Transduction employs the whole training set G to authenticate each new query. Based on the p-values defined earlier, Proedrou et al. [280] have proposed the TCM/k-nn (Transduction Confidence Machine/k-nearest neighbors), referred throughout this chapter as TCM, to serve as a formal transductive inference algorithm for classification purposes. In addition to classification/authentication, TCM provides NCM, such as credibility and confidence (see later). While TCM is most suitable for closed set recognition, it does not address the detection aspect needed for open set recognition. Toward that end, we introduce in the next section the Transduction Confidence Machine for Detection and Recognition (TCM-DR). It is the solution we advance for open set recognition as it facilitates outlier detection, in general, and impostor detection, in particular.

The p-values are used to assess the extent to which the biometric data supports or discredits the null hypothesis H0 (for some specific subject ID authentication). Large random deficiency, which shows up as large p-values, suggests them as most credible ID labelings. When the null hypothesis is rejected for each identity class known, one records that the test image lacks mates in the gallery and therefore the identity query is answered with "none of the above." This corresponds to forensic exclusion with rejection, and it is characteristic of open set recognition (see Section 10.7). The largest p-value defines the credibility of the classification chosen. The confidence measure is the difference between the top two p-values. It indicates how close to each other the first two classifications are and it measures ambiguity. The larger the confidence the smaller the ambiguity is. Both credibility and confidence are examples of information quality suitable for decision-making and data fusion, and are complementary outputs of TCM beyond classification/authentication. Assuming that closed face recognition takes place using either Eigenfaces (PCA) or Fisherfaces to encode facial signatures, the corresponding Cartesian products of confidence and credibility, derived using TCM for closed set recognition, correctly segregate authentication outcomes between Correct/Hit and False Accept Recognition, respectively (see Figure 10.2) [375].

Note that the basic TCM seeks for authentication the label that is most consistent with the training set composing the gallery. The intuition behind TCM is to model the working ("test") exemplar set Q in a fashion most similar to the training set G while minimally change the original (predictive) model learned from and for G, or alternatively enable the prediction model to accommodate learning from the augmented set $G \cup Q$. "The difference between the classifications that induction and transduction

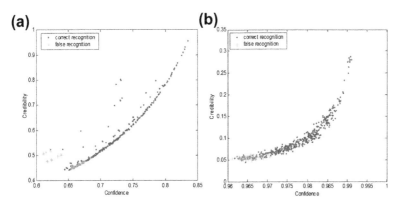

FIGURE 10.2

Closed set recognition for (a) Eigenfaces and (b) Fisherfaces using (confidence, credibility) for non-conformity measures.

yield for some working exemplar approximates its randomness deficiency. The intuitive explanation is that one disturbs a classifier (driven by G) by inserting a new working exemplar in a training set. A magnitude of this disturbance is an estimation of the classifier's instability (unreliability) in a given region of its problem space" [187] and supports inductive conformal predictors (ICP) (see Section 10.12).

10.7 Open and Closed Set Face Recognition

The two operation modes for face recognition, those of closed and open set recognition, were introduced earlier (see Section 10.3). The basic difference between them is that open set recognition considers the possibility that a query posed against the gallery cannot be processed to completion if the subject of the query is not enrolled. This corresponds to lack of familiarity and the authentication query needs to be duly rejected. Informally, the unfamiliar subject lacks a mate in the gallery and plays the role of impostor. Another reason for lacking a mate happens when the image quality is greatly impaired and no reliable matches are available to answer the query. In both cases, the search for familiarity corresponds to "detection" and lack of familiarity is recorded as an impostor attempt for authentication. This requires empirical determination of an optimal detection threshold driven by some similarity distance. The combined macro for (open and closed) face categorization method (see later) TCM-DR (Transduction Confidence Machine for Detection and Recognition/k-nn) expands on the basic TCM (see Section 10.6) as it supports both detection and recognition (steps d and e; whereas TCM supports only recognition in step d)

(a) Strangeness computation
(b) (Randomness deficiency) p-values derivation and rankings
(c) (Confidence, Credibility) computation of nonconformity measures (NCM)

(d) (Detection) *a priori* setting for impostor threshold and detection decisions (for rejection) in terms of (low) p-values using PSR (peak-side-ratio) with $PSR = (p_{max} - p_{mean})/p_{sd}$ and $PSR > \theta$

(e) (Recognition) TCM (Transduction Confidence Machine)/k-nn (k nearest neighbors) recognition

The proposed solution for the detection step involves using the peak-to-side ratio (PSR) distribution of p-values. p_{mean} and p_{sd} are the mean and standard deviation for the p-values distribution without the p_{max} value. p-values rankings and NCM are used for "detection" (see step d, earlier) and then for "recognition" (see step e, earlier) but only for faces found familiar in step d. PSR implements the equivalent of the likelihood ratio (LR) used in detection theory and hypothesis testing, with LR playing the role of the ratio between the null hypothesis H0 (that the unknown face is enrolled in the gallery) and the alternative hypothesis H1 (that the face has never enrolled). PSR determines the optimal threshold needed for accepting or rejecting the null hypothesis H0 concerning the particular working exemplar z. Toward that end and integral to TCM-DR, we have to (re)label the training examples, one at a time, with all the putative labels except the one originally assigned to them. This is characteristic of revision using "ghost" or "virtual" examples subsumed by the symmetrization lemma (see Section 10.5).

The PSR distribution derived in such a manner is characteristic of negative identification or rejection. Implementationwise, each training exemplar g has its mates first removed from the gallery and treated as a probe to derive its p-value and corresponding PSR. The PSR values found for such examples are low since they play the role of impostors and lack mates, compared to the PSR values derived for legitimate ("enrolled") subjects. Low PSR values call thus for rejection. Furthermore, if all p-values are randomly distributed and no p-values outscore other p-values enough, any recognition choice will be questionable and the new exemplar should be rejected. The PSR distribution obtained over the training set provides then a robust method for deriving the rejection threshold without access to negative examples, characteristic of impostors. The threshold for rejection can now be learned *a priori* using only the composition and structure of the training data set G at enrollment time. The proposed PSR distribution for presumed impostors provides therefore a method for empirically deriving *a priori* the sought-after rejection threshold for detection as $\theta = PSR_{mean} + 3 \times PSR_{sd}$ with PSR_{mean} and PSR_{sd} characteristic of the PSR distribution of presumed impostors. A new test face z is rejected if $PSR_{new} \leq \theta$ holds true, and authentication takes place only for (large) PSR_{new} values that exceed θ. We note that detection for open set recognition (see step d for TCM-DR) and verification operations are complementary to each other in the use of PSR for setting rejection thresholds. TCM-DR further facilitates outlier detection in general, and impostor detection in particular.

Biometric systems in general, and face recognition engines in particular, require significant calibration and tuning for setting detection thresholds before any plug-and-play can take place. Setting thresholds is not easy to automate due to their strong dependency on image quality and the composition of the gallery. Note also that "much more is known about the population of genuine customers than it is known about adversaries, i.e., the imposters that need be rejected. Consequently, the probability of a false alarm rate (FAR), a false match (for screening and positive identification), is hard to estimate. Hence, the false reject rate (FRR), that concerns open set negative identification, is easier to estimate than the false alarm rate, because the biometric samples of the enemy population are not available" [33]. The thresholds needed for field deployment and operation have to be set up ahead of time, *a priori*, and without resorting to additional impostor data. The alternative of setting the thresholds *a posteriori* using the ground truth available from the aggregate similarity scores recorded for matching the probe set against the gallery set is not appropriate because the ground truth is not available during system operation (see also Section 10.9 on score normalization).

Open set face recognition expands the scope of traditional face identification. It involves both detection and recognition [204] (see Figure 10.3a). Detection means familiarity rather than finding faces in an image or tracking them in a crowd. When detection fails, the face is rejected using the "none of the above" option rather than misclassified as the most similar face in the gallery, as closed set face recognition does by default. Rejection can be due among other things to a deliberate attempt made by an impostor to penetrate a secure facility. Watch list/surveillance (see Section 10.9), a special instance of open set face recognition, corresponds to the scenario when the overlap between the gallery and probe sets is the gallery (watch list) itself and the probe set size is much larger than the gallery (see Figure 10.3b). Watch list surveillance corresponds to the case when subjects are matched for negative identification against some WANTED list.

The experimental design and results on open set face recognition using transduction reported next follow Li and Wechsler [204]. The biometric data set comes from the FERET database developed by the author at George Mason University [274], and consists of 750 frontal face images from 250 subjects (see Figure 10.4), where each column corresponds to one subject. 200 subjects come from the difficult FERET batch #15 that was captured under variable illumination and/or facial expressions,

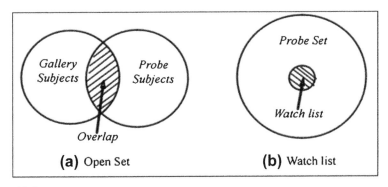

FIGURE 10.3

Open set face recognition and watch list surveillance.

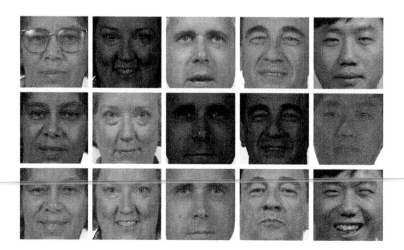

FIGURE 10.4

Face images for open set face recognition.

while the other 50 subjects are drawn from other FERET batches. There are three normalized (zero mean and unit variance) images of size 150×150 with 256 gray scale levels for each subject. The normalized 300 face images from 100 subjects are used to learn the PCA and Fisherfaces face bases. Toward that end, 50 subjects are randomly selected from batch #15, while the other 50 subjects are drawn from other batches. The remaining 450 face images from 150 different subjects are used for enrollment and testing (see Figure 10.1). The faces are projected on the face bases derived ahead of time to yield 300 PCA Eigenfaces and 100 Fisherfaces using LDA on the reduced 300 PCA space. For each subject, two images are randomly selected for training and one image for testing. Several well-known similarity measures are used to evaluate different (PCA and Fisherfaces) face representations in conjunction with TCM-DR (for $k = 1$). The nearest neighbor classifier completes the identification process using Mahalanobis $+L_2$ and cosine distances for PCA and Fisherfaces face representations, respectively.

Comparative performance of TCM-DR against Open Set {PCA, Fisherfaces} is presented next. The detection thresholds for TCM-DR are derived as explained earlier, while for Open Set {PCA, Fisherfaces} the thresholds are found as explained next. The Open Set {PCA (Eigenfaces) and Fisherfaces} classifiers derive their rejection threshold from the intra- and interdistance (similarity) distribution of training exemplars in a fashion similar to that used by FRVT2002. The statistics of intradistance (within) distribution set the lower bound of the threshold, while the statistics of interdistance (between) distribution set the upper bound. As the minimum distance of the new (test/probe) exemplar to the prototypes for each class becomes closer to or larger than the upper bound, the more likely it is that the test exemplar will be rejected.

The recognition rate reported below for Open Set {PCA and Fisherfaces} is the percentage of subjects whose probe is either correctly rejected or accepted and recognized. From the 150 subjects available, 80 subjects are randomly selected to form a fixed gallery, while another 80 subjects are randomly selected as probes such that 40 of them have mates in the gallery. The gallery and probe sets overlap thus over 40 subjects. The gallery consists of two (out of three) randomly selected images; the probes consist of the remaining image for faces that belong to the gallery and one (out of three) randomly selected image for faces that does not belong to the gallery. During testing different distance measurements are used and the threshold varies from the lower to the upper bound as explained earlier. The same experiment was run 100 times with different probe sets. The distance measurements d for Open Set {PCA, Fisherfaces} that yield the best results are Mahalanobis $+L_2$ and cosine, respectively. When ground truth is available, the thresholds θ are optimally set to yield maximum performance; rejection occurs when min $d > \theta$. The best average recognition rates (over 100 experiments) (i.e., correct rejection and identification) for Open Set {PCA, Fisherfaces} classifiers at FAR = 7% and $\theta \sim (intra_{mean} \times intra_{sd} + inter_{mean} \times inter_{sd})/(inter_{sd} + intra_{sd})$ were 74.3% (sd = 3.06%) for PCA and 85.4% (sd = 2.30%) for Fisherfaces.

For Open Set PCA, the results are quite similar when the number of components used varies from 150 to 300, while for Open Set Fisherfaces, the results are quite similar when the number of components used varies from 55 to 90. More experiments have been done by randomly varying the gallery set and the results obtained were similar. The optimal threshold, however, varies with the gallery and probe sets, and is hard to determine *a priori*. Attempts made to learn the threshold *a priori* without access to ground truth were unsuccessful. The same Open Set experiment was run then using TCM-DR for $k = 1$. The only difference now is that the rejection threshold θ is computed *a priori* as explained earlier. Detection requires large PSR. The average recognition (correct rejection and identification) rates for FAR = 6% are

- 81.2% (sd = 3.1%) for PCA using $\theta = 5.51$ and Mahalanobis $+L_2$ distance
- 88.5% (sd = 2.6%) for Fisherfaces using $\theta = 9.19$ and cosine distance

Using PCA, the results for TCM-DR are quite similar when the number of components used varies from 170 to 300, while using Fisherfaces the results for TCM-DR are quite similar when the number of components used varies from 55 to 80. More experiments were done in a random fashion by varying the gallery but the results obtained were similar. The threshold varies with the chosen gallery but it is always determined *a priori*. This is different from Open Set {PCA, Fisherfaces} where the threshold is derived *a posteriori* using ground truth. Keeping this significant difference in mind, TCM-DR outperforms the Open Set {PCA, Fisherfaces} classifiers both in performance and functionality.

10.8 Watch List and Surveillance

The gallery of wanted individuals now is very small compared to the number of subjects expected to flood the biometric system (see Figure 10.3b). Negative identification takes place for subjects not listed on the watch list for surveillance. Again there are 150 subjects, three images from each subject, for a total of 450 face images. Open Set {PCA, Fisherfaces} and TCM-DR are compared on small watch lists, whose size varies from 10 to 40 subjects. The mean (average) performance (detection and identification) rates obtained over 100 randomized runs are reported. Let the watch list size be n subjects, each of them having two images in the gallery. There are $(450 - 2n)$ face images in the probe set, n stands for the number of subjects on the watch list, and $(3 \times (150 - n))$ is the number of face images traced to subjects that are not on the watch list. The small size of the watch list requires that the threshold for rejection is derived from larger populations for stability purposes. The decision threshold is found in a manner similar to that used by cohort models for speaker verification. Toward that end, the gallery is augmented with different subjects randomly drawn from other FERET batches that include illumination and facial expression variation. The intra- and interdistance distributions and the PSR distributions determine as before the rejection thresholds for Open Set {PCA, Fisherfaces} and TCM-DR, respectively. The size of the gallery used to determine the threshold is kept constant at 80 throughout the runs so the number $(80 - n)$ of different subjects needed to augment it varies according to the size of the watch list.

When the watch list size is n, the accuracy (detection and identification rate) is (average correct rejection + average correct recognition)/$(450 - 2n)$. Since the watch list size is much smaller than the number of subjects that should be rejected, the (detection and identification rate) accuracy will be very high even if all the probes are rejected. The average results are better the closer the correct rejection number is to $(3 \times (150 - n))$, the closer the correct recognition number is to the watch list size, and the higher the accuracy is. The Fisherfaces representations outperform PCA regarding both rejection and identification decisions, with overall accuracies of 91% and 87%, respectively. As the watch list size increases, the performance drops as expected. TCM-DR is better than Open Set {PCA, Fisherfaces}, when the correct rejection, correct recognition, and the accuracy are taken into account, especially when the watch list size is large. PCA and Fisherfaces representations yield similar accuracy (around 92%). The overall performance for TCM-DR, which stays almost constant as the watch list size increases, is more stable than the performance observed for Open Set {PCA, Fisherfaces}. As expected the gallery size affects algorithmic performance [204].

10.9 Score Normalization

There are conceptual similarities between the use of PSR to approximate the likelihood ratio and score normalization methods used in speaker verification [111,285]. Score normalization models the alternative hypothesis H1 using either the cohort or the universal background model (UBM). The cohort approximates H1 using speech specific (same gender impostor) subjects, while UBM models H1 by pooling speech from several speakers and training a single speaker background model. PSR discussed earlier is conceptually related to the cohort model, as both implement the LR using local estimation for H1. The ability of the cohort model to discriminate the speaker's speech from those of similar, same gender impostors, is much better than that offered by UBM [220], and it leads to improved security at lower FAR (false acceptance rates). Similar arguments hold for other modalities, including human faces, whose authentication is sought. The same cohort model leads to an alternative definition for strangeness that was successfully used to implement and combine weak learners for recognition-by-parts (see Section 10.10).

The practice of score normalization in biometrics aims at countering subject/client pairwise variability during verification. It is used here to draw sharper class or client boundaries for better authentication by adjusting both the client dependent scores and the thresholds needed for decision-making during postprocessing. This should be compared to PSR where the thresholds are derived *a priori*. The context for score normalization includes clients CL and impostors $\neg CL$. Score normalization during postprocessing can be adaptive or empirical, and it requires access to additional biometric data during the decision-making process. The details for empirical score normalization and its effects are as follows [3]. Assume that the pdf of match (similarity) scores is available for both genuine transactions (for the same client; i.e., P_g) and impostor transactions (between different clients; i.e., P_i). Such information can be gleaned from sets maintained during enrollment or gained during the evaluation itself. One way to calculate the normalized similarity score ns for a match score m is to use Bayes' rule

$$ns = P(g|m) = P(m|g)P(g)/P(m) \qquad (10.4)$$

where $P(g)$ is the *a priori* probability of a genuine event and $P(m|g)$ is the conditional probability of match score m for some genuine event g. The probability of m for all events, both genuine and impostor transactions, is

$$P(m) = P(g)P_g(m) + (1 - P(g))P_i(m) \qquad (10.5)$$

The normalized score ns is then

$$ns = P(g)P_g(m)/[P(g)P_g(m) + (1 - P(g))P_i(m)] \qquad (10.6)$$

The accuracy for the match similarity scores depends on the degree to which the genuine and impostor pdf approximate ground truth. Bayesian theory can determine optimal decision thresholds for verification only when the two (genuine and impostor) pdf are known. To compensate for pdf estimation errors we should fit for the "overall shape" of the normalized score distribution, while at seeking to discount for "discrepancies at low match scores due to outliers" [279]. The normalized score serves to convert the match score into a more reliable value.

The motivation behind empirical score normalization using evaluation data can be explained as follows. The evaluation data available during testing attempts to overcome the mismatch between the estimated and the real conditional probabilities referred to earlier. New estimates are obtained for both $P_g(m)$ and $P_i(m)$, and the similarity scores are changed accordingly. As a result, the similarity score between a probe and its gallery counterpart varies. Estimates for the genuine and impostor pdf, however, should still be obtained at enrollment time and/or during training rather than during testing as is the case with PSR. One of the innovations advanced by FRVT 2002 was the concept of virtual image sets. The availability of the similarity (between queries Q and targets G) matrix S enables us to conduct different "virtual" experiments by choosing specific query Q^* and gallery G^* subsets of Q and G. Examples of virtual experiments include assessing the influence of demographics and/or elapsed time on face recognition performance. Performance scores relevant to a virtual experiment correspond to the $Q^* \times G^*$ similarity scores. Empirical score normalization compromises, however, the very concept of virtual experiments. The explanation is quite simple. Empirical score normalization has no access to the information needed to define the virtual experiment. As a result, the updated or normalized similarity scores depend now on additional information whose origin is outside the specific gallery and probe subsets.

The best practice/protocol of learning and tuning the face space (see Figure 10.1) needs to be completed prior to performance evaluation using cross-validation for enrollment and test data partitions. Consequently, under this protocol, score normalization is prohibited and the similarity score $s(q, g)$ between a query image q and a target image g does not depend on the other images in the target and query sets. Avoiding hidden interactions between images other than the two being compared at the moment provides the clearest picture of how algorithms perform. More formally, any approach that redefines similarity as $s(q, g; T)$ such that it depends upon the target (or query) image subset T is not allowed in the Good, Bad, and Ugly (GBU) Challenge Problem [273]. To maintain separation of learning and test sets, an algorithm cannot be tuned on images of any of the subjects in the GBU Challenge Problem. The motivation for score normalization is to redefine matching scores based on cohort data. As the matching scores m are related to NCM, score normalization edits the scores using local estimation of genuine and impostor distributions, and therefore affects both the validity and efficiency of the outcomes for any realization of conformal prediction. There are other ways that score normalization can be done but independent of target image subsets T. First the very diversity sought by standard score normalization can be implicitly achieved using diversity while learning the face space. Diverse biometric databases could be randomly sampled to provide the subjects needed for learning the face space. Diversity refers to age, gender, ethnicity, and even image quality. Importance sampling for specific demographics, wide coverage, and chorus of prototypes that encodes "representation is representation of similarity" [87], are additional props for implicit score normalization. This is related to conditional validity and suggests the use of K-conditional conformal predictors (see Chapter 2) with diversity defined relative to taxonomy induced categories. Diversity and conditional validity described earlier lead to better interoperability and identity management.

10.10 Recognition-by-Parts Using Transduction and Boosting

Recognition-by-parts is the method of choice for dealing with uncontrolled settings in general, and occlusion and disguise in particular. The combination rule for multilevel and/or multilayer fusion data fusion (e.g., features and modalities) is principled. It employs sequential aggregation of different components (parts), which are referred to as weak learners in the boosting framework. This corresponds to an ensemble method, which is interchangeable as terminology with a mixture of experts. Boosting is complementary to transduction using the strangeness for NCM. The motivation for boosting goes as follows. Logistic regression directly estimates the parameters of $P(y|\mathbf{x})$ to learn mappings when y is Boolean. Logistic regression supports discriminative methods and likelihood ratios (e.g., label $y = 1$ if $P\{y = 1|\mathbf{x}\}/P\{y = 0|\mathbf{x}\} > 1$) and it can be approximated using Support Vector Machines (SVM). AdaBoost [105] minimizes (using greedy optimization) some functional whose minimum defines logistic regression [107]. AdaBoost converges to the posterior distribution of y conditioned on x, and the strong but greedy boosted classifier H (see later) in the limit becomes the log-likelihood ratio test. Finally we note that AdaBoost and an ensemble of SVM are functionally similar [353].

The basic assumption behind boosting is that "weak" learners can be combined to learn any target concept with probability $1 - \epsilon$(see similarity to validity for conformal prediction). Weak learners, usually built around simple features, learn to classify at better than chance (with probability $1/2 + \epsilon$ for $\epsilon > 0$). AdaBoost works by adaptively and iteratively resampling the data to focus learning on samples that the previous weak (learner) classifier could not master, with the relative weights of misclassified samples increased (refocused) after each iteration. AdaBoost involves choosing T effective components h_t to serve as weak learners and using them to construct separating hyperplanes. The mixture of experts or final boosted (stump) strong classifier H is

$$H(\mathbf{x}) = \sum_{t=1}^{T} \alpha_t h_t(x) > \frac{1}{2} \sum_{t=1}^{T} \alpha_t \tag{10.7}$$

with α the reliability or strength of the weak learner. The constant 1/2 comes in because the boundary is located midpoint between 0 and 1. If the negative and positive examples are labeled as -1 and $+1$ the constant used is 0 rather than 1/2. The goal for AdaBoost is margin optimization with the margin viewed as a measure of confidence or predictive ability. The weights taken by the data samples are related to their margin and explain the AdaBoost generalization ability.

The multiclass extensions for AdaBoost are AdaBoost.M1 and .M2, the latter used to learn strong classifiers with the focus now on both difficult examples to recognize and labels hard to discriminate. The use of features or in our case components as weak learners is justified by their apparent simplicity. The drawback for AdaBoost.M1 comes from its expectation that the performance for the weak learners selected is better than chance. When the number of classes is $k > 2$, the condition on error is, however, hard to be met in practice. The expected error for random guessing is $1 - 1/k$; for $k = 2$ the weak learners need to be just slightly better than chance. AdaBoost.M2 addresses this problem by allowing the weak learner to generate instead a set of plausible labels together with their plausibility (not probability); that is, $[0, 1]^k$ (similar to efficiency for conformal prediction). The AdaBoost.M2 version focuses on the incorrect labels that are hard to discriminate. Toward that end, AdaBoost.M2 introduces a pseudo-loss e_t for hypotheses h_t such that for a given distribution D_t we seek those $h_t : \mathbf{x} \times Y \rightarrow [0, 1]$ that are better than chance. "The pseudo-loss is computed with respect to a distribution over the set of all pairs of examples and incorrect labels. By manipulating this distribution, the boosting algorithm can focus the weak learner not only on hard-to-classify examples, but more specifically, on the incorrect labels y that are hardest to discriminate" [105]. The use of Neyman-Pearson is complementary to AdaBoost.M2 training and can meet prespecified hit and false alarm rates during weak learner selection similar to cascade learning (for face detection).

The following discussion [205] is relevant to both multilevel and multilayer fusion in terms of functionality and granularity. Multilevel fusion involves feature/parts, score (match), and detection (decision), while multilayer fusion involves modality, quality, and method (algorithm). The components are realized as weak learners whose relative performance is driven by transduction using the strangeness, while their aggregation is achieved using boosting. The strangeness is the thread to implement both representation and boosting (learning, inference, and prediction regarding classification). The strangeness, which implements the interface between the biometric representation (including attributes and/or parts) and boosting, combines the merits of filter and wrapper classification methods. The coefficients and thresholds for the weak learners, including the thresholds needed for open set recognition and rejection, are learned using validation images, which are described in terms of components similar to those found during enrollment. The best feature correspondence for each component is sought between a validation and a training biometric face image over the component (parts or attributes) defining that component. The strangeness of the best component found during training is computed for each validation biometric image under all its putative class labels $c(c = 1, \ldots, C)$. Assuming M validation biometric images from each class, we derive M positive (genuine) strangeness values for each class c, and $M(C - 1)$ negative (imposter) strangeness values. The positive and negative strangeness values correspond to the case when the putative label of the validation and training image are the same or not, respectively. The strangeness values are ranked for all the components available, and the best weak learner h_i is the one that maximizes the recognition rate over the whole set of validation biometric images V for some component i and threshold θ_i. Boosting execution is equivalent to cascade classification [357]. A component is chosen as a weak learner on each iteration (see Figure 10.5).

The level of significance α determines the scope for the null hypothesis H0. Different but specific alternatives can be used to minimize Type II error or equivalently to maximize the power $(1 - \beta)$ of the weak learner [85]. During cascade learning each weak learner (classifier) is trained to achieve (minimum acceptable) hit rate $h = (1 - \beta)$ and (maximum acceptable) false alarm rate α. Upon completion,

Strangeness values from validation images of class c

Strangeness values from validation images of all other classes

FIGURE 10.5

Weak learners (biometric components) as stump functions.

boosting yields the strong classifier $H(\mathbf{x})$, which is a collection of discriminative biometric components playing the role of weak learners. The hit rate after T iterations is h^T and the false alarm α^T.

The basic recognition-by-parts method using transduction and boosting can be realized as follows [205]:

- Scale Invariant Feature Transform (SIFT) [Gabor] Patch Representation
- Feature (and Variable/Dimensionality) "Patch" Selection Using Strangeness and Iterative Backward Elimination (mutual information and Markov blankets; not necessary when using the Golden Ratio Template for frontal and boxed images)
- From Patches to (exemplar based) Parts Using K-Means Clustering
- Weak Learners (Parts) Compete to Assembly "Strong" Learners by Boosting

The experimental results [205] reported next illustrate the feasibility and utility of model-free and nonparametric recognition-by-parts using transduction and boosting. The first experiment **EXP1** shows that our boosting realization of face detection (corresponding to Layer 1 categorization for face versus background using Caltech101 database) confirms psychophysical findings reported in [326], among them Result 5 "that of the different facial features, eyebrows were indeed found most important for face detection" (see Figure 10.6). The best weak learner corresponds to the part that yields the largest coefficient when boosting starts. The explanation for this finding is straightforward. The eyebrows are highly discriminative due to their emotive contents, stability, and location above a convexity that makes them less susceptible to shadow, illumination changes and displacement due to movement.

Another experiment **EXP4** compares our strangeness (transduction) based boosting recognition-by-parts method against a voting recognition scheme based on TCM [204]. Authentication is determined for the voting scheme according to the number of parts (posed by query q) matched by the gallery. Each part is matched according to its putative class label c that yields the largest p-value. The class membership for the face is predicted by class voting (i.e., the putative class label c that enjoys the largest number of matched parts). Strangeness-based transduction and boosting outperform the voting approach, 97.5% and 98.1% versus 87.8% and 90.3% using first- and second-order patches (without symmetry) and 97.8% and 98.9% versus 88.1% and 89.2% using first- and second-order patches (with symmetry). The explanation for the comparative advantage shown by our method comes from its unique use of

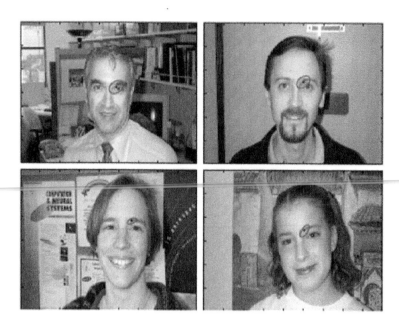

FIGURE 10.6

Eyebrows are best feature for face detection.

validation with competition between the parts playing the crucial role. The parts are not merely counted but rather their significance varies according to the categorization task accomplished.

In order to further evaluate the performance of boosting using transduction for face ID authentication, using uncontrolled settings, the next experiment **EXP6** considers tests images modified to simulate occlusion. A circle region with radius r is randomly chosen across the face image, the content of which is either set to zero or filled with random pixel values in [0, 255]. On the average the recognition rate decreases when the radius of occluded region increases but it does not drop too much. The occluded regions are randomly chosen and the performance observed is very stable when the occluded regions are not too large. The particular experiment reported next, **EXP7**, considers the case when the occluded regions are fixed (e.g., eyes, nose, and mouth). Figure 10.7 shows the recognition rates with respect to radius r when one eye, nose, or mouth is occluded and symmetry is used. The occlusion of nose affects the performance more than the mouth and eyes. This is consistent with the relative distribution found for the face parts' coefficients during training for boosting. It is also consistent with our earlier findings regarding the importance of the nose for biometric authentication using asymmetric faces [132]. Note the importance of the nose for Layer 2 categorization (identification) versus eyebrows importance (discussed earlier) for Layer 1 categorization (detection) (see **EXP1**).

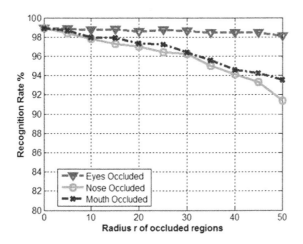

FIGURE 10.7

Recognition rates with respect to occlusion radius *r* when eye, nose, or mouth is occluded.

10.11 **Reidentification Using Sensitivity Analysis and Revision**

The reidentification problem is about matching objects in general, and faces in particular, across multiple but possibly disjoint fields of view for the purpose of sequential authentication over space and time. Detection and seeding for initialization do not presume known identity and allow for reidentification of objects and/or faces whose identity might remain unknown. Specific functionalities involved in reidentification include clustering and selection, recognition-by-parts, anomaly and change detection, sequential importance sampling and tracking, fast indexing and search, sensitivity analysis, and their integration for the purpose of identity management. Reidentification processes data streams, and involves change detection and online adaptation. The overall architecture is data-driven and modular on one side, and discriminative and progressive on the other (see Figure 10.8) [241]. The core of reidentification encompasses autonomic computing and W5+. Autonomic computing or self-management provides for closed-loop control. It provides among other things self-configuration (for planning and organization), self-optimization (for efficacy), and self-healing (to recover from misidentification and/or losing track of targets). W5+ answers questions related to functional dimensions such as *What* data to consider for sampling and collection, *When* to capture the data and from *Where*, and *How* to best process the data. The *Who* (is) query about identity becomes available for biometrics and identity management. Directed evidence accumulation also considers and documents the *Why* dimension for explanation purposes. The architecture intertwined challenges are those of (1) evidence-based management to progressively add value to data for

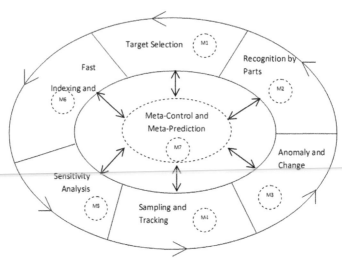

FIGURE 10.8

Prediction for reidentification online using semisupervised learning and transduction (PROUST).

upgrading it into knowledge leading to (2) purposeful and gainful action including active learning. Another dimension addressed is related to adversarial learning when reidentification becomes possibly "distracted" and sent off track due to deliberate injection of corrupt information.

Reidentification is characteristic of an overall hypothetical-deductive cycle of discovery, where an initial predictive model learned from data guides the iterative collection of new data, followed by model revision and new inferences (including labeling) that once again point the way to new data collection. This corresponds to an online hypothesis/observation and measurement/evaluation (validate/revision) loop of exploration and exploitation characteristic of intelligent control and discovery. Toward that end, three learning frameworks, characteristic of statistical learning, interface along the assumptions made to support conformal predictors. First, semisupervised learning stipulates the *smoothness assumption*, where similar examples share similar labels; the *cluster assumption*, where samples in the same cluster are likely to be of the same class; and the *low density separation assumption* that seeks for decision boundaries in low-density regions. Semisupervised learning spans the divide between supervised and unsupervised learning. Supervision is sparse and covers only some examples possibly using constraints, while the unsupervised aspect refers to clustering. Transduction, closely related to semisupervised learning and using nonconformity measures, mediates between randomness and prediction. Last, it is conformal prediction role to hedge and punt on putative labels for the purpose of validity and efficiency. This goes beyond bare predictions and includes reliability indexes for the specific choices made regarding reidentification.

Reliability indices include credibility and confidence for the predictions made, learning stability for the purpose of classification, and consistency in modeling the targets of interest and their recognizers. Along the same lines, Poggio et al. [278] suggest it is the stability of the learning process that leads to good predictions. The stability property says that "when the training set is perturbed by deleting one example, the learned hypothesis does not change much." The role of sensitivity analysis and revision is to engage the authentication system in continuous reidentification for the purpose of validation and efficiency and to set proper stopping criteria. The prediction regions narrow down and become smaller, and point prediction become feasible. One approach that addresses sensitivity analysis is that of inductive conformal predictors [114]. The divergence, characteristic of ICP, between inductive and transductive predictions, and the ensuing reliability attached to the recognition made, can be alternatively approached as discussed next.

Reliability indices are revised using information on class (label) such as priors, and the sensitivity and specificity of the classification method C used. Confidence intervals for both prediction and sequential importance sampling can be established accordingly. Toward that end assume a regression model where strangeness for some putative label y expands on (1.18) and is defined as

$$s(y) = \frac{p(x)|y - f(x)|}{e^{g(x)}} \tag{10.8}$$

with regression function f built using training data, error of regression function $|y - f(x)|$, estimate of accuracy for regression $g(x)$ built using Support Vector Regression (SVR) from data set $G = \{(x_i, ln(|y - f(x_i)|)), i = 1, \ldots, N\}$, and $p(x)$ characteristic of input data density. Given significance level and predictive region $\Gamma^\epsilon(T, x) = \{y \in Y : p_y > \epsilon\}$ or equivalently the set $\{y : s(y) < s_a\}$, which is a valid $(1 - a/(N + 1)) \times 100\%$ confidence region with $\epsilon = \#\{s_i : s_i \geq s_a\}/(N + 1)$. The predictive region is then

$$|y - f(x_{new})| < \frac{s_a e^{g(x)}}{p(x_{new})} \tag{10.9}$$

The obtained predictive region will be smaller for points at which SVR prediction is good and large for points where the prediction is bad, with more confidence in the regions of high input density [245].

10.12 Conclusions

Transduction is used throughout this chapter on problems related to categorization in general, and (biometrics) face recognition in particular. The on-line recognition aspect becomes paramount under reidentification scenarios, where characteristic of conformal prediction one hedges on progressive classification using incremental evidence accrual to decrease uncertainty (disambiguation) and increase efficiency vis-à-vis competitive (model-based) online nested prediction regions. Classification for the purpose of identification is efficient if the prediction region is relatively small and therefore informative [315]. The nonconformity measures used are those of strangeness driven p-values (for ranking) using k-nearest-neighborhood distances (for classification). The (closed and open set) classifiers advanced are TCM and TCM-DR, which operate under the assumption of randomness, when the objects (faces) and their labels are assumed to be generated independently from the same (but unknown) probability distribution (i.i.d) [114].

Similar to statistical learning we also stipulate throughout this chapter that the goal of learning is instrumentalism and generalization rather than estimation of true functions characteristic of system identification. Predictions choose that (putative) label y^* that corresponds to an online completion with the largest (p-value) randomness level referred to as the credibility of the choice made. Low credibility, possibly undermining validity, means that either the training set is nonrandom or the test object is not representative of the training set (i.e., not familiar). Open set recognition using cohort and impostor PSR methods expand on traditional TCM for the purpose of multilayer categorization leading to TCM-DR for both Detection (familiarity) and Recognition. The chapter also advances the scope for biometrics as it addresses adversarial learning vis-à-vis denial and deception in general, and occlusion and disguise in particular, employing recognition-by-parts using transduction and boosting. Note that boosting plays the role of metaprediction when combined with transduction for the purpose of prediction. In particular, it chooses among weak learners or parts using nonconformity measures such as the strangeness. The overall strategy followed throughout is characteristic of first guaranteeing validity under a relatively weak (rather than asymptotic) assumptions and then seeking efficiency under stronger assumptions [346].

As online transduction is local and incremental, computational drawbacks associated with k-nearest neighborhood classifiers readily surface. They can be alleviated using periodic updates, possibly informed by exchangeability for the purpose of change detection and/or distributed computation using MapReduce and Apache Hadoop. Another topic worth further study is the relation between boosting and conditionality. As boosting distinguishes between easy and hard-to-predict objects by iteratively ranking the stump (feature) weak learners, it becomes apparent that conformal prediction needs to be model-driven including reliability indices. The motivation for this observation comes from the local estimation aspect of transduction and it is reflected in the incremental approach sketched for online reidentification.

Reidentification leverages sensitivity analysis and revision for the purpose of recognition including increased efficiency. As reidentification involves sequential importance sampling, we can expand the scope of TCM and TCM-DR to include state trajectories for the purpose of behavior recognition, anomaly detection, and full-fledged spatial-temporal reasoning. The other side of the coin for recognition is deidentification, whose purpose is to provide for both security and privacy. As nonconformity measures support conformal prediction, their inverse measures (e.g., typicality) support anonymization purposes. Taken together identification and deidentification provide for enhanced and robust all-encompassing biometrics. We can translate the findings and suggestions made throughout this chapter to expand the scope of biometrics to cloud and fog (nearby) computing where behavior and intent compound appearance biometrics. Last but not least we note that the p-values distribution can indicate change or drift for online data streams. This is most important for proper evidence accumulation and authentication. In particular, the p-values from the conformal predictor on data generated from a source satisfying the exchangeability assumption are independent and uniformly distributed on [0, 1]. We note that when the observed data points are no longer exchangeable, the p-values have smaller value and the p-values are no longer uniformly distributed on [0, 1]. This is due to the fact that newly observed data points are likely to have higher strangeness values compared to the previously observed data points and the p-values therefore become smaller. This can be shown empirically using the Kolmogorov-Smirnov test (KS test). Note that the skewness, a measure of the degree of asymmetry of a distribution, deviates from close to zero (for uniformly distributed p-values) to more than 0.1 for the p-value distribution due to model change or drift occurs [151]. Alternatively, we can perform change detection approach driven by testing exchangeability described in Chapter 5.

Biomedical Applications: Diagnostic and Prognostic

11

Ilia Nouretdinov[*], **Tony Bellotti**[†], **and Alexander Gammerman**[*]

[*]*Computer Learning Research Centre, Department of Computer Science, Royal Holloway, University of London, United Kingdom*
[†]*Mathematics Department, Imperial College, London, United Kingdom*

CHAPTER OUTLINE HEAD

This chapter is devoted to medical applications of conformal predictors. Our main interest here is to review various nonconformity measures (NCMs) applied to different medical applications.

11.1 Introduction

There are several important advantages in applying conformal predictors (CP) in medical diagnostics. First of all, CPs provide valid measures of confidence in the diagnosis, and this is often a crucial advantage for medical decision-making since it allows the estimation of risk of an erroneous clinical decision for an individual patient. Moreover, the risk of clinical errors may be controlled by an acceptable level of confidence for a given clinical decision and therefore the risk of misdiagnosis is known. Another feature that makes CPs an attractive method in medical applications is that they are region predictors. This means that if we do not have enough information to make a definitive diagnosis, the method would allow us to make a number of possible (multiple) diagnoses and a patient may require further tests to narrow down the available options.

The core element of the CP is a nonconformity measure (NCM) that can be interpreted as an information distance between an object and a set. Selection of an appropriate NCM may improve efficiency of the prediction. The efficiency and validity are two main criteria in estimating success of the method. Validity in our approach means that for a given significance level, the probability of an error does not exceed the predetermined confidence threshold; and the efficiency means how many definitive diagnoses are made at a given confidence level.

Recall that NCM is defined by its equivariance equation (1.3):

$$(\alpha_1, \ldots, \alpha_n) = A(z_1, \ldots, z_n) \implies (\alpha_{\pi(1)}, \ldots, \alpha_{\pi(n)}) = A(z_{\pi(1)}, \ldots, z_{\pi(n)}).$$

This actually means that NCM can be defined as a distance between a set and one of its elements, reflecting relative strangeness of the element with respect to the set (or the strangeness of the data sequence continued by this example). The NCM values are usually converted to p-values by the formula 1.5:

$$p^z := \frac{|\{i = 1, \ldots, l + 1 \mid \alpha_i^z \geq \alpha_{l+1}^z\}|}{l + 1}$$

We review NCMs used in medical applications and consider them according to complexity and accessibility of features: from classical symptom-based clinical data to features obtained from more expensive high-throughput and high-dimensional techniques.

To begin, we present three examples that are related to proteomics, magnetic resonance images (MRI), and microarrays in order to give an interpretation of conformal prediction output and illustrate the main advantages of this approach. We use validity and efficiency as two main criteria to assess the results of applications.

After considering examples of conformal diagnostics, the paper reviews the NCMs used for diagnoses and we present an overall summary of the CP's medical applications.

11.2 Examples of Medical Diagnostics

Recall that a CP checks each of a set of hypotheses (possible diagnoses) when presented with a new example. The output—prediction set—is a list of diagnoses that are not discarded at a given significance level. If it consists of several possible diagnoses then the prediction is called uncertain (or multiple); if the prediction set consists of only a single diagnosis we shall call it *certain* (or definitive). The lower the significance level (higher confidence), the more predictions could become multiple. Sometimes, the conformal predictor makes errors. An *error* here means that the output prediction set does not contain the correct diagnosis of the new example. It is clear that using this setting we can actually control the number of errors by choosing an appropriate confidence level. The multiple predictions mean that there is not enough information in the data to make a single prediction, and the algorithm outputs several possible diagnoses. This is, of course, a very attractive feature of the algorithm since we are not forcing it to make an ultimate classification. Many "bare" prediction algorithms, including SVM, must assign a label irrespective of the circumstances. Different interpretation of errors makes the comparison with conventional algorithms more difficult, especially because the number of errors depends on the required confidence level. To compare the results in accuracy with conventional classification algorithms we also can use conformal predictor in its "bare" prediction form: the prediction is made by choosing the largest p-value for each individual example—so called "forced" predictions. Intuitively, the more difference between the highest and the second highest p-value, the more confident we are in our diagnosis. Hence we define confidence as a complement to 1 of the smallest significance level at which the prediction is *certain*. The certain prediction corresponds to the hypothesis that is assigned the highest p-value.

Another characteristic we use is *credibility*. It is the largest significance level at which the prediction set is not empty. If all the hypotheses are likely to be wrong, then we say that the prediction set is *empty* (or no diagnosis can be made) at the required level of confidence. This means that the new example is very unusual for any of the diagnostic groups presented in the training set. This may happen for example if the patient has a disease not from the list or if the data sample is collected or presented in a different way than the others.

How good our predictions are depends on the selected NCM, and its quality may be measured by the *certainty rate*.

Let us now introduce three examples of medical diagnostics using these concepts.

11.2.1 Proteomics: Breast Cancer

The proteomics data are usually presented as spectra, and machine learning methods are applied only after several steps of preprocessing (baseline substraction, smoothing, identification, and alignment of peaks). Typical details and data descriptions can be found in [113]. After the preprocessing each example is presented as a vector of intensities and we can form a list of the most frequent peaks. Only a few peaks are normally expected to be significant biomarkers for the discrimination between controls and cases.

An example of conformal methods applied to proteomic (breast cancer diagnosis) is presented in the work [112] that was a part of blind comparative assessment organized by Leiden University Hospital. The conformal predictor approach in this competition performed very well [138]. Data from 117 patients and 116 healthy volunteers were obtained. The data were divided into a calibration (or training) set and a validation (or testing) set. The training set consisted of 153 samples, 76 of which

Table 11.1   Conformal predictions for breast cancer diagnosis from Proteomics Mass Spectrometry Data: predictions, confidence, and credibility for individual samples.

No.	y_i	Pred	p(1)	p(2)	Conf.	Cred.
1	1	1	0.143	0.078	0.921	0.143
39	1	1	0.372	0.006	0.993	0.375
40	1	2	0.019	0.045	0.980	0.045

were cases and 77 controls. The test set consisted of 78 samples, 39 of which were cases (class 1) and 39 controls (class 2). One potential complicating factor mentioned in [138] is that the data for the training set were obtained from two plates, and the data for the test set were taken from a third plate. Since the mass spectrometer is recalibrated prior to the analysis of each plate, there is a potential for differences between the training and testing sets to be introduced.

Table 11.1 shows several individual examples with confident predictions. The first column is ID number, the second one is the true diagnosis (1 for cases and 2 for the controls), the third is the forced prediction, the fourth and fifth columns are p-values for the corresponding hypotheses, and the sixth and seventh are confidence and credibility.

To interpret the numbers in Table 11.1, recall that high (i.e., close to 100%) confidence means that we predicted a diagnosis and the alternative diagnosis is unlikely. If, say, the first example (No. 1) were classified wrongly, this would mean that a rare event (of probability less than 8%) had occurred; therefore, we expect the prediction to be correct (which it is).

In the case of the third example (No. 40), confidence is also quite high (more than 95%), but we can see that the credibility is low (less than 5%). From the confidence we can conclude that the other label (diagnosis) is excluded at level 5%, but the label 1 itself is also excluded at the same level of 5%. This shows that the unlabeled example itself is strange; perhaps the test example is very different from all examples in the training set. Unsurprisingly, the prediction for this example No. 40 is wrong.

Table 11.2 also demonstrates experimentally the property of validity of the conformal predictors. For example, at the 5% significance level that corresponds to 95% of confidence the error rate should not exceed 5%, and indeed, the experiments show that there are 4.5% of errors. Similar results can be seen for other significance levels.

In Table 11.3 we present a confusion matrix made from the forced diagnoses, where the corresponding specificity and sensitivity are given.

Nonconformity measures for this and other datasets will be defined in Section 11.3. Their performance (quality) has to be compared in terms of conformal predictions, as it is done in the Table 11.4, by the percentage of certain prediction (certainty rate) for the same significance level. Here it is set to 10% and from the

Table 11.2 Validity and accuracy for breast cancer diagnosis: significance level, certain predictions, and error rate.

Significance level	5%	10%	20%
Certain predictions	70%	80%	91%
Set prediction errors	4.5%	9.8%	19.6%

Table 11.3 Confusion matrix for predictions made by highest p-value.

True\classified as	1	2	
1	71	6	sensitivity 92%
2	8	68	specificity 88%

Table 11.4 Certainty rates (percent) at 10% significance level.

Data	Examples	Classes	kNN	SVM	RF
Competition breast cancer	153	2	80.4	80.0	88.9

three underlying algorithms the best one is Random Forest (RF), according to the comparison made in [74].

11.2.2 Magnetic Resonance Imaging: Clinical Diagnosis and Prognosis of Depression

The work [247] considers a conformal method to diagnoses and making clinical prognoses for patients who suffer from depression using preprocessed structural and functional magnetic resonance imaging (MRI) data.

For the diagnostic tasks using functional MRI (fMRI), there were 19 cases of depression and 19 controls. The attributes are 197484 MRI voxels (volume $2 \times 2 \times 2$ mm pixels of the three-dimensional map), each of them measuring a blood oxygenation signal that changes relative to baseline (crosshair fixation) during the observation of stimulus (standardized face expressing increasing levels of sadness).

For prognoses in depression, structured MRI (sMRI) was used. The data were split into two classes of size 9 according to their reaction to a treatment: depressed subjects who responded to an antidepressant treatment (class 1) and class 2 of nonresponders. The patients were examined by structural MRI scans while they were in an acute depressive episode, prior to the initiation of any treatment, and clinical response was assessed prospectively following eight weeks of treatment with an antidepressant medication.

Construction of the NCM will be discussed in Section 11.3.4. It required a detection of three-dimensional areas that showed significant reaction to a stimulus and

Table 11.5 Validity and accuracy for MRI diagnostic and prognostic: significance level, certain predictions, and error rate.

Significance level	5%	10%	20%
Functional MRI certain predictions	15.7%	57.9%	81.6%
error rate	2.6%	8.9%	13.9%
Structural MRI certain predictions	0%	10.5%	34.8%
error rate	0%	5.6%	17.6%

therefore were informative of separation between cases and controls or between two types of reaction to treatment.

The overall results are presented in Table 11.5. The validity property is demonstrated, in that prediction error rate is bounded by the significance level. Also, increasing the significance level results in an increase in the number of certain predictions. For example, for the structural MRI dataset at the 5% significance level the algorithm could not produce any definitive prognoses. Such result is due to the small sample sizes of this dataset.

11.2.3 Online Multiclass Diagnostics

As mentioned in Section 1.8, CPs have some additional useful properties in the online framework. Much of the theoretical work has been developed in the online setting.

Online learning is a procedure that presents the learner with new examples iteratively. The learner makes a prediction for each example, then the supervisor reveals the true label and adds it to the training set before proceeding to the next example. This procedure results in a sequence of predictions. At the n-th trial, the classifier has observed the previous examples $(x_1, y_1), ..., (x_{n-1}, y_{n-1})$ and the new object x_n and will try to predict y_n. It has been proved that conformal predictor is well-calibrated for online learning, in the sense that in the long run the predictions are wrong with relative frequency at most ϵ for a given significance level ϵ. The wrong prediction here means that the prediction set does not cover the true label. This happens when the p-value $p(y)$ corresponding to $y = y_n$ falls below ϵ. The average percentage of such events is determined by ϵ, this is guaranteed by an extended *validity* property.

At the same time the *efficiency* of the predictions (in the form of certainty rate) made by the classifier is expected to improve during the process of learning as more and more examples are accumulated. Cumulative certainty plots show how the learning depends on the training set size.

Following examples of online leukemia microarray diagnostics were originally presented in [20]. Four databases for acute leukemia were sourced from the following research groups: the Royal London Hospital (RLH), St. Jude Children's Research Hospital, Armstrong et al., Golub et al. A microarray measuring gene expression level was extracted for each patient, and a clinical diagnosis of leukemia subtype given in each case. The machine learning task is to classify each microarray by subtype. The

number of subtypes differs (from 2 to 6) for different databases. For example, in the
RLH data there are five types: AML, acute myeloblastic leukemia (14 cases), T-ALL,
T cell acute lymphoblastic leukemia (6 cases), TEL-AML1, precursor-B cell acute
lymphoblastic leukemia with chromosome 12;21 translocation (11 cases), H50, acute
lymphoblastic leukemia with hyperdiploidy more than 50 chromosomes (6 cases),
Others (7 cases).

For an individual example presented in [20] the corresponding p-values are 0.023
(AML, T-ALL, TEL-AML1), 0.23 (H50), 0.046 (Others), so it is classified as H50
with confidence 0.951. This prediction would be certain (H50 only) at 5% significance
level. If the significance level is set to $\epsilon = 2.5\%$, the prediction will be uncertain (i.e.,
H50, Others) but still informative (3 other classification are excluded). However, at
1% level the prediction set contains all five classifications so none of the classification
hypotheses could be excluded.

Figure 11.1 show the results using online TCM-NC with a 10% significance level.
The cumulative predictive errors are shown for increasing numbers of trials in relation
to the expected error calibration line. The cumulative certain and uncertain predictions
are also shown. The error calibration lines show the maximal wrong prediction rate
that for 10% significance level is expected to be 0.1 multiplied by the number of
current trial. Indeed, the number of wrong predictions is always below this line. In the
online setting, the region predictions become smaller during the process of learning,
with a decreasing number of uncertain predictions. On the plot this is reflected with
the increasing slope of the cumulative certain prediction rate. A saturation point shows
the moment where the learning actually stops as the best certainty rate is achieved
and further examples do not improve it.

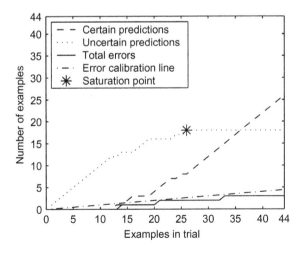

FIGURE 11.1

RHL data: cumulative error rate and numbers of certain and uncertain predictions in
online trial.

11.3 Nonconformity Measures for Medical and Biological Applications

In this section we present several nonconformity measures (NCMs) that have been used in medical and biological applications. Table 11.6 summarizes the results from

Table 11.6 Summary of conformal prediction applications in medicine and biology.

Task	Data type	Best NCM
(i) Plant promoter prediction [316]	Gene expression	SVM (Sec. 11.3.1)
(ii) Tea classifiction [250]	Time series	SVM (Sec. 11.3.1)
(iii) Heart diseases diagnosis [12]	Clinical symptoms	SVM (Sec. 11.3.1)
(iv) Cow TB diagnosis [2]	Skin test, symptoms	k Nearest Neighbors (Sec. 11.3.2)
(v) Various diagnosis (UCI rep.)[184,186]	Clinical symptoms	Bayesian NC (Sec. 11.3.3)
(vi) Abdominal pain diagnosis [262,261]	Clinical symptoms	**Neural Net** (Sec. 11.3.3) **Bayesian NC** (Sec. 11.3.3)
(vii) Atherosclerotic and stroke [191,192]	Ultrasound, symptoms	**Neural Net** (Sec. 11.3.3)
(viii) Thyroid, gastritis diagnosis [385,372]	Clinical symptoms	**Random Forest** (Sec. 11.3.3)
(ix) Breast, Colon, Lung cancer diagnosis [246]	Gene expression	k Nearest Neighbors (Sec. 11.3.2) with feature selection
(x) Leukemia diagnosis [20,19]	Microarrays	**Nearest Centroid** (Sec. 11.3.3) **with feature selection**
(xi) Depression diagnosis and treatment [247]	MRI results	**Featurewise T-test** (Sec. 11.3.4)
(xii) Breast cancer diagnosis [112,138]	Proteomics	**SVM** (Sec. 11.3.1)
(xiii) Ovarian cancer diagnosis [20,19]	Proteomics	Nearest Centroid (Sec. 11.3.3) with feature selection
(xiv) Lung, Colorectal cancer diagnosis [302]	Proteomics	Neural Gas [137] (Sec. 11.3.3)
(xv) Breast, Ovarian cancer diagnosis [190,189]	Proteomics; Breast mass	**Evolutionary** (Sec. 11.3.3); **SVM**(11.3.1)
(xvi) Breast, Ovarian cancer diagnosis [75,76,74]	Proteomics	**Rule search** (Sec. 11.3.3)
(xvii) Abdominal pain; Lung, Colon, Breast Cancer; Ovarian, Breast Cancer; Heart disease. [74] (Sec. 3)	Symptoms; Microarrays; Proteomics	**Random Forest** (Sec. 11.3.3)

different papers on the subject and if several measures have been used the best one (with the largest number of certain predictions) was chosen.

Recall that NCM is a way to measure how strange an element (data example) is with respect to a bag of other examples. Our problem is to find this measure of strangeness or nonconformity measure. Very often for this purpose we use the algorithms of classification—we call them underlying algorithms—to find an appropriate NCM.

In the medical context an example i is represented by a vector $x_i = (x_{i(1)}, \ldots, x_{i(m)})$ that may include symptoms or results of laboratory tests from various sources like proteomics or MRI scans or microarrays, and so on. Here m is the overall dimension of x_i.

The label y_i is a possible diagnosis for each observation i: usual notation is $y_i = 0$ for healthy or control, and $1, 2, \ldots$ for different diseases. Examples presented in this review are usually related to two-class problems (healthy vs diseases) for simplicity of presentation, although most of the algorithms can be easily extended to multiclass classification.

An NCM algorithm gets as its input a bag of examples $z_1 = (x_1, y_1), \ldots, z_{l+1} = (x_{l+1}, y_{l+1})$ and should output the NCM score α_j for each one of them, where $j = 1, \ldots, l + 1$. In other words, an algorithm inputs an unordered bag $\{z_1, \ldots, z_l\}$ as an input, a marked element $z_{(l+1)}$ as another input and has to produce α_j as an output. This is assumed in the Algorithms 11–13 presented in this section.

Once we calculated α we use them to figure out the corresponding p-values and can make predictions and estimate the confidence. Obviously, the accuracy of the classification depends on the measure we operate from the underlying algorithm. Most NCMs observed in this section are based on underlying classification algorithms. As the first approximation, we can say, that the efficiency of nonconformal predictor is high if the accuracy of the underlying algorithm is high.

Another idea of obtaining NCMs is based on the assumption that we are looking for the best separation of two (or more) classes. Here we extract each example in turn from the bag, and check at each step if our classification has improved (making less errors) or not. If it has improved, then this example has a high nonconformity score. Alternatively, a separability measure can be based on an underlying statistical test instead of an algorithm.

11.3.1 Support Vector Machine (SVM)

The main idea of a Support Vector Machine is to map the original set of vectors into a high-dimensional feature (attribute) space, and then to construct a linear separating hyperplane in this feature space. With every possible label (or diagnosis) $Y \in \{-1, 1\}$ for x_{l+1} we associate the SVM optimization problem for the $l + 1$ examples (the training examples plus one of test examples labeled with a hypothetical y):

$$\sum_{i=1}^{l+1} \alpha_i - \frac{1}{2} \sum_{i,j=1}^{l+1} \alpha_i \alpha_j y_i y_j K(x_i, x_j) \rightarrow \min_{\alpha_1, \ldots, \alpha_{l+1}} \tag{11.1}$$

under conditions $0 \leq \alpha_j \leq C$ and $\sum_{i=1}^{l+1} y_i \alpha_i = 0$. Here K is the kernel function, $C = \infty$ means strict separation, and $0 < C < \infty$ allows the hyperplane to make some separation mistakes. The solutions (Lagrange multipliers) $\alpha_1, \alpha_2, \ldots, \alpha_{l+1}$ to this problem reflect the "strangeness" of the examples (i.e., α_i being the strangeness of (x_i, y_i)). All α_i are nonnegative and, in practice, only some of them are different from zero, the so-called support vectors, that include misclassified and marginal examples.

These αs can be interpreted as our NCMs when using SVM as an underlying algorithm. One of its parameters is the *kernel function* that detects the type of surface making separation between classes: for example, higher degree d of a polynomial kernel $K(x_i, x_j) = (x_i x_j + 1)^d$ corresponds to more complex one.

Algorithm 11 Support Vector Machine NCM

Parameter: Kernel function $K : X \times X \to \mathbf{R}$ for SVM.
Extract Lagrange multipliers $\alpha_1^{SVM}, \ldots, \alpha_{l+1}^{SVM}$ by maximizing

$$\sum_{i=1}^{l+1} \alpha_i - \frac{1}{2} \sum_{i,j=1}^{l+1} \alpha_i \alpha_j y_i y_j K(x_i, x_j)$$

under $0 \leq \alpha_j \leq C$ and $\sum_{i=1}^{l+1} y_i \alpha_i = 0$.
Output $\alpha_j = \alpha_j^{SVM}$.

Actually, usage of SVM as an underlying algorithm is very popular: in the majority of the works presented here, it was either the main method or it was used for comparison. One example is the work [112] on breast cancer data collected in Leiden University hospital, discussed in Section 11.2.1. SVM was applied there with a polynomial kernel function.

Several other applications of conformal predictors based on SVM with feature selection to ovarian cancer diagnoses using proteomics and to diagnostic of acute leukemia using microarrays were made in [20]. Another work that used SVM as an underlying method in estimating a risk of heart disease by clinical symptoms can be found in [12].

11.3.2 *k* Nearest Neighbors (kNN)

The NCM for k nearest neighbors method can be defined as a ratio of k neighbors with the same label to k neighbors with the opposite label.

$$\alpha_i := \frac{\sum_{j=1}^{k} d_{ij}^{+}}{\sum_{j=1}^{k} d_{ij}^{-}}, \tag{11.2}$$

where d_{ij}^{+} is the jth shortest distance from x_i to other examples classified with the same label y_i, and d_{ij}^{-} is the jth shortest distance from x_i to the examples classified with a different label. Clearly, it requires a metric defined on the example space. For example, it may be Euclidean:

$$\Delta(x_i, x_j) = \sqrt{(x_i - x_j)^2}.$$

The parameter $k \in \{1, 2, \ldots\}$ in (11.2) is the number of nearest neighbors used in computing the prediction and associated confidence information; $k = 1$ often works very well in the examples presented here.

The intuition behind the formula (11.2) is as follows: in the binary case with class 1 and class 0, a typical 1 will tend to be surrounded by other 1s; if this is the case, the corresponding α_i will be small. In the "strange" case when there are 0s nearer to our example than 1s, α_i would become larger. Therefore, αs reflect the strangeness of examples, in the context of their neighbors. Notice that (11.2) works in the multiclass case as well.

Here (Algorithm 12) the strangeness of an example is the ratio of the average distance to k neighbors with same label and the average distance to k neighbors with other labels.

Algorithm 12 k Nearest Neighbors NCM

Parameter: Distance function $\Delta : X \times X \to \mathbf{R}$ for kNN.
find k objects $n_1(j), \ldots, n_k(j)$ such that $y_{n_i}(j) = y_j$ with the smallest $d_1 = \Delta(x_j, x_{n_1(j)}), \ldots, d_k = \Delta(x_j, x_{n_k(j)})$
find k objects $n'_1(j), \ldots, n'_k(j)$ such that $y_{n_i}(j) \neq y_j$ with the smallest $d'_1 = \Delta(x_j, x_{n'_1(j)}), \ldots, d'_k = \Delta(x_j, x'_{n_k(j)})$
Output $\alpha_j = (d_1 + \ldots + d_k)/(d'_1 + \ldots + d'_k)$

This method is usually not very robust to noise in data and is supplied with a feature selection step. An example is [246], where separation between different types of cancers (Breast, Colon, and Lung) was based on gene expression data.

11.3.3 NCM Based on Other Underlying Algorithms

In this section we shall consider several more NCMs that are used in conformal predictors medical applications, but we shall only outline the ideas behind them and provide a reference to the original papers. We provide a summary of published biomedical applications and the corresponding nonconformity measures used in Table 11.6.

- Linear Rule Search (LR) NCM [75,76]. Suppose that the underlying algorithm classifies two-classes data with a simple linear rule with parameters w, θ, that classifies x_n as $y_n = 1$ if $x_n \cdot w < \theta$ and $y = 0$ otherwise. Here w is a weighting vector of attributes and θ is a parameter. In this case $\alpha_j = (-1)^{y_i}(\theta - x_j \cdot w)$ is used as NCM.

- The Nearest Centroid (NC) NCM [20,19] is close to the kNN NCM. The NC algorithm compares distances from an object to different classes. NCM of an example is its distance to the average feature vector of the same class examples divided to the distance to the average feature vector of the alternative class (if there are only two classes) or to the smallest of such distances (it there are more than two classes). The average feature vector means that each of the attributes is averaged by different examples in a class. Also close to this is Supervised Relevance Neural Gas (SRNG) algorithm [302,137], which is a certain combination of Nearest Neighbors and Nearest Centroid.
- Naive Bayesian (NB) NCM [262,191] is inversely proportional to the probability of the example given the data. The probabilities are estimated according to the Bayesian model, which assumes conditional independence of the features with respect to the label. Another idea [184,186] is to use the Kullback-Leibler measure. It was suggested to use a distance (symmetric Kullback-Leibler divergence) between smoothed empirical distributions obtained from a dataset with and without the example whose nonconformity is measured.
- Neural Network (NNet) NCM [262,261,191,192]. Neural networks are a family of methods that construct a directed computational graph connecting input layers (attributes) with output layers (classifications) through one or more hidden layers. It is constructed using the training set and then may convert any feature vector (at the input layer) into a vector of numerical output layer units. The prediction is usually done by choice of the class with the highest corresponding output layer unit. NCM of an example can be defined as the ratio of the output layer unit corresponding to the correct class (its true label) divided by the highest of output layer units corresponding to the other (wrong) classes.
- Random Forest (RF) NCM [385,372,74]. Random Forest method provides a classifier in the form of decision trees, each of which provides a vote for a certain class. Each tree has its own training set, which is drawn with replacement from the original training set. The RF-NCM of an example can be defined as a number of votes against the true class. A combination with nearest neighbors algorithm (RF-kNN-NCM) can be found in [74].
- The evolutionary (genetic) algorithms (GA) NCM [190,189] are based on the idea of mutation (parameters of an algorithm are randomly changing). The optimization procedures are applied based on the random mutation as a step and the high accuracy as a goal. The whole process can be repeated many times with different results. The NCM of an example will be then defined as the number of repetitions that would misclassify this example.

11.3.4 NCM Based on Feature-Wise Two-Sample T-Test

In the analysis of neuroimages [247] (see Section 11.2.2) we define the NCM in the following way. As before, we are given $z_1 = (x_1, y_1), \ldots, z_n = (x_n, y_n)$ where examples x_i are m-dimensional vectors $x_i = (x_{i(1)}, \ldots, x_{i(m)})$ and labels y_i are binary-valued (e.g., 0 and 1). Actually, m in this example is a number of three-dimensional voxels and it can be very large. A featurewise T-test is applied that allows to check whether two sample sets come from the two distributions with equal means. An example is considered as strange if its exclusion from the set decreases accuracy of classification. This is calculated by Algorithm 13. The nonconformity score α_j of z_j is the number of voxels that are significantly different (from the point of view of the T-test giving low p-values) in examples z_i with the label $y_i = 0$ and in examples with the label $y_i = 1$, after z_j itself is excluded from the comparison ($i \neq j$).

Algorithm 13 T-test NCM

Parameter: significance level $\theta < 1$ for T-test.
$\alpha_j = 0$
for $k = 1, \ldots, m$ **do**
　$t(k) = T(\{x_{i(k)} : i \neq j, y_i = 0\}, \{x_{i(k)} : i \neq j, y_i = 1\})$
　if $t(k) < \theta$ **then**
　　$\alpha_j = \alpha_j + 1$
　end if
end for
Output α_j

11.4 Discussion and Conclusions

We described several measures of nonconformity and their applications in various medical problems. In all these applications is there a general method of designing nonconformity measures? Basically to construct a measure of nonconformity we usually use a loss function—a difference between the true label of an example and its label predicted by an underlying algorithm, $|y - \hat{y}|$. This is what we use for regression problems anyway. If we consider the algorithms presented here, we can see that the same idea, slightly expanded, is used for most of the classification problems. With the exception of the NCMs based on SVM and T-test, the rest of the algorithms also used the difference between true output and the predicted one. But unlike regression problems that deal with a real-valued output, in classification we have to find a way to make some more quantitative output than just $\{0, 1\}$. Thus, in the kNN method for two-classes problem we use distances between the new entry and the examples of both classes; a ratio of the distances would provide the NCM.

In addition to the work mentioned in the previous sections, there are some biomedical applications of different types of conformal predictors. Among them are conditional predictors (2.2) that are compatible with the same nonconformity measures but can make a stronger validity property: the validity can be guaranteed within each class and not just in general for all classes. This has been done in the applications [75] (OC), [2] (TB in cows).

Another interesting modification is the inductive conformal predictor (see Section 2.3). It is used in order to increase computational efficiency. The cost of this is that calculations of both NCM and p-values are based on smaller numbers of examples, but applications [262,191,246] show that they are still practical enough.

There are also some other works in biomedical applications that have not been covered in our review. Among them is the work on Venn predictors that was used in [248]. It also gives valid predictions, but the predictions are probabilistic: it outputs lower and upper bounds of probability of the label of a new example. Instead of a NCM it is based on a taxonomy function that is defined in a similar way and may also be based on an underlying algorithm (usually on a probabilistic one such as Logistic Regression in [248]).

Conformal predictors are also applied to biological problems other than diagnostic. One of them, included in Table 11.6, is the prediction of TATA and TATA-less plant promoters problem [316] by CP based on SVM. A multiclass version of SVM was applied in [250], where the task was to discriminate aroma of different types of tea using an electronic nose system based on gas sensors. In [249] a conformal predictor was used for the prediction of protein–protein interactions based on a list of interactions known from the literature. It was based on a special NCM that is using a featurewise approach (partially similar to one described in Section 11.3.4) reduced to a one-class problem, as there was no standard list of pairs without interactions, hence there is no second class for training.

We have presented various works where conformal methods are used in medical and biomedical applications. It is clear from the presented publications that CP are very useful in many of them and provide reliable diagnostics and efficient prognoses.

Acknowledgments

This work was supported by EraSysBio+ grant funds from the European Union, BBSRC, and BMBF, "Living with uninvited guests: Comparing plant and animal responses to endocytic invasions" to the Salmonella Host Interactions Project European Consortium; MRC grant G0802594 (Application of conformal predictors to FMRI research); MRC grant G0301107 (Proteomic analysis of the human serum proteome); EPSRC grant EP/K033344/1 ("Mining the Network Behaviour of Bots"); a grant from The National Natural Science Foundation of China (No. 61128003); and by the grant "Development of New Venn Prediction Methods for Osteoporosis Risk Assessment" from the Cyprus Research Promotion Foundation.

We are grateful to Vineeth N. Balasubramanian for the collection of references and to James Smith for his help.

Network Traffic Classification and Demand Prediction

12

Mikhail Dashevskiy and Zhiyuan Luo

Computer Learning Research Centre, Department of Computer Science,
Royal Holloway, University of London, United Kingdom

CHAPTER OUTLINE HEAD

Reliable classification of network traffic and accurate demand prediction can offer substantial benefits to service differentiation, enforcement of security policies, and traffic engineering for network operators and service providers. For example, dynamic resource allocation with the support of traffic prediction can efficiently utilize the network resources and support quality of service. One of the key requirements for dynamic resource allocation framework is to predict traffic in the next control time interval based on historical data and online measurements of traffic characteristics over appropriate timescales. Predictions with reliability measures allow service providers and network carriers to effectively perform a cost-benefit evaluation of alternative actions and optimize network performance such as delay and information loss. In this chapter, we apply conformal predictions to two important problems of the network resource management. First, we discuss reliable network traffic classification using network traffic flow measurement. Second, we consider the problem of time series analysis of network resource demand and investigate how to make predictions and build effective prediction intervals. Experimental results on publicly available datasets are presented to demonstrate benefits of the conformal predictions.

12.1 **Introduction**

The Internet is a global system of interconnected computer networks that use the standard Internet Protocol (IP) suite to serve billions of users all over the world. Various network applications utilize the Internet or other network hardware infrastructure to perform useful functions. Network applications often use a client-server architecture, where the client and server are two computers connected to the network. The server is programmed to provide some service to the client. For example, in the World Wide Web (WWW) the client computer runs a Web client program like Firefox or Internet Explorer, and the server runs a Web server program like Apache or Internet Information Server where the shared data would be stored and accessed.

The Internet is based on packet switching technology. The information exchanged between the computers are divided into small data chucks called packets and are controlled by various protocols. Each packet has a header and payload where the header carries the information that will help the packet get to its destination such as the sender's IP address. The payload carries the data in the protocols that the Internet uses. Each packet is routed independently and transmission resources such as link bandwidth and buffer space are allocated as needed by packets. The principal goals of packet switching are to optimize utilization of available link capacity, minimize response times, and increase the robustness of communication.

In a typical network, the traffic through the network is heterogeneous and consists of flows from multiple applications and utilities. Typically a stream of packets is generated when a user visits a website or sends an email. A traffic flow is uniquely identified by four-tuple {source IP address, source port number, destination IP address, destination port number}. Two widely used transport layer protocols are Transmission Control Protocol (TCP) and User Datagram Protocol (UDP). The main differences between TCP and UDP are that TCP is connection-oriented and a connection is established before the data can be exchanged. On the other hand, UDP is connectionless.

Many different network applications are running on the Internet. The Internet traffic is a huge mixture and thousands of different applications generate lots of different traffic. In addition to "traditional" applications (e.g., email and file transfer), new Internet applications such as multimedia streaming, blogs, Internet telephony, games, and peer-to-peer (P2P) file sharing have become popular [219]. Therefore, there are different packet sending and arrival patterns due to interaction between the sender and the receiver and data transmission behavior. Many of these applications are unique and have their own requirements with respect to network parameters such as bandwidth, delay, and jitter. Loss-tolerant applications such as video conferencing and interactive games can tolerate some amount of data loss. On the other hand, elastic applications such as email, file transfer, and Web transfer can make use of as much, or as little bandwidth as happens to be available. Elastic Internet applications have the greatest share in the traffic transported over the Internet today. Traffic classification can be defined as methods of classifying traffic data based on features passively observed in the traffic, according to specific classification goals. Quality of Service (QoS) is the ability to provide different priority to different applications, users, or data flows, or to guarantee a certain level of performance to a data flow.

The predictability of network traffic is of significant interest in many domains. For example, it can be used to improve the QoS mechanisms as well as congestion and resource control by adapting the network parameters to traffic characteristics. Dynamic resource allocation with the support of traffic prediction can efficiently utilize the network resources and support QoS. One of the key requirements for dynamic resource allocation framework is to predict traffic in the next control time interval based on historical data and online measurements of traffic characteristics over appropriate timescales. Machine learning algorithms are capable of observing and identifying patterns within the statistical variations of a monitored parameter such as resource consumption. They can then make appropriate predictions concerning future resource demands using this past behavior. There are two main approaches to predictions used in dynamic resource allocation: indirectly predicting traffic behavior descriptors and directly forecasting resource consumption.

In the indirect traffic prediction approach, it is assumed that there is an underlying stochastic model of the network traffic. Time-series modeling is typically used to build such a model from a given traffic trace. First, we want to determine the likely values of the parameters associated with the model. Then a set of possible models may be selected, and parameter values are determined for each model. Finally, diagnostic checking is carried out to establish how well the estimated model conforms to the observed data. A wide range of time series models has been developed to represent short-range and long-range dependent behavior in network traffic. However, it is still an open problem regarding how to fit an appropriate model to the given traffic trace. In addition, long execution times are associated with the model selection process.

The direct traffic prediction approach is more fundamental in nature and more challenging than indirect traffic descriptor prediction. This is because we can easily derive any statistical traffic descriptors from the concrete traffic volume, but not vice versa. Different learning and prediction approaches, including conventional statistical methods and machine learning approaches such as neural networks, have been applied to dynamic resource reservation problems [61]. Despite the reported success of these methods in asynchronous transfer mode and wireless networks, the learning and prediction techniques used can only provide simple predictions; that is, the algorithms make predictions without saying how reliable these predictions are. The reliability of a method is often determined by measuring general accuracy across independent test sets. For learning and prediction algorithms, if we make no prior assumptions about the probability distribution of the data, other than that it is identically and independently distributed (i.i.d.), there is no formal confidence relationship between the accuracy of the prediction made with the test data and the prediction associated with a new and unknown case.

Network behavior can change considerably over time and space. Learning and prediction should ideally be adaptive and provide confidence information. In this chapter, we apply conformal predictions to enhance the learning algorithms for network traffic classification and demand prediction problems. The novelty of conformal predictions is that they can learn and predict simultaneously, continually improving their performance as they make each new prediction and ascertain how accurate it is. Conformal predictors not only give predictions, but also provide additional information about reliability with their outputs. Note that in the case of regression the predictions output by such algorithms are intervals where the true value is supposed to lie.

The reminder of this chapter is structured as follows. Section 12.2 discusses the application of conformal predictions to the problem of network traffic classification. Section 12.3 considers the application of conformal predictions to the network demand predictions and presents a way of constructing reliable prediction intervals (i.e., intervals that include point predictions) by using conformal predictors. Section 12.4 shows experimental results of the conformal prediction on public network traffic datasets. Finally, Section 12.5 presents conclusions.

12.2 Network Traffic Classification

Network traffic classification is an important problem of network resource management that arises from analyzing network trends and network planning and designing. Successful classification of network traffic packets can be used in many applications, such as firewalls, intrusion detection systems, status reports and Quality of Service systems [175]. Approaches to network traffic classification vary according to the properties of the packets used. Following [175], the following approaches will be briefly examined and discussed: port-based approach, payload-based approach, host behavior-based approach, and flow features-based approach.

12.2.1 Port-Based Approach

Port-based approach is the fastest and the simplest method to classify network traffic packets and as such has been extensively used [388]. Many applications, such as WWW and email, have fixed (or traditionally used) port numbers and, thus, traffic belonging to these applications can be easily identified. However, since there are many applications (such as P2P, games, and multimedia) that do not have fixed port numbers and instead use the port numbers of other widely used applications (e.g., HTTP/FTP connections), this approach sometimes yields poor results (see [84,219,308]).

12.2.2 Payload-Based Classification

Payload-based classification algorithms look at the packets' contents to identify the type of traffic [308]. When a set of unique payload signatures is collected by an algorithm, this approach results in high performance for most types of traffic, such as HTTP, FTP, and SMTP. However, payload-based classification methods often fail to correctly identify the type of traffic used by P2P and multimedia applications [237] due to the fact that these applications use variable payload signatures.

12.2.3 Host Behavior-Based Method

Algorithms that classify traffic by analyzing the profile of a host (i.e., the destinations and ports the host communicates with) to determine the type of the traffic are called host behavior-based methods [128]. Some newly developed methods (such as BLINC [170]) rely on capturing host behavior signatures. An advantage of these methods is that they manage to classify traffic even when it is encrypted. A disadvantage is the fact that host behavior-based methods require the number of flows specific to a particular type of traffic to reach a certain threshold before they are able to be classified.

12.2.4 Flow Feature-Based Method

Flow feature-based methods employ machine learning techniques to find a pattern in the packets and thus identify the type of traffic based on various statistical features of the flow of packets. Examples of flow-level features include flow duration, data volume, number of packets, variance of these metrics, among others. The machine learning methods that can be used include Naive Bayes, k-nearest neighbors, neural networks, logistic regression, clustering algorithms, and Support Vector Machines (SVM) [9,93,95,237,92,236,268,213]. This chapter considers only this approach to network traffic classification.

12.2.5 Our Approach

Many machine learning algorithms have been successfully applied to the problem of network traffic classification [237,243,392,380], but usually these algorithms provide bare predictions (i.e., predictions without any measure of how reliable they are). Algorithms that do provide some measure of reliability with their outputs usually make strong assumptions on the data. Bayesian predictors, for example, require the *a priori* distribution on the data [116]. It was shown in [226] that if this *a priori* distribution is wrong, the algorithm provides unreliable confidence numbers (measures of reliability).

This section considers the problem of reliable network traffic classification. The aim is to classify network traffic flows and to provide some measure of how reliable the classification is by applying conformal predictors [69,68,67]. Conformal predictors is a machine learning technique of making predictions (classifications) according to how similar the current example is to representatives of different classes [114,365]. In machine learning, given a training set of $n - 1$ labeled examples $(z_1, \ldots, z_{n-1})$ where each example z_i consists of an object $\mathbf{x_i}$ and its label y_i, $z_i = (\mathbf{x_i}, y_i)$, and a new unlabeled example $\mathbf{x_n}$, we would like to say something about its label y_n [231]. The objects are elements of an object space $\mathbf{X}$ and the labels are elements of a finite label space $\mathbf{Y}$. For example, in traffic classification, $\mathbf{x_i}$ are multidimensional traffic flow statistics vectors and y_i are application groups taking only finite number of values such as {WWW, FTP, EMAIL, P2P}. It is assumed that the example sequence is generated according to an i.i.d. unknown probability distribution P in $\mathbf{Z}^\infty$.

Conformal predictors are based on a *Nonconformity Measure*, a function that gives some measure of dissimilarity between an example and a set of other examples. The higher the value of this function on an example, the more unlikely it is that this example belongs to the selected group of examples. To exploit this idea, we can assign different labels to the current object $\mathbf{x_n}$, calculate the dissimilarity between this example and other examples with the same label, calculate the dissimilarity between this example and examples with other labels, and then use these values to classify the object. In order to describe conformal predictors more precisely we need to introduce some formal definitions.

For each $n = 1, 2, \ldots$ we define function

$$A_n : Z^{n-1} \times Z \to \overline{\mathbb{R}}$$

as the restriction of A to $Z^{n-1} \times Z$. Sequence $(A_n : n \in \mathbb{N})$ is called a *nonconformity measure*. To provide a more intuitive idea of what a nonconformity measure is, we need to use the term *bag*, which was defined in the previous subsection. Given a nonconformity measure (A_n) and a bag of examples $(z_1, \ldots, z_n)$ we can calculate the nonconformity score for each example in the bag:

$$\alpha_i = A_n\left((z_1, \ldots, z_{i-1}, z_{i+1}, \ldots, z_n), z_i\right). \tag{12.1}$$

The nonconformity score is a measure of how dissimilar one example is from a group of examples. If, for example, the one-nearest neighbor algorithm is used as the underlying algorithm (the algorithm used to calculate the nonconformity score) for conformal predictors, the nonconformity score can be calculated as

$$A_n\left((z_1, \ldots, z_n), z\right) = \frac{\min_{i \in \{1,\ldots,n\}, y_i = y} d(x_i, x)}{\min_{i \in \{1,\ldots,n\}, y_i \neq y} d(x_i, x)}.$$

This formula represents the idea that we consider an example as nonconforming if it lies much further from the selected group of examples than from all other examples outside the selected group. In this thesis, we compare two reliable predictors, which make only weak assumptions on the data. In addition, we provide some guidelines on how to choose between the algorithms in practical applications.

Unlike the nearest neighbors algorithm, the nearest centroid (NC) algorithm (see [24]) does not require computing the distances between each pair of objects. Instead, it measures the distance between an object and the centroid (i.e., the average) of all objects belonging to the same class. The nonconformity measure can be calculated as follows:

$$\alpha_i = \alpha_i(x_i, y_i) = \frac{d(\mu_{y_i}, x_i)}{\min_{y \neq y_i} d(\mu_y, x_i)},$$

where μ_y is the centroid of all objects with the label y.

Now, to use the nonconformity scores we must compare the current object (which we are trying to classify) with the examples from the training set. In this way, we can see how the current object fits into the "big picture" of the dataset. Now we introduce the term p-value. The number

$$\frac{\#|\{j = 1, \ldots, n : \alpha_j \geq \alpha_n\}|}{n}$$

is called p-value of object $z_n = (\mathbf{x_n}, y_n)$. Conformal predictor receives a significance level (a small positive real number reflecting the confidence we want to achieve; it equals one minus the confidence level) as a parameter, and makes predictions. Basically, conformal predictor calculates the p-values of the pairs $(\mathbf{x_n},$ possible label) and outputs all pairs where the p-value is greater than the significance level. Algorithm 14 outlines the scheme by which conformal predictors make predictions.

Algorithm 14 Conformal Predictor Algorithm for Classification

---

Input: Parameters ϵ {significance level}

  for $n = 2, 3, \ldots$ {at each step of the algorithm} **do**

    for $j = 1, \ldots, NumberOfLabels$ {for each possible label} **do**

      Assign $y_n = j$ {let us consider that the current example has label j}

      Calculate $\alpha_i, i = 1, \ldots, n$ {calculate nonconformity scores using (12.1)}

      Calculate $p_j = \dfrac{|\{i = 1, \ldots, n : \alpha_i \geq \alpha_n\}|}{n}$ {calculate p-value corresponding to the current possible label}

      Output j as a predicted label of the current example with p-value p_j if and only if $p_j > \epsilon$

    end for

  end for

Conformal predictors can output multiple (region) predictions, sets of possible labels for the new object. The main advantage of conformal predictors is their property of validity in an online setting: the asymptotic number of errors, that is, erroneous region predictions, can be controlled by the significance level—the error rate we are ready to tolerate, which is predefined by the user [365]. Given an error probability ϵ, conformal predictor produces a set of labels that also contains the true label with probability $1 - \epsilon$ [365]. If we want to choose only one label as the prediction (single prediction), it is reasonable to choose the label corresponding to the highest p-value. In this case, however, we do not have any theoretical guarantee on the performance of the algorithm.

12.3 Network Demand Prediction

The need for a network demand model arises as the importance of access to the Internet increases for the delivery of essential services. The ability to predict bandwidth demand is critical for efficient service provisioning and intelligent decision-making in the face of rapidly growing traffic and changing traffic patterns [268,308].

Accurate estimates for message quantity and size directly imply network resource requirement for bandwidth, memory, and processor (CPU) cycles. For efficient management of resources such as network bandwidth, an accurate estimate of the bandwidth demand of the traffic flowing through the network is required. The bandwidth demand patterns have to be learned to predict the future behavior of the traffic. Because the Internet is based on packet switching technology, the duration of time connected to the Internet greatly depends on the efficiency of the movement of packets between different IP addresses. One way to estimate the demand for network resources is to estimate the number of packets in a specific time period. Since each packet in the Internet carries a certain number of bytes' worth of information, network traffic demand could be defined in terms of bytes.

When a traffic flow is transmitted via a network, usually there are several routes that can be used for this purpose. We can consider a network as a graph where the nodes are network clients, such as routers, and the edges are communication links. The problem of routing packets in a network belongs to resource management and is important to the performance of a network. A decision-making system that routes packets usually relies on a prediction module to estimate future network demand. Network demand can be typically characterized as the bandwidth measured in bytes or number of packets over a particular source destination pair. The behavior of the traffic is usually modeled in terms of its past statistical properties. For short-term estimates of traffic behavior the statistical properties are assumed to vary slowly and hence daily, weekly, and seasonal cycles are not considered. The demand is often obtained by measuring traffic at regular time periods such as seconds or minutes. Therefore, we deal with data in terms of time series. In the time series model, the forecast is based only on past values and assumes that factors that influence the past, present, and future traffic demand will continue.

To model and predict network traffic demand a number of algorithms can be used. Currently researchers use traditional statistical methods of prediction for time series, such as Auto-Regressive Moving Average (ARMA) [42], which is a general linear model, or machine learning algorithms, such as neural networks [343,61]. The goal of time series forecasting is to model a complex system as a black box, predicting its behavior based on historical data. However, the neural network method requires human interaction throughout the prediction process (see [260]) and for this reason the approach is not considered in this chapter.

Note that the fact that network traffic demand exhibits long-range dependence means that linear models cannot predict it well. It has also been noted that network traffic demand is self-similar [202]); that is, the traffic behaves in a similar manner regardless of the time scale. This statement, however, has to be adapted so that it takes into account trends in the traffic demand, such as daily (e.g., at 3 a.m. the demand is lower than at noon) or yearly (e.g., toward the end of a year the demand is higher due to its constant increase) trends. The slight difference in the data distribution can be attributed to the daily trend; for example, when the time scale is 100 seconds and 1000 observations represent approximately 28 hours of traffic, the daily trend becomes noticeable [65,66]. This topic is out of the scope of the chapter and for more information, see [65,70] .

12.3.1 Our Approach

An important property of time series prediction that is useful for decision-making systems is the reliability of prediction intervals. The problem of applying conformal predictors (a method that could not originally be used for time series) to time series prediction in general and to the network traffic demand prediction problem in particular is considered. For network traffic demand prediction, it is particularly important to provide predictions quickly; for prediction algorithms to have low computational complexity, Quality of Service systems need to react to changes in a network in a timely manner.

We consider conformal predictors for regression and particularly conformal predictors for time series analysis. The challenge of applying conformal predictors to the problem of time series analysis lies in the fact that observations of a time series are dependent and, therefore, do not meet the requirement of exchangeability. The aim of this section is to investigate possible ways of applying conformal predictors to time series data and to study their performance. We will show that conformal predictors provide reliable prediction intervals even though they do not provide a theoretical guarantee on their performance.

Conformal predictors for regression

The difference between conformal predictors for classification and conformal predictors for regression begins with the definition of the p-value: since in regression there are an infinite number of possible labels, the definition must change slightly. To see how the current example (depending on y, its possible label) fits into the "big picture" of the other examples we compare the nonconformity scores. We again denote objects as x_i and labels as y_i. Now we introduce the term p-value calculated for the example $z_n = (x_n, y)$ as

$$p(y) = \frac{\#|\{j = 1, \ldots, n : \alpha_j(y) \geq \alpha_n(y)\}|}{n}, \qquad (12.2)$$

where $\alpha_i(y)$ is the nonconformity score of object $\mathbf{x_i}$ when the current observation has label y.

Conformal predictors (as described by Algorithm 15) receive a significance level (a small positive real number equal to the error rate we can tolerate, with the confidence level equal to one minus the significance level) as a parameter. To predict label y for the new example x_n, the conformal predictor solves an equation on the variable y so that the p-value of the new example is greater than or equal to the significance level.

Usually, the nonconformity measure for regression is designed in such a way that the equation is piecewise linear. For example, we can define $\alpha_i = |y_i - \hat{y}_i|$, where $\hat{y}_i$ is the prediction calculated by applying to x_i the decision rule found from the dataset without the example z_i [365]. Nonconformity measures were developed for Ridge Regression (and, as a corollary, Least Squares Regression) in [365].

Algorithm 15 Conformal Predictor Algorithm for Regression

Input: significance level ϵ and $z_1 = (x_1, y_1)$

   for $n = 2, 3, \ldots$ **do**

      Get x_n

      Calculate $\alpha_i(y), i = 1, \ldots, n$ {calculate nonconformity scores using Equation (12.1)}

      Calculate $p(y) = \dfrac{\#|\{i = 1, \ldots, n : \alpha_i(y) \geq \alpha_n(y)\}|}{n}$ {calculate p-value}

      Output $\Gamma_n := \{y : p(y) \geq \epsilon\}$

      Get y_n

   end for

As we can see, Algorithm 15 receives feedback on the true label of the object x_n after each prediction is made. This setting "object → prediction → true label" is called online mode. When conformal predictors are run in online mode, they are said to be valid as long as they satisfy the assumption of exchangeability of the data. Validity means that the algorithm made a wrong prediction at step n, is independent, and has probabilities equal to the pre-defined significance level ϵ.

Conformal predictors for time series

A time series is a collection of observations typically sampled at regular intervals. Time series data occur naturally in many application areas such as economics, finance, and medicine. A time series model assumes that past patterns will occur in the future. Many network traffic traces are represented as time series. Conformal predictors are designed to be applied to those datasets for which the assumption of exchangeability holds: the elements in the dataset have to be exchangeable. In other words, if we suppose that the elements are the outputs of a probability distribution, then the probability of the occurrence of sequences should not depend on the ordering of the elements in those sequences and, thus, the output of an algorithm applied to such a dataset should not depend on the ordering of the elements. However, in the case of time series, the ordering of the elements of a dataset is essential as the future observations depend only on the current and previous observations.

We extend conformal predictors to the case of time series. To do this, however, we have to either violate or change the restriction on the data required by the algorithm. Thus, we lose the guarantee of validity given by conformal predictors. However, our experiments show that the error rate line is close to a straight line with the slope equal to the significance level (a parameter of the algorithm), which indicates empirical validity.

One way of using conformal predictors for time series data is to assume that there is no long-range dependence between the observations. In this scenario, we use a parameter $T \in \mathbb{N}$, which specifies how many of the previous observations the current observation can depend on.

Conformal predictors do not fit the framework of time series as they look for the dependence between objects and labels (they predict the new object's label). To apply them to time series data, we artificially create objects as sets of previous observations.

Suppose we have time series data $a_1, a_2, a_3, \ldots$ where $a_i \in \mathbb{R}$ $\forall i$. We employ two methods to generate pairs (object, label) from the time series data. If we want to generate as many pairs as possible and at the same time we do not mind violating the exchangeability requirement, we use the rule

$$\forall i, T + 1 \leq i \leq n : z_i = (\mathbf{x_i}, y_i) := \left((a_{i-T}, \ldots, a_{i-1}), a_i\right),$$

where n is the length of the time series data. We call these observations *dependent*. If, on the other hand, we want to achieve validity, then we use the rule

$$\forall 0 \leq i \leq \left[\frac{n}{T+1}\right] - 1 : z_i = (\mathbf{x_i}, y_i) :=$$
$$\left((a_{n-i(T+1)-T}, \ldots, a_{n-i(T+1)-1}), a_{n-i(T+1)}\right),$$

where $\left[k\right]$ is the integer part of k. These observations are called *independent*.

After transforming the time series data into pairs (object, label) by one of the rules described earlier, we apply conformal predictors with a nonconformity measure based on some existing algorithm such as Ridge Regression or the nearest neighbors algorithm [365]. Now the ordering of the observations is "saved" inside the objects.

To calculate a nonconformity score for object $\mathbf{x_n}$ with possible label y, we use prediction $\hat{y}$ made by an underlying algorithm. We then take function $|y - \hat{y}|$ as the nonconformity score, where y is a variable. Note that the only nonconformity score dependent on y is the one for the new example $\alpha_n(y)$ and that to find the prediction interval it is enough to solve a linear equation on y (see Eq. 12.2).

To show an example of how conformal predictors can be applied to time series data, we provide an implementation of conformal predictors based on the one nearest neighbor algorithm (see Algorithm 16). In this algorithm, r is a possible nonconformity score for the current example and the calculation of $\hat{y}_n$ is provided by the underlying algorithm. To build conformal predictors for time series data using another underlying algorithm, the calculation of $\hat{y}_n$ will be changed accordingly. For example, $\hat{y}_n$ can be a prediction made by an ARMA model [42] or by the Ridge Regression algorithm [365]. In this way, conformal predictors can use the outputs of any time series prediction model to build prediction intervals without constructing objects; in this chapter, we will use this idea to run experiments on conformal predictors for time series analysis.

Algorithm 16 Conformal predictors for time series data based on the one nearest neighbor algorithm

---

Input: Parameters ϵ and y_1, y_2

   $x_2 := y_1$
   $\alpha_2(y) := 0$
   for $n = 3, 4, 5, \ldots$ **do**
      $x_n := y_{n-1}$
      $\hat{y}_n := y_{\arg\min_{i,2 \le i \le n-1}\{|x_i - x_n|\}}$
      $p := \max\{r \in \mathbb{R} : \frac{\#\{\alpha_i \ge r, 2 \le i \le n-1\}}{n-2} \ge \epsilon\}$
      Output $\Gamma_n := [\hat{y}_n - p, \hat{y}_n + p]$ as prediction for y_n
      Get y_n
      $\alpha_n(y) := |y_n - \hat{y}_n|$
   end for

12.4 Experimental Results

The effectiveness of conformal predictions can be evaluated on publicly available datasets by using two performance metrics: validity and efficiency [365]. Validity means that the error rate is close to the expected value, which is equal to a predefined constant (one minus the confidence level). Efficiency reflects how useful the prediction's output by a conformal predictor are. For a classification problem, a conformal predictor ideally outputs a single prediction at each step, but in practice this does not always happen. We call an algorithm efficient if the average number of output labels is close to one. For time series prediction, we want to make conformal predictors output efficient (narrow) prediction intervals that are empirically valid. We conducted our experiments on two tasks: network traffic classification and traffic demand prediction.

12.4.1 Network Traffic Classification Datasets

The Network Traffic Classification Datasets (NTCD) is a collection of thousands of examples of hand-classified TCP flows (we used the datasets after feature selection, performed by other researchers [237]). The datasets are publicly available at http://www.cl.cam.ac.uk/research/srg/netos/nprobe/data/papers/sigmetrics/index.html [235]. Flows are labeled according to the type of traffic they represent, for example WWW, EMAIL, FTP, or P2P traffic. For each flow, there are 248 features describing simple statistics about packet length and interpacket timings, and information derived from the TCP protocol such as SYN and ACK count; for details see [238,209,210]. There are 11 datasets and Table 12.1 shows the number of TCP flows in each dataset. Eight types of network applications are considered: WWW (1), EMAIL (2), FTP (3), ATTACK (4), P2P (5), DATABASE (6), MULTIMEDIA (7), and SERVICES (8).

Table 12.1 Traffic types by dataset.

Dataset	1	2	3	4	5	6	7	8	Total
NTCD-1	18211	4146	1511	122	339	238	87	206	24860
NTCD-2	18559	2726	1701	19	94	329	150	220	23798
NTCD-3	18065	1448	2736	41	100	206	136	200	22932
NTCD-4	19641	1429	600	324	114	8	54	113	22283
NTCD-5	18618	1651	928	122	75	0	38	216	21648
NTCD-6	16892	1618	521	134	94	0	42	82	19383
NTCD-7	51982	2771	484	89	116	36	36	293	55807
NTCD-8	51695	2508	551	129	289	43	33	220	55468
NTCD-9	59993	3678	1577	367	249	15	0	337	66216
NTCD-10	54436	6592	930	446	624	1773	0	212	65013
NTCD-12	15597	1799	1513	0	297	295	0	121	19622

Table 12.2 Selected features.

Index	Meaning
1	Server Port Number.
11	First quartile of bytes in (Ethernet) packet.
39	The total number of sack packets seen that carried duplicate SACK (D-SACK) blocks. $(S \rightarrow C)$
57	The count of all the packets observed arriving out of order. $(C \rightarrow S)$
66	If the endpoint requested Time Stamp options as specified in RFC 1323 a "Y" is printed on the respective field. If the option was not requested, an "N" is printed. $(C \rightarrow S)$
102	The missed data, calculated as the difference between the TTL stream length and unique bytes sent. If the connection was not complete, this calculation is invalid and an "NA" (Not Available) is printed. $(S \rightarrow C)$

Feature selection was applied to these datasets in an attempt to optimize the performance of the prediction systems. The Fast Correlation-Based Filter (FCBF) was chosen as the feature selection method, using symmetrical uncertainty as the correlation measure [389]. The FCBF method has been shown to be effective in removing both irrelevant and redundant features [390]. This methods is based on the idea that the goodness of a feature can be measured based on its correlation with the class and other good features. The Weka environment [381] was used to perform feature selection and the dataset NTCD-1 was chosen as the training set. Based on the FCBF method, six features out of 248 features were selected and are presented in Table 12.2, where $S \rightarrow C$ and $C \rightarrow S$ mean the flow direction Server to Client and Client to Server, respectively, and "index" represents features in the original datasets. These six features are used in the experiments. Table 12.3 shows the performance of

Table 12.3 Performance comparison between kNN and kNN with feature selection (accuracy as ratio of correct predictions, %).

Dataset	NTCD-2	NTCD-3	NTCD-4	NTCD-5	NTCD-6	NTCD-7	NTCD-8	NTCD-9	NTCD-10	NTCD-12
1NN	96.60	91.37	97.42	97.34	98.34	94.68	94.70	93.83	92.22	66.43
1NN FS	96.69	99.05	98.59	99.06	98.34	96.19	96.36	94.89	92.75	96.78
2NN	96.93	92.17	97.72	97.41	98.50	96.53	96.34	95.38	93.30	67.86
2NN FS	96.79	99.18	98.81	99.01	98.48	96.43	96.73	95.21	94.88	96.41
3NN	96.91	90.77	97.49	97.28	98.41	95.40	95.26	94.43	92.38	63.86
3NN FS	96.86	99.14	98.80	98.99	98.42	96.45	96.65	95.12	95.71	96.29
4NN	96.93	93.30	97.61	97.23	98.26	96.18	96.44	95.37	93.78	64.39
4NN FS	98.87	99.08	98.98	98.44	99.23	97.90	98.02	96.68	97.81	96.31
5NN	96.83	90.93	97.55	97.11	98.25	95.47	96.78	94.89	92.95	62.94
5NN FS	98.88	98.97	98.91	98.40	99.18	98.00	98.02	96.69	97.12	96.76
6NN	96.77	90.78	97.50	97.08	98.18	96.13	96.63	95.21	93.40	63.65
6NN FS	98.88	98.96	98.91	98.06	99.20	98.00	98.06	96.75	97.85	96.52
7NN	96.64	90.45	96.82	96.87	98.12	95.70	96.11	94.91	92.48	63.76
7NN FS	98.90	98.94	98.88	98.03	99.18	98.01	98.03	96.71	97.84	97.00
8NN	96.59	92.33	97.21	96.82	98.07	96.17	96.81	95.22	93.48	64.00
8NN FS	98.85	98.92	98.90	97.93	99.15	97.98	98.01	96.69	97.85	96.83
9NN	96.11	93.88	96.78	96.78	98.03	95.81	96.57	94.96	93.08	63.84
9NN FS	98.86	98.89	98.88	97.89	99.07	98.00	97.91	96.71	97.82	96.85
10NN	96.17	94.62	97.11	96.72	97.94	96.06	96.64	95.15	93.32	64.76
10NN FS	98.82	98.87	98.88	97.89	99.05	97.98	97.82	96.69	97.81	96.83

the k-nearest neighbors algorithm on the datasets with and without feature selection. The table clearly shows the advantages of using feature selection for these datasets.

In the case of multiple predictions, if the true label is a member of the prediction set, then the prediction is correct; otherwise, we have a prediction error. As we mentioned earlier, we are interested in validity and efficiency. Validity means that the error rate is close to the expected value, which is equal to a predefined constant (one minus the confidence level). Conformal predictors provide guaranteed validity (when the assumption of exchangeability holds) [365]. Efficiency reflects how useful the prediction's output by a reliable predictor are. Ideally, a reliable predictor outputs a single prediction at each step, but in practice this does not always happen. In this chapter, we call an algorithm efficient if the average number of output labels is close to one.

Figures 12.1 and 12.2 show two examples of experimental results with different significance level. Figure 12.1 shows that the higher the confidence level is, the lower the total number of errors will be. The graphs of the number of errors over time should be straight lines and the error rates at each point should be approximately equal to the significance level. Figure 12.2 shows that the higher the confidence level is, the higher the number of output labels will be.

Tables 12.4 and 12.5 show the error rates and average number of labels observed when applying conformal predictors to NTCD-1 and NTCD-2 in an online setting, respectively. Two underlying algorithms, k-nearest neighbors (NN) and nearest centroid (NC) are used and both region (multiple) predictions and single prediction

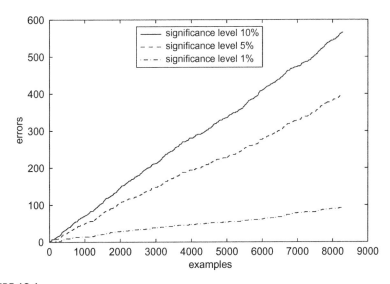

FIGURE 12.1

Number of errors for different significance levels (NTCD-1, 3 nearest neighbors, multiple predictions).

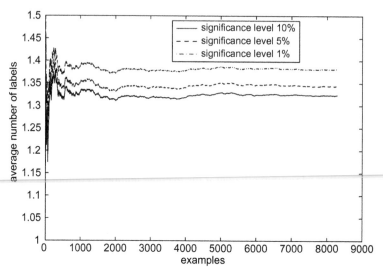

FIGURE 12.2

Average number of labels for different significance levels (NTCD-1, 3 nearest neighbors, multiple predictions).

Table 12.4 Performance on dataset NTCD-1.

Underlying algorithm	Error rate, %				Number of labels		
	1%	5%	10%	single	1%	5%	10%
1NN	1.13	4.88	6.25	0.66	1.38	1.34	1.33
2NN	1.10	4.89	6.67	0.62	1.38	1.34	1.33
3NN	1.12	4.79	6.83	0.68	1.38	1.34	1.32
4NN	1.16	4.88	6.94	0.69	1.38	1.34	1.32
5NN	1.19	4.85	7.02	0.71	1.38	1.34	1.32
6NN	1.17	4.94	7.11	0.72	1.38	1.34	1.32
7NN	1.17	4.84	7.23	0.78	1.38	1.34	1.32
8NN	1.16	4.92	7.35	0.81	1.36	1.33	1.30
9NN	1.16	4.90	7.47	0.84	1.36	1.32	1.30
10NN	1.17	4.92	7.54	0.86	1.36	1.32	1.29
NC	0.53	0.53	9.26	92.16	7.10	7.10	4.50

are considered. The number of nearest neighbors does not significantly affect the performance of the NN algorithm. For both underlying algorithms, the error rates can be controlled by the preset confidence level subject to statistical fluctuations. However, the efficiency of the algorithms changes depending on the dataset. On these two

Table 12.5   Performance on dataset NTCD-2.

Underlying algorithm	Error rate, %				Number of labels		
	1%	5%	10%	single	1%	5%	10%
1NN	0.96	5.18	7.58	0.34	1.90	1.85	1.83
2NN	0.98	5.16	7.87	0.38	1.89	1.85	1.82
3NN	0.96	5.22	8.06	0.38	1.88	1.84	1.81
4NN	1.01	5.22	8.14	0.40	1.88	1.84	1.81
5NN	1.05	5.22	8.19	0.42	1.88	1.84	1.81
6NN	1.03	5.24	8.24	0.42	1.88	1.84	1.81
7NN	1.02	5.23	8.31	0.43	1.88	1.84	1.81
8NN	1.02	5.27	8.38	0.44	1.88	1.84	1.81
9NN	1.02	5.29	8.46	0.45	1.84	1.80	1.77
10NN	1.00	5.23	8.53	0.47	1.66	1.62	1.59
NC	0.50	4.83	7.80	88.94	6.68	6.31	2.32

particular datasets, NC does not perform as well as the NN algorithm, in particular when single predictions are made.

12.4.2 Network Demand Prediction Datasets

For time series prediction experiments, we used 22 datasets that contained both the number of packets and the number of bytes arriving at (or transmitted to and from) a particular facility. The datasets are publicly available at http://ita.ee.lbl.gov/html/ traces.html. Here we briefly describe the datasets, their labeling and some of their properties. Datasets A, B, C, and D represent Wide Area Network traffic arriving at the Bellcore Morristown Research and Engineering facility. Datasets E, F, D, and H were collected at the same facility and represent only local traffic. Datasets I through P each represent the traffic between Digital Equipment Corporation and the rest of the world during an hour of observation. Similarly, datasets Q, R, S, and T each represent the traffic transmitted between the Lawrence Berkeley Laboratory and the rest of the world during an hour of observation. Datasets U and V contain information about the TCP traffic between the same facility and the rest of the world during two hours of observation.

These datasets have been extensively used in research [202,269]. Table 12.6 describes the correspondence between the notation of this chapter and the notation used by other researchers, and the values used to create datasets (i.e., the number of bytes or the number of packets transmitted in a network). The original datasets contain the number of bytes in packets and their corresponding timestamps. Our datasets contain the aggregated number of bytes and the aggregated number of packets in a network during time intervals of one second. Table 12.6 also shows the number of observations contained in the datasets when the time scale is fixed at one observation per second.

Table 12.6   Network traffic demand datasets.

Dataset	Name used in literature	Measurement	No. of observations
A	BC_Oct89Ext4	no of bytes	75945
B	BC_Oct89Ext4	no of packets	75945
C	BC_Oct89Ext	no of bytes	122798
D	BC_Oct89Ext	no of packets	122798
E	BC_pAug89	no of bytes	3143
F	BC_pAug89	no of packets	3143
G	BC_pOct89	no of bytes	1760
H	BC_pOct89	no of packets	1760
I	dec_pkt_1_tcp	no of bytes	3601
J	dec_pkt_1_tcp	no of packets	3601
K	dec_pkt_2_tcp	no of bytes	3601
L	dec_pkt_2_tcp	no of packets	3601
M	dec_pkt_3_tcp	no of bytes	3600
N	dec_pkt_3_tcp	no of packets	3600
O	dec_pkt_4_tcp	no of bytes	3600
P	dec_pkt_4_tcp	no of packets	3600
Q	lbl_pkt_4_tcp	no of bytes	3600
R	lbl_pkt_4_tcp	no of packets	3600
S	lbl_pkt_5_tcp	no of bytes	3600
T	lbl_pkt_5_tcp	no of packets	3600
U	lbl_tcp_3	no of bytes	7200
V	lbl_tcp_3	no of packets	7200

Figure 12.3 shows dataset A (the number of bytes arriving at the Bellcore facility) before preprocessing. Figure 12.4 shows the first 100 entries of the same dataset after preprocessing, which involved subtracting the mean value of the dataset and dividing by the maximum absolute value entry in the dataset. The entries are negative because they are just the first 100 values and in the original dataset they were below the mean value.

Before being used in the experiments, the datasets were preprocessed. For each dataset, we performed the following operations: from each observation, we subtracted the mean value of the dataset and then divided by the largest in absolute value entry. These operations guarantee that the mean value of the datasets is zero and the largest in absolute value entry is 1. If a prediction made for such data exceeds 1 in absolute value, then ether 1 or −1 (whichever is closer to the original prediction) is output as the prediction. During the experiments, the datasets were used with different time scales (i.e., measurement time intervals): 1 second, 2 seconds, and 5 seconds, for demonstration purposes.

A single long time series can be converted into a set of smaller time series by sliding a window incrementally across the time series. Window length is usually a user-defined parameter. Each dataset was divided into subdatasets of approximately 300

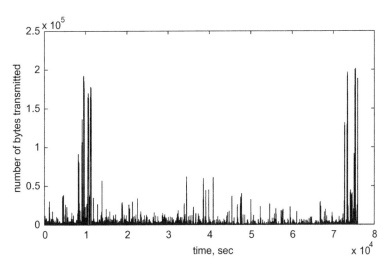

FIGURE 12.3

Dataset A before preprocessing.

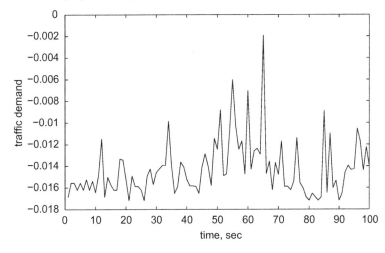

FIGURE 12.4

Dataset A after preprocessing, first 100 seconds of observation.

observations. Each of the subdatasets was used as follows: the first 200 observations were used to build a model and then this model was used to make predictions on the next 100 observations in the online mode; after each prediction was made, the true value of the observation was passed on to the prediction system. Next, the last 200 observations were used to build another model and this model was used to make predictions on the next 100 observations. Then the process was repeated. This so-called moving window setting divided the experiments into cycles.

There were two purposes to the experiments described in this section. First, we wanted to make sure that conformal predictors output efficient (narrow) prediction intervals and second, that they are empirically valid. Empirical validity means that the error rate equals a predefined level, where the error rate is the number of wrong predictions (i.e., predictions that do not contain the real observation of the process) divided by the total number of predictions.

Efficient prediction with confidence

To show that conformal predictors are empirically valid and have high efficiency, we experimented with artificial datasets generated by using the Autoregressive Moving Average (ARMA) model [42]. The ARMA model has two parts, an autoregressive (AR) part and a moving average (MA) part. The model is defined as the ARMA(p, q) model where p is the order of the autoregressive part and q is the order of the moving average part [42]. In our artificially generated datasets, the optimal width of prediction intervals could be calculated and thus we could estimate the efficiency of conformal predictors applied to these datasets [66,65].

For illustrative purposes, four datasets, X1, X2, X3, and X4 were artificially generated with different parameters p and q. Dataset X1 was generated by an ARMA$(2,0)$ process, dataset X2 by an ARMA$(1,2)$ process, dataset X3 by an ARMA$(2,1)$ process, and dataset X4 by an ARMA$(0,2)$ process. All these processes have the variance of the white noise sequence equal to 1, which means that the best possible value for the width of a prediction interval with confidence level of 95% is 3.92, as this is the width of the prediction interval (with the same confidence level) for a normally distributed random variable with variance 1. Of course, the value 3.92 is optimal, but in reality is subject to statistical fluctuations. Therefore, algorithms in the experiments might achieve lower or higher values for the widths of the prediction intervals and still be considered efficient.

We used eight underlying algorithms before applying conformal predictors to their outputs. The underlying algorithms were the nearest neighbors (NN) algorithm with the number of neighbors equal to 1 (with the window size equal to 10) and 3 (with the window size equal to 20), Ridge Regression (RR) with the window size equal to 10 and 20, and the ARMA model with sets of parameters equal to $(0,2), (1,1), (2,0)$, and $(2,1)$.

Table 12.7 shows the widths of the prediction intervals for the last predictions made by conformal predictors based on different underlying algorithms. It can be seen that for the NN algorithm, the widths are much greater than the desired value of 3.92. This is probably due to the fact that the data were generated by linear models and the NN algorithm does not take the linearity of the data into account. Other algorithms, however, are designed to make predictions for data with linear dependence and, with rare exceptions, according to our experimental results, are highly efficient.

Table 12.8 shows the error rates for different algorithms with the significance level of 5%. It can be seen that with few exceptions the error rate of these conformal predictors is close to 5%. It is interesting to note that even though conformal predictors do not provide any guaranteed theoretical validity, the experimental results are still empirically valid.

Table 12.7 Width of the prediction intervals of the last prediction.

Dataset	X1	X2	X3	X4
NN1-WS10	9.22	6.96	7.50	6.71
NN3-WS20	7.66	5.72	6.16	6.93
RR-WS10	4.02	4.01	3.87	4.04
RR-WS20	4.01	3.97	3.90	4.12
ARMA(0, 2)	5.20	4.01	4.27	4.02
ARMA(1, 1)	5.46	4.95	5.08	4.03
ARMA(2, 0)	3.99	4.41	3.92	4.37
ARMA(2, 1)	4.00	4.36	3.87	4.03

Table 12.8 Error rates of conformal predictors with significance level of 5%.

Dataset	X1	X2	X3	X4
NN1-WS10	0.048	0.048	0.050	0.046
NN3-WS20	0.050	0.056	0.050	0.050
RR-WS10	0.045	0.047	0.046	0.046
RR-WS20	0.043	0.044	0.046	0.038
ARMA(0, 2)	0.049	0.048	0.052	0.047
ARMA(1, 1)	0.045	0.048	0.052	0.045
ARMA(2, 0)	0.050	0.050	0.049	0.046
ARMA(2, 1)	0.049	0.051	0.047	0.046

An interesting property of conformal predictors is that the better the underlying algorithm is, the more efficient the conformal predictor based on this algorithm is. Indeed, since the error rate for conformal predictors is guaranteed (in the case where the assumption of exchangeability holds), only the efficiency is important in assessing how successful an underlying algorithm is. Table 12.9 shows the cumulative square errors of different algorithms. It is clear that the algorithms with large errors (such as the NN) have low efficiency whereas the algorithms with small errors (such as the RR) have high efficiency.

To demonstrate that conformal predictors for time series prediction are empirically valid, we draw the graph of the cumulative number of errors for different algorithms applied to dataset X1 and the theoretical line to which we want the error rates to converge. Figure 12.5 shows that the cumulative number of errors of different algorithms with significance level of 5% are close to the theoretical value (i.e., the line with the inclination of 0.05).

Figure 12.6 shows the average widths of the prediction intervals for conformal predictors based on different underlying algorithms applied to dataset X1 and the theoretical bound on the width (derived from the properties of the process generating the data). The graph shows that for four out of eight algorithms (namely, RR-WS10,

Table 12.9 Cumulative square errors of different algorithms.

Dataset	X1	X2	X3	X4
NN1-WS10	19510	11186	13121	10700
NN3-WS20	14144	7661	8952	11026
RR-WS10	3759	3726	3540	3963
RR-WS20	3769	3629	3568	3938
ARMA(0, 2)	6238	3642	4314	3792
ARMA(1, 1)	6955	5460	5912	3817
ARMA(2, 0)	3702	4434	3541	4505
ARMA(2, 1)	3707	4315	3502	3807

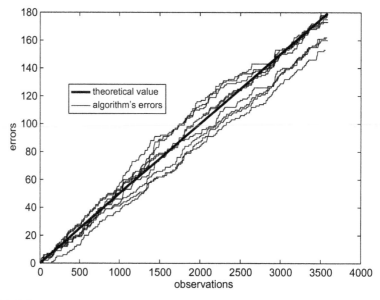

FIGURE 12.5

Cumulative number of errors for conformal predictors with significance level of 5%, dataset X1.

RR-WS20, ARMA(2, 0), and ARMA(2, 1)), the widths quickly converge to the optimal value. The remaining four algorithms did not have high performance and thus did not result in efficient conformal predictors.

Prediction with confidence and guaranteed performance

The next set of experiments involved building conformal predictors on top of different underlying algorithms. The purpose of the study was to check the experimental validity and efficiency of the algorithm on 22 real network demand traces. We considered three

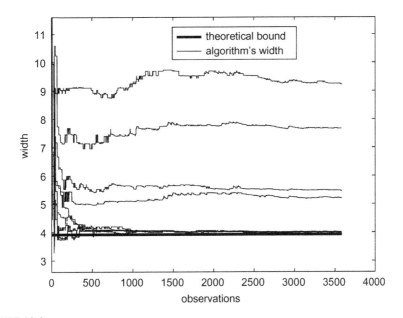

FIGURE 12.6

Average widths of prediction intervals for conformal predictors, dataset X1.

Table 12.10 Conformal predictors built on top of different algorithms.

Algorithm	Performance	SL-2%	SL-5%	SL-10%
CONST	Error rate	0.019	0.049	0.098
	Interval width	1.096	0.773	0.588
PREV	Error rate	0.020	0.052	0.102
	Interval width	1.143	0.802	0.595
LSR	Error rate	0.018	0.051	0.101
	Interval width	1.060	0.716	0.524

underlying algorithms: outputting the mean value of the dataset as the prediction (we call this predictor CONST as it outputs constant values), outputting the last observation as the prediction on the next observation (this predictor is called PREV), and Least Squares Regression (LSR) applied to pairs of two consecutive observations. For each of the datasets we again used time scales of 1, 2, and 5 seconds and made predictions. We built conformal predictors on top of these three algorithms and ran them with the significance level equal to 2%, 5%, and 10%. We then averaged the error rates and prediction widths over all datasets and time scales.

Table 12.10 shows the performance of the three conformal predictors for different algorithms and different significance levels (SL), including the average value over all

Table 12.11 Performance on datasets A–H (timescale = 1 second).

Algorithm	Performance	SL	A	B	C	D	E	F	G	H
CONST	Error Rate	2%	0.01	0.01	0.01	0.01	0.02	0.02	0.01	0.01
		5%	0.02	0.02	0.03	0.03	0.05	0.04	0.04	0.04
		10%	0.04	0.04	0.05	0.05	0.09	0.09	0.09	0.10
CONST	Interval Width	2%	0.57	0.59	0.60	0.64	1.27	1.30	1.32	1.43
		5%	0.27	0.30	0.28	0.33	0.90	1.00	1.05	1.16
		10%	0.17	0.19	0.16	0.22	0.68	0.80	0.85	0.97
PREV	Error Rate	2%	0.02	0.02	0.02	0.02	0.02	0.02	0.02	0.01
		5%	0.06	0.05	0.05	0.05	0.05	0.05	0.04	0.04
		10%	0.11	0.09	0.10	0.10	0.10	0.10	0.09	0.10
PREV	Interval Width	2%	0.55	0.57	0.60	0.63	1.27	1.29	1.19	1.32
		5%	0.24	0.27	0.28	0.32	0.90	0.94	0.88	0.99
		10%	0.13	0.15	0.15	0.20	0.68	0.72	0.68	0.75
LSR	Error Rate	2%	0.02	0.02	0.02	0.02	0.02	0.02	0.01	0.02
		5%	0.05	0.05	0.05	0.05	0.05	0.04	0.05	0.04
		10%	0.10	0.10	0.10	0.10	0.09	0.09	0.09	0.09
LSR	Interval Width	2%	0.55	0.57	0.59	0.62	1.18	1.18	1.14	1.26
		5%	0.24	0.26	0.27	0.31	0.83	0.86	0.83	0.94
		10%	0.13	0.15	0.15	0.19	0.62	0.67	0.65	0.73

Table 12.12 Performance on datasets A–H (timescale = 2 seconds).

Algorithm	Performance	SL	A	B	C	D	E	F	G	H
CONST	Error Rate	2%	0.01	0.01	0.01	0.01	0.01	0.02	0.01	0.01
		5%	0.03	0.03	0.03	0.03	0.04	0.04	0.03	0.05
		10%	0.08	0.07	0.06	0.06	0.09	0.08	0.07	0.10
CONST	Interval Width	2%	0.58	0.60	0.60	0.63	1.36	1.25	1.32	1.48
		5%	0.28	0.30	0.28	0.32	1.01	0.98	1.05	1.24
		10%	0.18	0.20	0.17	0.21	0.79	0.80	0.89	1.09
PREV	Error Rate	2%	0.02	0.02	0.02	0.02	0.02	0.02	0.01	0.02
		5%	0.06	0.05	0.06	0.05	0.05	0.04	0.05	0.04
		10%	0.11	0.10	0.11	0.10	0.09	0.09	0.10	0.10
PREV	Interval Width	2%	0.55	0.57	0.60	0.62	1.41	1.23	1.17	1.30
		5%	0.24	0.26	0.28	0.30	1.07	0.95	0.87	1.03
		10%	0.13	0.15	0.15	0.18	0.83	0.73	0.69	0.82
LSR	Error Rate	2%	0.02	0.02	0.02	0.02	0.01	0.01	0.02	0.02
		5%	0.05	0.05	0.06	0.05	0.04	0.04	0.04	0.04
		10%	0.11	0.10	0.10	0.10	0.08	0.08	0.10	0.10
LSR	Interval Width	2%	0.55	0.57	0.60	0.61	1.29	1.14	1.12	1.27
		5%	0.24	0.26	0.27	0.30	0.95	0.88	0.83	0.98
		10%	0.13	0.15	0.15	0.18	0.75	0.69	0.65	0.77

Table 12.13 Performance on datasets A–H (timescale = 5 seconds).

Algorithm	Performance	SL	A	B	C	D	E	F	G	H
CONST	Error	2%	0.02	0.02	0.02	0.02	0.03	0.03	0.02	0.02
	Rate	5%	0.05	0.05	0.05	0.04	0.06	0.07	0.02	0.05
		10%	0.11	0.10	0.09	0.09	0.11	0.11	0.05	0.06
CONST	Interval	2%	0.59	0.61	0.64	0.70	1.32	1.33	1.77	1.82
	Width	5%	0.29	0.31	0.32	0.39	0.98	1.02	1.52	1.69
		10%	0.18	0.20	0.19	0.27	0.77	0.79	1.41	1.54
PREV	Error	2%	0.02	0.02	0.03	0.02	0.02	0.02	0.00	0.00
	Rate	5%	0.06	0.05	0.06	0.05	0.04	0.06	0.04	0.03
		10%	0.11	0.10	0.11	0.10	0.12	0.11	0.11	0.11
PREV	Interval	2%	0.56	0.58	0.63	0.67	1.40	1.48	1.34	1.38
	Width	5%	0.24	0.26	0.30	0.35	1.07	1.12	0.96	1.03
		10%	0.13	0.14	0.17	0.21	0.77	0.81	0.69	0.82
LSR	Error	2%	0.02	0.02	0.02	0.02	0.03	0.02	0.00	0.00
	Rate	5%	0.06	0.05	0.06	0.05	0.04	0.06	0.04	0.03
		10%	0.11	0.10	0.11	0.10	0.11	0.11	0.09	0.08
LSR	Interval	2%	0.56	0.58	0.62	0.66	1.23	1.27	1.43	1.47
	Width	5%	0.24	0.26	0.29	0.34	0.92	0.95	1.01	1.16
		10%	0.13	0.14	0.16	0.21	0.68	0.73	0.79	0.90

Table 12.14 Performance on datasets I–P (timescale = 1 second).

Algorithm	Performance	SL	I	J	K	L	M	N	O	P
CONST	Error	2%	0.02	0.02	0.02	0.02	0.02	0.02	0.02	0.02
	Rate	5%	0.05	0.05	0.05	0.05	0.05	0.05	0.05	0.05
		10%	0.10	0.10	0.10	0.10	0.10	0.10	0.10	0.10
CONST	Interval	2%	1.13	1.02	1.23	1.19	1.04	1.27	1.31	1.29
	Width	5%	0.79	0.70	0.92	0.89	0.71	0.96	1.03	1.01
		10%	0.60	0.54	0.73	0.70	0.54	0.77	0.82	0.81
PREV	Error	2%	0.02	0.02	0.02	0.02	0.02	0.02	0.02	0.02
	Rate	5%	0.05	0.05	0.05	0.05	0.05	0.05	0.05	0.04
		10%	0.10	0.10	0.09	0.09	0.10	0.10	0.10	0.09
PREV	Interval	2%	1.10	0.94	1.25	1.12	1.09	1.27	1.35	1.28
	Width	5%	0.77	0.62	0.94	0.79	0.74	0.91	1.04	0.98
		10%	0.57	0.44	0.74	0.61	0.55	0.72	0.83	0.78
LSR	Error	2%	0.02	0.02	0.02	0.02	0.02	0.01	0.02	0.02
	Rate	5%	0.06	0.05	0.05	0.05	0.04	0.06	0.04	0.03
		10%	0.10	0.10	0.10	0.10	0.11	0.11	0.09	0.08
LSR	Interval	2%	1.06	0.91	1.16	1.07	1.00	1.18	1.25	1.19
	Width	5%	0.71	0.58	0.84	0.74	0.66	0.84	0.93	0.88
		10%	0.52	0.42	0.65	0.55	0.49	0.65	0.73	0.70

Table 12.15   Performance on datasets I–P (timescale = 2 seconds).

Algorithm	Performance	SL	I	J	K	L	M	N	O	P
CONST	Error	2%	0.03	0.02	0.02	0.02	0.02	0.02	0.02	0.02
	Rate	5%	0.05	0.05	0.05	0.05	0.05	0.05	0.05	0.05
		10%	0.11	0.11	0.10	0.10	0.10	0.10	0.11	0.11
CONST	Interval	2%	1.13	0.99	1.20	1.35	1.11	1.46	1.23	1.34
	Width	5%	0.79	0.68	0.88	1.04	0.80	1.17	0.91	1.05
		10%	0.61	0.50	0.69	0.81	0.62	0.97	0.72	0.85
PREV	Error	2%	0.02	0.03	0.02	0.02	0.01	0.01	0.02	0.02
	Rate	5%	0.05	0.06	0.06	0.06	0.05	0.04	0.05	0.04
		10%	0.11	0.10	0.10	0.11	0.10	0.09	0.10	0.09
PREV	Interval	2%	1.11	0.92	1.17	1.28	1.14	1.44	1.27	1.38
	Width	5%	0.74	0.57	0.85	0.94	0.79	1.13	0.93	1.03
		10%	0.55	0.42	0.68	0.71	0.59	0.89	0.72	0.81
LSR	Error	2%	0.02	0.03	0.02	0.02	0.01	0.01	0.02	0.02
	Rate	5%	0.05	0.06	0.06	0.05	0.05	0.04	0.04	0.05
		10%	0.11	0.10	0.10	0.10	0.10	0.09	0.09	0.09
LSR	Interval	2%	1.06	0.89	1.14	1.22	1.05	1.33	1.17	1.27
	Width	5%	0.69	0.55	0.80	0.88	0.72	1.01	0.84	0.94
		10%	0.52	0.40	0.61	0.67	0.54	0.80	0.65	0.74

Table 12.16   Performance on datasets I–P (timescale = 5 seconds).

Algorithm	Performance	SL	I	J	K	L	M	N	O	P
CONST	Error	2%	0.03	0.03	0.02	0.01	0.02	0.02	0.04	0.02
	Rate	5%	0.06	0.06	0.05	0.04	0.04	0.04	0.07	0.06
		10%	0.11	0.11	0.10	0.08	0.08	0.09	0.13	0.10
CONST	Interval	2%	1.28	0.94	1.51	1.61	1.27	1.51	1.24	1.44
	Width	5%	0.97	0.64	1.15	1.29	0.90	1.23	0.96	1.16
		10%	0.74	0.47	0.97	1.00	0.69	0.99	0.78	0.95
PREV	Error	2%	0.02	0.03	0.01	0.01	0.01	0.02	0.03	0.02
	Rate	5%	0.06	0.06	0.04	0.06	0.03	0.04	0.07	0.06
		10%	0.11	0.11	0.11	0.09	0.07	0.08	0.13	0.12
PREV	Interval	2%	1.21	0.89	1.46	1.53	1.33	1.58	1.26	1.43
	Width	5%	0.85	0.57	1.16	1.19	0.99	1.31	0.87	1.08
		10%	0.67	0.44	0.90	0.99	0.75	1.06	0.65	0.80
LSR	Error	2%	0.03	0.03	0.02	0.02	0.01	0.02	0.03	0.02
	Rate	5%	0.08	0.07	0.04	0.05	0.03	0.03	0.07	0.05
		10%	0.12	0.12	0.08	0.10	0.08	0.09	0.11	0.10
LSR	Interval	2%	1.15	0.86	1.44	1.50	1.20	1.43	1.15	1.32
	Width	5%	0.77	0.54	1.05	1.18	0.86	1.15	0.81	1.00
		10%	0.60	0.39	0.82	0.89	0.65	0.90	0.61	0.78

Table 12.17   Performance on datasets Q–V (timescale = 1 second).

Algorithm	Performance	SL	Q	R	S	T	U	V
CONST	Error	2%	0.02	0.02	0.02	0.02	0.02	0.02
	Rate	5%	0.05	0.05	0.05	0.05	0.05	0.05
		10%	0.11	0.10	0.10	0.10	0.10	0.10
CONST	Interval	2%	0.98	0.92	0.80	0.88	0.81	0.82
	Width	5%	0.64	0.59	0.48	0.57	0.48	0.50
		10%	0.44	0.42	0.33	0.42	0.32	0.36
PREV	Error	2%	0.02	0.02	0.02	0.02	0.02	0.02
	Rate	5%	0.05	0.05	0.05	0.05	0.06	0.05
		10%	0.09	0.10	0.10	0.09	0.10	0.10
PREV	Interval	2%	0.95	0.93	0.80	0.86	0.77	0.79
	Width	5%	0.62	0.60	0.48	0.54	0.43	0.47
		10%	0.42	0.42	0.32	0.38	0.28	0.33
LSR	Error	2%	0.02	0.02	0.02	0.02	0.02	0.02
	Rate	5%	0.05	0.05	0.05	0.05	0.05	0.05
		10%	0.09	0.10	0.10	0.09	0.10	0.10
LSR	Interval	2%	0.93	0.88	0.77	0.83	0.75	0.77
	Width	5%	0.57	0.54	0.44	0.51	0.41	0.44
		10%	0.39	0.38	0.29	0.35	0.26	0.31

Table 12.18   Performance on datasets Q–V (timescale = 2 seconds).

Algorithm	Performance	SL	Q	R	S	T	U	V
CONST	Error	2%	0.02	0.01	0.02	0.02	0.02	0.02
	Rate	5%	0.05	0.05	0.05	0.04	0.06	0.06
		10%	0.10	0.09	0.08	0.09	0.11	0.10
CONST	Interval	2%	1.19	1.12	0.91	1.02	0.93	0.89
	Width	5%	0.79	0.78	0.59	0.72	0.54	0.56
		10%	0.54	0.59	0.42	0.57	0.37	0.40
PREV	Error	2%	0.02	0.01	0.02	0.02	0.02	0.02
	Rate	5%	0.05	0.04	0.05	0.05	0.06	0.05
		10%	0.10	0.10	0.10	0.09	0.10	0.09
PREV	Interval	2%	1.17	1.16	0.90	0.98	0.88	0.86
	Width	5%	0.79	0.83	0.56	0.67	0.51	0.53
		10%	0.53	0.60	0.40	0.50	0.33	0.37
LSR	Error	2%	0.02	0.01	0.03	0.02	0.02	0.02
	Rate	5%	0.05	0.04	0.05	0.05	0.05	0.05
		10%	0.10	0.09	0.10	0.09	0.10	0.10
LSR	Interval	2%	1.11	1.09	0.85	0.94	0.84	0.83
	Width	5%	0.70	0.73	0.52	0.62	0.49	0.50
		10%	0.47	0.51	0.36	0.46	0.31	0.35

Table 12.19   Performance on datasets Q–V (timescale = 5 seconds).

Algorithm	Performance	SL	Q	R	S	T	U	V
CONST	Error	2%	0.02	0.02	0.01	0.01	0.03	0.02
	Rate	5%	0.04	0.04	0.04	0.03	0.07	0.06
		10%	0.09	0.10	0.08	0.07	0.13	0.12
CONST	Interval	2%	1.64	1.22	1.20	1.38	1.03	1.02
	Width	5%	1.03	0.84	0.75	0.96	0.63	0.67
		10%	0.64	0.62	0.49	0.69	0.46	0.49
PREV	Error	2%	0.01	0.02	0.02	0.02	0.03	0.02
	Rate	5%	0.04	0.04	0.04	0.04	0.06	0.05
		10%	0.09	0.08	0.09	0.09	0.10	0.10
PREV	Interval	2%	1.72	1.30	1.09	1.18	1.03	0.95
	Width	5%	1.20	0.94	0.73	0.87	0.59	0.62
		10%	0.79	0.71	0.48	0.66	0.40	0.46
LSR	Error	2%	0.01	0.02	0.01	0.01	0.03	0.02
	Rate	5%	0.04	0.04	0.04	0.02	0.06	0.05
		10%	0.08	0.08	0.09	0.06	0.11	0.10
LSR	Interval	2%	1.59	1.18	1.06	1.20	0.97	0.93
	Width	5%	0.93	0.81	0.65	0.80	0.56	0.58
		10%	0.66	0.60	0.42	0.59	0.37	0.41

the datasets. From the table we can see that the error rates are relatively close to the significance levels. The detailed performance measurements on these datasets can be found in Tables 12.11–12.19. For example, Tables 12.11, 12.12, and 12.13 show the performance of the different underlying algorithms on the datasets A through H for the timescale of 1, 2, and 5 seconds, respectively. Similarly the performance of the different underlying algorithms on the datasets I through P and Q through V can be found in Tables 12.14–12.19. It seems that the performance of conformal predictors is not dependent on the measurement used: the number of bytes or the number of packets. The measurement interval can affect the performance of conformal predictors slightly.

Table 12.10 also shows the average widths of the prediction intervals for different algorithms. It is worth noting that at the beginning of the prediction process, conformal predictors output the whole range of possible outcomes as the prediction interval and hence the width of the prediction intervals at later steps is smaller than the average width. it can be seen that the width of the prediction interval decreases when the level of the desired error rate increases, which is somewhat intuitive. Indeed, if we want to make fewer mistakes we have to output a wider prediction interval. The table shows that the average prediction widths of successful algorithms are smaller than those of less successful algorithms. If we let the algorithm make 10% of predictions incorrectly, then the average prediction width is less than a quarter of the width of the interval of possible outcomes, since the observed values are between −1 and 1 after preprocessing.

12.5 **Conclusions**

In this chapter, we described two applications of conformal prediction to network resource management problems: network traffic classification and network demand prediction. The introduction of prediction algorithms based on conformal predictors into a network management system can lead to significant improvements in the way a network is managed. For example, the confidence information associated with predictions can be used when evaluating plausible alternative resource allocations over a continuum of timescales. Unlike conventional machine learning techniques, the predictions these conformal predictors make are hedged: they incorporate an indicator of their own accuracy and reliability. These accuracy reliability measures allow service providers and network carriers to choose appropriate allocation strategies by eliminating unlikely resource demands. Therefore, the resource management process can effectively perform a cost-benefit evaluation of alternative actions.

When analyzing network traffic flows through classification, it is important to add some measure of how reliable the classifications are. Most currently used methods either do not provide such a measure of reliability or they make strong assumptions on the data. It has been shown that when these assumptions are violated traditional methods (such as Bayesian methods) become invalid and thus cannot be trusted [226]. On the other hand, conformal predictors make weak assumptions on the data generation process and therefore can be applied more widely.

The second problem considered in the chapter is the prediction of future network traffic demand. It is a challenging and important problem and a successful solution leads to great improvements in a network's performance. Conformal predictors offer a method of providing some measure of confidence placed on top of traffic demand predictions that can be used by higher level decision-making systems. The resulted network management system becomes more efficient and has higher performance according to a variety of measures.

Other Applications

13

Shen-Shyang Ho

School of Computer Engineering, Nanyang Technological University, Singapore

CHAPTER OUTLINE HEAD

In the previous three chapters, we see how the conformal prediction (CP) framework is adapted to handle real-world problems for face recognition, medical applications, and also network traffic/demand prediction. The theoretically proven *validity* property of conformal predictor makes it an extremely attractive prediction tool for many real-world prediction tasks for both the online and offline settings. Moreover, the ability of the conformal predictor to return prediction region (or interval) based on user-defined confidence level, instead of just returning a single point prediction, is an attractive capability that other conventional machine learning techniques and statistical models cannot provide. These are the two main reasons more practitioners are seriously considering using conformal predictors for their real-world applications.

In this final chapter, we provide a review on other real-world applications that directly utilized the CP framework for classification/regression tasks or its adaptations to tasks not discussed in the previous three chapters. In Section 13.1, we describe how the CP framework is utilized in various prediction tasks related to the investigation on clean and safe fusion power generation. In Section 13.2, we describe three different prediction tasks based on sensor readings. In Section 13.3, we describe three tasks related to applications pertaining, in general, to issues on sustainability and environment. In Section 13.4, we describe security problems, namely network intrusion and sea surveillance. Finally, In Section 13.5, we describe how people used the CP framework for estimation, identification, and modeling tasks in software engineering, forensic science, machine translation, and pharmaceutical industry. As new diverse applications are constantly being proposed and implemented, the author apologizes for the exclusion of any current developed applications utilizing the CP framework or its related theory.

13.1 Nuclear Fusion Device Applications

13.1.1 Image Classification for a Nuclear Fusion Diagnostic Device

Recently, the conformal prediction framework has been extensively tested on the recognition of images in the Thomson Scattering Diagnostic of the TJII fusion device. In this section, developments on this application are described.

Vega et al. [354] reported on their successful integration of a multiclass image classifier based on conformal prediction to the TJ-II Thomson Scattering (TS) charged coupled device (CCD) camera to automate the data processing system in the camera. After classification process, specific data analysis is, then, automatically carried out depending on the image class. The new classifier, a new independent software component in the camera "replaces a previous one that has become obsolete due to major modifications in both the TJ-II TS optics and TJ-II plasma injected NBI power" [354].

Five types of images can be captured by the TJ-II TS CCD camera, namely: (1) CCD camera back- ground (BKG), (2) measurement of stray light (STR) without plasma or in a collapsed discharge, (3) images during electron-cyclotron heating phase (ECH), (4) during natural beam injection phase (NBI), and (5) after reaching the cut-off density during electron-cyclotron heating (COFF).

The conformal predictor used in the TJ-II TS CCD camera is based on the 1-NN nonconformity measure defined in (1.17) and the p-value function (1.5).

Vega et al. [354] demonstrated the feasibility of conformal prediction for the image classification problem using a set of 165 images (576 × 385 pixels) consisting of 17 BKG, 18 STR, 56 ECH, 32 NBI, and 42 COFF. To reduce the data dimensionality,

Table 13.1 Classification results for TJ-II images [354].

Level	ER (%)	AM (%)	CO (%)	CR (%)
3	1.87	1.25	0.964	0.605
4	1.87	1.25	0.947	0.610
5	3.75	1.87	0.950	0.600

each image is represented by a feature vector that is the Haar wavelet transform of the original image. As the wavelet transform decomposition is multiscale, images can be characterized by a set of approximation coefficients and three sets of detailed coefficients (horizontal, vertical, and diagonals). Three different decomposition levels have been tested: levels 3, 4, and 5. With these selections, the number of attributes are reduced to 72×48 (1.59% of the original) 36×24 (0.39%), and 18×12 (0.10%) respectively. This compression process is a standard procedure used with images to reduce their dimensionality. For their experiments, the initial training set consisting of a unique object in each class is randomly selected. During the experiments, the images are sequentially classified and they are added to their respective classes.

Table 13.1 shows the classification errors (ER), ambiguities (AM; more than one class predicted), the average confidence (CO), and the average credibility (CR) for the three decomposition levels.

To overcome computational issues related to large data set and high dimensionality, Makili et al. [223] applied the approach proposed in [298] by creating a hash function that splits the training set into smaller subsets of roughly equal sizes to generate several "one versus the rest" SVM classifiers for the TJ-II image recognition task. To further improve the computational efficiency of the conformal predictor using SVM as the underlying classifier, a standard SVM is replaced by an incremental SVM. The processing of the training data is improved by as much as seven times the original speed on a large dataset [222].

To further improve on the image classification task, a region selection approach based on the nonconformity measure is used to select the most suitable region in an image for the classification of each class [122].

13.1.2 Classification of L-mode/H-mode Confinement Regimes in a Tokamak Device

To enable controlled nuclear fusion for clean and safe generation of energy, the biggest challenge is confinement. Most current research focuses on controlled fusion reaction using magnetic fields to confine the hot hydrogen isotope plasma according to the Tokamak principle. There are two types of confinement mode: low-confinement mode (L-mode) and the high-confinement mode (H-mode). The H-mode is characterized by "an enhanced plasma temperature, density and average confinement time of the plasma energy and particles." It has a better confinement time than L-mode. The H-mode is the reference plasma scenario for the next-step device machine ITER.

The transition mechanism of a plasma into H-mode is currently a subject of active research. For practical purposes, we can identify the confinement mode from some conventional plasma diagnostic signals. In fact, it can be used as an important tool for real-time plasma control to stabilize complex plasma and magnetic configurations and maximize the performance. A conformal predictor is based on a geometric-probabilistic modeling framework to the classification of confinement regimes, the L(ow)-mode and the H(igh)-mode plasmas [356].

The International Tokamak Physics Activity (ITPA) Global H-mode Confinement Database (DB3, version 13f) is used in the experiment. The ITPA database contains more than 10,000 validated measurements of various global plasma and engineering variables at one or several time instants during the discharges in 19 tokamaks. Eight plasma and engineering parameters: plasma current, vacuum toroidal magnetic field, total power loss from the plasma, central line-averaged electron density, plasma major radius, plasma minor radius, elongation, and effective atomic mass, are used for the classification task. All database entries with a confinement mode labeled as H, as well as related high-confinement regimes labeled HGELM, HSELM, HGELMH, HSELMH, and LHLHL, were considered to belong to the H-mode class. Those labeled with L, OHM, and RI were assigned to the L-mode class.

13.1.3 Reliable L-mode/H-mode Transition Time Estimation

Nowadays, there is not a single theory to describe the transition from the L-mode to the H-mode confinement regime. There are many competing theoretical models but no one has proven to completely explain the transition. A typical approach to acquire knowledge about the physics involved in the L/H transition has been to determine the time when it occurs and to generate scaling laws with several physical quantities. Unfortunately, the transition time estimation can be a very tedious and time-consuming process without ensuring accurate estimations, because it requires human intervention to perform visual data analysis.

A novel technique for the determination of L/H transition times in a completely automatic way without human intervention is using Inductive Conformal Prediction with SVM as the underlying classifier to provide a level of reliability for the probability confidence interval for the estimated transition time from L-mode to H-mode [121]. The technique is used to develop an automated transition detector (ATD) that can be used to create large databases of L/H transition times to understand L/H transition physics.

13.2 Sensor Device Applications

13.2.1 Tea (Smell) Classification

Traditionally, tea flavor is measured through the use of a combination of conventional analytical instrumentation and human organoleptic profiling panels. These methods are expensive in terms of time and labor. There is inaccuracy due to a lack of both sensitivity and quantitative information [250]. Electronic nose has been successfully used for tea classification and grading. However, such classification used only bare predictions without any confidence estimation. In general, an electronic nose is a smart instrument that is designed to detect and discriminate among complex odors using an array of sensors. The array of sensors is exposed to volatile odor vapor through a suitable odor handling and delivery system that ensures constant exposure rate to each sensors. The response signals of these sensors are recorded and processed for analysis and classification. For tea classification, the objective is to discriminate the aroma of different tea types.

Nouretdinov et al. [250] proposed a nonconformal measure derived from multiple Lagrange multipliers to link binary-class SVM to multiclass SVM. Suppose there are $q > 2$ classes. One constructs $\frac{q(q-1)}{2}$ binary-class SVMs using examples that have the two classes of the binary-class SVM_r. If an example x_j has a class label of the two classes, it will have the Lagrange multiplier $\alpha_j^{SVM_r}$, else $\alpha_j^{SVM_r} := 0$. The nonconformal measure is

$$\alpha_j := \max_r \alpha_j^{SVM_r} \qquad (13.1)$$

Metal Oxide Semiconductor (MOS) sensors are commonly used in electronic nose applications for their convenience in operating and steadiness in features. An array of seven gas sensors were used for the tea classification experiments. Four types of tea available from the market—Japanese Green Tea (JG), Chinese Green Tea (CG), Indian Black Tea (IB), and Chinese Black Tea (CB)—were used and they are labeled from 1 to 4, respectively. Each tea sample is heated before data acquirement. There are 68 data samples in total obtained in the experiments (15 for Indian Black Tea, 19 for Chinese Black Tea, 17 for Chinese Green Tea, and 17 for Japanese Green Tea). Each data sample is described by seven features obtained from the seven gas sensors. Each sensor returns time series data and the maximum value during time of measurement is used as the feature value for the classification task.

Empirical results have shown good performance for the conformal predictor on the tea classification task. More experimental results and their discussions are found in [250].

13.2.2 Total Electron Content Prediction

Total Electron Content (TEC) is the total amount of electrons along a particular line of sight and is measured in total electron content units ($1 TECu = 10^{16} el/m^2$). TEC prediction is useful in the application of mitigation techniques for the reduction of ionospheric imposed errors on communication, surveillance, and navigation systems. Since solar activity has a strong effect on the variability of TEC, the objective for [263] is to have reliable TEC estimates on typical days during low, medium, and high sunspot periods.

Papadopoulos and Haralambous [263] applied the Inductive Conformal Prediction (ICP) (see Section 2.3) for regression based on neural network (NN) to the total electron content prediction using a normalized nonconformality measure

$$\alpha_i = \frac{|y_i - \hat{y}_i|}{\exp(\mu_i)} \tag{13.2}$$

where μ_i is the prediction of the value $\ln(|y_i - \hat{y}_i|)$ produced by a trained linear NN.

The TEC measurements used in the experiment consist of 60421 values recorded between 1998 and 2009. A two-fold cross-validation was performed such that the data was split into two equal parts, one with 30211 and one with 30210. The testing step was repeated twice. The above cross-validation was repeated 10 times with different random splitting of the dataset. The underlying NN used in the experiment had a fully connected two-layer structure, with five input, 13 hidden, and one output neurons. The hidden layer consisted of neurons with hyperbolic tangent activation functions, while the output neuron had a linear activation function. The number of hidden neurons was determined by trial and error on the original NN. The training algorithm used was the Levenberg- Marquardt backpropagation algorithm with early stopping based on a validation set created from 10% of the training examples. The main observations from the experimental result are (1) (13.2) achieves tighter bound compared to using the nonconformality measure $|y_i - \hat{y}_i|$, and (2) the estimated interval corresponds to the specified significance level for almost all trials.

More experimental results and their discussions are found in [263].

13.2.3 Roadside Assistance Decision Support System

Smirnov et al. [329] applied a variant of the CP framework called single-stacking conformal predictors to a roadside assistance clinical decision support system. The objective of this work was to predict the status of a car, given the symptoms identified from its off-/on-board diagnosis system. Details of this application can be found in Section 9.3 of Chapter 9.

13.3 Sustainability, Environment, and Civil Engineering

13.3.1 Wind Speed Prediction

Similar to the fusion power generation investigation described in Section 13.1, the ability to tap into wind power as an alternative source of clean and inexhaustive energy has also attracted a lot of research. Wind power (i.e., speed) prediction/forecasting in wind farms is an important issue to enable efficient wind power utilization. Unlike conventional power generation based on fossil fuels such as coal, oil, natural gas, or nuclear power, wind generation is not easily adjustable on demand. The ability to predict wind speed well, in turns, ensures that variability of wind generation can be managed for optimal integration of wind energy into electricity grids. Meyn et al. [229] argued that volatility (i.e., uncertainty and variability) of wind generation may affect the value of wind power generation. To overcome this issue, we need to provide a reliable estimation of wind speed prediction uncertainty. There are many machine learning methods applied to wind speed prediction (see references in [292]). But they do not provide reliable and theoretical sound uncertainty quantification.

Ji et al. [292] proposed using Inductive Conformal Predictor with support vector regression as the underlying prediction algorithm developed by Papadopoulos et al. [266] for wind speed prediction. Experiments were carried out on 90 days of mean hourly wind speed data from a wind farm in China. The results showed that the proposed approach provides good predictions with high confidence values. However, the efficiency (i.e, size of the prediction region) of the proposed conformal predictor could be improved.

13.3.2 Air Pollution Assessment

Air pollution occurs when unnatural chemicals, particulates, or biological compounds introduced into the atmosphere cause harm to humans (and other living things) and/or to the environment. Accurate assessment of air pollution level or contamination level of a particular harmful compound is critical for decision/policy makers to design policies to control and reduce the air pollution problem in urban and industrial areas. Many methods have been proposed ([159,160] and references therein) for air pollution assessment. However, the assessments are point estimates and lack theoretical sound confidence measures.

Ivina et al. [159,160] proposed using conformal predictor with ridge regression as the underlying prediction algorithm (called RRCM) developed by Nouretdinov et al. [251] for air pollutant concentration estimation. RRCM was applied to data collected in the Barcelona Metropolitan Region (BMR) on the concentrations of nitrogen dioxide measured at 49 locations across BMR from 1998 to 2009, excluding 2003. According to the experimental results, RRCM is comparable to ordinary kriging [368] with the additional advantage of a confidence measure. Moreover, RRCM only requires an i.i.d. assumption to be satisfied while kriging requires the stochastic process to be Gaussian.

13.3.3 Pavement Structural Diagnostics

Inverse analysis of pavement systems is used to determine the structural condition of roads or pavements. Backcalculation is an evaluation approach to determine the moduli or stiffness of pavement by using pavement surface deflection basins generated by various pavement deflection devices. The evaluation approach takes a measured surface deflection and matches it with a calculated surface deflection generated from an identical pavement structure. Several artificial intelligence techniques were proposed to handle this task [125]. However, these techniques only provide point estimations without reporting the credibility or confidence of the prediction.

Gopalakrishnan and Papadopoulos [125] proposed using Inductive Conformal Predictor using neural networks regression as the underlying prediction algorithm (called NNR-CP) developed by Papadopoulos and Haralambous [264] (used in Section 13.2.2 for the total electron content prediction). A comprehensive set of synthetic data consisting of moduli-deflection solutions for various layer thickness and layer stiffness are used in the experiment. The training set has 28,000 records and the testing set has 1,500 records. The authors demonstrated the ability of NNR-ICP to return prediction intervals for the HMA (hot-mixed asphalt) surface layer moduli given a fixed confidence level or credibility specified by the pavement engineer.

13.4 Security Applications

13.4.1 Network Intrusion Detection

The goal of a network intrusion detection system is to discover unauthorized access to a computer network by analyzing traffic on the network for signs of malicious activity. The intrusion detection task is to build a predictive model capable of distinguishing between intrusions or attacks, and normal network connections. There are four main categories of attacks, namely: denial-of-service (DOS), unauthorized access from a remote machine, unauthorized access to local superuser (root) privileges, and probing.

Li et al. [212] proposed using Conformal Predictor using KNN as the underlying prediction algorithm (called TCM-KNN [280]) with a slight modification in the nonconformity measure for detecting anomalies in network traffic. The modified nonconformal measure considers only the sum of the distances from the nearest K data points from the same label. Moreover, Li and Guo [211] considered using the active learning strategy described in Chapter 3 to select small number of relevant training data in order to reduce computational cost and labeling cost. The KDD Cup 1999 data (described in [334]), a standard benchmark data that includes a wide variety of intrusions simulated in a military network environment, was used in [212,211] to demonstrate that the proposed approach is competitive against conventional machine learning intrusion detection approaches such as SVM, neural network, and K-NN.

13.4.2 Surveillance

Surveillance of moving objects for abnormal behavior is getting more attention with the availability of huge amounts of trajectory data based on sensor systems. For maritime surveillance, abnormal behaviors include "unexpected stops, deviation from standard routes, speeding, [and] traffic direction violations" that point to possible "threats and dangers related to smuggling, sea drunkenness, collisions, grounding, terrorism , hijacking, [and] piracy" [195]. Timely identification of anomalies and intervention of these threats and danger can reduce the possible loss of life, occurrences of crime, and number of accidents.

Laxhammer and Falkman [196] proposed a conformal anomaly detector (CAD) (see Chapter 4) using KNN as the underlying prediction algorithm and nonconformity measure similar to [212] for trajectory data. Laxhammer [195] proposed SNN-NCM (Similarity-based Nearest Neighbor Nonconformity Measure) that is based on any similarity instead of the Euclidean distance. In particular, the similarity (or more precisely, the dissimilarity) measure does not need to be symmetric; that is, $S(z_i, z_j) \neq S(z_j, z_i)$ such that $S(\cdot, \cdot)$ is the similarity function, and z_i and z_j are two different trajectories. The SNN-CAD [195], using the SNN-NCN as the nonconformity measure, is a generalization of CAD.

Unlabeled (i.e., no information either the trajectories are anomalies) vessel trajectories were extracted from the AIS (Automatic Identification System) database provided by Saab Transponder Tech. The attributes are MMSI (Maritime Mobile Service Identity), latitudinal and longitudinal position, course, speed, timestamp, and vessel class. These trajectories show three weeks of continuous sea traffic along the west coast of Sweden. In addition, trajectories are extracted from a confined area outside the port of Gothenburg. Trajectories extracted from IR surveillance videos, together with the two sea traffic datasets, are also used to demonstrate the feasibility of CAD [196].

13.5 Applications from Other Domains

13.5.1 Software Engineering: Cost Estimation

An accurate cost estimation, especially during the early stages of the software project life cycle, provides more efficient project resource management. The estimation task is extremely challenging even for well-planned projects because of the different degree of complexity and the uniqueness of the software engineering process for different projects.

Most conventional cost models and techniques provide a single estimate for cost and effort [265]. Thus, it would be helpful to handle the uncertainty of the estimate using prediction intervals based on user-defined confidence levels. Papadopoulos et al. [265] proposed using conformal predictors with ridge regression as the underlying prediction algorithm developed by Nouretdinov et al. [251] for the software cost estimation task that provides a cost/effort prediction interval. The predictor is applied to three software effort estimation datasets, namely: COCOMO 81 (Constructive Cost Model) [32], Desharnais [72], and ISBSG.[1] The COCOMO dataset contains information about 63 software projects. The dataset from Desharnais includes observations for more than 80 systems developed by a Canadian Software Development House in the late 1980s. The ISBSG dataset contains information on the software project costs for a group of projects from different industries and range in size, effort, platform, languages and development techniques. It was shown to obtain reliable and narrow predictive interval for practical use.

13.5.2 Forensic Science: Striation Pattern Identification

Tool mark impression evidences have been used in courts for decades. A tool mark examiner verbally states that a particular set of tool mark evidence is associated to a specific tool without any scientific and statistical justification that would "independently corroborate conclusions based on morphology characteristics" [271].

---

[1]International Software Benchmarking Standards Group: The ISBSG estimating, benchmarking & research suite release 9 (2005). http://www.isbsg.org/.

There are no standard statistical or machine learning methods for the analysis of tool mark evidence. The application of classification methods for tool mark evidence analysis are of particular interest for their potential to assign objective quantitative measures to the words "sufficient agreement" and "comparative examination" in a court case [271].

A screwdriver marks dataset was created to demonstrate the feasibility of a CP framework for a tool mark identification task. Nine identical screwdrivers were purchased at a local hardware store. The screwdrivers were used to generate multiple reproducible striation patterns that were digitally photographed. The positions and widths of a small number of striation lines and grooves were measured with a stage micrometer. Seven hundred and thirty-two striation patterns were simulated for testing purposes based on 75 actual patterns created from the nine screwdrivers.

Petraco et al. [271] proposed applying conformal prediction using SVM and 3-NN as the underlying algorithms based on mean Lagrange multiple values and the standard nonconformity measure for nearest neighbor classifier, respectively. They expect to extend the CP framework methodology to any kind of striated tool mark identification or firearm evidence to be used in court cases.

13.5.3 Machine Translation: Quality Estimation

Machine translation (MT) is an instrument to save time for human translators. A human translator would apply a MT system and manually postedit its translation to correct mistakes. However, there is no guarantee that a given translated segment from the MT system is good enough for postedition. A human translator may need to read the segment many times to find out whether to use the segment or to redo the translation. This is an extremely unpredictable and inefficient process.

The inability to provide information about the quality of the translation from a MT system is one reason hampering the use of these systems [332]. The task of MT confidence estimation (CE) is concerned with quality (e.g., fluency or adequacy, postediting requirements, etc.) prediction of a MT output for a given input, without any information about the expected output.

Specia et al. [332] proposed the use of Inductive Confidence Machines [266] with partial least square regression [382] as the underlying prediction algorithm to dynamically define the threshold to filter out bad translations under a certain expected level of confidence. Translation data produced by three MT systems: Matrax [325], Portage [164], and Sinuhe [168] are used to test the effectiveness of the CP solution. For each system, translations are manually annotated by professional translators with quality scores from one to four to indicate the quality of translations with respect to the need for postedition: (1) requires complete retranslation, (2) postediting quicker than retranslation, (3) little post editing needed, and (4) fit for purpose. The regression algorithm produces a continuous score that is then thresholded into the two classes: good and bad translation. With translation datasets produced by the three MT systems, Specia et al. [332] showed that the proposed CP solution improves results over conventional regression and classification algorithms with better precision or recall.

The CP solution allows control of both the expected precision and recall according to the needs of a translation task.

13.5.4 Pharmaceutical Industry: QSAR Modeling

Quantitative Structure-Activity Relationships (QSAR) is a framework for employing statistical learning methods to predict the pharmacological effect (cure or alleviate a disease) and the toxicity from chemical compounds structures [89] for applications such as drug development. To make reliable decisions based on predictions from a QSAR model, knowledge about the confidence for a prediction and the interpretation is required.

Eklund et al. [89] proposed using Inductive Conformal Predictor with K-nearest neighbor regression as the underlying prediction algorithm developed by Papadopoulos et al. [267] with a slight modification on the nonconformity measure. Instead of using Euclidean distance between data points, the distances between points in the feature space is used. Moreover, a SVM is used to obtain prediction used in the nonconformity measure. Five datasets (two publicly available and three in-house) are used in the experiments. The two publicly available datasets include the aqueous solubilities for a diverse set of 1297 organic compounds[2] and the US Food and Drug Administration (FDA) recommended daily doses for 1215 pharmaceuticals.[3] The other three datasets are proprietary in-house AstraZeneca datasets.

According to Eklund et al. [89], one of the nonconformity measures provides prediction intervals with almost the same width as the size of the QSAR models prediction errors, showing that the prediction intervals obtained by conformal prediction are efficient and useful. Moreover, conformal prediction provides an intuitive interpretation (p-values and prediction intervals) of the QSAR modeling reliability.

---

[2] http://cheminformatics.org/.
[3] http://www.epa.gov/ncct/dsstox/sdf_fdamdd.html.

Bibliography

[1] Abe N, Mamitsuka H. Query learning strategies using boosting and bagging. In: Proceedings of the 15th international conference on machine learning (ICML); 1998.

[2] Adamskiy D, Nouretdinov I, Mitchell A, Coldham N, Gammerman A. Applying conformal prediction to the bovine TB diagnosing. In: Proceedings of 12th INNS EANN-SIG international conference and seventh IFIP WG 12.5 international conference, vol. II; 2011. p. 449–54.

[3] Adler A. Sample images can be independently restored from face recognition templates. In: IEEE Canadian conference on electrical and computer engineering, 2003, vol. 2; 2003. p. 1163–6.

[4] Aggarwal CC. A framework for change diagnosis of data streams. In: Halevy AY, Ives ZG, Doan A., editors. Proceedings of the ACM SIGMOD international conference on management of data. ACM; 2003. p. 575–86.

[5] Alt H. The computational geometry of comparing shapes. In: Albers S, Alt H, Näher S, editors. Efficient algorithms. Lecture notes in computer science, vol. 5760. Berlin: Springer; 2009. p. 235–48.

[6] Ambroise C, McLachlan GJ. Selection bias in gene extraction on the basis of microarray gene-expression data. In: Proceedings of the national academy of sciences of the USA, vol. 99; 2002. p. 6562–6.

[7] Ambroladze A, Parrado-Hernández E, Shawe-Taylor J. Tighter PAC-Bayes bounds. In: Proceedings of advances in neural information processing systems; 2006.

[8] Bache K, Lichman M. UCI machine learning repository. University of California, Irvine, school of information and computer sciences; 2013. <http://archive.ics.uci.edu/ml>.

[9] Auld T, Moore AW, Gull S. Bayesian neural networks for internet traffic classification. IEEE Trans Neural Netw 2007;18:223–39.

[10] Axelsson S. The base-rate fallacy and the difficulty of intrusion detection. ACM Trans Inf Syst Secur 2000;3(3):185–205.

[11] Balasubramanian V, Chakraborty S, Panchanathan S. Generalized query by transduction for online active learning. In: IEEE international conference on computer vision (ICCV), workshop on online learning for computer vision; 2009.

[12] Balasubramanian VN, Gouripeddi R, Panchanathan S, Vermillion J, Bhaskaran A, Siegel RM. Support vector machine based conformal predictors for risk of complications following a coronary drug eluting stent procedure. In: Proceedings of the IEEE conference on computers in cardiology; 2009.

[13] Baram Y, El-Yaniv R, Luz K. Online choice of active learning algorithms. J Mach Learn Res 2004;5.

[14] Barbará D, Domeniconi C. Detecting outliers using transduction and statistical testing. In: Proceedings of the 12th annual SIGKDD international conference on knowledge discovery and data mining; 2006. p. 55–64.

[15] Barlow HB. Unsupervised learning. Neural Commun 1989;1:295–311.

[16] Baskiotis N, Sebag M. C4. 5 competence map: a phase transition-inspired approach. In: Proceedings of the 21st international conference on machine learning. ACM; 2004. p. 10.

[17] Basseville M, Nikiforov IV. Detection of abrupt changes: theory and application. Prentice Hall; 1993.

[18] Bay SD, Pazzani MJ. Characterizing model errors and differences. In: Proceedings of the 17th international conference on machine learning. San Francisco, CA: Morgan Kaufmann; 2000. p. 49–56.

[19] Bellotti T, Luo Z, Gammerman A. Reliable classification of childhood acute leukaemia from gene expression data using confidence machines. In: Proceedings of IEEE international conference on granular computing; 2006. p. 148–53.

[20] Bellotti T, Luo Z, Gammerman A, Van Delft FW, Saha V. Qualified predictions for microarray and proteomics pattern diagnostics with confidence machines. Int J Neural Syst 2005;15:247–58.

[21] Bellotti T. Confidence machines for microarray classification and feature selection [Ph.D. thesis]. Royal Holloway University of London; 2005.

[22] Bellotti T, Crook J. Support vector machines for credit scoring and discovery of significant features. Expert Syst Appl 2009;36:3302–8.

[23] Bellotti T, Luo Z, Gammerman A. Strangeness minimisation feature selection with confidence machine. In: Intelligent data engineering and automated learning IDEAL; 2006. p. 978–85.

[24] Bellotti T, Luo Z, Gammerman A, van Delft FW, Saha V. Qualified predictions for microarray and proteomics pattern diagnostics with confidence machines. Int J Neural Syst 2005;15:1–12.

[25] Bender R, Berg G, Zeeb H. Tutorial: using confidence curves in medical research. Biomed J 2005;47:237–47.

[26] Benjamini Y, Hochberg Y. Controlling the false discovery rate: a practical and powerful approach to multiple testing. J Roy Stat Soc Ser B 1995;57:289–300.

[27] Birattari M, Bontempi H, Bersini H. Local learning for data analysis. In: Proceedings of the eighth Belgian-Dutch conference on machine learning, Wageningen, The Netherlands; 1998. p. 55–61.

[28] Blok HJ. On the nature of the stock market: simulations and experiments [Ph.D. thesis]. Canada: University of British Columbia; 2000.

[29] Blum A, Chawla S. Learning from labeled and unlabeled data using graph mincuts. In: Proceedings of international conference on machine learning (ICML); 2001.

[30] Blum A, Langley P. Selection of relevant features and examples in machine learning. Artif Intell 1997;97:245–71.

[31] Blum A, Mitchell T. Combining labeled and unlabeled data with co-training. In: Bartlett P, Mansour Y, editors. Proceedings of the 11th annual conference on computational learning theory, Madison, Wisconsin. New York, USA: ACM Press; 1998. p. 92–100.

[32] Boehm B. Software engineering economics. Prentice Hall; 1981.

[33] Bolle RM, Connell JH, Pankanti S, Ratha NK, Senior AW. Guide to biometrics. Springer; 2004.

[34] Bonwell C, Eison J. Active learning: creating excitement in the classroom. ASHE-ERIC higher education report; 1991.

[35] Boser BE, Guyon IM, Vapnik VN. A training algorithm for optimal margin classifiers. In: Proceedings of the fifth annual workshop on computational learning theory. Pittsburgh: ACM; 1992. p. 144–52.

[36] Bosnić Z, Kononenko I. Estimation of individual prediction reliability using the local sensitivity analysis. Appl Intell 2007;29:187–203.

[37] Bosnić Z, Kononenko I. Comparison of approaches for estimating reliability of individual regression predictions. Data Knowl Eng 2008;67:504–16.

[38] Bosnić Z, Rodrigues PP, Kononenko I, Gama J. Correcting streaming predictions of an electricity load forecast system using a prediction reliability estimate. Man Mach Interact 2011;2:343–50.

[39] Bosnić Z, Vračar P, Radović MD, Devedžić G, Filipović N, Kononenko I. Mining data from hemodynamic simulations for generating prediction and explanation models. IEEE Trans Inf Technol Biomed 2012;16:248–54.

[40] Bosnič Z, Kononenko I. Estimation of individual prediction reliability using the local sensitivity analysis. Appl Intell 2008;29(3):187–203.

[41] Bousquet O, Elisseeff A. Stability and generalization. J Mach Learn Res 2002;2: 499–526.

[42] Box G, Jenkins GM, Reinsel GC. Time series analysis: forecasting and control. 3rd ed. Prentice-Hall; 1994.

[43] Breierova L, Choudhari M. An introduction to sensitivity analysis. MIT System Dynamics in Education Project; 1996.

[44] Breiman L, Friedman JH, Olshen RA, Stone CJ. Classification and regression trees. Chapman and Hall; 1984.

[45] Brinker K. Incorporating diversity in active learning with support vector machines. In: Proceedings of the international conference on machine learning (ICML); 2003.

[46] Campbell C, Cristianini N, Smola A. Query learning with large margin classifiers. In: Proceedings of the international conference on machine learning (ICML); 2000.

[47] Carney J, Cunningham P. Confidence and prediction intervals for neural network ensembles. In: Proceedings of the international joint conference on neural networks, Washington, USA; 1999. p. 1215–8.

[48] Cauwenberghs G, Poggio T. Incremental support vector machine learning. In: Advances in neural information processing systems (NIPS); 2000.

[49] Champod C, Meuwly D. The inference of identity in forensic speaker recognition. Speech Commun 2000;31:193–203.

[50] Chandola V, Banerjee A, Kumar V. Anomaly detection: a survey. ACM Comput Surv 2009;41(3):1–58.

[51] Chang C.-C., Lin C.-J. LIBSVM: a library for support vector machines; 2001. <http://www.csie.ntu.edu.tw/~cjlin/libsvm>.

[52] Chapelle O, Scholkopf B, Zien A. Semi-supervised learning. MIT Press; 2006.

[53] Chapelle O, Vapnik VN. Model selection for support vector machines. In: Proceedings of advances in neural information processing systems, vol. 12; 1999. p. 230–7.

[54] Cheng J, Wang K. Active learning for image retrieval with Co-SVM. In: Pattern recognition; 2007.

[55] Chu F, Wang Y, Zaniolo C. An adaptive learning approach for noisy data streams. In: Proceedings of the fourth IEEE international conference on data mining. IEEE Computer Society; 2004. p. 351–4.

[56] Chu F, Zaniolo C. Fast and light boosting for adaptive mining of data streams. In: Dai H, Srikant R, Zhang C, editors. PAKDD. Lecture notes in computer science, vol. 3056. Springer; 2004. p. 282–92.

[57] Cohn D. Neural network exploration using optimal experiment design. In: Advances in neural information processing systems (NIPS); 1994.

[58] Cohn D, Atlas L, Ladner R. Improving generalization with active learning. Mach learn 1994;15(2):201–21.

[59] Cohn D, Ghahramani Z, Jordan M. Active learning with statistical models. J Artif Intell Res 1996;4:129–45.

[60] Corani G, Zaffalon M. Credal model averaging: an extension of bayesian model averaging to imprecise probabilities. In: Machine learning and knowledge discovery in databases. Springer; 2008. p. 257–71.

[61] Cortez P, Rio M, Rocha M, Sousa P. Multiscale internet traffic forecasting using neural networks and time series methods. Expert Syst 2012;29(2):143–55.

[62] Cover TM, Hart P. Nearest neighbor pattern classification. IEEE Trans Inf Theory 1967;13:21–7.

[63] Cox DR, Hinkley DV. Theoretical statistics. London: Chapman and Hall; 1974.

[64] Dasgupta S, Hsu D. Proceedings of the international conference on machine learning (ICML); 2008.

[65] Dashevskiy M. Prediction with performance guarantees [Ph.D. thesis]. Royal Holloway, UK: Department of Computer Science, University of London; 2010.

[66] Dashevskiy M, Luo Z. Network traffic demand prediction with confidence. In: GLOBECOM; 2008. p. 1453–7.

[67] Dashevskiy M, Luo Z. Reliable probabilistic classification and its application to internet traffic. In: Fourth international conference on intelligent computing. Lecture notes in computer science, vol. 5226. Springer; 2008. p. 380–8.

[68] Dashevskiy M, Luo Z. Predictions with confidence in applications. In: The sixth international conference on machine learning and data mining (MLDM 2009); 2009. p. 775–86.

[69] Dashevskiy M, Luo Z. Reliable probabilistic classification of internet traffic. Int J Inf Acquisition 2009;6(2):133–46.

[70] Dashevskiy M, Luo Z. Time series prediction with performance guarantee. IET Commun 2011;5:1044–51.

[71] Feres de Souza B, de Carvalho ACPLF, Calvo R, Ishii RP. Multiclass SVM model selection using particle swarm optimization. In: Proceedings of the sixth international conference on hybrid intelligent systems; 2006.

[72] Desharnais JM. Analyse statistique de la productivite des projects de development en informatique a partir de la technique de points de fonction [M.Sc. thesis]. Montreal Universite du Quebec; 1988.

[73] Dessimoz D, Champod C. Handbook of biometrics. In: Linkages between biometrics and forensic science. Springer; 2008.

[74] Devetyarov D. Confidence and Venn machines and their applications to proteomics [Ph.D. thesis]. Royal Holloway: University of London; 2011.

[75] Devetyarov D, Nouretdinov I, Burford B, Camuzeaux S, Gentry-Maharaj A, Tiss A, et al. Conformal predictors in early diagnostics of ovarian and breast cancers. Prog Artif Intell 2012;1:245–57.

[76] Devetyarov D, Nouretdinov I, Gammerman A. Confidence machine and its application to medical diagnosis. In: BIOCOMP; 2009. p. 448–54.

[77] Devroye L, Györfi L, Lugosi G. A probabilistic theory of pattern recognition. Applications of mathematics, vol. 31. New York: Springer; 1996.

[78] Diaconis P, Freedman D. On the consistency of Bayes estimates (with discussion). Ann Stat 1986;14:1–67.

[79] Diacu F. Is failure to predict a crime? October 2012. New York Times; October 2012. <http://www.nytimes.com/2012/10/27/opinion/a-failed-earthquake-prediction-a-crime.html>.

[80] Diamond GA, Forester JS. Analysis of probability as an aid in the clinical diagnosis of coronary artery disease. New Eng J Med 1979;300:3–50.

[81] Diehl C, Cauwenberghs G. SVM incremental learning, adaptation and optimization. In: International joint conference on neural networks (IJCNN); 2003.

[82] Ding C, Peng H. Minimum redundancy feature selection from microarray gene expression data. In: Proceedings of the computer society bioinformatics conference. IEEE; 2003.

[83] Domingos P, Pazzani M. Beyond independence: conditions for the optimality of the simple bayesian classifier. In: Proceedings of the 13th international conference on machine learning; 1996. p. 105–12.

[84] Dreger H, Feldmann A, Mai M, Paxson V, Sommer R. Dynamic application-layer protocol analysis for network intrusion detection. In: Proceedings of the 15th conference on USENIX security symposium, Berkeley, CA, USA, vol. 15. USENIX Association; 2006.

[85] Duda RO, Hart PE, Stork DG. Pattern classification. 2nd ed New York: Wiley; 2000.

[86] Džeroski S, Ženko B. Is combining classifiers with stacking better than selecting the best one? Mach Learn 2004;54(3):255–73.

[87] Edelman S. Representation is representation of similarity. Behav Brain Sci 1998;21: 449–98.

[88] Efroymson MA. Multiple regression analysis. Wiley; 1960.

[89] Eklund M, Norinder U, Boyer S, Carlsson L. Application of conformal prediction in QSAR. In: Artificial intelligence applications and innovations. Springer; 2012. p. 166–75.

[90] Elidan G, Ninio M, Friedman N, Schuurmans D. Data perturbation for escaping local maxima in learning. In: Proceedings of the 18th national conference on artificial intelligence and 14th conference on innovative applications of artificial intelligence, Edmonton, Alberta, Canada. AAAI Press; 2002. p. 132–9.

[91] Elomaa T, Mannila H, Toivonen H, editors. Proceedings of the 13th European conference on machine learning (ECML 2002), Helsinki, Finland, August 19–23. Lecture notes in computer science, vol. 2430. London: Springer; 2002.

[92] En-Najjary T, Urvoy-Keller G, Pietrzyk M, Costeux J-L. Application-based feature selection for internet traffic classification. In: 22nd international teletraffic congress (ITC); 2010. p. 1–8.

[93] Erman J, Mahanti A, Arlitt M. Traffic classification using clustering algorithms. In: Proceedings of the 2006 SIGCOMM workshop on mining network data; 2006. p. 281–6.

[94] Eskin E. Anomaly detection over noisy data using learned probability distributions. In: Proceedings of the seventh international conference on machine learning; 2000. p. 255–62.

[95] Este A, Gringoli F, Salgarelli L. Support vector machines for TCP traffic classification. Comput Netw 2009;53(14):2476–90.

[96] Fawcett T. An introduction to ROC analysis. Pattern Recogn Lett 2006;27(8): 861–74 [special issue: ROC analysis in pattern recognition].

[97] Fedorova V, Gammerman A, Nouretdinov I, Vovk V. Plug-in martingales for testing exchangeability on-line. In: Proceedings of the 29th international conference on machine learning (ICML); 2012.

[98] Ferri C, Hernández-Orallo J. Cautious classifiers. In: Proceedings of the first international workshop on ROC analysis in artificial intelligence (ROCAI-2004); 2004. p. 27–36.

[99] Fleuret F. Fast binary feature selection with conditional mutual information. J Mach Learn Res 2004;5:1531–55.

[100] Frank A, Asuncion A. UCI machine learning repository; 2010.

[101] Fraser DAS. Sequentially determined statistically equivalent blocks. Ann Math Stat 1951;22:372–81.

[102] Fraser DAS. Nonparametric tolerance regions. Ann Math Stat 1953;24:44–55.

[103] Fraser DAS, Wormleighton R. Nonparametric estimation IV. Ann Math Stat 1951;22: 294–8.

[104] Freund Y, Sebastian Seung H, Shamir E, Tishby N. Selective sampling using the query by committee algorithm. Mach learn 1997;28(2–3):133–68.

[105] Freund Y, Shapire RE. Experiments with a new boosting algorithm. In: Proceedings of the 13th international conference on machine learning (ICML); 1996. p. 148–56.

[106] Freund Y, Schapire RE. A decision-theoretic generalization of on-line learning and an application to boosting. J Comput Syst Sci 1997;55:119–39.

[107] Friedman FH, Hastie T, Tibshirani R. Additive logistic regression: a statistical view of boosting. Ann Stat 2005;28:337–407.

[108] Friedman JH. Greedy function approximation: a gradient boosting machine. Ann Stat 2001;29:1189–232.

[109] Friedman JH. Stochastic gradient boosting. Comput Stat Data Anal 2002;38: 367–78.

[110] Fujii A, Tokunaga T, Inui K, Tanaka H. Selective sampling for example-based word sense disambiguation. Comput Linguist 1998;24(4):573–97.

[111] Furui S. Recent advances in speaker recognition. Pattern Recogn Lett 1997;18:859–72.

[112] Gammerman A, Nouretdinov I, Burford B, Chervonenkis A, Vovk V, Luo Z. Clinical mass spectrometry proteomic diagnosis by conformal predictors. Stat Appl Genet Mol Biol 2008;7(2).

[113] Gammerman A, Vovk V, Burford B, Nouretdinov I, Luo Z, Chervonenkis A, et al. Serum proteomic abnormality predating screen detection of ovarian cancer. Comput J 2009;52(3):326–33.

[114] Gammerman A, Vovk V. Hedging predictions in machine learning: the second Computer Journal lecture. Comput J 2007;50:151–63.

[115] Gammerman A, Vovk V, Vapnik V. Learning by transduction. In: Cooper GF, Moral S, editors. Proceedings of the 14th conference on uncertainty in artificial intelligence, Madison, WI. San Francisco, USA: Morgan Kaufmann; 1998. p. 148–55.

[116] Gelman A, Carlin JB, Stern HS, Rubin DB. Bayesian data analysis. Chapman and Hall/CRC; 2003.

[117] Giacinto G, Roli F. Dynamic classifier selection based on multiple classifier behaviour. Pattern Recogn 2001;34:1879–81.

[118] Gibbs AL, Su FE. On choosing and bounding probability metrics. Int Stat Rev 2002; 70(3):419–35.

[119] Girshik MA, Rubin H. A Bayes approach to a quality control model. Ann Math Stat 1952;23(1):114–25.

[120] Gold C, Sollich P. Model selection for support vector machine classification. Neurocomputing 2003;55:221–49.

[121] Gonzalez S, Vega J, Murari A, Pereira A, Dormido-Canto S, Ramirez JM, JET-EFDA contributors. Automatic location of l/h transition times for physical studies with a large statistical basis. Plasma Phys Control Fusion 2012;54(6):065009.

[122] Gonzalez S, Vega J, Pereira A, Pastor I. Region selection and image classification methodology using a non-conformity measure. Prog Artif Intell 2012;1(3):215–22.

[123] Gonzalez-Rodriguez J, Rose P, Ramos D, Toledano DT, Ortega-Garcia J. Emulating DNA: rigorous quantification of evidential weight in transparent and testable forensic speaker recognition. IEEE Trans Audio Speech Lang Process 2007;15:2104–15.

[124] Goodrich M, Tamassia R. Data structures and algorithms in JAVA. John Wiley and Sons, Inc.; 1998.

[125] Gopalakrishnan K, Papadopoulos H. Reliable pavement backcalculation with confidence estimation. Sci Iran 2011;18(6):1214–21.

[126] Granger CWJ, Joyeux R. An introduction to long-memory time series models and fractional differencing. J Time Ser Anal 1980;1:15–29.

[127] Grother P. Face recognition vendor test (FRVT). Supplemental report NISTIR 7083; 2004.

[128] Gu C, Zhang S, Xue X. Encrypted internet traffic classification method based on host behavior. Int J Digit Content Technol Appl 2011;5(3):167–74.

[129] Guo Y. Active instance sampling via matrix partition. In: Advances of neural information processing systems (NIPS); 2010.

[130] Guo Y, Greiner R. Optimistic active learning using mutual information. In: Proceedings of the international joint conference on artificial intelligence (IJCAI); 2007.

[131] Guo Y, Schuurmans D. Discriminative batch mode active learning. In: Advances of neural information processing systems (NIPS); 2007.

[132] Gutta S, Wechsler H. Face recognition using asymmetric faces. In: First international conference on biometric authentication (ICB); 2004.

[133] Guttman I. Statistical tolerance regions: classical and Bayesian. London: Griffin; 1970.

[134] Guyon I, Elisseeff A. An introduction to variable and feature selection. J Mach Learn Res 2003;3:1157–82.

[135] Guyon I, Weston J, Barnhill S, Vapnik V. Gene selection for cancer classification using support vector machines. Mach Learn 2002;46(1–3):389–422.

[136] Halck OM. Using hard classifiers to estimate conditional class probabilities. In: Elomaa T, Mannila H, Toivonen H, editors. Proceedings of the 13th European conference on machine learning. Berlin: Springer; 2002. p. 124–34.

[137] Hammer B, Strickert M, Villmann T. Supervised neural gas for learning vector quantization. In: Proceedings of the fifth German workshop on artificial life (GWAL-5), Berlin: Akademische Verlagsgesellschaft-infix-IOS Press; 2002. p. 9–16.

[138] Hand DJ. Breast cancer diagnosis from proteomic mass spectrometry data: a comparative evaluation. Stat Appl Genet Mol Biol 2008;7(2).

[139] Hastie T, Rosset S, Tibshirani R, Zhu J. The entire regularization path for the support vector machine. J Mach Learn Res 2004;5:1391–415.

[140] Hastie T, Tibshirani R, Friedman J. The elements of statistical learning: data mining, inference, and prediction. 2nd ed New York: Springer; 2009.

[141] Hastie T, Tibshirani R, Friedman J, Franklin J. The elements of statistical learning: data mining, inference and prediction. Math Intell 2005;27(2):83–5.

[142] Hawkins D. Identification of outliers. London: Chapman and Hall; 1980.

[143] Heskes T. Practical confidence and prediction intervals. Adv Neural Inf Process Syst 1997;9:176–82.

[144] Ho SS, Wechsler H. Transductive confidence machine for active learning. In: Proceedings of the international joint conference on neural networks'03, Portland, OR; 2003.

[145] Ho S-S. A martingale framework for concept change detection in time-varying data streams. In: De Raedt L, Wrobel S, editors. ICML. ACM; 2005. p. 321–7.

[146] Ho S-S. Learning from data streams using transductive inference and martingale [Ph.D. thesis]. George Mason University; 2006.

[147] Ho S-S, Wechsler H. Adaptive support vector machine for time-varying data streams using martingale. In: Kaelbling LP, Saffiotti A, editors. IJCAI. Professional Book Center; 2005. p. 1606–7.

[148] Ho S-S, Wechsler H. On the detection of concept changes in time-varying data stream by testing exchangeability. In: Proceedings of the 21st annual conference on uncertainty in artificial intelligence (UAI-05). AUAI Press; 2005. p. 267–74.

[149] Ho S-S, Wechsler H. Detecting change-points in unlabeled data streams using martingale. In: 20th international joint conference on artificial intelligence (IJCAI), Hyderabad, India; 2007.

[150] Ho S-S, Wechsler H. Query by transduction. IEEE Trans Pattern Anal Mach Intell 2008;30(9):1557–71.

[151] Ho S-S, Wechsler H. A martingale framework for detecting changes in data streams by testing exchangeability. IEEE Trans Pattern Anal Mach Intell 2010;32(12):2113–27.

[152] Hofmann T, Buhmann J. Active data clustering. In: Advances in neural information processing systems (NIPS); 1998.

[153] Hoi Steven CH, Jin R, Lyu M. Batch mode active learning with applications to text categorization and image retrieval. IEEE Trans Knowl Data Eng 2009;21(9):1233–48.

[154] Hoi S, Jin R, Zhu J, Lyu M. Batch mode active learning and its application to medical image classification. In: International conference on machine learning (ICML); 2006.

[155] Hoi SCH, Jin R, Zhu J, Lyu MR. Semi-supervised SVM batch mode active learning for image retrieval. In: IEEE CVPR; 2008.

[156] Holub A, Perona P, Burl M. Entropy-based active learning for object recognition. In: IEEE conference on computer vision and pattern recognition (CVPR) workshops; 2008.

[157] Hüllermeier E. Case-based approximate reasoning, vol. 44. Springer; 2007.

[158] Hulten G, Spencer L, Domingos P. Mining time-changing data streams. In: Proceedings of the seventh ACM SIGKDD international conference on knowledge discovery and data mining. ACM; 2001. p. 97–106.

[159] Ivina O. Conformal prediction of air pollution concentrations for the barcelona metropolitan region [Ph.D. thesis]. University of Girona; 2012.

[160] Ivina O, Nouretdinov I, Gammerman A. Valid predictions with confidence estimation in an air pollution problem. Prog Artif Intell 2012;1(3):235–43.

[161] Jaeger J, Sengupta R, Ruzzo WL. Improved gene selection for classification of microarrays. In: Pacific symposium of biocomputing, vol. 8; 2003. p. 53–64.

[162] Joachims T. Transductive inference for text classification using support vector machines. In: International conference on machine learning (ICML), Bled, Slowenien; 1999. p. 200–9.

[163] John GH, Langley P. Estimating continuous distributions in Bayesian classifiers. In: Besnard P, Hanks S, editors. Proceedings of the 11th conference on uncertainty in artificial intelligence. San Francisco, USA: Morgan Kaufmann; 1995.

[164] Johnson H, Sadat F, Foster G, Kuhn R, Simard M, Joanis E, et al. Portage: with smoothed phrase tables and segment choice models. In: Proceedings of the workshop on statistical machine translation. Association for Computational Linguistics; 2006. p. 134–7.

[165] Joshi A, Porikli F, Papanikolopoulos N. Breaking the interactive bottleneck in multi-class classification with active selection and binary feedback. In: IEEE conference on computer vision and pattern recognition (CVPR); 2010.

[166] Joshi A, Porikli F, Papanikolopoulos N. Multi-class batch-mode active learning for image classification. In: International conference on robotics and automation (ICRA); 2010.

[167] Jost L. Combining significance levels from multiple experiments or analyses. <http://www.loujost.com/statistics> and <http://www.physics/statsarticlesindex.htm>; 2009.

[168] Kääriäinen M. Sinuhe: statistical machine translation using a globally trained conditional exponential family translation model. In: Proceedings of the 2009 conference on empirical methods in natural language processing, vol. 2. Association for Computational Linguistics; 2009. p. 1027–36.

[169] Kapoor A, Hua G, Akbarzadeh A, Baker S. Which faces to tag: adding prior constraints into active learning. In: IEEE international conference on computer vision (ICCV) workshops; 2009.

[170] Karagiannis T, Papagiannaki K, Faloutsos M. BLINC: multilevel traffic classification in the dark. In: Proceedings of ACM SIGCOMM; 2005. p. 229–40.

[171] Kearns M, Ron D. Algorithmic stability and sanity-check bounds for leave-one-out cross-validation. Neural Comput 1999;11(6):1427–53.

[172] Kemperman JHB. Generalized tolerance limits. Ann Math Stat 1956;27:180–6.

[173] Keogh E, Lin J, Fu A. HOT SAX: efficiently finding the most unusual time series subsequence. In: Proceedings of the fifth IEEE international conference on data mining; 2005. p. 226–33.

[174] Kifer D, Ben-David S, Gehrke J. Detecting change in data streams. In: Nascimento MA, Özsu MT, Kossmann D, Miller RJ, Blakeley JA, Bernhard Schiefer K, editors. Proceedings of the 13th international conference on very large data bases. Morgan Kaufmann; 2004. p. 180–91.

[175] Kim H, Claffy KC, Fomenkov M, Barman D, Faloutsos M, Lee K. Internet traffic classification demystified: myths, caveats, and the best practices. In: Proceedings of the 2008 ACM CoNEXT conference, New York, USA. ACM; 2008.

[176] Kleijnen J. Experimental designs for sensitivity analysis of simulation models. In: Eurosim 2001 conference; 2001.

[177] Klinkenberg R. Learning drifting concepts: examples selection vs example weighting. Intell Data Anal 2004;8(3):281–300 [special issue on incremental learning systems capable of dealing with concept drift].

[178] Klinkenberg R, Joachims T. Detecting concept drift with support vector machines. In: Langley P, editor. Proceedings of the 17th international conference on machine learning. Morgan Kaufmann; 2000. p. 487–94.

[179] Kolter JZ, Maloof MA. Dynamic weighted majority: a new ensemble method for tracking concept drift. In: ICDM. IEEE Computer Society; 2003. p. 123–30.

[180] Kononenko I, Šimec E, Robnik-Šikonja M. Overcoming the myopia of inductive learning algorithms with RELIEFF. Appl Intell 1997;7:39–55.

[181] Kononenko I. Semi-naive Bayesian classifier. In: Kodratoff Y, editor. Proceedings of the European working session on learning-91, Porto, Portugal. Berlin-Heidelberg-New York: Springer-Verlag; 1991. p. 206–19.

[182] Kothari R, Jain V. Learning from labeled and unlabeled data using a minimal number of queries. IEEE Trans Neural Netw 2003.

[183] Krishnamurthy B, Sen S, Zhang Y, Chen Y. Sketch-based change detection: methods, evaluation, and applications. In: Proceedings of the 3rd ACM SIGCOMM conference on Internet measurement. ACM; 2003. p. 234–47.

[184] Kukar M. Transductive reliability estimation for medical diagnosis. Artif Intell Med 2003;29:81–106.

[185] Kukar M. Quality assessment of individual classifications in machine learning and data mining. Knowledge and information systems 2006;9(3):364–84.

[186] Kukar M, Groselj C. Transductive machine learning for reliable medical diagnostics. J Med Syst 2005;29(1):13–32.

[187] Kukar M, Kononenko I. Reliable classifications with machine learning. In: Elomaa T, Mannila H, Toivonen H, editors. Proceedings of 13th European conference on machine learning, ECML 2002. Berlin: Springer-Verlag; 2002. p. 219–31.

[188] Lachiche N, Flach P. Improving accuracy and cost of two-class and multi-class probabilistic classifiers using ROC curves. In: Proceedings of the 20th international conference on machine learning (ICML 2003); 2003. p. 416–23.

[189] Lambrou A, Papadopoulos H, Gammerman A. Evolutionary conformal prediction for breast cancer diagnosis. In: Information technology and applications in biomedicine; 2009.

[190] Lambrou A, Papadopoulos H, Gammerman A. Reliable confidence measures for medical diagnosis with evolutionary algorithms. IEEE Trans Inf Technol Biomed 2011;15(1):93–9.

[191] Lambrou A, Papadopoulos H, Kyriacou E, Pattichis CS, Pattichis MS, Gammerman A, et al. Assessment of stroke risk based on morphological ultrasound image analysis with conformal prediction. In: Proceedings of the sixth IFIP international conference on artificial intelligence applications and innovations, IFIP AICT 339. Springer; 2010. p. 146–53.

[192] Lambrou A, Papadopoulos H, Kyriacou E, Pattichis MS, Gammerman A, Nicolaides A. Evaluation of the risk of stroke with confidence predictions based on ultrasound carotid image analysis. Int J Artif Intell Tool 2012;21(4).

[193] Lambrou A, Papadopoulos H, Nouretdinov I, Gammerman A. Reliable probability estimates based on support vector machines for large multiclass datasets. In: Iliadis L, Maglogiannis I, Papadopoulos H, Karatzas K, Sioutas S. editors. Proceedings of the AIAI 2012 workshop on conformal prediction and its applications. IFIP advances in information and communication technology, vol. 382. Berlin: Springer; 2012. p. 182–91.

[194] Langford J. Tutorial on practical prediction theory for classification. J Mach Learn Res 2005;6:273–306.

[195] Laxhammar R. Conformal anomaly detection: Detecting abnormal trajectories in surveillance applications [Ph.D. thesis]. University of Skövde; 2014.

[196] Laxhammar R, Falkman G. Conformal prediction for distribution-independent anomaly detection in streaming vessel data. In: Proceedings of the first international workshop on novel data stream pattern mining techniques. ACM; 2010. p. 47–55.

[197] Laxhammar R, Falkman G. Sequential conformal anomaly detection in trajectories based on Hausdorff distance. In: Proceedings of the 14th international conference on information fusion; 2011. p. 153–60.

[198] Laxhammar R, Falkman G. Inductive Conformal Anomaly Detection for Sequential Detection of Anomalous Sub-Trajectories. In Annals of Mathematics and Artificial Intelligence: Special Issue on Conformal Prediction and its Applications 2013. September 2013.

[199] Laxhammar R, Falkman G. Online Learning and Sequential Anomaly Detection in Trajectories. In IEEE Transactions on Pattern Analysis and Machine Intelligence, 99, (2013) PrePrints, September 2013.

[200] Lei Jing, Robins James, Wasserman Larry. Distribution free prediction sets. Journal of the American Statistical Association 2013;108:278–287. Preliminary version published as Technical Report arXiv:1111.1418 [math.ST].

[201] Lei Jing, Wasserman Larry. Distribution free prediction bands. Technical Report arXiv:1203.5422 [stat.ME], arXiv.org e-Print archive, March 2012. Published in the Journal of the Royal Statistical Society B, 2014;76:71-96.

[202] Leland WE, Taqqu MS, Willinger W, Wilson DV. On the self-similar nature of ethernet traffic (extended version). IEEE/ACM Trans Netw 1994;2(1):1–15.

[203] Lewis D, Gale W. A sequential algorithm for training text classifiers. In: Proceedings of the ACM SIGIR conference; 1994.

[204] Li F, Wechsler H. Open set face recognition using transduction. IEEE Trans Pattern Anal Mach Intell 2005;27:1686–97.

[205] Li F, Wechsler H. Face authentication using recognition-by-parts, boosting and transduction. Int J Artif Intell Pattern Recogn 2009;23:545–73.

[206] Li H, Wang S, Qi F. SVM model selection with the VC bound. Comput Inf Sci 2005;3314:1067–71.

[207] Li M, Sethi Ishwar K. Confidence-based active learning. IEEE Trans Pattern Anal Mach Intell 2006;28(8):1251–61.

[208] Li M, Vitányi P. An introduction to Kolmogorov complexity and its applications. 2nd ed. New York: Springer-Verlag; 1997.

[209] Li W, Abdin K, Dann R, Moore AW. Approaching real-time network traffic classification. Technical report RR-06-12. Department of Computer Science, Queen Mary, University of London; 2006.

[210] Li W, Canini M, Moore AW, Bolla R. Efficient application identification and the temporal and spatial stability of classification schema. Comput Netw 2009;53(6): 790–809.

[211] Li Y, Fang B, Guo L, Chen Y. Network anomaly detection based on TCM-KNN algorithm. In: Proceedings of the second ACM symposium on information, computer and communications security, ASIACCS '07, New York, NY, USA. ACM; 2007. p. 13–9.

[212] Li Y, Guo L. An active learning based TCM-KNN algorithm for supervised network intrusion detection. Comput Secur 2007;26(7–8):459–67.

[213] Li Z, Yuan R, Guan X. Accurate classification of the internet traffic based on the SVM method. In: Proceedings of IEEE international conference on communications, ICC; 2007. p. 1373–8.

[214] Liere R, Tadepalli P. Active learning with committees for text categorization. In: Proceedings of the 14th national conference on artificial intelligence; 1997.

[215] Lindenbaum M, Markovitch S, Rusakov D. Selective sampling for nearest neighbor classifiers. Mach Learn 2004;54(2):125–52.

[216] Lomasky R, Brodley C, Aernecke M, Walt D, Friedl M. Active class selection. In: Proceedings of the European conference on machine learning (ECML); 2007.

[217] Loughin TM. A systematic comparison of methods for combining p-values from independent tests. Comput Stat Data Anal 2004;47(3):467–85.

[218] MacKay David JC. Information-based objective functions for active data selection. Neural Comput 1992;4(4):590–604.

[219] Madhukar A, Williamson C. A longitudinal study of p2p traffic classification. In: Proceedings of the 14th IEEE international symposium on modeling, analysis, and simulation (MASCOTS'06); 2006. p. 179–88.

[220] Mak MW, Zhang WD, He MX. A new two-stage scoring normalization approach for speaker verification. In: International symposium on multimedia, video and speech processing; 2001.

[221] Makili L, Vega J, Dormido-Canto S. Active learning using conformal predictors: application to image classification. In: Seventh workshop on fusion data processing validation and analysis; 2012.

[222] Makili L, Vega J, Dormido-Canto S. Incremental support vector machines for fast reliable image recognition. Fusion Eng Des 2013;88(6):1170–73.

[223] Makili L, Vega J, Dormido-Canto S, Pastor I, Murari A. Computationally efficient {SVM} multi-class image recognition with confidence measures. Fusion Eng Des 2011;86(6–8):1213–6. Proceedings of the 26th symposium of fusion technology (SOFT-26).

[224] McCallum A, Nigam K. Employing EM and pool-based active learning for text classification. In: Proceedings of the international conference on machine learning (ICML); 1998.

[225] McCullagh P, Vovk V, Nouretdinov I, Devetyarov D, Gammerman A. Conditional prediction intervals for linear regression. In: Proceedings of the eighth international conference on machine learning and applications, Miami, FL, December 13–15; 2009. p. 131–8. <http://www.stat.uchicago.edu/~pmcc/reports/predict.pdf>.

[226] Melluish T, Saunders C, Nouretdinov I, Vovk V. Comparing the Bayes and typicalness frameworks. In: De Raedt L, Flach PA, editors. Proceedings of the 12th European conference on machine learning. Lecture notes in computer science, vol. 2167. Heidelberg: Springer; 2001. p. 360–71.

[227] Melville P, Mooney R. Diverse ensembles for active learning. In: Proceedings of the international conference on machine learning (ICML); 2004.

[228] Melville P, Yang S, Saar-Tsechansky M, Mooney R. Active learning for probability estimation using Jensen-Shannon divergence. In: European conference on machine learning (ECML); 2005.

[229] Meyn S, Negrete-Pincetic M, Wang G, Kowli A, Shafieepoorfard E. The value of volatile resources in electricity markets. In: 2010 49th IEEE conference on decision and control (CDC); 2010. p. 1029–36.

[230] Miettinen OS. Theoretical epidemiology: principles of occurrence research in medicine. New York: Wiley; 1985.

[231] Mitchell TM. Machine learning. Boston, MA: McGraw-Hill; 1997.

[232] Mitra P, Murthy CA, Pal Sankar K. A probabilistic active support vector learning algorithm. IEEE Trans Pattern Anal Mach Intell 2004;26(3):413–18.

[233] Momma M, Bennett KP. Pattern search method for model selection of support vector regression. In: Proceedings of the second SIAM international conference on data mining; 2002.

[234] Monteleoni C, Kaariainen M. Practical online active learning for classification. In: IEEE conference on computer vision and pattern recognition (CVPR); 2007.

[235] Moore AW., Discrete content-based classification – a data set. Technical report. Cambridge: Intel Research; 2005.

[236] Moore AW, Papagiannaki D. Toward the accurate identification of network applications. In: Proceedings of the sixth passive and active measurement workshop; 2005. p. 50–60.

[237] Moore AW, Zuev D. Internet traffic classification using bayesian analysis techniques. In: Proceedings of the 2005 ACM SIGMETRICS, New York, USA. ACM; 2005. p. 50–60.

[238] Moore AW, Zuev D, Crogan M. Discriminators for use in flow-based classification. Technical report RR-05-13. Department of Computer Science, Queen Mary, University of London; 2005.

[239] Morris BT, Trivedi MM. A survey of vision-based trajectory learning and analysis for surveillance. IEEE Trans Circuits Syst Video Technol 2008;18(8):1114–27.

[240] Musicant DR. Normally distributed clustered datasets. Madison: Computer Sciences Department, University of Wisconsin; 1998. <http://www.cs.wisc.edu/dmi/svm/ndc/>.

[241] Nappi M, Wechsler H. Robust re-identification using randomness and statistical learning: Quo Vadis. Pattern Recogn Lett 2012;33:1820–7.

[242] National Institute of Standards and Technology. Digital library of mathematical functions. <http://dlmf.nist.gov/>; 6 May 2013.

[243] Nguyen TTT, Armitage G. A survey of techniques for internet traffic classification using machine learning. IEEE Commun Surv Tutor 2008;10(4):56–76.

[244] Nigam K, McCallum AK, Thrun S, Mitchell T. Text classification from labeled and unlabeled documents using EM. Mach Learn 2000;39(2–3):103–34.

[245] Nischenko I, Jordaan EM. Confidence of SVM predictions using a strangeness measure. In: International joint conference on neural networks (IJCNN); 2006. p. 1239–46.

[246] Nouretdinov I, Burford B, Gammerman A. Application of inductive confidence machine to ICMLA competition data. In: Proceedings of the eighth international conference on machine learning and applications; 2009. p. 435–8.

[247] Nouretdinov I, Costafreda SG, Gammerman A, Chervonenkis A, Vovk V, Vapnik V. Machine learning classification with confidence: application of transductive conformal predictors to MRI-based diagnostic and prognostic markers in depression. Neuroimage 2011;56:809–13.

[248] Nouretdinov I, Devetyarov D, Vovk V, Burford B, Camuzeaux S, Gentry-Maharaj A, et al. Multiprobabilistic prediction in early medical diagnoses. Ann Math Artif Intell 2013:1–20. http://dx.doi.org/10.1007/s10472-013-9367-5.

[249] Nouretdinov I, Gammerman A, Qi Y, Klein-Seetharaman J. Determining confidence of predicted interactions between HIV-1 and human proteins using conformal method. Pacific symposium on biocomputing, vol. 17; 2012. p. 311–22.

[250] Nouretdinov I, Li G, Gammerman A, Luo Z. Application of conformal predictors to tea classification based on electronic nose. In: Proceedings of the sixth conference on artificial intelligence applications and innovations; 2010. p. 303–10.

[251] Nouretdinov I, Melluish T, Vovk V. Ridge regression confidence machine. In: Proceedings of the 18th international conference on machine learning, San Francisco. Morgan Kaufmann; 2001. p. 385–92.

[252] Nouretdinov I, Vovk V, V'yugin V, Gammerman A. Transductive confidence machine is universal. Technical report CLRC-TR-02-05. Computer Learning Research Centre, Royal Holloway, University of London; 2002.

[253] Nouretdinov I, V'yugin V, Gammerman A. Transductive confidence machine is universal. In: Gavaldà R, Jantke KP, Takimoto E, editors. Proceedings of the 14th international conference on algorithmic learning theory. Lecture notes in artificial intelligence, vol. 2842. Berlin: Springer; 2003.

[254] Nouretdinov IR. Offline Nearest Neighbour Transductive Confidence Machine. In: Poster and workshop proceedings of the eighth industrial conference on data mining; 2008. p. 16–24.

[255] Olona-Cabases M. The probability of a correct diagnosis. In: Candell-Riera J, Ortega-Alcalde D, editors. Nuclear cardiology in everyday practice. Dordrecht, NL: Kluwer; 1994. p. 348–57.

[256] Osugi T, Kun D, Scott S. Balancing exploration and exploitation: a new algorithm for active machine learning. In: IEEE international conference on data mining (ICDM); 2005.

[257] Özöğür S, Shawe-Taylor J, Weber GW, Ögel ZB. Pattern analysis for the prediction of fungal pro-peptide cleavage sites. Discrete Appl Math 2008. http://dx.doi.org/10.1016/j.dam.2008.06.043 [special issue on Netw Comput Biol].

[258] Özöğür-Akyüz S, Hussain Z, Shawe-Taylor J. Prediction with the SVM using test point margins. Data Min 2010:147–58.

[259] Page ES. On problem in which a change in a parameter occurs at an unknown point. Biometrika 1957;44:248–52.

[260] Papadimitriou S, Brockwell A, Faloutsos C. Adaptive, hands-off stream mining. In: Proceedings of the 29th international conference on very large data base; 2003. p. 560–71.

[261] Papadopoulos H, Gammerman A, Vovk V. Confidence predictions for the diagnosis of acute abdominal pain. Artificial Intelligence Applications and Innovations 2009;vol. III:175–84.

[262] Papadopoulos H, Gammerman A, Vovk V. Reliable diagnosis of acute abdominal pain with conformal prediction. Eng Intell Syst 2009;17:127–37.

[263] Papadopoulos H, Haralambous H. Neural networks regression inductive conformal predictor and its application to total electron content prediction. In: Diamantaras K, Duch W, Iliadis L, editors. Artificial neural networks ICANN 2010. Lecture notes in computer science, vol. 6352. Berlin/Heidelberg: Springer; 2010. p. 32–41.

[264] Papadopoulos H, Haralambous H. Reliable prediction intervals with regression neural networks. Neural Netw 2011;24(8):842–51.

[265] Papadopoulos H, Papatheocharous E, Andreou AS. Reliable confidence intervals for software effort estimation. In: Proceedings of the workshops of the fifth IFIP conference on artificial intelligence applications and innovations (AIAI-2009), April 23–25, Thessaloniki, Greece; 2009. p. 211–20.

[266] Papadopoulos H, Proedrou K, Vovk V, Gammerman A. Inductive confidence machines for regression. In: ECML; 2002. p. 345–56.

[267] Papadopoulos H, Vovk V, Gammerman A. Regression conformal prediction with nearest neighbours. J Artif Intell Res 2011;40(1):815–40.

[268] Park J, Tyan H-R, Kuo CJ. Ga-based internet traffic classification technique for QOS provisioning. In: Proceedings of the 2006 international conference on intelligent information hiding and multimedia (IIH-MSP '06); 2006. p. 251–4.

[269] Paxson V, Floyd S. Wide-area traffic: the failure of poisson modeling. IEEE/ACM Trans Netw 1995;3:226–44.

[270] Davis RA, Brockwell PJ. Time series: theory and methods. Springer; 1991.

[271] Petraco NDK, Shenkin P, Speir J, Diaczuk P, Pizzola PA, Gambino C. Addressing the national academy of sciences challenge: a method for statistical pattern comparison of striated tool marks. J Forens Sci 2012;57(4):900–11.

[272] Pfahringer B, Bensusan H, Giraud-Carrier C. Meta-learning by landmarking various learning algorithms. In: Proceedings of the 17th international conference on machine learning. San Francisco, CA: Morgan Kaufmann; 2000.

[273] Phillips PJ. The Good, the bad, and the ugly face challenge problem. Image Vis Comput 2012;30:177–85.

[274] Phillips PJ, Wechsler H, Huang J, Rauss P. The FERET database and evaluation procedure for face recognition algorithms. Image Vis Comput 1998;16:295–306.

[275] Piatetsky-Shapiro G. Data scientists responsibility for predictions, October 2012. KDD Nuggets; October 2012. <http://www.kdnuggets.com/polls/2012/responsibility-for-predictions.html>.

[276] Piciarelli C, Micheloni C, Foresti GL. Trajectory-based anomalous event detection. IEEE Trans Circuits Syst Video Technol 2008;18(11):1544–54.

[277] Platt J. Probabilistic outputs for support vector machines and comparisons to regularized likelihood methods. In: Advances in large margin classifiers; 1999.

[278] Poggio T, Rifkin R, Mukherjee S, Niyogi P. General conditions for predictivity in learning theory. Nature 2004;428:419–22.

[279] Poggio T, Smale S. The mathematics of learning: dealing with data. Notices of ASM 2003:537–44.

[280] Proedrou K, Nouretdinov I, Vovk V, Gammerman A. Transductive confidence machines for pattern recognition. In: Elomaa T, Mannila H, Toivonen H, editors. Proceedings of the 13th European conference on machine learning. London: Springer; 2002. p. 381–390. (Lecture Notes in Computer Science).

[281] Qi G, Hua X, Rui Y, Tang J, Zhang H. Two-dimensional active learning for image classification. In: IEEE conference on computer vision and pattern recognition (CVPR); 2008.

[282] Quinlan JR. C4.5: programs for machine learning, vol. 1. Morgan kaufmann; 1993.

[283] Reiner A, Yekutieli D, Benjamini Y. Identifying differentially expressed genes using false discovery rate controlling procedures. Bioinformatics 2003;19(3):368–75.

[284] Rényi A. Théorie des éléments saillants d'une suite d'observations. Annales Scientifiques de l'Université de Clermont-Ferrand 2, Série Mathématiques 1962;8: 7–13. <http://www.numdam.org/>.

[285] Reynolds DA, Quatieri TF, Dunn RB. Speaker verification using adaptive Gaussian mixture models. Digit Signal Process 2000;10:19–41.

[286] Rigollet P, Vert R. Optimal rates for plug-in estimators of density level sets. Bernoulli 2009;14:1154–78.

[287] Riveiro M. Visual analytics for maritime anomaly detection [Ph.D. thesis]. Örebo University; 2011.

[288] Ross ME, Mahfouz R, Onciu M, Liu H-C, Zhou X, Song G, et al. Gene expression profiling of pediatric acute myelogenous leukaemia. Blood 2004;104(12):3679–87.

[289] Ross ME, Zhou X, Song G, Shurtleff SA, Girtman K, Williams WK, et al. Classification of pediatric acute lymphoblastic leukaemia by gene expression profiling. Blood 2003;102:2951–9.

[290] Roy N, McCallum A. Toward optimal active learning through sampling estimation of error reduction. In: Proceedings of the international conference on machine learning (ICML); 2001.

[291] Rubinstein YD, Hastie T. Discriminative vs. informative learning. Knowledge and data discovery (KDD) 1997:49–53.

[292] Ji G-R, Dong Z, Wang D-F, Han P, Xu D-P. Wind speed conformal prediction in wind farm based on algorithmic randomness theory. 2008 international conference on machine learning and cybernetics, vol. 1; 2008. p. 131–5.

[293] Rumelhart DE, McClelland JL. Parallel distributed processing. Foundations, vol. 1. Cambridge: MIT Press; 1986.

[294] Ryabko D. Relaxing i.i.d. assumption in online pattern recognition. Technical report CS-TR-03-11. Department of Computer Science, Royal Holloway, University of London; 2003.

[295] Saar-Tsechansky M, Melville P, Provost F. Active feature-value acquisition. Manage Sci 2009;55(4):664–84.

[296] Sanderson C. Biometric person recognition: face, speech and fusion. VDM Verlag; June 2008.

[297] Saunders C, Gammerman A, Vovk V. Transduction with confidence and credibility. In: Dean T, editor. Proceedings of the 16th international joint conference on artificial intelligence, vol. 2. San Francisco, CA: Morgan Kaufmann; 1999. p. 722–6.

[298] Saunders C, Gammerman A, Vovk V. Computationally efficient transductive machines. In: Proceedings of the 11th international conference on algorithmic learning theory. Lecture notes in computer science, vol. 1968. Berlin: Springer; 2000. p. 325–33.

[299] Scheffé H, Tukey JW. Nonparametric estimation I: validation of order statistics. Ann Math Stat 1945;16:187–92.

[300] Scheffer T, Decomain C, Wrobel S. Active hidden Markov models for information extraction. In: Proceedings of the international conference on advances in intelligent data analysis (CAIDA); 2001.

[301] Schleif F-M, Villmann T, Kostrzewa M, Hammer B, Gammerman A. Cancer informatics by prototype networks in mass spectrometry. Artif Intell Med 2009;45(2-3):215–28.

[302] Schohn G, Cohn D. Less is more: Active learning with support vector machines. In: Proceedings of the international conference on machine learning (ICML); 2000.

[303] Schölkopf B, Smola A. Learning with kernels. Cambridge, MA: MIT Press; 2002.

[304] Schölkopf B, Williamson R, Smola A, Shawe-Taylor J, Platt J. Support vector method for novelty detection. In: Advances in neural information processing systems 12. Morgan Kaufmann; 1999. p. 582–8.

[305] Sculley D. Online active learning methods for fast label-efficient spam filtering. In: Fourth conference on email and antispam; 2007.

[306] Seber GAF, Lee AJ. Linear regression analysis. 2nd ed Hoboken, NJ: Wiley; 2003.

[307] Seewald A, Furnkranz J. An evaluation of grading classifiers. In: Proceedings of the fourth international symposium on advances in intelligent data analysis; 2001. p. 115–24.

[308] Sen S, Spatscheck O, Wang D. Accurate, scalable in-network identification of p2p traffic using application signatures. In: Proceedings of the 13th international conference on World Wide Web (WWW'04); 2004. p. 512–21.

[309] Settles B. Active learning literature survey. Technical report 1648. University of Wisconsin-Madison; 2010.

[310] Settles B. From theories to queries: active learning in practice. In: JMLR workshop on active learning and experimental design; 2011.

[311] Settles B, Craven M. An analysis of active learning strategies for sequence labeling tasks. In: Proceedings of the conference on empirical methods in natural language processing (EMNLP); 2008.

[312] Settles B, Craven M, Friedland L. Active learning with real annotation costs. In: Proceedings of the neural information processing systems (NIPS) workshop on cost-sensitive learning; 2008.

[313] Settles B, Craven M, Ray S. Multiple-instance active learning. In: Advances in neural information processing systems (NIPS); 2008.

[314] Shafer G, Vovk V. Probability and finance: it's only a game! New York: Wiley; 2001.

[315] Shafer G, Vovk V. A tutorial on conformal prediction. J Mach Learn Res 2008;9:371–421.

[316] Shahmuradov I, Solovyev V, Gammerman A. Plant promoter prediction with confidence estimation. Nucleic Acid Res 2005;33(3).

[317] Shannon CE. A mathematical theory of communication. ACM SIGMOBILE Mobile Comput Commun Rev 2001;5(1):3–55.

[318] Shawe-Taylor J. Classification accuracy based on observed margin. Algorithmica 1998;22:57–172.

[319] Shawe-Taylor J, Cristianini Nello. Kernel methods for pattern analysis. Cambridge, UK: Cambridge University Press; 2004.

[320] Shewhart WA. The application of statistics as an aid in maintaining quality of a manufactured products. J Am Stat Assoc 1925;20:546–8.

[321] Shewhart WA. Economic control of quality of manufactured product. American Society for Quality Control; 1931.

[322] Shi L, Zhao Y. Batch mode sparse active learning. In: IEEE international conference on data mining (ICDM) workshops; 2010.

[323] Shi L, Zhao Y, Tang J. Batch mode active learning for networked data. In: ACM transactions on embedded computing systems; 2011.

[324] Shiryaev AN. On optimum methods in quickest detection problems. Theory Probab Appl 1963;8:22–46.

[325] Simard M, Cancedda N, Cavestro B, Dymetman M, Gaussier E, Goutte C, et al. Translating with non-contiguous phrases. In: Proceedings of the conference on human language technology and empirical methods in natural language processing. Association for Computational Linguistics; 2005. p. 755–62.

[326] Sinha P, Balas B, Ostrovsky Y, Russell R. Face recognition by humans: nineteen results all computer vision researchers should know about. Proc IEEE 2006;94(11):1948–62.

[327] Smirnov E, Sprinkhuizen-Kuyper I, Nalbantov G, Vanderlooy S. Version space support vector machines. Front Artif Intell Appl 2006;141:809.

[328] Smirnov EN, Nalbantov GI, Kaptein AM. Meta-conformity approach to reliable classification. Intell Data Anal 2009;13(6):901–15.

[329] Smirnov E, Nikolaev N, Nalbantov G. Single-stacking conformity approach to reliable classification. In: Dicheva D, Dochev D, editors. Artificial intelligence: methodology, systems, and applications. Lecture notes in computer science, vol. 6304. Springer; 2010. p. 161–70.

[330] Smyth P, Gray A, Fayyad U. Retrofitting decision tree classifiers using kernel density estimation. In: Prieditis A, Russell SJ, editors. Proceedings of the 12th international

conference on machine learning, Tahoe City, California, USA. San Francisco, USA: Morgan Kaufmann; 1995. p. 506–14.

[331] Specht DF, Romsdahl H. Experience with adaptive probabilistic neural networks and adaptive general regression neural networks. In: Rogers SK, editor. Proceedings of IEEE international conference on neural networks, Orlando, USA. Piscataway, USA: IEEE Press; 1994.

[332] Specia L, Saunders C, Turchi M, Wang Z, Shawe-Taylor J. Improving the confidence of machine translation quality estimates. In: Proceedings of MT summit XII; 2009.

[333] Steele M. Stochastic calculus and financial applications. Springer Verlag; 2001.

[334] Stolfo SJ, Fan W, Lee W, Prodromidis A, Chan PK. Cost-based modeling for fraud and intrusion detection: results from the jam project. In: Proceedings of the DARPA information survivability conference and exposition, 2000 (DISCEX '00), vol. 2; 2000. p. 130–44.

[335] Sugiyama M, Rubens N. Active learning with model selection in linear regression. In: SIAM data mining conference (SDM); 2008.

[336] Šajn L, Kukar M. Image processing and machine learning for fully automated probabilistic evaluation of medical images. Comput Method Prog Biomed 2011;104:75–86.

[337] Štrumbelj E, Bosnić Z, Kononenko I, Zakotnik B, Grašič C. Explanation and reliability of prediction models: the case of breast cancer recurrence. Knowl Inf Syst 2010;24:305–24.

[338] Taneja IJ. On generalized information measures and their applications. Adv Electron Elect Phys 1995;76:327–416.

[339] Nguyen Hieu T, Smeulders A. Active learning using pre-clustering. In: Proceedings of the twenty-first international conference on machine learning. ACM; 2004. p. 79.

[340] Tong S. Active learning: theory and applications [Ph.D. thesis]. Stanford University; 2001.

[341] Tong S, Chang E. Support vector machine active learning for image retrieval. In: Proceedings of the ninth ACM international conference on multimedia; 2001.

[342] Tong S, Koller D. Support vector machine active learning with applications to text classification. J Mach Learn Res 2002;2:45–66.

[343] Topuz V. Traffic demand prediction using ann simulator. In: Proceedings of the 11th international conference, KES 2007 and XVII Italian workshop on neural networks conference on knowledge-based Intelligent Information and Engineering Systems: Part I; 2007. p. 864–70.

[344] Tsuda K, Raetsch M, Mika S, Mueller K. Learning to predict the leave-one-out error of kernel based classifiers. In: Lecture notes in computer science. Berlin/Heidelberg: Springer; 2001. p. 227–331.

[345] Tsybakov AB. Introduction to nonparametric estimation. New York: Springer; 2010.

[346] Tukey JW. Sunset salvo. Am Stat 1986;40:72–6.

[347] Tukey JW. Nonparametric estimation II: statistically equivalent blocks and tolerance regions – the continuous case. Ann Math Stat 1947;18:529–39.

[348] Tukey JW. Nonparametric estimation III: statistically equivalent blocks and tolerance regions – the discontinuous case. Ann Math Stat 1948;19:30–9.

[349] Tusher VG, Tibshirani R, Chu G. Significance analysis of microarrays applied to the ionising radiation response. Proc Natl Acad Sci USA, 98; 2001. p. 5116–21.

[350] Vanderlooy S, Sprinkhuizen-Kuyper IG. A comparison of two approaches to classify with guaranteed performance. In: Kok JN, Koronacki J, López de Mántaras R, Matwin S, Mladenic D, Skowron A, editors. Proceedings of the 11th European conference on

principles and practice of knowledge discovery in databases, September 17–21, 2007, Warsaw. Lecture notes in computer science, vol. 4702. Berlin: Springer; 2007. p. 288–99.

[351] Vanderlooy S, Sprinkhuizen-Kuyper IG, Smirnov EN, Jaap van den Herik H. The ROC isometrics approach to construct reliable classifiers. Intell Data Anal 2009;13(1):3–37.

[352] Vapnik V. Statistical learning theory. New York: Wiley; 1998.

[353] Vapnik V. The nature of statistical learning theory. 2nd ed. Springer; 2000.

[354] Vega J, Murari A, Pereira A, Gonzalez S, Pastor I. Accurate and reliable image classification by using conformal predictors in the TJ-II thomson scattering. Rev Sci Instrum 2010;81(10):10E118–10E118–4.

[355] Venn J. The logic of chance. London: Macmillan; 1866.

[356] Verdoolaege G, Vega J, Murari A, Van Oost G. Identification of confinement regimes in tokamak plasmas by conformal prediction on a probabilistic manifold. In: Iliadis LS, Maglogiannis I, Papadopoulos H, Karatzas K, Sioutas S, editors. AIAI (2). IFIP advances in information and communication technology, vol. 382. Springer; 2012. p. 244–53.

[357] Viola P, Jones M. Rapid object detection using a boosted cascade of simple features. In: Proceedings of the computer vision and pattern recognition conference (CVPR); 2001.

[358] Vovk V. Aggregating strategies. In: Proceedings of the third annual workshop on computational learning theory; 1990.

[359] Vovk V. On-line confidence machines are well-calibrated. In: Proceedings of the 43rd annual symposium on foundations of computer science, Los Alamitos, CA. IEEE Computer Society; 2002. p. 187–96.

[360] Vovk V. Conditional validity of inductive conformal predictors. Mach Learn 2013;92:349–76.

[361] Vovk V. Cross-conformal predictors. Ann Math Artif Intell 2013;(1012–2443):20. http://dx.doi.org/10.1007/s10472-013-9368-4.

[362] Vovk V. Kernel ridge regression. In: Schölkopf B, Luo Z, Vovk V, editors. Empirical inference: festschrift in honor of Vladimir N. Vapnik. Heidelberg: Springer; 2013 [chapter 11].

[363] Vovk V, Fedorova V, Nouretdinov I, Gammerman A. Criteria of efficiency for conformal prediction, in preparation.

[364] Vovk V, Gammerman A, Saunders C. Machine-learning applications of algorithmic randomness. In: Proceedings of the 16th international conference on machine learning, San Francisco, CA. Morgan Kaufmann; 1999. p. 444–53.

[365] Vovk V, Gammerman A, Shafer G. Algorithmic learning in a random world. New York: Springer; 2005.

[366] Vovk V, Nouretdinov I, Gammerman A. Testing exchangeability on-line. In: Fawcett T, Mishra N, editors. ICML. AAAI Press; 2003. p. 768–75.

[367] Vovk V, Petej I. Venn–Abers predictors, in preparation.

[368] Wackernagel H. Multivariate geostatistics: an introduction with applications. Berlin: Springer; 2003.

[369] Wald A. Sequential analysis. NY: Wiley; 1947.

[370] Wald A. An extension of Wilks' method for setting tolerance limits. Ann Math Stat 1943;14:45–55.

[371] Wand MP, Jones MC. Kernel smoothing. London: Chapman and Hall; 1995.

[372] Wang H, Lin Ch, Yang F, Hu X. Hedged predictions for traditional chinese chronic gastritis diagnosis with confidence machine. Comput Biol Med 2009;39(5).

[373] Wang H, Fan W, Yu PS, Han J. Mining concept-drifting data streams using ensemble classifiers. In: Getoor L, Senator TE, Domingos P, Faloutsos C, editors. Proceedings of the ninth ACM SIGKDD international conference on knowledge discovery and data mining. ACM; 2003. p. 226–35.

[374] Wasserman L. Frasian inference. Stat Sci 2011;26:322–5.

[375] Wechsler H. Reliable face recognition methods. Springer; 2007.

[376] Weigend AS, Nix DA. Predictions with confidence intervals (local error bars). In: Proceedings of the international conference on neural information processing, Seoul, Korea; 1994. p. 847–52.

[377] Weston J, Mukherjee S, Chapelle O, Pontil M, Poggio T, Vapnik V. Feature selection for SVMs. In: Proceedings of NIPS; 2000. p. 668–74.

[378] Widmer G, Kubat Miroslav. Learning in the presence of concept drift and hidden contexts. Mach Learn 1996;23(1):69–101.

[379] Wilks SS. Determination of sample sizes for setting tolerance limits. Ann Math Stat 1941;12:91–6.

[380] Williams N, Zander S, Armitage G. A preliminary performance comparison of five machine learning algorithms for practical ip traffic flow classification. SIGCOMM Comput Commun Rev 2006;36(5):5–16.

[381] Witten IH, Frank E, Hall MA. Data mining: practical machine learning tools and techniques. Morgan Kaufmann; 2011.

[382] Wold S, Ruhe A, Wold H, Dunn III WJ. The collinearity problem in linear regression. the partial least squares (PLS) approach to generalized inverses. SIAM J Sci Stat Comput 1984;5(3):735–43.

[383] Wolpert DH. Stacked generalization. Neural Netw 1992;5:241–59.

[384] Xu Z, Yu K, Tresp V, Xu X, Wang J. Representative sampling for text classification using support vector machines. In: European conference on information retrieval; 2003.

[385] Yang F, Zhen Wang H, Mi H, de Lin C, Wen Cai W. Using random forest for reliable classification and cost-sensitive learning for medical diagnosis. BMC Bioinf 2009;10(1).

[386] Yang M, Nouretdinov I, Luo Z, Gammerman A. Feature selection by conformal predictor. In: Proceedings of 12th INNS EANN-SIG international conference and seventh IFIP WG 12.5 international conference, vol. II; 2011. p. 449.

[387] Yeoh E-J, Ross ME, Shurtleff SA, Williams WK, Patel D, Mahfouza R, et al. Classification, subtype discovery, and prediction of outcome in pediatric acute lymphoblastic leukaemia by gene expression profiling. Cancer Cell 2002;1:133–43.

[388] Yoon S-H, Park J-W, Park J-S, Oh Y-S, Kim M-S. Internet application traffic classification using fixed ip-port. In: Proceedings of the 12th Asia-Pacific network operations and management conference on management enabling the future internet for changing business and new computing services; 2009. p. 21–30.

[389] Yu L, Liu H. Feature selection for high-dimensional data: a fast correlation-based filter solution. In: Proceedings of the 20th international conference on machine learning (ICML-2003); 2003. p. 856–63.

[390] Yu L, Liu H. Efficient feature selection via analysis of relevance and redundancy. J Mach Learn Res 2004;5:1205–24.

[391] Zaffalon M, Wesnes K, Petrini O. Reliable diagnoses of dementia by the naive credal classifier inferred from incomplete cognitive data. Artif Intell Med 2003;29(1):61–79.

[392] Zander S, Nguyen T, Armitage G. Automated traffic classification and application identification using machine learning. In: IEEE conference on local computer networks; 2005. p. 250–7.

[393] Zhang T. A leave-one-out cross validation bound for kernel methods with application in learning. Lecture notes in computer science: 14th annual conference on computation learning theory 2001;2111:427–43.

[394] Zhang X, Zhao D, Chen L, Min W. Batch mode active learning based multi-view text classification. In: International conference on Fuzzy systems and knowledge discovery; 2009.

[395] Zhu X. Semi-supervised learning literature survey. Computer sciences technical report 1530. University of Wisconsin-Madison; 2005.

[396] Zhu X, Lafferty J, Ghahramani Z. Combining active learning and semi-supervised learning using gaussian fields and harmonic functions. In: Proceedings of the ICML workshop on the continuum from labeled to unlabeled data; 2003.

Index

03/10/2024

01040324-0013